871.

THE JUDICIAL PROCESS

In the absence of a sound conception of the judicial role, judges at present can be said to be 'muddling along'. They disown the declaratory theory of law but continue to behave and think as if it had not been discredited. Much judicial reasoning still exhibits an unquestioning acceptance of positivism and a 'rulish' predisposition. Formalistic thinking continues to exert a perverse influence on the legal process.

Written by a practising judge, this book dismantles these outdated theories and seeks to bridge the gap between legal theory and judicial practice. The author propounds a coherent and comprehensive judicial methodology for modern times.

Founded on the truism that the law exists to serve society, and adopting the twin criteria of justice and contemporaneity with the times, a methodology is developed that is realistic and pragmatic and that embraces a revised conception of practical reasoning, including in that conception a critical role for legal principles.

THE RT HON. E. W. THOMAS DCNZM, practised law as a trial and appellate lawyer for thirty-two years, first in a large law firm and then as a Queen's Counsel at the independent bar. He was a Judge of the High Court of New Zealand for five years and subsequently a Judge of the Court of Appeal for six years. He is a member of the Privy Council. He has been a Visiting Fulbright Scholar at Harvard Law School; a Visiting Scholar at the Centre for Socio-Legal Studies at Wolfson College, Oxford; an Inns of Court Fellow at London University; a Visiting Fellow in the Law Program at the Research School of Social Sciences at the Australian National University, Canberra; and a Visiting Fellow at Wolfson College, Cambridge. He has written numerous articles and delivered many lectures on a wide range of legal topics, including jurisprudence. He is currently a Distinguished Visiting Fellow at the Law School, Auckland University, and an Acting Judge of the newly established Supreme Court of New Zealand.

THE JUDICIAL PROCESS

Realism, Pragmatism, Practical Reasoning
and Principles

E. W. THOMAS

CAMBRIDGE
UNIVERSITY PRESS

CAMBRIDGE UNIVERSITY PRESS
Cambridge, New York, Melbourne, Madrid, Cape Town, Singapore, São Paulo

CAMBRIDGE UNIVERSITY PRESS
The Edinburgh Building, Cambridge CB2 2RU, UK
Published in the United States of America by Cambridge University Press, New York
www.cambridge.org
Information on this title: www.cambridge.org/9780521855662

© E. W. Thomas 2005

This book is in copyright. Subject to statutory exception
and to the provisions of relevant collective licensing agreements,
no reproduction of any part may take place without
the written permission of Cambridge University Press.

First published 2005

Printed in the United Kingdom at the University Press, Cambridge

A catalogue record for this book is available from the British Library

ISBN-13 978-0-521-85566-2 hardback
ISBN-10 0-521-85566-7 hardback

Cambridge University Press has no responsibility for
the persistence or accuracy of URLs for external or
third-party internet websites referred to in this book,
and does not guarantee that any content on such
websites is, or will remain, accurate or appropriate.

To my wife, Margaret

CONTENTS

Preface   *page* xv

1 Introduction   1
Practical skills and legal theory   1
Judges make law – endlessly   3
And judges also make policy – regularly   4
The interpretative approach is wanting   6
Judges and legal theory   7
Theorists and legal practice   9
Bridging the divide   12
A précis – more or less   14
Conclusion   23

2 Muddling along   24
Practical muddling along   24
The declaratory theory of law   25
Positivism   27
    Die Meistersinger von Nürnberg   27
    Positivism and its stubborn survival   29
    Aspirational positivism   34
    Romantic positivism   37

Natural law   42
    Superstition and/or speculation   42
    Natural law and human rights jurisprudence   45
    Natural law and parliamentary supremacy   49
Conclusion   52

3 The 'curse' of formalism   54
Timur, the barbarian   54
The lingering legacy of formalism   55
Formalism will not stay dead   56
The formalism of 'presumptive positivism'   58
A short portrait of the formalist judge   62
A case study: *Sevcon Ltd* v *Lucas CAB Ltd*   66
Conclusion   73

4 Legal fundamentalism   75
Legal fundamentalism   75
The democratic legitimacy of the judiciary   77
    Judicial independence and impartiality   77
    The will of the people   79
    The judge's values!   84
    Other considerations   86
'Judicial activism'   88
    The parable of the activist judge   88
    An ersatz concept   91
    And Lord Denning?   94
    Conservative activism   99

A 'political' process!   101
Conclusion   104

5 **The idolatry of certainty**   108
   A conversation in chambers   108
   An uncertain world   115
   The law is inherently uncertain   115
   Acknowledged causes of uncertainty   122
      The uncertainty of the facts   122
      The uncertainty in defining the legal dispute   123
      The uncertainty of the *ratio*   123
      The uncertainty of exceptions   124
      The uncertainty as to what other jurisdictions are up to   124
      The uncertainty arising from an abundance of riches   125
   Some underlying causes of uncertainty   125
      The imprecision of language   125
      The need for finality in judicial adjudication   126
      The 'status' of justice   128
   Two critical consequences   130
   Certainty and precedent   131
   Certainty as a relevant consideration   135
   Conclusion   137

6 **The piety of precedent**   139
   A foolish consistency ...   139
   The doctrine of precedent   141
   The perceived value of precedent unmasked   144

Stability   145
Reliance   148
Legitimacy   150
Judicial craftsmanship and so on   151
Efficiency   153
'Non-binding' precedents?   153
    Persuasive precedents   154
    'Famous dicta'   154
Relevance and justice   155
The 'attitude of mind'   157
Conclusion   161

7   The foibles of precedent – a case study   164
Lewis v *Attorney-General of Jamaica*   164
An assessment, a rebuke and a note of optimism   173
Postscript; don't speak too soon!   176

8   There is no impersonal law   184
A shout from the rooftops   184
An internal logic and coherence?   186
The doyen – Ronald Dworkin   188
Dworkin's implausible distinction betweenprinciples and rules   192
Dworkin's implausible distinction between principles and policy   195
Dworkin's implausible rejection of judicial discretion   202
Dworkin's implausible justification for precedent   205

Trigwell's case: Hercules J confronts Athena J   208
Conclusion   214

9 **So, what is the law?**   217
'The law' is essentially a process   217
Is 'the law' what the courts ultimately decide?   219
A more fluid concept   222
The 'as is' and 'ought to be' distinction dissimulated   224
The rule of law in the scheme of things   225
Rechtsstaat or *justizstaat*?   231
The judicial oath   238
Conclusion   239

10 **The constraints on the judiciary**   241
The significance of judicial constraints   241
The external constraints   243
Internalised constraints   245
Some structural constraints   249
   A legitimate role for certainty   250
   A justifiable role for precedent   251
   'Leave it to Parliament'   254
   Minimalism   265
   Vanquishing general discretions   266
Conclusion   267

11 **Towards a new judicial methodology**   270
A methodology for the twenty-first century   270
Justice and relevance   272

The reality of justice   272

But is justice 'knowable'?   281

The imperative to be relevant   287

A case study: *Fletcher Challenge Energy* v *ECNZ Ltd*   289

Conclusion   299

12 Of realism and pragmatism   302

Hard realism   302

   A new realism   302

   Realism in practice   305

Determined pragmatism   307

   Legal pragmatism   307

   Pragmatism in practice   312

Conclusion   314

13 Of . . . practical reasoning and principles   316

Practical reasoning   316

   The theory of practical reasoning   316

   Practical, practical reasoning   320

   The all-important facts   321

   The legal issue   327

   The initial premise   329

   A community of considerations   329

   Community values   331

   Principles to the forefront   334

   Common sense   334

   A summary   338

Principles   339
  Principles and reason   339
  Legal principles   343
Conclusion   347

14 Taking law seriously   349

So, will there be a difference?   349
  Making overt that which is covert   349
  The flow of the river ...   350
  The main differences   351
Taking law seriously   354

15 A theory of ameliorative justice   358

Our Lady of Justice ... why the sword?   358
The precept of non-exploitation   360
The ground is cleared – a reconciliation   364
The ground is further cleared – justice?   367
Liberal individualism   371
Equity   375
The common law   379
  Contract   382
  Tort   386
  Public and administrative law   387
  ... of Marxism and Critical Legal Studies   388
Justice and fairness   392
Conclusion   394

Subject index   396
Authors index   411

PREFACE

Alexander M. Bickel said:

> Judges have, or should have, the leisure, the training, and the insulation to follow the ways of the scholar in pursuing the ends of government. This is crucial in sorting out the enduring values of a society ...[1]

Although unaware of this aphorism at the time, it is nevertheless an exhortation I sought to follow as a judge. Regrettably, the training of a judge is essentially practical, the insulation is imperfect and the leisure is effectively non-existent. As an overworked judge at first instance for five years and a frantically overworked judge of an appellate court for just over six years,[2] my aspirations at scholarship fell short of the 'ways of the scholar'. But in that estate I am in splendid company.

In 1992, after I had been a Judge at first instance for two years, I presumed to write a Monograph with the long title: *A Return to Principle in Judicial Reasoning and an Acclamation of Judicial Autonomy*.[3] But the work did not emanate from my two short years on the Bench. It reflected the thinking of a practitioner, only lately a Judge, who had spent some thirty-four years in the practice of the law in and around the courts. An irresistible propensity to observe and analyse the legal process in which I was a participant, and an equally irresistible bent to perceive the reality of that process, dictated the conclusions that I expressed in that Monograph. I suffered, I felt, the self-imposed mantle of the proverbial man from Mars.

The thrust of the Monograph was simple enough. It urged a departure from an overly rigid approach to precedent and its fellow traveller, *stare decisis*, and a deliberate return to a more principle-oriented approach.

---

[1] Alexander M. Bickel, *The Least Dangerous Branch: The Supreme Court at the Bar of Politics* (2nd edn, Yale University Press, New Haven and London, 1962), at 25–26.
[2] The High Court of New Zealand and the Court of Appeal of New Zealand.
[3] (1993) 4 VUWLR Mono. 5 ('Monograph').

Principles, and not precedent, would be dominant in judicial reasoning. No longer would the past predict the future.[4] *Stare decisis* would give way to a more flexible approach. Before it would be accorded precedential force the validity and authority of a prior decision would require to be justified as being just, or fair, in the circumstances of the particular case and relevant to the contemporary needs and expectations of the community.

At the same time, the reality of the judicial process would be recognised, principally, the inherent uncertainty and vagueness of the law. This uncertainty vests judges with vast discretion and confronts them with limitless choices in the course of reaching a decision. Judicial autonomy, I urged, is not only inevitable, but also is essential to ensure that justice is done in the individual case and that the law is applied and developed to meet current requirements. I recognised that it is this judicial autonomy that gives the common law its dynamic.

I sought to place this dissertation in a tenable jurisprudential setting based on the truism that the law exists to serve society.

Contrary to what was probably sound scholarly advice, I decided to publish the work rather than allow a draft to be circulated for the valuable comments of those who could be persuaded to read it, and to then let it stand for the benefit of further reflection. Immediate publication, however, did not indicate finality. It was my expressed intention to return to the subject in the fullness of time and to modify and expand my thinking in the light of my added experience, further reflection, any critical observations that the Monograph may have prompted, and the advances made in relevant legal theory. This book seeks to give effect to that intention.

All these factors; further experience and reflection, comments received and current legal theory have caused me to recast much of my thinking. Further articles that I have written on the subject of the judicial process while on the Court of Appeal indicate a progression of thought.[5]

---

[4] As my argument has developed, it might be more correct to say that, although the past will no longer predict the future, proper regard for and use of the past will assist in the task of predictability.

[5] 'Fairness and Certainty in Adjudication: Formalism v Substantialism' (1999) Vol. 9, No. 3, Otago LR 459 ('Fairness and Certainty in Adjudication'); 'The "Invisible Hand" Prompts a Response' [1999] Pt II, NZLR 227; 'The Relationship of Parliament and the Courts: A Tentative Thought or Two for the New Millennium', Victoria University of Wellington Law Faculty's Centennial Lecture, (2000) 31 VUWLR 5 ('Centennial Lecture'); 'Judging in the Twenty-First Century' (2000) NZLJ 228; 'The Conscience of the Law' (2000) Vol. 8, No. 1, Waikato LR; and 'A Critical Examination of the Doctrine

Such is that progression that I cannot be confident further time would not cause me to revise my thinking yet again. But I am satisfied any such revision, while probably inevitable, would be at the periphery of my vision. My core beliefs are firmly held. Indeed, believing that to be the case, I have utilised parts of these earlier writings, with much modification certainly, in this book. Self-plagiarism, I claim, is not plagiarism at all. But the great bulk of the book is new – if not novel! In addition, the opportunity I was given following my retirement from the Court of Appeal decrees that I complete the task that I began in 1992.

I was fortunate to have been awarded a Visiting Fellowship in the Law Program of the Research School of Social Sciences at the Australian National University in Canberra for the year 2002. This book was substantially completed during my visit. My indebtedness to the Program is unbounded.

My time as an appellate Judge revealed that my exhortation to the judiciary to revert to principles in determining cases and my focus on the rigidity of precedent was incomplete. An increasing number of judges, I found, seek to unearth the principle underlying the case or cases cited in argument. The question from the bench to counsel confidently claiming the direct advantage of a precedent: 'Yes, but what is the principle behind that decision', or words to that effect, is being voiced more often than in the past. Admittedly, the question is often prompted by the fact that counsel's confidence that the precedent is directly in point is misplaced. Perceptions of the evident principle may then vary. But however the principle is discerned, it is what the judges choose to do with it that is critical. Some judges will confine or restrain the principle, even to the extent of modifying and redefining its breadth and application. Others will construe and apply the principle liberally, extending it where that is thought necessary to serve the interests of justice or to bring the law into harmony with the current needs and expectations of the community. While, therefore, many judges search for the relevant principle on which to base their decision, only some adopt the approach that I sought to prescribe in my Monograph.

I also found that cases in which the application of a precedent was directly in issue were extremely rare. In my six years on the Court of Appeal, during which time the Court delivered just under 3000 judgments, a binding precedent was directly in issue and reviewed in less

---

of Precedent' in Rick Bigwood (ed.), *Legal Method in New Zealand* (Butterworths, Wellington, 2001), at 141 ('*Legal Method*').

than a handful of cases. I realised that it was not the doctrines of precedent or *stare decisis*, as such, that were the problem as I had earlier opined, but a deep-rooted predisposition that those doctrines engender in judges. Certainty is pursued as a goal of adjudication. Without being bound by a precedent, many judges hugged the skirts of the established body of law, or, rather, the body of law that they held had been established. The coercive element in the doctrines continued to exert a dominant influence as a consequence of this latent predisposition.

At the same time, however, I was confirmed in my view that judicial autonomy is an undeniable reality. The scope for choice in judicial reasoning is of mammoth proportions. It is ever-present and all-pervading. These choices are directed by the preconceptions and predilections of the individual judge. Included among these preconceptions and predilections are evident prejudices, which, although perhaps not of the order of the prejudices at times aired on 'talk-back' radio, are or should be wholly alien to judicial decision-making. Such preconceptions (in which term I will throughout this book include the judge's predilections, predispositions, prejudices, vanities, passions, obsessions, preoccupations and biases) frame the value judgements that underlie the judges' decisions and determine whether they will be more or less formalistic in their approach.

I came to see that it is the lingering judicial penchant for formalism that is the real obstacle to the application of the principle-oriented approach that I had earlier endorsed. The true antithesis in legal reasoning is the tension between formalism, on the one hand, and an approach that favours the reality and substance of an issue, on the other. Contrary to the claims of any number of legal theorists, formalism is far from dead. My experience confirmed that it is very much alive and, indeed, that from time to time it exhibits a vitality capable of exerting a coercive influence on judicial thinking. It harbours its own aberrant logic and distracts its adherents from the realism or realistic approach that must be an early and essential element in any competent legal process. I concluded that it is, in fact, the lingering impact of formalism that has provoked much uncertainty in the law and that impedes delivery of the Justinian precept of rendering to every person their due in the individual case.

Over further time, however, I came to appreciate that even this analysis is incomplete. If judicial reasoning and the value judgements underlying its exposition are driven by the judge's preconceptions, the formalistic approach is no more than the means by which a given end is achieved. Certainly, I have never underestimated the panoramic compass for rationalisation in judicial reasoning. But the formalistic approach is more than a means to an end. Because it is deeply imbedded in their psyche, the value judgements of many judges are directed and shaped by that formalistic methodology. The means infects the end. There is, in other words, an interplay or symbiotic relationship between the preconceptions of a judge and the methodology adopted by that judge.

I also observed that the value judgement that a judge will make in a particular case cannot be divorced from the judge's perception of the function of the law and the role of a judge. For example, a judge who has not escaped the residual influence of formalism will favour leaving a proposed change in the law to Parliament even though, objectively considered, the change could properly be made by the courts, or the judge will decide that a particular outcome would foment uncertainty in the law, even though the judge might never be able to explain how uncertainty would result from that outcome, or the judge will decide the case on a minimalist basis, notwithstanding that the articulation of general principles in the particular case would provide much needed guidance to the community and enhance certainty and predictability in the law, and so on.

It is this lingering judicial commitment to formalism that explains why so much judicial reasoning is still legalistic, strained or mechanical. Formalism, or a formalistic approach, inspires its own laboured or artificial responses to a legal problem. The stilted logic of formalism has both directed the judge's value judgement and dominated or confined his or her thinking. All too often the approach is adopted blindly, as if a creed, in which case the judge's reaction is automatic and prevents a distinction being drawn between the judge's preconceptions and the methodology that he or she has pursued.

I therefore came to accept that the judicial methodology that is adopted is critically important in determining the substantive decisions that are reached. Judges will by nature be more or less conservative, or more or less orthodox, or more or less liberal, or more or less creative, or more or less many other human characteristics, but the adoption of a methodology that is more reasoned, deliberate and transparent than that of the past should, I felt, reduce the disparity between them. The alternative, instinctively unpalatable to even an ardent realist, is that the outcome of legal disputes is dependent solely on the personal preconceptions of the individual judge. It became my view that, if the chains of formalism could be finally broken and the vast scope for choice in judicial reasoning accepted, judicial decision-making could be harnessed to an approach that is realistic, pragmatic and yet principle-oriented in its implementation. It is that approach or methodology that is explored in this book.

I am conscious that it could be said that my experience is peculiar to me and the appellate Court of which I was a member. It is true that for the last five years I sat on a notably conservative Court and that a number of the Court's judgments reflect a determined formalism and all that this intuitive commitment entails. But experience as an appellate judge has a universality that cannot be abridged in this fashion. To a greater or lesser extent, appellate courts in all common law jurisdictions are beset by the vestiges of formalism. Formalism, for example, is still readily evident in the judgments of a number of their Lordships in the House of Lords in the United Kingdom. Under the guise of 'legalism' it is the proclaimed wisdom of many, if not most, of the Judges of the High Court of Australia.[6] It is much less evident, but still present, in the judgments of a number of the Judges of the Supreme Court of Canada. I therefore believe that what I have to say in this book is applicable to judicial reasoning in all common law jurisdictions.

Nor is the judicial methodology that I advance, and the conception of the judicial role that it embraces, restricted to appellate judges. It is directed to all judges, both appellate judges and judges at first instance alike. Nevertheless, I anticipate that the reaction of many will be to seek to restrict what I have to say to judges of appellate courts only. Any such restriction would be unfortunate. Obviously, the methodology will be more pertinent to appellate judges who are higher in the judicial hierarchy and who are called upon to deal with more pure questions of law. They will have more scope to give effect to the recommended approach and conception of the judicial role than judges at first instance. But this does not mean that the methodology is not applicable to judges at first instance. The only reservation that need be made is in connection with the doctrines of precedent and *stare decisis*, which are dealt with in Chapter 6. Where a precedent is directly in point a judge at first instance will need to be more circumspect in re-evaluating the validity of the precedent, particularly if it is a case determined by a higher court within the same jurisdiction. I have, however, included in that chapter a section which may prove of particular value to judges at first instance in

---

[6] See Leslie Zines, *The High Court of Australia* (4th edn, Butterworths, Sydney, 1997).

determining whether they need feel bound to apply a purported precedent.[7] I may add that, when a judge at first instance, I followed my own advice in this regard, and the world as we know it did not come to an end.[8]

In casting the rethinking in this book at common law jurisdictions generally I do not exclude the United States or any other country that has a written constitution. But my work is not directed at constitutional interpretation. Because of its dominant role in the interpretation of the Constitution, the Supreme Court of the United States is necessarily oriented to the resolution of constitutional issues. Consequently, scholars in the United States, almost to a person, have concentrated on the judiciary's approach to constitutional issues to the exclusion of the vast range and volume of judicial work involving nothing more than the application and development of the common law. Yet, focusing almost exclusively on the judicial process at the level of constitutional interpretation tends to reduce the relevance of legal theory to the bulk of the law and legal practice. Constitutional issues and theories of interpretation that compete for ascendancy create their own particular scholarly domain. It is, for example, much easier to portray the judicial process at that level as a process of interpretation. Dworkin, for one, can describe law as an 'interpretive practice'. But, as I will assert in Chapter 1, the judicial process is much more than an interpretive exercise. It is irrevocably creative. While sections of this book will no doubt be relevant to constitutional interpretation, its primary focus remains the judicial process and the application and development of the common law generally.

I am not therefore directly concerned with statute law. This does not mean that I am unaware of or indifferent to the immense volume of statute law generated in modern parliamentary democracies. I freely acknowledge the extent and impact of statutory law in contemporary society, especially on commercial activity, and that it necessarily overrides and modifies the common law. But I decline to demean the importance of the common law simply because of the emergence of a mountainous body of statutory law. Vast areas of human activity of vital significance to the interests and well-being of citizens who are affected remains subject to the vagaries of the common law and the vicissitudes of the judicial process. Moreover, it must be borne in mind that the approach and principles that guide courts in interpreting statutes is

---

[7] See below, Chapter 10, at 251–254.
[8] See, for examples, Chapter 10, nn. 20 and 22.

largely the product of the common law. Reference need only be made to a penetrating article by Professor A. T. H. Smith for concrete illustrations of the extensive development of the criminal law in the framework of statutory interpretation.[9] Formalism has beset the process of statutory interpretation just as much as it has the development of the common law, and the judicial methodology that I advance in this book can be applied to that process with such minimal modification as may be necessary.

Nor have I sought to burden the treatise with references to cases. Where it is helpful to illustrate a point, however, I have seen fit to cite a case and generally to deal with it in some detail. The risk with this economy is that, if the relevance of the case is accepted, it may prompt the response that the case is an exception, and the point it illustrates may then be dismissed with the comment that one swallow does not make a summer. Such a reaction would be unfortunate. Suitable cases to illustrate the various points abound. They reflect the prevailing judicial methodology. Indeed, the exceptions are the rare cases that reflect the approach endorsed in this book. Many more, and probably better, examples of the points that are illustrated can be found in any volume of any law report in any law library. Law students will discover them from day one of their studies at law school.

I have also deliberately refrained from restricting the cases used to illustrate various points to New Zealand decisions and, in particular, decisions in which I was involved as a judge. One exception proved inevitable. But, for the most part, I refer to cases in the United Kingdom and Australia and, to a lesser extent, Canada and the United States. If cases from the United Kingdom loom large it is simply because that jurisdiction provides the most fertile ground for the judicial failings that are censured in this book. The United States, on the other hand, has supplied by far the bulk of the jurists and legal theorists whose work is addressed.

In taking up the Visiting Fellowship at the Law Program in the Research School of Social Sciences for the purpose of writing this book, I initially intended to adopt the style of modern legal theorists. The book would be an essay in jurisprudential theory laden with copious footnotes. It soon became clear, however, that a theoretical dissertation is not what is required and would not lend itself to what I want to say. Although the work has, as it must have, a theoretical perspective, I am

---

[9] A. T. H. Smith, 'Judicial Law Making in the Criminal Law' (1984) 100 LQR 46.

essentially speaking from the standpoint of a working judge. While my target audience is anyone interested in jurisprudence, particularly the judicial process and judicial reasoning, the groups I most want to influence are judges and lawyers, for it is through them that the law is practised and administered. Consequently, and contrary perhaps to my natural inclination, I have sought to write this book in a way that accords with that objective. The possibly over-ambitious desire to redirect judges' approach and reasoning in judicial decision-making is not concealed.

I am, of course, conscious of the fact, as the late Professor Peter Birks, for one, was wont to emphasise, that an increasing source of law are the articles and commentaries of academic lawyers. The epistemology of judicial reasoning is of signal interest to them. For that reason I do not discount the possibility that this book may serve a useful purpose for those academics who seek to influence the substance and development of the law.

Furthermore, because I believe that legal theory is an important adjunct to the judicial process and that, to be effective in practice, judges must acquire a greater knowledge of legal theory, jurisprudence will never be far beneath the surface. At times, no doubt, it will break the surface. This surfacing is to be expected of one who has in the past claimed, perhaps tongue in cheek, that he has always aspired to be a good lawyer, but jurisprudence kept on getting in the way! I therefore hope legal theorists may find the work of some value, even if not quite of the same value as I have obtained from their own writings in the performance of my judicial duties. If nothing else, it may provide an insight into the assumptions, perceptions and philosophy, never wholly perfect, but never, I trust, wholly imperfect, of one working judge.

Finally, I harbour the fond hope that the book may be of real benefit to students. Law students seemingly come to their law schools as putative, if not committed, positivists. Law is about rules and cases, and learning the law is about learning those rules and cases. It is as ingenuous as that. Too often, it seems, this simplistic predisposition is confirmed in the lecture room. All would be well with the world and, in particular, certainty and predictability in the law would be assured and stability and continuity in society enhanced, if only the judges would apply the rules, adhere to precedent, and suppress any urge to be creative. Alas, the legal process is not so simple or straightforward. The fond hope of which I speak, therefore, is that this book will provide students with a more realistic introduction to the judicial process, and one that will stand them in better stead in the practice of the law and the service of their clients.

I should add, having referred to students as a desirable class to read this book that it is not written as a textbook. No settled effort is made to expound the various legal theories mentioned in the text. The student must look elsewhere for an exposition of these theories. For the most part, no more explanation is included than is necessary for me to develop the argument being advanced at the time.

I should also add an apology of sorts. At the outset I observed that, as an overworked judge for just over eleven years, my aspirations at scholarship fell short of the 'ways of the scholar'. The same can be said of the time that I was in practice. Before accepting appointment to the Bench I was an overly busy practitioner. I therefore wish to reiterate the disclaimer. Without enjoying the opportunity for the long and deep study, reflection and discussion that an academic environment would have provided, it would be pretentious for me to lay claim to undue scholarship. My knowledge of legal theory has been picked up 'on the run', so to speak, and often when a Le Carré novel lay unopened begging for attention.[10] I can only hope that this lack of scholarship is less evident than I fear; that it does not provoke exasperation, or worse, irritation, in the learned reader; that any shortcomings in my learning will lead to compassion rather than frenzied exposure; and that those shortcomings are more than made up for by my direct experience in the process of which I write.

In writing and completing this book I have received considerable assistance from many learned and able people. First, I am grateful to the inhabitants of the Law Program corridor of the Research School of Social Sciences at the Australian National University; Peter Cane, John Braithwaite, Jane Stapleton, Leslie Zines, Sarah Harding, Carol Harlow, George Christie, Ernst Willheim, Gary Edmond, Christos Mantziaris, Chris Finn, Adrienne Stone, Collin Scott and Imelda Maher for their constant encouragement and support. In truth, I became so fond of them all that I would express such gratitude even if it were not their due. But it undoubtedly is their due. They created for me an environment

---

[10] The difficulty that I have highlighted is not peculiar to me, and reveals a problem outside the scope of this book. If judges are to obtain a greater understanding of legal theory they must be given the time – what Bickel called 'the leisure' – to acquire the knowledge that will give rise to that understanding. Judicial administration needs to provide that time. If senior judges are treated like 'work horses', with judicial efficiency measured by output alone, judges cannot be held venal for behaving like work horses.

that I found both stimulating and productive, at times exhilaratingly so. To the names of those wonderful folk I must add Nicola Piper, a sociologist, and Maria Barge, a political scientist, both also from the Research School of Social Sciences. Their refreshing insights were a great benefit to me and a constant reminder that all wisdom in matters legal is not the sole prerogative of lawyers.

Secondly, I thank all those persons who volunteered to peruse and comment on a draft manuscript or who, before they had the opportunity to volunteer, were cajoled into doing so, for their valuable and constructive comments. I am acutely conscious of the task that they confronted and I am overwhelmed by their response. My unbounded thanks (in alphabetical order and without regard to titles) are extended to Sarah Allen, David Baragwanath, Rick Bigwood, John Braithwaite, Peter Cane, George Christie, Gary Edmond, Emma Finlayson-Davis, Rodney Hansen, Stephen Hunter, Daniel Kalderimis, Christos Mantziaris, Simon Mount, Jane Stapleton, Hanna Wilberg, Ernst Wilheim and Leslie Zines. Quite late in the piece, the comments of an anonymous Cambridge reader proved exceptionally helpful. My friend from University days, Gordon Cruden, deserves special mention for his invaluable encouragement and advice. The depth and force of the comments of another good friend, Robin Congreve, did not surprise me, but the measure of his agreement with my manuscript did.

The fact that I may not have made all the recommended corrections, modifications or deletions or incorporated all the suggested additions that commentators have made does not mean that their recommendations and suggestions were not valid. Those recommendations and suggestions are simply the casualties of the author's ultimate autonomy. Needless to say, none of those worthy commentators are responsible for what remains.

I am particularly indebted to Simon Mount and Emma Finlayson-Davis for there research and help in tying up the remaining bits and pieces of the manuscript that I brought back from Canberra. Prudence dictated that I submit my piece on Richard Wagner's *Die Meistersinger* to Heath and Liz Lees, the President and Secretary respectively of The Wagner Society of New Zealand. Their enthusiastic support was in no way diminished by their surprise that a book on the law could be, to quote them, 'singable'. Katherine Lee is to be mentioned for typing up the bulk of this book. Nor could I have done without the typing assistance of Cynthia Koks after I had returned to New Zealand. Finally, I must thank my daughter, Helen, and her husband, Robert Scott, for their determined persistence and tireless patience in assisting me conquer the machinations of my computer when, with a mind of its own, it sought to thwart my reasonable demands.

Just as none of the above persons are to be held responsible for the opinions advanced in this book, so too none are to be saddled with the criticisms that it will provoke. That criticism is for me and me alone. Criticism there will be, and plenty of it, for the shibboleths that I challenge are too deeply ingrained in the psyche of too many judges, lawyers and legal academics for it to be otherwise.

Yet, I must confess that I will be dismayed at much of the criticism. By my own lights, I have done nothing more than bring to the study of the judicial process a determined realism and a relentless determination to pursue that realism through to its logical conclusion. Experienced judges, in particular, will acknowledge, for example, that the law is contentiously vague and uncertain, that judges make and remake the law, that judicial decisions are impregnated with policy considerations, that there is no impersonal or transcendental law to which judges can conveniently defer responsibility, that multiple choices are integral to the process of judicial decision-making, that a rule-bound or 'rulish' approach is inadequate to explain the application and development of the common law, and that resting at the base of much judicial decision-making is the value judgement of the particular judge; but they, no less than practitioners and academics generally, will resolutely decline to press these premises to their logical conclusion. If I am right in what I have written and the reader is about to read, it is only because I have sought to do just that; to take premises that are founded in a realistic appreciation of the judicial process and drive them to their logical destination.

1

Introduction

Practical skills and legal theory

Judges undoubtedly bring immense practical skills to the practise of their craft. Practical skills are encouraged and developed in the service of clients by the practising lawyer in the law firm or the barrister at the bar, and finally elevated to an art form by those who ascend the bench and are required to make a final determination. That final determination must be reached in disputes where, as often as not, the evidence is conflicting, the issue or issues elusive, and the law to apply uncertain or vague. The judge's practical skills are utilised to resolve and stabilise the facts of the case, to analyse and identify the question in issue, to arrive at a decision on that issue and, then, to justify with reasons the decision that has been reached.

But practical skills alone are not enough. Those skills must be anchored in a conception of the judicial role. Legal theory is fundamental to that conception. Without a clearly thought out conception of the judicial role, a judge is in no better position than a mariner at sea without a compass or, perhaps, a mariner at sea with a defective compass. The practical skills are exercised with either an apparent indifference to any considered purpose for their exercise, or blindly or intuitively as if the purpose were self-evident or innate to those skills and need not be comprehended. Judges risk the charge that they are simply 'muddling along'.

I am not suggesting that judges should become philosophers, or worse, that philosophers should become judges, but merely contending that a basic understanding of legal theory is essential for the complete performance of the judicial function. Plumbers may plumb for a lifetime without perplexing themselves as to what their trade is all about. But the administration of justice in accordance with the law is far removed from plumbing. A judge cannot simply judge as a plumber may plumb. To fulfil their judicial function, and to be able to assess whether they are fulfilling that function, judges must explore, examine and know the theoretical framework for their judicial thinking.

Yet, judicial scepticism, if not distrust, of legal theory is commonplace. Andrew Halpin has identified the various strands of practitioners' scepticism towards theory.[1] These strands are encountered often enough in legal practice. Scepticism is first apparent in the belief that the law has no need of theory. Legal practice is regarded as being sufficiently rich to make theory redundant. The second strand of scepticism is that practice has only a limited need for theory. While it is acknowledged that theory can provide an ancillary role in limited areas of practical skills, those skills remain transcendent. Theory, in other words, may assist to manage the long-term strategy but it is not to be permitted to detract from the opportunities practitioners have to excel in performing their practical skills. The third strand of scepticism is that theory has overstepped the mark altogether. It fails to represent practice and often takes the form of an alien rhetoric. To which, one may add, all of the above.

While the language, relevance and remoteness of much legal theory undoubtedly contributes to this reaction, scepticism of theory in itself is misplaced and, indeed, dangerous. Intuition and unquestioned assumptions replace a personal theory of law or a conception of the judicial role. If the judge does have a personal theory, it may be largely unarticulated, or incomplete, or even unsound, or it may be no more than a felt approach reflecting a vaguely understood legal theory. Judges of this description are reluctant to abandon the mythology that clings to the judicial process because they have nothing articulate, complete or sound with which to replace it. More often than not they become wedded to a crude form of positivism that does not exhibit any of the refinements of reconstructed positivist theory; to a black letter approach that is sustained by some sort of lingering faith in the discredited declaratory theory of law; and to an impoverished formalism or quasi-formalism that is dismissive of the breadth of factors and societal demands external to the formal expression of the law.

A basic understanding of legal theory provides an antidote to these ill-informed preconceptions and perceptions of the legal process. It provides the judge with the concepts and vocabulary with which to describe the judicial decision-making process. More importantly, it enables the judge to formulate a conception of the judicial role, and it is that conception that will inform and influence the decisions that the judge will make in the course of carrying out the judicial task.

---

[1] *Reasoning with Law* (Hart Publishing Oxford and Portland Oregon, 2001), at 20–21.

The impact of the judge's underlying conception of the judicial role is apparent when reference is made to the breadth of the judicial function. Where the judicial duties are of a routine nature, theory may not matter greatly, if at all. But judges' tasks do not stop at the routine. Judges are regularly called upon to make law, and in the course of doing so, to formulate policy. It is these aspects of judicial activity that most require the benefaction of legal theory to obtain legitimacy.

Judges make law – endlessly

The notion that judicial law-making is restricted to innovative or adventurous decisions and that judicial policy-making is an aberration that some judges only indulge in at the expense of proper interpretative principle needs to be dispelled at once. This notion does not reflect reality.

None, other than the uninitiated who seemingly lack an understanding of the dynamic of the common law, seriously question the fact that judges make law. The belief that judges do not make law is hopelessly out of date. As Lord Reid famously said as long ago as 1972: 'We do not believe in fairy-tales anymore.'[2]

What is not, perhaps, so widely appreciated is that judges make law, not only when they expand a legal doctrine or extend a legal principle to a new situation, but also when they confine a legal doctrine or restrict a legal principle. Whenever the question before the court could be called novel, and at the appellate level that is frequently the case, the law is made just as much when the judge's decision may be characterised as orthodox or 'negative' as when it may be described as creative or 'positive'. The idea that the law is only made when a decision is creative or positive presumes that there is a 'law' from which to depart. It is that presumption, of course, which is misplaced.

Donoghue v *Stevenson*[3] provides an example. Lord Bingham has observed that no-one could fail to recognise that the decision of the majority of three to two had made law.[4] Most would have little doubt that it made good law. The decision, Lord Bingham continues, would still have made law even if the majority's decision had been to the opposite effect. Such a decision, he observes, might not have stood the test of time and one might incline to see it as a bad decision. But the

---

[2] Lord Reid, 'The Judge as Lawmaker' (1972) 12 JSPTL 22.   [3] [1932] AC 56.
[4] Tom Bingham, *The Business of Judging: Selected Essays and Speeches* (Oxford University Press, Oxford, 2000), at 29.

critical point is that, until reversed or modified, it would have precluded a plaintiff bringing a successful proceeding in a similar situation. While a negative decision would have been less innovative than the decision actually made, it would have placed a highly authoritative roadblock in the path of the plaintiff, and so, Lord Bingham concludes, would have made law.

This perception follows inescapably from the fact that there is no 'law' to declare. Because there is no law to declare and the law is largely indeterminate, it is made, either conservatively or less conservatively, by the decision in the instant case. In their outstanding work, *Judicial Policy Making and the Modern State*,[5] Malcolm M. Feeley and Edward L. Rubin confirm that, if legal doctrine is largely indeterminate, judges are creating law perhaps as often as every time they reach a decision. Some judgments may be more creative than others, but this difference does not exclude the law-making property of the less creative decision. Judicial resistance to this analysis simply indicates that the declaratory theory of law still loiters in judicial chambers.

Appreciation of the fact that judicial law-making is not only restricted to the more progressive judges, but embraces the judiciary as a whole, emphasises the need for all judges to be directed by a judicial philosophy that is articulated and transparent. Judges, as regularly proclaimed, are not elected officials and they have no mandate to make law outside or beyond that which can be justified by sound legal theory. It is the underlying theory, and nothing else, which provides judicial law-making with its legitimacy.

And judges also make policy – regularly

Equally inevitable is the fact that, in the process of making law, judges frequently formulate public policy. Legal theorists who condemn legal policy-making as an aberrant departure from the true judicial interpretative function also ignore this reality. To some extent, judges have always made policy. They have done so, for example, when having regard to the social impact of their decisions. Judges are influenced by their perception whether their decision will achieve a socially desirable end or bring in its train socially undesirable consequences. They seek,

---

[5] Malcolm M. Feeley and Edward L. Rubin, *Judicial Policy Making and the Modern State: How the Courts Reformed America's Prisons* (Cambridge University Press, Cambridge, 1998).

consciously or unconsciously, to reflect socially acceptable norms and to utilise social policy to inform their thinking. Admittedly, reference to policy considerations may not always be overt. Those considerations may be forced to fit the configuration of formalism. Judges will seek to show that the new policy somehow emerges from the existing body of law, or is implied in it, rather than to justify the policy on the basis of the socially desirable outcome it will achieve. Such terms as 'experience', 'reason', 'self-evident', and the like, often conceal – or reveal – the weight placed upon policy considerations.

A number of judges, of course, have acknowledged the presence of policy considerations in judicial decision-making. Who, other than Lord Denning, could be expected to be at the forefront in doing so? In *Dutton v Bognor Regis UDC*,[6] Lord Denning confirmed that the question, what is the best policy for the law to adopt, may not have been openly asked, but has always been there in the background. It has, he said, been concealed behind such questions as: Was the defendant under any duty to the plaintiff? Was the relationship between them sufficiently proximate? Was the injury direct or indirect? Was it foreseeable or not? Was it too remote? And so forth. Lord Denning concluded emphatically, 'Now-a-days, we direct ourselves to considerations of policy . . .'[7] Many judges today, and certainly many more than in his day, would not be at all abashed at acknowledging the truth of Lord Denning's observations. Indeed, and by way of example, in *Fairchild* v *Glenhoven Funeral Services Ltd*,[8] the House of Lords in 2003 openly referred to policy considerations in determining the question of causation where the plaintiffs were unable to prove which of two employers had caused the disease arising from inhalation of asbestos dust from which the deceased had died.

Any residual doubts that judicial policy-making is exceptional, or incoherent, or avoidable by better legal reasoning have been put to rest by the study reported in the book I have already described as

---

[6] [1972] 1 QB 373, at 397.
[7] See also Bingham, *The Business of Judging*, at 28. Lord Cooke has spoken in similar vein; 'The New Zealand National Legal Identity' (1987) 3 Cant. LR 171.
[8] [2003] 1 AC 32. See, e.g., Lord Bingham at para. 33 and Lord Nicholls at paras. 40–43 for admirable treatment of the policy issues. The policy considerations and accompanying value judgements undoubtedly determined the outcome of the appeal. Why, then, in this case as in many others, is it seen to be necessary for the judgment writers to expand upon the case law (with often conflicting interpretations) at such inordinate length? (But see the case note by Jonathan Morgan in (2003) 66 MLR at 277–284, in which their Lordship's acknowledgement of the influence of policy is approved but their analysis of the policy reasons for their decision is said to be disappointing!)

outstanding.[9] Professors Feeley and Rubin carried out an exhaustive study of how Federal Judges in most of the States of the United States of America, acting largely independently of each other, overturned rules and precedents to reform the prison system throughout the country. Having described this judicial enterprise, the authors enter upon a remarkable exercise in jurisprudential analysis, and extract from the study a perception of the decision-making process that closely accords with my own. Central to their work is the argument that judges are not passive adjudicators of conflicts but active policy-makers. They point out that judges treat the text of the applicable law as a grant of jurisdiction, and then fashion a decision that they believe will yield the most socially desirable results. Judges will initiate a policy-making effort when motivated by strong moral sentiments in the community. But the authors are at pains to point out that policy-making is not unconstrained. They assert that the constraints that are intrinsic to the judicial policy-making process yield decisions that are just as principled and legitimate as decisions that purport to interpret the legal texts.

Feeley and Rubin's conclusions cannot be dismissed on the basis that they are peculiar to the United States or to jurisdictions having a written constitution. Their description of the legal process is too close to my own experience in a jurisdiction where there is no supreme law for me to permit of that escape route. In examining the judges' motivations, their departure from previous rules and precedents, their formulation of policy, and the constraints that operate within the discipline and methodology of the law, Feeley and Rubin entered upon an examination of a process of judicial reasoning that is generic to all common law jurisdictions. Jurisprudentially speaking, the judicial process is highly ecumenical.

The interpretative approach is wanting

In disclosing the full extent of policy-making in judicial decision-making, Feeley and Rubin explode the interpretivist theories of law, that is, the notion that the legal process is a matter of interpreting a constitution (where there is a constitution) or the text of statute law or the common law. This demolition of the interpretivist theory is to be welcomed for the theory is but one or two steps up from the discredited declaratory theory of law. It necessarily suggests that there is a law to interpret or that interpretation will provide a decision whenever the law is

---

[9] Feeley and Rubin, *Judicial Policy Making*.

indeterminate. Timothy Endicott has pointed out the hollowness of this view. In cases where there is a rule to be applied there is no need for interpretation. In cases where it is necessary to invent a new rule, either there is nothing to interpret or a rule that might have been applied without interpretation is overturned, or derogated from, or ignored.[10]

Interpretivist theory nevertheless remains dear to many legal theorists. I believe that this affection is due, in part at least, to the focus many North American theorists give to decisions of the Supreme Court of the United States relating to the Constitution of that country. But as a general theory, the interpretivist theory must founder on a number of realities. The first reality is the indeterminacy of the law. That which is indeterminate cannot be interpreted, at least not in any sensible sense. What is there may be extended or restricted, but that is not a process of interpretation. In either case it is a process of creativity. As Feeley and Rubin have commented,[11] at some point the law or legal text is so vague, and the law which the judge then makes so comprehensive and precise, that the term 'interpretation' seems like more of a conceit than a description.

Secondly, the interpretivist theory is inconsistent with the measure of judicial autonomy enjoyed by judges in practice. As I will press in argument further, choice is endemic to judicial decision-making. Certainly, interpretation itself allows for choice. A legal rule or principle may be interpreted differently by different judges. But what is defective in this limited view is the implication that there was an applicable law in existence for the judges to interpret differently. More often than not, the judges have made law or formulated policy simply because there was no applicable law or, certainly, no applicable law beyond a starting point. Essentially, the interpretivist theory denies the role of creativity in the judicial process and, therefore, the true extent of judicial autonomy.

Judges and legal theory

Once it is recognised that in the course of making law judges move beyond any sensible concept of interpretation and formulate policy, it becomes important that they have some familiarity with legal theory in order to define their judicial role. A conception of the judicial role that does not acknowledge the extent of judicial law-making or policy-making cannot be

---

[10] Timothy A. O. Endicott, *Vagueness in Law* (Oxford University Press, Oxford, 2000), at 182.
[11] Feeley and Rubin, *Judicial Policy Making*, at 205–206.

conducive to sound judicial reasoning. Indeed, there is no logical reason to believe that policy-making without an underlying conception of the judicial role will be other than random, incoherent or irrelevant. Nor, without a basic understanding of legal theory, will the judges be able to enter into any sensible discourse about judicial policy-making. Discourse will also proceed among legal theorists and academics without the benefit of the direct experience that judges can provide. The task of defining the legitimate metes and bounds of adjudication becomes that much more difficult.

Further, law is not an end in itself but exists to serve the needs of society. Society will not be served or its needs met by judges who make law or policy for that society without the guidance legal theory can provide. Not just the metes and bounds of policy-making in adjudication, but the purpose and substance of the policy made, will be shaped by the judge's conception of the judicial role. It is surely an oxymoron to speak of law as being an instrument of social policy and yet have judges administer the law and make policy ill-informed or indifferent to the theoretical foundations of their task. A sound conception is likely to deliver sound policy; a poor conception is likely to deliver poor policy.

As already intimated, the immediate value of a basic knowledge of legal theory is that it serves as an antidote to intuitive, ill-informed and ill-considered perceptions of legal theory and the preconceptions that those intuitive, ill-informed and ill-considered perceptions engender. Familiarity with legal theory will in itself encourage a judge consciously to disregard any sort of lingering faith in the discredited declaratory theory of law; inhibit judges from determinedly adopting a positivist bent; and disabuse judges of any tendency to adhere to the formalism of the past or any more modern mutation of it.

At the same time, the preconceptions that these intuitive, ill-informed and ill-considered judicial attitudes generate will be shed. They cannot coexist with a more realistic and comprehensive theory of the judicial function. Of course, it would be unrealistic to expect that a judge's preconceptions will be entirely eliminated by such enlightenment. What would be shed will be those preconceptions that survive, or thrive, simply because the judge nurtures an inadequate or outdated theory of law and the legal process. In short, the blind, intuitive approach to adjudication would be annulled, the charm of legalism would be wasted, and the simplicity of mechanical reasoning would be spurned.

Of course, it can be said that judges who are or become familiar with legal theory will be likely to adopt different theories of law and the legal process and will develop different conceptions of the judicial role as a result. That is so, and is for the good. Indeed, it would detract from the vitality of the law if this were not the case. Any theory and resulting conception of the judicial role is almost certain to be an advance on an unconscious adherence to the notion that the law is there to be declared, a committed positivist dogma, or a self-satisfied formalistic bent. Whatever the theory, judges would naturally express their reasoning in the context of their conception of the judicial role and overtly seek to make their decision accord with that conception. Judicial reasoning would be more sincere and transparent as a result. Further, because judges' greater familiarity with legal theory would permit them to enter into a discourse about the proper conception of the judicial role, differences in judgments will tend to be directed to the basic beliefs of the judges as to the proper conception and why that conception directs the outcome which they favour. More open appeal to the judges' true motivation and reasoning, and much less rationalisation, can be expected in judgment writing.

Theorists and legal practice

If judges' practical skills are to be harnessed to a sound conception of the judicial role based on legal theory, it follows that legal theory should be readily accessible to judges. Regrettably, that is not always the case.[12] Many legal theorists seem to write to and for each other. In the result, jurisprudential theory has become burdened with a surfeit of theories and sub-theories. These theories and sub-theories attract numerous counter-theories, some of which misrepresent and distort the subject theory, which in turn provokes further critical comment.

Unpalatable though it may be, it has to be said that there have been too many rather than too few contributions to legal theory, to the point

---

[12] In referring to legal theory, I am effectively referring to jurisprudence or legal philosophy. I acknowledge that there are vast areas of legal theory that bear directly on the substantive law, such as the law of contract, torts, equity, or administrative law, which are of immense assistance to judges in the application and development of the law. No-one could complain that contributions of this kind are expressed in anything other than plain and readable language. See, for example, the work of the late John Fleming, who was described in *Hunter v Canary Wharf Ltd* [1997] AC 655 by Lord Cooke of Thorndon as 'the doyen of living tort writers' (at 717). Fleming saw the prime function of the academic commentator as being to counteract the inherent conservatism of the law by measuring it against 'modern' conditions. See Peter Cane, 'Fleming on Torts: A Short Intellectual History' (1998) 6 Torts LJ 216, at 216. Cane points out that Fleming engaged in a forty-year conversation with the higher judiciary of the common law world.

where the subject has generated its own somewhat self-conscious and introspective industry. Within this industry, legal terms are defined and redefined and inspire theories that may be perceived to have both their footing and their reach in the given definition; legal concepts are classified and reclassified until the classification or reclassification seems to become the end of the discourse in itself; and hypotheses are advanced and readvanced until they break down under the weight of their own linguistic genesis. Jurisprudence has come to possess the variety of a giant supermarket. Small wonder that the practitioner is bemused as to what to take from the shelf.

Hand in hand with this jurisprudential rampage is the development of a jargon that may be helpful to the initiated, but which is bewildering to the novice. Legal positivism, for example, may be 'analytical positivism', 'imperative positivism', 'classical positivism', 'linguistic positivism', 'positive legal positivism', 'presumptive positivism', 'soft positivism', 'modern positivism', 'normative positivism', 'ethical positivism', 'democratic positivism', 'exclusive positivism', 'inclusive positivism', 'negative positivism' and, no doubt, as many other positivisms as there are colours in Joseph's spectacular multicoloured coat.

Built into this heady promiscuity of concepts is the phenomenon of naming rights. After explaining the concept, insight or phenomenon advanced the theorist will add, 'I will call this ...', and will then insert the brand name. Having one's name associated with an accepted concept identified by other theorists is no doubt appealing, but if the theory advanced will not hold up in its own right, coining a phrase for it will be to no avail. I fell foul of this temptation myself when I invented the term 'substantialism' in an effort to express the opposite of formalism.[13] Today, that term does not seem particularly apt to describe the work of those judges who, in their judicial approach, have a penchant for justice and modernity in the law and who prefer substance over form.

Nor can there be any excuse for the legal theorist writing in obscure and obtuse language that cannot be reasonably understood. It is disturbing that, in seeking to understand some jurisprudential work, it is at times necessary to read a sentence or paragraph two or three times over to understand it, and even more disturbing to find that one still cannot understand what the author is trying to say. Judges and lawyers are intelligent people, well equipped to handle and evaluate concepts and

---

[13] 'Fairness and Certainty in Adjudication: Formalism v Substantialism' (1999) Vol. 9, No. 3, Otago LR 459.

ideas. They do not come to the work unfamiliar with the law and legal process. If they cannot readily understand what the legal theorist is saying, the delinquency lies, not so much with them, as with the theorist. It is for the theorist who wishes his or her work to infiltrate the legal system to write in a style and language that can be comprehended by the reasonably intelligent reader.

This censure does not mean that there is no place in the legal firmament for pure legal philosophy. Legal philosophers may advance pure knowledge no less than philosophers generally may advance our understanding of the universe, our existence, the meaning of life and human behaviour. Knowledge for knowledge's sake is not to be decried, but it must be preferable for that knowledge to be expanded intelligibly. Addressing themselves to a universal audience, philosophers must necessarily strive for universality and, in so doing, endeavour to persuade that universal audience to accept their premises.[14] It must therefore be allowed that legal philosophers may need to exchange ideas among themselves in a manner that is unintelligible to intelligent practitioners in the law before distilling an insight of undoubted value, which can then be presented in a more accessible fashion. Ultimately, however, legal philosophy is directed at a particular human activity and cannot be soundly developed in isolation from that activity. Unless it is based on the reality of that activity, it is not about the law or legal process. If, then, legal philosophical exercises are to possess a value beyond internecine philosophical discourse, those exercises, or the outcome of those exercises, must be grounded in the practice of the law. Only then can they be measured for their validity or relevance to the real world or have a value independent of their expression. Legal theory belongs on this earth, not on another planet.

More critical than these strictures, perhaps, are the recurring more substantive shortcomings of legal theory, which, to the experienced judge immersed in the reality of the legal process, are likely to seem somewhat remote. One such shortcoming is the vain but persistent efforts of legal theorists to unearth a predetermined or impersonal law. A second is the failure to recognise the full extent of judicial autonomy necessary to resolve the vast array of choices confronting a judge in reaching a decision, and the essential place of that judicial

---

[14] Ch. Perelman, *Justice, Law, and Argument: Essays in Moral and Legal Reasoning* (D. Reidal Publishing Co., and Dordrecht, Holland Boston, 1980), at 71. See also George C. Christie, 'The Universal Audience and Predictive Theories of Law' (1986) 5 Law & Phil. 343.

autonomy in the legal system. A third is the distance seemingly placed between theory and the basic requirement that the law exists to serve the needs of society. It is not and never can be an end in itself. Legal theory that departs from or obscures this basic truism does a disservice to the law and legal process. But more on these points anon.

Bridging the divide

For the moment, it will suffice to say that these shortcomings do not excuse judges from obtaining a basic understanding of legal theory. Any number of admirable textbooks and selected works will serve that purpose.[15] All the main schools of jurisprudence have much to offer. From Bentham to Hart, Kelsen to Llewyllen and Dworkin to Unger, the leading theorists offer valuable insights into the congenitally ambiguous question: 'What is law?', the workings of the legal process and the mystique of legal reasoning. Jurisprudence is not a single-question subject and no one theory can purport to be a complete theory. But judges are acutely equipped to select that which appeals to their reason and reject that which does not.

It will be clear that I do not accept the view advanced by Stanley Fish that theory can be made to disappear in the solvent of an enriched notion of practice.[16] Theory provides more than an enriched notion of practice. As I have already argued, only a grounding in jurisprudence provides, or is capable of providing, judges with a sound conception of the judicial role, and it is that conception that is basic to their judging. Theory not only enriches judicial practice but also inspires the very core of a judge's judiciousness. Fish's view that theory 'can never be strong enough to validate theory's strongest claim, the claim to be a special kind of activity in relation to which practice is, or should be, derivative and as a consequence of which practice can be transformed',[17] fails to recognise that judicial practice is derivative because it cannot be validly divorced

---

[15] See, e.g., Hilaire McCoubrey and Nigel White, *Textbook on Jurisprudence* (3rd edn, Blackstone Press Limited, London, 1999); J. W. Harris, *Legal Philosophies* (2nd edn, Butterworths, London, 1980); Ian Ward, *An Introduction to Critical Legal Theory* (Cavendish Publishing Ltd., London, 1998); Brian Bix, *Jurisprudence: Theory and Context* (3rd edn, Sweet and Maxwell, London, 1996); Roger Cotterrell, *The Politics of Jurisprudence* (Butterworths, London, 1989); George P. Fletcher, *Basic Concepts of Legal Thought* (Oxford University Press, Oxford and New York, 1996).

[16] Stanley Fish, *Doing What Comes Naturally: Change, Rhetoric and the Practice of Theory in Literary and Legal Studies* (Clarendon Press, Oxford, 1989), at IX. For an enlightened commentary on Fish's views see Halpin, *Reasoning with Law*, at 7–14.

[17] Halpin, ibid., at 8.

from a conception of the judicial role and that the conception is in large part dependent on theory. As a consequence, practice can be transformed by an advance in that conception resulting from a greater understanding of legal theory.

Certainly, particular theories may be consigned to a long overdue oblivion, but legal theory of itself cannot be relegated to the role of an academic or rhetorical side show. The changes that I am urging in the succeeding chapters of this book must be permitted and encouraged to inform judges' perception of their judicial role. In achieving this transformation it is just as important for the judge to know what theory or parts of a theory to reject as it is to know what theory of parts of a theory to accept. As will become plain, it is this knowledge that will allow judges to eradicate the remnants of the formalism that continues to dog the practice of the law.

It follows from what I have said that I do not, for the most part, accept that there is or should be any tension between judicial practice and legal theory. One should merge into the other. There should be no divide between the practising judge and the academic theorist. The existing divide, at times approaching a gulf, can only be bridged if judges are prepared to assimilate enough theory to be able to expound a sound conception of the judicial role and legal theorists are persuaded to found their theory of the legal process on the reality of judicial practice and express it in reasonably comprehensible language.

Focusing on legal theory with a view to forming a sound conception of the judicial role must necessarily lead judges to more consciously examine and analyse exactly what it is that they are doing. They will be inclined to monitor more closely their performance of the judicial function. In encouraging greater judicial introspection I would not, of course, wish on judges the fate of the centipede:

> The centipede was happy, quite
> Until a toad in fun
> Said, 'Pray, which leg goes after which?'
> This worked his mind to such a pitch
> He lay distracted in a ditch,
> Considering how to run.[18]

---

[18] Justice Sandra Day O'Connor, 'Reflections on Preclusion of Judicial Review in England and the United States', (1986) 27 Wm & Mary LR 643, relating in Justice O'Connor's case, however, to judicial review of administrative action.

Judges need not harbour a fear of such a fate. Indeed, it would be mischievous to align the orderly and dignified gait of your average judge with the frenzied flurry of a centipede's hundred tiny feet. Self-education in itself cannot craze or warp one's thinking. Judges will not become confused by the enlightenment obtained from familiarity with legal theory and a more deliberate assessment of the judicial role.

With judges more receptive to legal theory what, then, is the conception of the judicial role that is likely to eventuate? This book seeks to provide what I hope will be received as a tenable answer to that question.

A précis – more or less

The starting point has to be a more extensive examination of the present judicial process and practice. How are judges reasoning at present? I undertake that examination in the next chapter under the title, 'Muddling Along'. The title may seem rather harsh, especially as judges possess considerable practical skills. It is intended to indicate, however, that in the absence of a sound conception of law, judicial reasoning lacks a coherent or comprehensive base. The declaratory theory of law has been discredited; natural law is generally perceived to be other worldly; positivism and the realities of the law and legal process are an ill-fitting mismatch; and formalism strenuously resists a long-standing death sentence. No theory has emerged to replace these outdated hypotheses.

In the vacuum that remains, judges make do with intuitive beliefs that are never adequately questioned. The critical point is that, although accepting that the declaratory theory of law is a fairy tale, many judges continue to behave and reason as if the theory still held sway. Rules continue to be seen as prescriptive and precedents tangibly coercive. The outcome is a judicial practice that retains all the hallmarks of formalism. Disowned it may be, but experience confirms that formalism exerts a lingering impact on the judicial process.

A fundamental theme of this work recurs in most, if not all, the subsequent chapters in this book, at times as an unspoken assumption, at times as an articulated premise, and at times as the pivotal objective of the law and legal process. The theme is founded in the belief, ranking as a truism, that the law is not an end in itself but a social institution that exists to serve the needs and expectations of society. As such, its justification is to be found in the manner and extent to which the law meets those needs and expectations. Central to this quest are justice and contemporaneity. The needs and expectations of society will not be met unless the law is just and the courts administer justice, and the law is responsive to the ever-changing requirements of the times. Justice and relevance are the leitmotifs of this work.

In Chapter 3, I examine the consequences of residual formalism and the preconceptions it engenders. Formalism, or its lingering influence, I argue, obscures the reality of the judicial process, particularly the scope and extent of choice in judicial decision-making. It results in a 'rulish' or rule-bound approach and undue deference to the coercive element in the doctrine of precedent. In this context, the belief or assumption that the law is an internally coherent and rational phenomenon is examined and found wanting. Nor does the notion that the law can be equated with legal analysis fare any better. I conclude that the true curse of formalism is that it inhibits judges developing a sound conception of the judicial role. Before the Chapter is closed, however, the observable attributes of the modern day 'formalist' judge are reviewed and condemned – or condemn themselves in the very act of being stated. The decision of the House of Lords in *Sevcon Ltd* v *Lucas CAB Ltd*[19] provides a stark example of inveterate formalistic thinking.

Chapter 4 contains a pointed attack on legal fundamentalism. The attack is made necessary because judges will fail to develop a sound conception of the judicial role unless and until they are able to resist the overt and constant pressure of legal fundamentalism. The 'blandishments and bluster' of legal fundamentalists are every bit as effective in retarding the development of a contemporary methodology as is the influence of outdated and discredited legal theories, the survival of which legal fundamentalism in turn abets. The right of people to be concerned about the boundaries and nature of judicial power in a democracy is fully acknowledged, but legal fundamentalism is identified as the creed that builds on those concerns and, notwithstanding its extreme, simplistic and incomplete candour, ultimately obtains ideological force. Under this heading I discuss three topics: the democratic legitimacy of the judiciary, so-called 'judicial activism' and the 'political' aspect of the judicial function. I seek to bring a more balanced perspective to these topics.

In order to move from formalism to the judicial methodology and conception of the judicial role advanced in this book certain chimeras must be banished. One is the present judicial proclivity to treat certainty as a major goal of adjudication. The other is the penchant for an over-strict approach to the doctrine of precedent. Judicial idolatry of

[19] [1986] 2 All ER 104.

certainty is dealt with in Chapter 5. The expectation prevalent in the community that the legal process should deliver certainty and predictability in the law is acknowledged, and the drive for certainty fully examined. While suggesting that much legal theory describing certainty as a myth or illusion is exaggerated, I nevertheless argue that the law is inherently uncertain in that no law is so complete or absolute as to be beyond challenge. The answer to this vagueness in the law is not to blindly subjugate legal reasoning to the goal of certainty. Rather, it is to recognise that certainty has a legitimate but less monumental role in judicial decision-making. Where in a particular case the impact of the decision on the community's ability to organise its affairs is discernible, certainty should, of course, be taken into consideration. But certainty should require a particular relevance to the case in hand before being permitted to influence the outcome of a dispute. Generally speaking, it would be subordinate to the dictates of justice and the need to keep the law abreast of the times.

In the following chapter, Chapter 6, I subject the doctrines of precedent and *stare decisis* to critical examination. Few cases coming before the courts actually require a precedent to be reviewed. Contrary to popular thought, a 'binding' precedent is seldom directly in issue. Rather, the problem with the doctrine of precedent is that it engenders in the judge an 'attitude of mind' that inhibits the proper application and development of the law.[20] Judges adhere as closely as possible to the perceived pre-existing corpus of rules so that the choices and value judgements that must be made emanate from a narrower base. While acknowledging that some system of precedent is inevitable and desirable, I argue that the doctrine of *stare decisis*, certainly at the appellate level, should be abandoned and the precedential force of pre-existing case law should be relaxed. In considering a precedent, the court should re-evaluate its validity and authority and if, and only if, it can be justified as being in accord with justice and as meeting the contemporary needs of the community, should it be applied.

To demonstrate the foibles of precedent, I launch upon an extensive case study in a separate chapter, Chapter 7. In *Lewis* v *Attorney-General of Jamaica*,[21] the Privy Council overruled five of its previous decisions in respect of three different issues. The poverty of the attitude of mind which I condemn, however, is not to be attributed to the majority in

---

[20] The phrase 'attitude of mind' is that of the Hon. Sir Anthony Mason; see 'The Use and Abuse of Precedent' (1988) 94 Aust. Bar Rev. 93, at 106. See also below at 157 *et seq.*
[21] [2001] 2 AC 50; [2000] 3 WLR 1785.

Lewis, but to those Judges who struggled within the framework of the doctrine of precedent in the cases that preceded it. The narrative presents a sorry saga; the administration of justice languished simply because of the coercive force of precedent. But there is some cause for optimism in the approach adopted by the majority in *Lewis*. A 'postscript' to this chapter is required, however, having regard to the fact that the approach of the majority in *Lewis* was effectively reversed by an enlarged Board in a trilogy of appeals relating to the constitutionality of the mandatory death penalty. Five of their Lordships adopt a 'legalistic' approach in sharp contrast to the 'generous' approach pursued by the minority.

With the excesses of certainty and precedent dispatched, the theme of this work is renewed in the next chapter. It is fundamental to a sound conception of the judicial role that any notion of an impersonal or transcendent law, or any notion that the law possesses a logic and coherence that is impersonal to the individual judge, be rejected. In Chapter 8, I seek to reaffirm positively that there is no such impersonal law. It is only when judges recognise that there is no impersonal law that they will cease behaving as if the declaratory theory of law still prevails and will rid themselves of a rule-bound approach and precedent-dominated thinking. In this context, I describe the reality of judicial autonomy and conclude that it is not only inevitable but also desirable.

As the leading advocate of a theory of law that embraces the notion that there is a 'right' answer is Ronald Dworkin, I pursue an examination of various aspects of Dworkin's theory of law in this chapter. I find that Dworkin's distinction between principles and rules, his distinction between principles and policy, his rejection of judicial discretion, and his justification for precedent, are all sadly misguided. The decision of the High Court of Australia in *State Government Insurance Commissioner* v *Trigwell and Ors*[22] provides a convenient illustration of the points made in this chapter.

If there is no impersonal law, then, what do we mean by 'the law'? In Chapter 9 I seek to provide an answer to that question. Underlining the conjunctive, I suggest that 'the law' is nothing more nor less than that which the judges of yesterday proclaimed to be the law *and* which the judges of today or tomorrow are prepared to apply or extend. One must add, of course, that where the judges of yesterday have had nothing relevant to say, the law is what the judges of today or tomorrow are

---

[22] (1979) 26 ALR 67; (1979) 142 CLR 617.

prepared to create. The law is always in a state of transition; that is, predictive rather than subsisting. I therefore argue for a perception that views 'the law' as primarily a process or continuum, which embraces the text of the law but is not dominated by it. Viewing the law as essentially a process overcomes many of the difficulties faced by those judges and theorists of a formalist persuasion; it accommodates the fact that the law is inherently uncertain; it avoids the impossible conundrum of trying to reconcile some rule of recognition with the reality of judicial decision-making; it points to the conclusion that the true and effective constraints on the judiciary are not to be found in the text or content of the law, but in a sound judicial methodology; and it confirms that the law 'as it is' cannot be sensibly separated from the law 'as it ought to be'.

I conclude that judicial creativity is central to the process of applying, extending or inventing 'the law' but argue that this perception does not render the law formless or undisciplined. What takes the place of a non-existent impersonal law is a judicial methodology in which judicial reasoning is more structured and judicial discretion is constrained by procedural, institutional and substantive constraints. Past rules and precedents remain relevant, not as constraints on judicial decision-making, but as tools, and often the primary tools, by which judges fashion 'the law' to serve the ends of justice and keep the law relevant to the times. The rule of law requires a corresponding adjustment to accord with reality and that subject, together with the terms of the judicial oath, are addressed before the chapter closes.

Having denied the judiciary an impersonal law, eliminated the residual impact of formalism, relegated certainty to a consideration only where directly relevant, subdued *stare decisis*, relaxed the coercive element in the strict doctrine of precedent and recognised the full extent of judicial autonomy in the operation of the legal process, it is necessary to spell out the constraints that curb judicial errancy and individual aberration. This task is undertaken in Chapter 10. The constraints are described at length and, as I show, are both real and effective. This chapter, possibly more than any other, reinforces my contention that judicial behaviour is constrained, not by the text of the law, but by the judicial methodology and discipline that make up the legal process. The rule of law is satisfied by the constraints that are part of that methodology and discipline.

Constraints external to the judiciary, such as the fact that judges operate within a judicial hierarchy containing an appellate structure, are outlined first. What may be called self-imposed or self-generated constraints are then examined and found to be equally real and effective. I point out that further substantive constraints would arise with the utilisation of a structured framework to resolve critical questions that underlie judicial decision-making. These questions: whether certainty should be considered a relevant consideration in any particular case; whether a precedent should be re-evaluated and given or denied precedential force; whether a change in the law should be left to Parliament or made by the courts; whether the court should adopt a minimalist approach in deciding a particular case or articulate more general principles; and whether and to what extent the courts should lay down guidelines to control the exercise of a general statutory discretion, are examined in turn. The constraints are in total more extensive and deep-rooted than commonly appreciated. They are interlocking in that they reinforce one another, and they form a matrix of judicial control precluding any serious possibility of errant or aberrant judicial behaviour.

In Chapters 11 to 14, I set out the positive features of the conception of the judicial role that I favour. The conception necessarily begins with the fundamental plank that the law is an instrument of social policy. As the law exists to serve society, each decision must further or be consistent with that end. Chapter 11 focuses on the need for the law to do justice in the individual case and meet the needs and expectations of the community. The twin criteria of justice and relevance therefore assume prominence in this chapter. The reality of justice as a legitimate value in the decision-making process is explained and the problem of translation; that is, the process by which judges discern and apply the sense of justice immanent in the community, is confronted – with greater or lesser success.

The imperative for the law to be responsive to the needs of the times is accorded equal treatment. Relevance is achieved by ensuring, not only that the law develops to meet the changing needs of society, but also, as far as the incremental system of adjudication and incremental law-making permits, that it does so without an enduring time lag between society's changed needs and the revised law. In particular, the law or legal process must strive to meet the requirements of the commercial community or fail in its basic function. An unrealistic expectation that the commercial community will slavishly conform to whatever rules judges magisterially choose to lay down is commercially unrealistic. The decision of the Court of Appeal of New Zealand in *Fletcher Challenge Energy Ltd v Electricity Corporation of New Zealand Ltd*[23] provides an

---

[23] [2002] 2 NZLR 433.

acute example of a case in which commercial reality and judicial wisdom failed to coincide.

Chapter 12 is the vehicle for a discussion on realism and pragmatism. The realism that is endorsed is not that of the American Realist Movement but a revised version, which includes, not only a realistic appraisal of the judicial process, but also a realistic evaluation of the legal theories that inform or infect the process. This attempt to rejuvenate realism, however, does not seek to implant a new legal theory divorced from reality in the place of those that have been dismantled. The realism that is endorsed remains basically a mood or attitude, and with that mood or attitude firmly embedded, I take a hard look at the judicial process in practice.

Pragmatism is also pursued in both theory and practice. The legal pragmatism that is advanced retains the essential characteristics of philosophical pragmatism: it is essentially functional; it embraces realism; it shuns abstract theories and a doctrinaire approach; it is alert to the practical consequences and impact of the law; and the judgments that are made in its name are irrevocably practical judgments designed to further the objectives of a law obligated to serve the needs and expectations of society. The ways in which legal pragmatism of this order will manifest itself in practice and permeate judicial decision-making is then addressed.

This emphasis on reality and pragmatism leads to an excursion into practical reasoning in Chapter 13. I examine the relevant epistemology at some length. Existing practical reasoning theory is valuable in recognising that judges depart from or extend the perceived existing body of law when they are dissatisfied with the outcome that would result, and that they will then seek to place their decision in the context provided by that existing body of law. But the existing theory is deficient in a number of respects. I examine these respects and suggest that the criteria which may give rise to that sense of dissatisfaction in any given case should be introduced into the reasoning process itself. The perceived existing rules, I argue, should not presumptively apply. A rule, principle or the relevant body of law may provide a starting point for judges' reasoning, but should nevertheless be open to re-evaluation. Dissatisfaction, I assert, may arise at the outset simply because the existing law is uncertain.

I then proffer a practical discourse on the effect of practical reasoning in the determination of the choices that must be made in the course of judicial decision-making. What I term a community of considerations emerges, each consideration vying for predominance and acceptance in the judicial balancing exercise that leads to a decision. Prime among these considerations are legal principles, and the remainder of Chapter 13 is taken up with a discussion of the definition, content and role of principles in judicial decision-making.

Although principles dominate fixed rules and prevail over precedent, principles in the conception I advance enjoy a greater elasticity than is customarily conferred upon them. But I vest principles with a critical role in the judicial process notwithstanding this greater elasticity. Principles provide the law or legal process with cohesion and continuity. They become the means by which a mass of disparate and at times conflicting considerations are hobbled into a coherent whole.

In Chapter 14, entitled 'Taking Law Seriously', the difference that greater judicial familiarity with legal theory and the development of a comprehensive conception of the judicial role would make in practice is explored. I point out the respects in which this development would make overt much that is now being done covertly by the judiciary. Much more than greater transparency, however, can be expected to occur. Disregarding, as for practical reasons I must, the substantive developments that are possible in the law, I focus on the changes that may be expected in the judicial process and in judicial methodology. Finally, I conclude Chapter 14 with a plea to cease likening the law to a 'game', as so many legal theorists have done, and too many practitioners of the law are inclined to do. The impact of the law on peoples' lives is too great for judges to do otherwise than treat the law seriously. My closing claim is that the adoption of the conception of the judicial role and the judicial methodology advanced in this book will result in judges discharging that responsibility.

A keen observer will note that the work as it progresses utilises theory in three different respects. In the first place, theory is harnessed to dispel the myths and shibboleths that impair the administration and development of the common law. Untenable and outdated theories are challenged, if not debunked. Secondly, theory is utilised to provide a constructive forum in which different, but nevertheless plausible, views of the judicial role can be discussed more effectively. Finally, the concluding chapters of the book advance a theory of judicial methodology that incorporates a richer understanding of the judicial role.

This book could therefore finish with Chapter 14. Within the recommended approach, however, there is scope for a judge to nurture a personal theory of justice. Not all judges will develop theories, and among those that do so there will be differences, but those differences can properly occur and will, as I have said, enhance and enrich the administration of the law. For completeness, therefore, I proceed in the final chapter, almost in the nature of an addendum, to develop a theory of justice. I have chosen to call it: 'A theory of ameliorative justice'.

I had long cherished a quotation that seemed to me to emphasise what was so often happening in the courts: 'Justice is the right of the weaker.' The quotation is from Joseph Joubert, an eighteenth-century philosopher, moralist and writer. It was with that quotation in mind that I concluded an address in 2000 with this musing:

> It may well be that the law has no higher calling than to defend the poor against the mighty, the powerless against the powerful, and the weak against the strong.[24]

A year later I answered that question in the affirmative.[25] A rhetorical musing had become a theory of justice, and it is that theory that I expound and elaborate in the final chapter. The theory that I proffer is an extension of the concept of corrective justice. In returning the parties to the position they were in before the impeached transaction it seeks to ameliorate the harsh extremes of individual liberalism and, in particular, the economic order, capitalism. I articulate what I perceive to be the underlying precept of the common law, including equity. It is the law's ultimate abhorrence of exploitation: no person may exploit another in the sense of taking or obtaining an unfair advantage at the other's expense. The law serves to protect the weak and vulnerable from the machinations and unfair domination of the strong and powerful. It takes a stand when a person seeks to take advantage of another in a manner or to an extent where it can fairly be said that he or she is abusing the freedom that individual liberalism confers on them. The deep and extended prevalence of the precept of non-exploitation in all branches of the law is revealed and, it is argued, its implementation becomes an integral and intrinsic part of the judicial function.

---

[24] 'The Relationship of Parliament and the Courts: A Tentative Thought or Two for the New Millennium', Victoria University of Wellington Law Faculty's Centennial Lecture, (2000) 31 VUWLR 5.
[25] 'The Conscience of the Law' (2000) Vol. 8, No. 1, Waikato LR.

Conclusion

As a general proposition it must be accepted that practice divorced from theory is necessarily directionless, and theory divorced from practice is necessarily unrealistic. Yet, there is a remarkable divide between judicial practice and legal theory or jurisprudence. Although not its only aim, this book seeks to bridge that divide.

While the practical skills of judges are impressive, those skills need to be augmented by an edified conception of the judicial role and that conception requires, at the very least, a basic knowledge and understanding of legal theory. Apart from the will and effort required on the part of the judiciary, judges will not obtain that familiarity unless judicial scepticism towards legal theory is dispelled and legal theory becomes more accessible to practitioners of the law, including judges. Both these requirements will be assisted if legal theory is expressed in reasonably comprehensible language. It would be unfortunate if the practice of the law were separated from jurisprudence by an artificial barrier created by nothing more than the choice of words.

With judicial practice and legal theory in closer harmony, judicial reasoning aimed at advancing the ends of justice and contemporaneity in the law will become more prevalent. Formalism, or its lingering influence, will be replaced by a judicial methodology that is every bit as disciplined in the service of the law as that outmoded creed. Realism, pragmatism, practical reasoning and principles will become the order of the judicial day. Or, so, that is my hope.

2

Muddling along

Practical muddling along

As a description of the incremental, intuitive decision-making of judges in general, the title to this chapter is not unduly harsh. It is taken from Charles Lindlom's article, 'The Science of Muddling Through'.[1] Harsh or not, it is apt.[2] To decide cases that usually make law and often formulate policy on the basis of an intuitive conception of the judicial role that, at best, only begrudgingly acknowledges the reality of judicial autonomy, and to act as if discredited and out-of-date theories still prevailed, is to muddle along. The trend to a better judicial order is there, but it is incomplete.

At the turn of the twentieth century a basic form of positivism dominated legal thinking. The law was perceived as a closed and cloistered edifice, an independent and autonomous discipline, and a sovereign, self-contained system of internally rational and predictable rules to which the judge, having no or little discretion, would mechanically apply deductive reasoning. Such dogmatic formalism embraced the declaratory theory of law and fostered the belief that the law could be determined with quasi-mathematical precision. Idolatry of certainty and predictability in the law displaced the search for justice and relevance. Justice, if justice was to be done, would be systemic – the product of adhering to rules and form. Fastidious adherence to the doctrine of precedent overwhelmed the emphasis that the judges of old accorded underlying principles[3] and reinforced the technical and linguistic purity of the formalism that prevailed.

---

[1] (1959) 19 Publ. Admin. Rev. 79.
[2] But not as harsh as Duncan Kennedy's description of judges as 'half-conscious, in a state of denial in respect of the ideological element in their judicial behaviour, and therefore acting in "bad faith" '; *A Critique of Adjudication* (Harvard University Press, Cambridge, Mass., 1998), at 20, 23, and Chapter 8.
[3] See E. W. Thomas, *A Return to Principle in Judicial Reasoning and an Acclamation of Judicial Autonomy* (1993) 4 VUWLR Mono. 5, at 1.

At least, judges who practised this more pure form of formalism knew, or believed that they knew, what they were doing. The 'muddling' emanated from the simplistic cast and rigidity of the theory. Today, the 'muddling' results from the lack of any theory on which to base a sound conception of the judicial function. Overtly, there is little support for the rigid doctrines of the past. Many judges pointedly reject them as valid theories of the law or judicial decision-making. A progressive few assail them as adolescent dogmas that the judiciary has outgrown and discarded as it seeks to bring greater maturity to the process of reaching a decision. But the functional and practical realism that should come with the denial of these dogmas remains but a promise.

The fact that these dogmas remain influential in judicial decision-making today is not simply due to the theoretical vacuum that their rejection leaves. A lingering belief that they are valid or have some redeeming value remains. Judges are accustomed to weigh and assess competing propositions and arguments in the belief that there is likely to be something of value in every proposition or argument. Ideas or arguments bandied about in the courtroom may be weak at times but they are generally not without some redeeming value. As a result, judges are predisposed to believe that there must also be something of value in these discredited theories. They seek to assume the advantage of that value. But the assumption is lopsided in the absence of a theory to contest these dogmas. Add to this the judiciary's traditional perceived need for restraint and the 'institutional' pressures to conform and it is fair to say that the judiciary remains unduly shackled to these discredited theories.

The declaratory theory of law

Consequently, it is important that these discredited theories are consciously discarded. The declaratory theory of law for one collapses once it is accepted that judges make law. Simply stated, judges cannot exercise the choice or choices that make law and at the same time be declaring a pre-existing law. The two notions are incompatible.

The 'institutional' pressure that leads judges to remain committed to the outdated declaratory theory or, if not committed to it, to continue to act as if it were a valid theory, is readily evident. It assists to absolve judges from personal responsibility for their decisions. Responsibility can be transferred to that amorphous corpus, 'the law', which they are merely interpreting. It also militates against the criticism that the judges are setting themselves above the law. The charge of arbitrariness is avoided when judges purport to propound, or make the pretence of propounding, a pre-existing law. Finally, the theory also deflects the charge that judicial decisions are retrospective and undemocratic.

The problem, as Professor Dias has observed,[4] arises because of an inability to think other than exclusively in the present time-frame. It is all too easy for judges to believe that there must be some rule in existence, which, even with the aid of some tinkering, is waiting to be discovered or deduced. Judges import their own law-making step or extension into the 'pre-existing' law as if it were part of that law. So it is 'declared'. What enables this wayward thinking to take hold is essentially the absence of a perception of the law as a process, and an appreciation that a decision is not only a reflection of what has gone before, but also a step in the process of what is yet to come. Immediate influences will bear on the instant decision with the result that the law is constantly on the move. It simply will not stand still long enough to be 'declared'.

In addition, the declaratory view, or any less absolute derivative of that view, makes it appear that the outcome of a case is unrelated to the identity of the particular judge. The decision can be presented as a decision that is neither personal to the judge nor an arbitrary exercise of the law-making power. Even if it must be accepted that the judge has made the law, the judge can profess that the pre-existing law moulded or dictated his or her modest law-making accretion. In other words, his or her accretion was inherent in the established law and, therefore, could be 'declared' in this looser sense.

Lord Radcliffe spelt this deception out with unseemly approbation. He suggested that judges should deny their law-making capacity in public in order to retain the semblance of legitimacy for the law they administer. 'If', he said, 'judges prefer the formula – for that is what it is – that they merely declare the law and do not make it, they do no more than show themselves wise men in practice . . .' 'Men's respect for it will be greater', he added, 'the more imperceptible its development'.[5] Yet, later, the illustrious Law Lord posed the question whether anyone would now deny that judicial decisions are creative and not merely an expository contribution to the law. 'There are', he said, 'no means by which they can be otherwise, so rare is the occasion upon which a decision does

---

[4] R. W. M. Dias, *Jurisprudence* (5th edn, Butterworths, London, 1985), at 152.
[5] Lord Radcliffe, *The Law and its Compass* (Faber & Faber, London, 1961), at 39, quoted in Alan Paterson, *The Law Lords* (Macmillan, London, 1982), at 140–141.

not involve choice between two admissible alternatives ...' Yet, Lord Radcliffe insisted, judges 'cannot run the risk of finding the archetypal image of the judge confused in men's minds with the very different image of the legislator ...' 'Personally', he later clarified, 'I think that judges will serve the public interest better if they keep quiet about their legislative function.'[6]

Such an approach, of course, should be utterly unthinkable. As Alan Paterson observes,[7] Lord Radcliffe's façade did not solve the problem of the legitimacy of the law. It simply ruled it out of existence by judicial fiat and swept it under the carpet. By refusing to discuss judicial law-making it left the limits of law-making and practice undefined. More than that, it is a basically dishonest device in that it seeks to perpetuate a false process by a pretence that cannot survive public scrutiny. While Lord Radcliffe's sentiments might not be voiced out loud in respectable legal circles today, however, they retain an unspoken force in the innate desire of judges to distance themselves from personal responsibility for their decisions or from the criticism that they are setting themselves above the law. But they cannot achieve this distance; they are responsible for the law that they make. In short, judges cannot set themselves above the law that they make.

The answer, then, is for judges to accept that the declaratory theory of law is discredited, and to totally and consciously disown it. They make the many choices necessary to arrive at an outcome, and in the process of making choices make the law. They do not then declare or find the law. They pronounce it for what it is, judge-made law, and they must seek to justify it on that basis.

Positivism

Die Meistersinger von Nürnberg

Richard Wagner sets his famous opera, The Mastersingers, in sixteenth-century Nuremberg. The city is home to the most prestigious of the city's guilds, the Mastersingers. They are a pompous, stodgy lot. They are able to boast of years of training and experience, and they are bent on protecting the rules of musical composition. Musical certainty, as it were, emanates from their rigid tones and firmly set phrases, to say

---

[6] Lord Radcliffe, 'The Lawyer and His Times' in Arthur E. Sutherland (ed.), *The Path of the Law* (Harvard University Press, Cambridge, Mass., 1968), at 14–15.
[7] Alan Paterson, *The Law Lords*, at 142.

nothing of their obsessive reliance on rudimentary scales and arpeggios, and their constant fear of too much musical decoration. There must be the correct number of verses, each verse must consist of two parts, each part must consist of a given number of lines and be followed by an aftersong, each aftersong must contain a set number of lines and have a melody not to be found in the parts, and so on, and so on, and so on. The Mastersingers were no strangers to musical positivism.

One Pogner, a rich and cultured goldsmith (who allows that it is God who has made him a wealthy man) wishes to donate a more valuable prize than usual to the winner of the annual song contest. The prize is the hand in marriage of his only daughter, Eva, along with all his material wealth. We can assume that Eva is beautiful for she seems to attract much more interest than Pogner's not inconsiderable worldly goods.

The Town Clerk, Beckmesser, is besotted with Eva. A Mastersinger himself, he is confident that he can win the prize. But Eva cannot abide the fellow and she endeavours to persuade the genial Hans Sachs to enter the competition and so save her from the drooling clutches of Beckmesser.

Hans Sachs was a real historical person, a shoemaker, a famous poet and composer, and a fine bass baritone to boot. As he is without doubt the most influential and gifted Mastersinger, Hans Sachs would be certain to win the contest if he could be persuaded to enter. But he is old enough to be Eva's father or, possibly, even her grandfather, and being of a noble disposition, is reluctant to compete. His reluctance, however, is starting to wilt.

But then the tenor, Walther von Stolzing, a handsome young knight, hits town. He meets Eva, and it is love at first sight.

Not unexpectedly, Walther wants to enter the competition and win Eva's fair hand. He takes steps to join the Mastersingers. Walther has a truly great voice, but he has had no formal training. He learned the art of poetry by reading some old book and learned about songs from the birds in the forest. From these lessons he fashions his own songs.

Walther agrees to submit a trial song to the Mastersingers. But it is far too novel for them. They are appalled. His song confounds all the rules. Beckmesser, who is appointed to mark Walther's effort by making chalk marks for every fault on a slate, quickly runs out of both chalk and slate. Amid scornful laughter Walther is rejected by the Mastersingers. His song is perceived to be nothing more than a collection of mistakes from beginning to end, an outright affront to orthodox musical learning, composition and tradition.

But the more enlightened Hans Sachs, while acknowledging the hefty transgression of the rules, is uncomfortable with the Mastersingers' condemnation of the novelty of Walther's song. He urges them to forget their old rules and try to understand the freedom and flexibility inherent in Walther's improvisation. But the pompous, stodgy Mastersingers remain committed to their rules and will have none of that left-wing nonsense. They huff; acceptance of such innovation and creativity would open the doors to musical anarchy.

Well, Wagner's opera moves on, extremely slowly it must be said, and the song competition finally dawns. The Mastersingers and a sizeable crowd assemble. Beckmesser goes first. The tricky Town Clerk has stolen the score of Walther's song but, being steeped in the Mastersingers' rules, he does not know how to handle the flexibility and freedom it allows. His performance is an abysmal failure and the crowd hiss and hoot with derisive laughter. Beckmesser exits stage left in a fury.

Sachs calls upon the creator of the song to reveal himself and, his moment having arrived, Walther steps forward. It is at once no contest. His improvisation breaks all the rules and, yet, his song draws any number of over-acted nods and murmurs of approbation from the Masters. It is a triumph. The Master assigned to check Walther's performance against the written score is so transfixed by the sheer beauty of the song that he lets his hand holding the score card drop to his side, and the 'technical' faults go unmarked. With one voice the Mastersingers exult: 'Your song has won the Masters' prize.'

If only positivism's reification of rules could be so gloriously dispatched.

Positivism and its stubborn survival

Positivism today has come to bear many of the hallmarks of an ideology. Its adherents will not let it go, preferring instead to add refinement after refinement until it bears little resemblance to a law that is 'posited'. As such, it sustains in the mind of the populace, as well as the judicial mind, a crude form of the theory. Firm rules and certainty become both the end and the means. It needs to be said that in practice, rules, or a rule-bound approach, have an irresistible appeal to many judges. These judges rejoice in rules because they appear to provide certainty, and their recitation can conveniently box the facts into comfortable categories. The expenditure of energy in thought is reduced.[8]

---

[8] John T. Noonan Jr. *Narrowing the Nation's Power: The Supreme Court Sides with the States*, (University of California Press, Berkley, Calif. 2002), at 144.

Positivism must be decomposed or reconstructed. Principally directed at explaining the authority of law to govern, positivism necessarily embraces the notion of law as a set of rules. Contemporary positivists who follow H. L. A. Hart take the view that legal authority is made possible by an interdependent convergence of behaviour and attitude expressed, as if an 'agreement' among individuals, in a duty-imposing social or conventional rule.[9] For Hart, this convergence is his famous 'rule of recognition'. It follows from the perception that decisions can be deduced from predetermined rules without recourse to simple aims, policy or morality. Morality, for example, is not a condition of legality. Principles do not fit into positivism other than as a set of background values that judges may choose to take into consideration when confronted with rules that are vague or in conflict.

It should be borne in mind that much positivist thought is a reaction to the natural law theorist's claim that what might be regarded as law by any formal standard is not law if it is sufficiently unjust. The purpose of the positivists' inquiry therefore dictates its direction.[10] It is when the theory is applied to legal reasoning that it becomes disoriented. Of course, if law is by definition restricted to those elements that create a binding obligation or confer a power, the law is almost certainly to be perceived in terms of a set of rules. But that perception is simply a matter of definition. The boundaries of the law will be drawn tightly and other contributing factors, such as the source of rules, legal principles, standards, the source of legal principles, the source of standards, and the infinite variety of considerations and influences that lead to the outcome of a decision will be relegated to the background. The chorus line will not feature as part of the show.

The positivists' analysis is ultimately superficial. The statement of a rule in a decision is the manifestation of all the factors that contribute to that decision, and it is shallow to depict that manifestation as the binding element comprising the law when all the factors that led to the final formulation of the rule contributed directly to its binding quality. In other words, what gives a rule, or the expression of a rule, such binding or compelling force is not the degree of recognition it commands but the underlying community value that prompts the rule. As

---

[9] Jules Coleman, *The Practice of Principle: In Defence of a Pragmatist Approach to Legal Theory* (Oxford University Press, Oxford, 2001), at 70–71.

[10] See E. P. Soper, 'Legal Theory and the Obligation of a Judge; the Hart/Dworkin Dispute' (1977) 75 Mich. LR 473, at 479–480.

the underlying value provides the reason for the rule in the first place, the force of the rule cannot be separated from or extended beyond the reason for its existence. It is this feature that determines whether or not the rule will command the 'force of law' and foreclose the judge's decision.

Positivists do not, of course, deny that judges make the law. Most admit that to be the case. The influence of moral and ethical considerations of judges is now widely acknowledged and, indeed, it is recognised that it is because a proposition is thought to be just that a judge is likely to adopt it. No such external precepts become law, however, until incorporated in a statute, precedent or custom; that is, until they satisfy the 'rule of recognition' or its modern equivalent. But the acknowledgement that judges make law is grudging and reserved. To Hart, for instance, 'the life of the law consists to a very large extent in the guidance both of officials and private individuals by determinant rules which, unlike the application of variable standards, do not require from them a fresh judgement from case to case'.[11] Hart mitigated this view of 'mechanical jurisprudence' by accepting that rules are 'open textured' and that in 'hard cases' judges must assume a creative role in developing the law.[12]

The description of rules as 'open textured', however, is somewhat inadequate to describe the inherent indeterminacy and vagueness of the law. Because it must be acknowledged that the law changes, precedent-derived rules must necessarily be regarded as incomplete.[13] Every time a rule is extended or contracted the incompleteness of the previous rule is confirmed. Yet, if the rules are incomplete they must necessarily also be uncertain. As an experienced Judge has said; 'the powers of distinguishing and overruling mean that the last word has never been said'.[14] But this is not quite what Hart had in mind in conceding that rules are 'open textured'. That august jurist did not intend to undermine his positivist commitment.

The extent of indeterminacy in the law, however, effectively undermines the positivist approach. Certainly, there is a body of rules which,

---

[11] H. L. A. Hart, *The Concept of Law* (Oxford University Press, Oxford and New York, 1961), at 77–132.

[12] Ibid., at 124–125.

[13] T. M. Benditt, 'The Rule of Precedent', in L. Goldstein (ed.), *Precedent in Law* (Clarendon Press, Oxford, 1987), at 103.

[14] The Hon. Justice W. D. Baragwanath, 'The Dynamics of the Common Law' (1987) 6 Otago LR 355, at 355.

in Hart's words, guide both officials and private individuals. Undoubtedly, there is a large body of relatively settled rules that could be described as relatively determinate, but they remain 'determinate' in the sense that they have not been, or are not likely to be, challenged in a court of law. Officials and private individuals are therefore guided by rules that may or may not prove to be the law in the next case in which they are in issue. Any 'determinacy' is contingent. While the rules as they stand may vest 'the law' with authority and may, unless revoked or modified, be enforced, they do not thereby acquire the permanence to justify the positivist's limited perception of the role of creativity in judicial decision-making.

Nor can judges' creativity be confined to 'hard' cases. In all the jurisprudential literature there is a tendency to focus on the 'hard' case as if it comprised a distinct and identifiable category of cases. The presumption is that it is a 'hard' case because there is no applicable precedent giving rise to a determinate rule in that case. Because it represents a 'novel' case it is, for that reason, difficult to adjudicate. The reality is not so simple. Notwithstanding the infinite variety of factual situations that arise, most cases reach court with a formidable baggage of purported authority and doctrine in train. Generally, it is the baggage that creates the difficulty, not the novelty of the facts or question in issue. Moreover, it is wrong to assume that a case for which there is no apparently binding precedent is more difficult to decide. Indeed, the opposite is more likely to be the case. Untrammelled by allegedly binding authority, the judge is free to bypass much unproductive argument and revert to fundamental principles. Shorn of the legal process' argumentative focus on the scope and applicability of the purported authority, the decision may not be hard at all. Any 'hardness' judges' experience in reaching a decision in such cases tends to reside in making the value judgement that must be made in the course of arriving at a decision; not in the presence or otherwise of a so-called determinate rule.

The positivist's perception also suffers from another serious drawback. Unless the rules are predetermined and a judge is bound to apply them, they cannot be said to create binding obligations or possess binding or compelling force. This is why the doctrine of precedent in its more unbending form is so important in positive thought. But the prodigious difficulty in predicting that any asserted rule will be upheld or applied in a particular case is demonstrated in Chapter 6 dealing with precedent. The outcome, in short, is that uncertain rules can only impose uncertain obligations, and that is a patently flimsy basis for determining what is or is not the law.

The point may be expressed in another way by reverting to Hart's basic rule of recognition. Rules can have no value for their own sake. Their rationale rests in their capacity to provide the basis on which the activity and intercourse of the community may be ordered; that is, as a guide for the conduct of human affairs. But if in the real world rules are inevitably subject to a measure of uncertainty, they can only provide an uncertain guide for human conduct. What, then, has been recognised in terms of Hart's test? A test that is qualified by the proviso that it relates to rules that will be upheld or applied when put in issue in an actual case is not a rule of recognition at all. The recognition is forever being deferred until the next case.

Nor can positivists ignore the leviathan scope for choice in judicial decision-making and the fact that creativity exists in the choices that must be made in all but the most routine of cases. As we have seen, law is created and developed whether the judge chooses to opt for a 'positive' or 'negative' outcome. At best, therefore, positivism may usefully be referred to as a theory seeking to explain the authority of 'law'. But positivism is inadequate as a description of judicial decision-making. As a matter of reality, judges just do not follow Hart's precept or any modern variant of the positivist theory. Modern legal theorists who endorse positivism are left to rail against judges for not applying an uncertain law as if it were certain and therefore binding.

Positivism nevertheless continues to exercise a remarkably adverse influence on judicial reasoning. Because of their limited or intuitive understanding of the theory, judges tend to confuse the positivists' explanation as to why 'the law' is authoritative with the decision-making process. They are led to believe or act as if there is a law to be declared. The art, they believe, is to 'recognise' what constitutes the law, and the process therefore tends to become one of determining the strength of that recognition rather than determining the merit of the particular law or rule.

Inevitably, judges who are prone to adopt this approach develop a rule-bound mentality and an undue deference for precedents. Their penchant for formalism, that is, to regard the law as a system of self-contained internally rational and predictable rules, is reinforced. Furthermore, the positivist's insistence on separating law from morality leads judges to adopt a narrow view of the law and the function of a judge. The notion that the law must have some term of reference external to the law itself, other than recognition, falls by the wayside unnoticed. Discarded as well is a broader perception of the law as being, just not rules, but the source of rules, legal principles, standards, the source of legal principles, the source of standards and the infinite variety of societal considerations and concerns, which, as a matter of reality, can and do influence the outcome of adjudication.

Judges must therefore approach their conception of the judicial role with a clear view of the shortcomings of positivist theory and the disparity between that theory and the reality of judicial practice. Positivists, themselves, can be left to fall by the wayside, immediately adjacent, it is to be hoped, to a roadside sign pointing the way to the reality of the legal process.

Aspirational positivism

Curiously, an idealistic element has entered positivist thinking. The encroachment is called 'normative positivism' or 'ethical positivism'. Not to be outdone, I call it 'aspirational positivism'. It is almost as if the positivists were saying: 'Alas and alack, legal positivism as a conceptual thesis separating law and morality cannot survive in the real world; we must rehabilitate it by recasting it as a normative thesis about the law.' The moral element is injected by proclaiming that the separability of law and morality is a good thing, perhaps even indispensable from a moral, social or political point of view, and certainly something to be valued and encouraged.[15]

Tom Campbell is forthright in his attempt to rescue positivism.[16] Campbell acknowledges that legal positivism is generally regarded as an inadequate analytical and empirical theory whose distinctive feature is the avoidance of moral commitment. Critics identify it 'with empty formalism, theorising by definition, morally detached linguistic analysis, and the unreflective science of calculable observations'.[17] But these criticisms, says Campbell, present positivism in a crude and caricatured form.[18] Legal positivism can be viewed as at base a morally grounded

---

[15] Jeremy Waldron, 'Normative (or Ethical) Positivism' in Jules Coleman (ed.), *Hart's Postscript: Essays on the Postscript to the Concept of Law* (Oxford University Press, Oxford, 2001), at 411.
[16] 'Legal Positivism and Deliberative Democracy' (1998) Current Legal Problems, Vol. 51, 65–69. See also Tom Campbell, *The Legal Theory of Ethical Positivism* (Dartmouth Pub. Co., Aldershot, 1996).
[17] 'Legal Positivism and Deliberative Democracy', ibid., at 65 and 66.
[18] Ibid., at 68.

approach to law that sets out 'an ideal type of legal system'.[19] In other words, legal positivism is not just an account of the way law 'is', it is the way law 'ought' to be. Campbell calls this mode of positivism 'ethical positivism', principally to make it clear that the theory involves an evaluative commitment to a certain type of law, that is, positive law framed in such a way that it can be identified and followed or applied without recourse to contentious moral and political judgements.[20] The term 'ethical positivism' also serves to denote that the law, so conceived, is an institution in which the roles of judge, legislator and citizen bear moral duties of an ethical kind. Thus, judges are under a judicial duty to recognise and enforce only positive law; legislators under a duty to enact laws that can be applied more or less without recourse to controversial moral or political judgements; and citizens under a duty to participate in an ongoing process of fair bargaining and open debate to determine the rules that are to be binding within their communities and to be loyal to the outcome of such a democratic process. Undoubtedly, Campbell's choice of the word 'ethical' is apposite for this theory.

Ethical positivism, then, is represented as a normative political philosophy about the manner in which political power should be exercised. In simplified terms, it is an 'aspirational model of law' based on a presumptive condition as to the legitimacy of governments. Governments must function through the medium of specific rules capable of being applied by citizens and officials without recourse to contentious personal or group political presuppositions, beliefs and commitments.[21] Ethical positivism is irrevocably an 'ideal'. Campbell's theory also leads him to articulate a 'theory of democratic positivism'. The theory would curb 'judicial activism' beyond certain limited circumstances that give the courts delegated power to deal with ambiguities and gaps in existing law where it is unnecessary or unjust to await legislative clarification and development.[22]

Waldron rejects the term 'ethical'. He believes that it connotes normative standards for personal behaviour, as opposed to normative standards for evaluating institutions. Waldron makes clear that, to

---

[19] Ibid., 65–66.   [20] Ibid., at 66.
[21] Ethical positivism 'is about striving towards the rule of law, specifically, the rule of positive law, as a set of constitutional norms, a model which requires political power be rule governed, and in which we seek to establish rather than presuppose a body of ordinary and constitutional mandatory rules that can be recognised and applied in a value-neutral manner'. Ibid., at 69.
[22] Ibid., at 72–75.

him, normative positivism is something more than the idea of a system of norms. Legal positivism is squarely propounded as a normative thesis. In this proclamation he is at one with Campbell. Indeed, Waldron claims in support in modern jurisprudence, not only Tom Campbell, but also Gerald Postema, Neil MacCormick, Stephen Perry and, perhaps, Joseph Raz.[23] The normative positivists' essential claim is that decision-making without a moral component cannot be secured unless the law is structured in such a way as to enable the law on any given subject to be determined without the exercise of a moral or political judgement.

One can have no objection to legal theorists or philosophers proclaiming that a particular perception of law is desirable and should be aspired to by the judiciary, legislators and citizens alike. But the claim of normative or ethical positivists struggles for credibility.

In the first place, normative positivism (or ethical positivism) is not an independent theory. It does not replace legal positivism, it presupposes it. Consequently, all the defects of positivism, which I have highlighted above,[24] apply with equal force to normative positivism. The lack of realism is now compounded by the pain of futility. Positivists' failure to comprehend the inherent uncertainty of the law, the vast scope for choice open to judges in decision-making, and the extent of judicial autonomy taints the normative positivists' perception of what is attainable. No-one would deny that the law should be as certain as possible, but it is unacceptable to found a theory on an unrealistic premise. Because legal positivism fails so, too, must normative positivism fail.

In the second place, normative positivism seems to fall foul of its own rhetoric. In seeking to sustain legal positivism on a normative basis, normative positivists reintroduce a moral element into the law. Reaching a decision because there is an established rule applicable to the instant facts becomes morally justified. It matters not that the application of the rule may work an injustice or be out of step with the needs of the times; its application is now underlined by a 'moral' imperative. In this way, I suggest, the contentious moral and political judgement that Campbell and Waldron seek to eliminate has been replaced by an even more contentious moral judgement. Judges who decline to apply or develop the law in a particular case in accord with the dictates of fairness or contemporary requirements because there is an

---

[23] Waldron, 'Normative Positivism', at 412.   [24] See above at 29–34.

apparently established rule that could be applied are preferring one 'moral' compunction to another.

In the third place, the reification of rules is a decrepit aspiration. Rules and more rules do not lead to greater certainty or the elimination of the moral and political element in the law. As will be argued later,[25] a rule-bound approach must give way to a realistic and pragmatic approach; the shreds of formalism, nurtured as it is by positivism, must defer to practical reasoning; and rules must bow to principles in judicial adjudication. A 'rulish' approach is just what we should aspire to bury, not honour.

I will not, however, anticipate what is to come in Chapters 11 to 14. Suffice to conclude by observing that normative and ethical positivists seek a utopia that is unrealistic and undesirable. Indeed, there is no such utopia.

Romantic positivism

An illuminating example of the way in which an academic's theoretical discourse can reinforce positivism is to be found in Jeremy Waldron's book, *Law and Disagreement*.[26] Waldron extols the legislative process and disparages the judicial process. Writing with power and clarity, his description of the legislative process is nevertheless incorrigibly romantic and his corresponding perception of the judicial process equally cynical. But Waldron's advocacy has acquired a dedicated following among a number of academics and lawyers, particularly those of a positivist bent. So it may be useful to briefly touch upon Waldron's thesis.

Approximately the first two-thirds of *Law and Disagreement* are devoted to the rehabilitation of legislation. The remaining one-third is directed to the demolition of judicial review (using that phrase as it is understood in the United States). For present purposes, it is the former aspect that calls for attention.

Waldron has coined the phrase, 'the circumstances of politics', to describe the necessity of reaching agreement in a community in which disagreements about policies, ethics and basic questions of political structure and individual rights are rife.[27] The proper forum for the resolution of these intractable disagreements is the legislature. Only the legislature can resolve disputes in such a way as to preserve the dignity and self-respect of

---

[25] See below, Chapter 12.   [26] Clarendon Press, Oxford, 1999.   [27] Ibid., at 107–118.

those who come off second best in the political struggle. Citizens search, not for a just consensus, but for a political framework that will accord equal respect for their differing views. Majoritarian government meets this prescription. Waldron articulates democratic, pluralistic and proceduralist values,[28] and only laws enacted in accordance with those values will have authority. No other mechanism for settling disputes can have that authority because they do not treat each view and each vote equally. Decision-making by majority vote therefore becomes the principle by which the divergent views of every individual are ascribed equal weight, that is, the means of giving each person's view the greatest possible weight compatible with an equal weight being given to the views of every other person. 'It accords maximum decisiveness to each, subject only to the constraint of equality.'[29] Waldron asserts that the defects of majoritarianism do not count in favour of the courts as they themselves decide disputed questions by majority vote.

Waldron's denies that the legislative process is 'an unholy scramble for personal advantage',[30] preferring to describe it as 'a noisy scenario in which men and women of high spirit argue passionately and vociferously about what rights we have, what justice requires, and what the common good amounts to, motivated in their disagreement not by what is in it for them but by a desire to get it right'.[31] Richard Posner pointedly observes that Waldron has a 'too starry-eyed a view' of the legislative process.[32] Waldron's notion that people of diverse perspectives are 'capable of pooling these perspectives to come up with better decisions than any of them could make on their own'[33] is a 'pious proposition' that ignores the fact that deliberation among people with such disagreements may tend to entrench rather than dissolve their disagreements.[34]

While I would not deny that such virtues as altruism and high-mindedness can motivate legislators, one should not go overboard. Waldron, in my view, does so. He goes too far in diminishing the element of self-interest in the political process.[35] Lawrence Sager has forcibly argued that Waldron's perception is 'thin and dangerous' simply because political representatives are inevitably drawn to a substantial degree to respond to the power of votes or of dollars as opposed to the

---

[28] Ibid., at 32. [29] Ibid., at 113. [30] Ibid., at 304. [31] Ibid., at 305.
[32] Richard A. Posner, 'Book Review: Review of Jeremy Waldron, *Law and Disagreement*' (2000) 100 Colum. LR. 582, at 590.
[33] Waldron, *Law and Disagreement*, at 72. [34] Posner, 'Book Review', at 591.
[35] See below, Chapter 4, at 80–82.

force of an individual or group's claim that they have right on their side.[36] Sager acknowledges that competition among political contenders for support might often push the powerful to include the less powerful in their political agendas, and that 'discrete and insular minorities'[37] may, through coordinating their determination and energy, acquire substantial political muscle. But this is a function of what is expedient in shifting political circumstances in a process that proceeds far more readily by the logic of accumulated power than by that of reflective justice. The point is that no individual or group can demand to be heard or have their interest taken into account unless they can make themselves strategically valuable in the political process. Sager concludes that in the real world of popular politics, power, not truth, speaks to power.[38]

Further, Waldron's description of majority voting as a manifestation of a principle according respect for persons because it ascribes equal weight to the divergent view of every individual is highly theoretical in the context of the legislative process. Divergent views may have equal weight in an abstract sense, but that does not mean that in practice they have equal weight in the political arena. Try, for example, telling a member of a racial minority, or a member of the gay community or even a disabled person on a pension, that his or her vote has equal weight with the votes of those who make up the majority! Moreover, the apathetic and indifferent voter's vote is weighed equally with that of the voter who is intensely interested in or caring about a particular issue.[39] Again, people may vote without having the incentive to undertake research or to give significant consideration to the choices they make when voting. In all, the system permits, if not encourages, voters to act on the basis of their personal self-interest.[40] No adage has displaced the maxim proffered by Dr Lindsay over half a century ago in describing democratic control: '... only the wearer knows where the shoe pinches'.[41] It is for such reasons that Waldron cannot successfully defend 'majority rule' on the ground that it is neutral among competing

---

[36] Lawrence G. Sager, 'Article, Comments and Speeches: Constitutional Justice' 6 NYUJ Legis. & Pub. Pol'y 11, at 17.
[37] Justice Stone's famous footnote 4 in *United States* v *Carolene Products Co* 304 U.S. 144; 58 S. Ct. 778 (1938).
[38] Ibid. [39] Posner, 'Book Review', at 589.
[40] Christopher L. Eisgruber, 'Democracy and Disagreement: A Comment on Jeremy Waldron's *Law and Disagreement*' NYUJ Legis. & Pub. Pol'y, Vol. 6, No. 1, at 42.
[41] A. D. Lindsay, *The Modern Democratic State* (Oxford University Press, Oxford, 1943), Vol. 1, at 269.

conceptions of equal respect.[42] Nor is Waldron's claim that the people ought to be able to govern themselves by their own judgements unassailable. For the reasons I spell out below,[43] the 'people' cannot be equated with 'the legislature'. The implementation of the people's will by their representatives is imperfect.

Waldron's 'tit for tat' deprecation of the judicial process is no more realistic than his 'rosy' view of the legislative process. Take, for example, his portrayal of the judicial process as a process sharing majoritarian rule. While it is true that the decisions of multi-member courts where they are not unanimous are decided by a majority, there is a vast difference in the manner in which that majority evolves. The majority in a contested decision emerges following an objective, deliberative and reflective process in which the judges are constrained by a distinct methodology and discipline and distinguished by their independence and impartiality.[44] It cannot be said that cases are decided on the basis of personal self-interest. Judges are not representatives of or beholden to any particular faction in the community. Nor are they vicariously attached to the immediate interests of those participating in the political community. They are detached from their own immediate interests and projects by the demands of the adjudicatory role and from the vicarious interests of the members of their political community by the absence of political accountability.[45]

Waldron seems to nurture an underlying predilection that the legislature is 'us' and the judiciary is 'them'. This predilection leads to the portrayal of the judiciary as an intruder in the affairs of the people and to a corresponding failure to appreciate the constitutional and democratic role of the judiciary. I have sought to establish the constitutional and democratic legitimacy of the judiciary elsewhere.[46] Suffice here to attest to the complementary role of the judiciary in Posner's terms. Realism, he asserts in a sentence as substantial as it is long, would include recognition of the fact judges are insulated from most of the political pressures that beset elected legislatures; that these pressures sometimes reflect selfish, parochial interests, ugly emotion, ignorance, irrational fears and prejudice; and that the judges' insulation, together with the traditions and usages of the courts and the screening of judges for competence and integrity, may confer on the judiciary a power of detached and intelligent reflection on policy issues that is a valuable

---

[42] Eisgruber, 'Democracy and Disagreement', at 38. [43] See below, Chapter 4, at 79–81.
[44] See below, at 77–79. [45] Sager, 'Constitutional Justice', at 15.
[46] See below, at 77–85.

complement to the consideration of these issues by the ordinary lawmakers.[47] The fact that individuals and minority groups can seek to obtain redress, however popularly ridiculed and deplored they may be, based on the strength or merit of their argument, means that the adjudication process offers its own distinct – and distinctly valuable – form of equality, particularly in relation to contested rights.[48]

I would prefer an approach that is equally laudable – or equally cynical – about both the legislative process and the judicial process. The legislative process is not as good, and the judicial process is not as bad, as Waldron seeks to portray them, and this lack of balance necessarily infects his thesis. They are different processes, existing and operating within the constitutional framework of a democracy, suitable for the resolution of essentially different kinds of disagreement. While there will be an overlap and controversy as to where the boundary should be drawn, the art is to ensure that agreements and disputes are allocated between the two processes according to the respective strengths of those processes. While in a representative democracy, most disagreements will fall to be resolved by the legislative branch of government, those disputes that require an objective, deliberative and reflective process directed by an independent and impartial adjudicative body immune to the disparate power and strength of the contestants will more naturally be drawn to the courts.[49]

Nor, although it may be something of a digression, do I consider that the debate typified by Waldron's book occupies the whole picture. It is a truism that society is made up of many different people with many different views. Without any doubt, there is and, I suspect, will remain, a substantial body of people who hold dear to a vision of society in which individual and minority rights are truly respected, and where this respect is ingrained in the community without threat of pressure or coercion. A popular legislature may or may not advance their vision. For them, the legal process provides a forum in which they can express and pursue their deeply felt beliefs. Without that forum they are deprived, or are likely to see themselves as being deprived, of an effective voice. Argument as to the respective merits of the legislative and judicial processes and the legitimacy of the judiciary to resolve disagreements of the kind Waldron addresses can, for the moment, be put to one side.

---

[47] Posner, 'Book Review', at 591. I have omitted Posner's qualification that in certain respects he is referring to Federal Judges.
[48] Sager, 'Constitutional Justice', at 14 and 19.
[49] See below, Chapter 4, at 78–79 and Chapter 15, at 366–367.

Rather, we are here dealing with a phenomenon that bears on the health of society; possibly, the core of a civilised society. We are confronted by a sociological question rather than a legal or philosophical question. Can the best of human aspirations be indefinitely bottled up in frequently indecisive and inconclusive compromises? The people who hold dear to these aspirations can look to a forum which, although having its fair share of predilections and prejudices, is less endowed with those qualities by virtue of its methodology and discipline than any other forum. It is just possible that the right of ultimate recourse to the courts to resolve the tension between the finer aspirations of men and women, on the one hand, and the baser instincts of men and women, on the other, and the hope of realisation that comes with that access, is necessary for the health and harmonious functioning of a civilised society.

Natural law

Superstition and/or speculation

As positivism was essentially a reaction to natural law theory, it is appropriate to touch briefly on that ethereal phenomenon and its impact on the legal process.

Essentially, in natural law theory, authority is explained in terms of moral authority. Morality is an immanent property of the law. Beyond and superior to the laws made by humans is a higher or more fundamental law propounding moral principles or ideals that are immutable and eternal, and that exist apart from and are logically prior to legal institutions and statutes and enacted human law. Thus, human enactments must reflect these principles and ideals to possess the validity and authority of law. At different times over a long history this 'natural law' has been proclaimed to be derived from human nature, the natural condition of humanity, the natural order of the universe, the eternal law of God or correct political morality. The method of discovering it is usually claimed to be human reason.[50] Rather than being a normative theory to describe the legal system, natural law provides guidance as to what the law 'should' be and a means of judging the worth of human law.

I share the scepticism of Oliver Wendell Holmes about natural law. Indeed, I believe that Jeremy Bentham was closer to being right than

---

[50] For an excellent short account of natural law theory, see Cotterrell, *The Politics of Jurisprudence* (Butterworths, London, 1989), at 119 *et seq.*

wrong when he described natural law as 'nonsense' and the allied notion of natural rights as 'nonsense on stilts'. Natural law, to Bentham, was a 'formidable non-entity' and natural law reasoning a 'labyrinth of confusion' based on moral prejudice or unproveable speculations about human nature.[51] I acknowledge that my own occasional censure of natural law does not approximate the invective of the great Bentham – but perhaps that is due to the different times.

Irrespective of its long historical tradition it is difficult to analyse natural law theory as anything other than a mix of superstition and speculation. It can no longer be thought possible to discern the immutable principles and ideals of natural law by the use of reason. Far from being vested with some sort of metaphysical dignity, the law is an instrument of social policy squarely in the hands of the law-makers in a political process, a process that does not exclude the judiciary. The law is required to change, and does change, to reflect the needs of a society continually in a state of flux in a manner that is less than deferential to the purported timeless principles and ideals of natural law.

Such firm censure of natural law theory may be awkward in that there are obviously times in this book when I flirt with the outer, or even the inner, folds of the skirts of natural law theory. Perhaps it is a charge that anyone who rejects the positivists' view of the law may encounter.[52] Ronald Dworkin, for example, has at times admitted to being a natural lawyer, and in the sense that he believes that legality is to be explained in terms of moral and political theory, and not as a normative description of law in operation, that may be so. But I continue to harbour the realist's reluctance to ascribe to morality the decisive role in determining what is and is not law. The law can be judged according to an external term of reference without that external term of reference being an innate property of the law. Moral ideals may influence the law simply because they are likely to influence judges, and the law can be evaluated from a moral standpoint, but that does not mean that the 'essential character' of law is to be explained in moral terms.[53]

The key point to make is that, as with positivism, natural law theory is essentially directed to explaining the authority and validity of law. It examines the nature of legal authority and how far that authority may be

---

[51] Jeremy Bentham, *A Comment on the Commentaries and a Fragment on Government*; J. H. Burns and H. L. A. Hart (University of London, Athlone Press, London, 1977).
[52] See James Allan, 'The Invisible Hand in Justice Thomas's Philosophy of Law' (1999) Pt II, NZLR, 213.
[53] Cotterrell, 'Politics of Jurisprudence', at 124.

pressed against the moral authority derived from a metaphysical view of human nature, or the human order, or from God. It is directed at the source of the law's authority. In deciding a case, however, the judge is undertaking an exercise of authority, not determining the source of that authority. A judge cannot consciously set out to reach a decision in accordance with some metaphysical view of human nature, or of human order, or of God.

Nor do the modern variations of natural law theory alter this perception. Lon Fuller, a legal theorist at the edge of natural law theory, has argued against a sharp separation of law and morality. He introduced the notion of 'fidelity to law'. To work, a legal system must embrace the citizen's need for cooperation and reciprocal obligations. The legal order will then provide coherence, logic and order. Fidelity to the system is achieved through what Fuller calls the 'inner morality of the law'. This internal morality of the law consists of a series of eight requirements any system of rules must meet, or substantially meet, before the system can be said to constitute a valid legal system or the rules rank as law. These requirements need not be set out. Suffice to say that they are essentially 'procedural' in nature, and would find a place in almost any lawyer's broad conception of the rule of law. But where these requirements are present the citizen is obliged to obey the laws of that system.

John Finnis provides the most recent and substantive statement of natural law theory. In his view, the authority of a legal system is founded on its promotion of the 'common good'. He bases natural law, not in reason, but in intuition, in what is 'self-evident', although he also stresses that knowledge of what is self-evident only comes to us if we have sufficient experience and are willing to engage in reason and reflection; that is, practical reason or 'practical reasonableness'.

If natural law theory of these kinds held sway among judges it could be expected that their reasoning would exhibit a greater mix of law and morality than is the case. At present, any moral considerations are almost invariably kept covert. In fact, positivism's insistence on the analytical separation of law and morality has overwhelmed any semblance of natural law reasoning in judicial practice. If anything, the conviction that the law can be determined without overt reference to morality has meant that judges have also tended to exclude from consideration any external term of reference and sought to deal with the law as its own hermetic discipline. Traces of natural law theory that are consonant with a positive or more formalistic approach can, however, be detected in judicial thinking. Bentham, for instance, thought that natural law theory fomented in the minds of many a confusion of legal and moral authority, that is, that law possessed not only authority as law but also moral authority. Complacency that the law was 'right' followed. Blackstone was severely criticized for the tendency in his *Commentaries* to merge legal and moral authority with the implication that English law was intrinsically superior to all others.[54]

Few, if any, judges today think that there is a 'right' answer to any legal problem. But there is nevertheless an observable air of complacency among many judges with the law as they find it. Notwithstanding that they have forsworn any conviction that their decisions must be 'right', or necessarily right, they are less critical of the precedents that they are called upon to apply than the merits of those decisions might deserve. The notion persists that the common law reflects a transcendent wisdom built up by the reasoning of the judges of yesteryear. Subjecting themselves to this wisdom without question vests the perceived existing law with an aura akin to natural law.

Nevertheless, while respect for the wisdom of the past and a confidence in reason to unearth the law may in part have its origins in natural law theory, my own perception is that the present day attitude of judges, including the complacency and unquestioning satisfaction with much existing law, is due in far greater measure to the triumph of positivism and the formalistic approach that positivism has nurtured.

Natural law and human rights jurisprudence

A caveat to the above thinking may be required, however, to account for the judiciary's earnest adoption of human rights jurisprudence over the past two or more decades. Human rights are vested with much of the panoply of natural law. Natural law embraces natural rights, and those rights become, or are, related to human rights. The supremacy of human rights is then verified by the enactment of constitutions and bills of right giving hallowed expression to those rights. Almost invariably, the rights will be proclaimed as if they are self-evident, eternal and immutable truths. The language will be broad and emphatic. There is little doubt that rights are expected to 'trump' the general law, and to that extent they implicitly constitute a superior law.

Nor is it possible to read the numerous decisions relating to human rights without concluding that judges have warmly and earnestly accepted that rights 'trump' the existing law. There is a crusading or missionary zeal

---

[54] Bentham, *A Comment on the Commentaries*, at 498–499.

about many judgments in this area, particularly at first instance, which is a trifle discomforting. The judges, it seems, have found their natural habitat; enforcing fundamental rights for the protection of the individual who is different or the minority that is repressed. In a democratic setting in which the people want the rights of individuals and minorities in the abstract respected and are yet, as a majority, liable to demonstrate something less than that respect in a particular situation, the judiciary sees itself as the guardians of the community's enduring values.

This setting only has to be stated for it to be seen that human rights jurisprudence is fertile ground for the growth of natural law theory. With the rights in the constitution or legislation expressed in the broadest of terms, where do the judges' perceptions of the rights of the individual or the minority in a particular case come from? Where does their articulation of the community's enduring values derive? Then, in the inevitable inquiry into these questions, expansive concepts such as the dignity of the human person and the values of a civilised society will be introduced as a basis for 'interpreting' the right. Small wonder that judges in the heat of the forensic battle are from time to time prone to cast their eyes upwards to the heavens in the hope of procuring inspiration. Where else will the judge get the divine creative impulse he or she so badly needs?

Human rights litigation is a setting in which judges are virtually forced to be creative. The broad statutory language of the rights in itself necessitates that creativity. Moreover, judges are also free to discard or modify prior case law. Indeed, as already indicated, in most cases it would be contrary to the will of the makers of a constitution or the legislators of bills of right to crimp the spirit of the constitution or proclaimed rights with case law that those makers or legislators presumably thought inadequate for the protection of those rights.[55] Of course, as decisions build up, so is the pristine freedom of judges deciding human rights cases curtailed, but with a novel claim, judges must still strive, creatively or otherwise, to give some practical meaning to the broad rights and expansive concepts that are their human rights stock in trade.

Do judges therefore assume that human rights are founded in natural law? If they do so it is an unarticulated assumption. Most are content not to

---

[55] Courts have universally given constitutional provisions and bills of right a generous interpretation. See, e.g., *Collins* v *Lewis* (1869) LR 8 Eq 708, at 709; *Vere* v *Cawdor and King* (1809) 11 East 568; 103 ER 1125; *Wickes* v *Gordon* (1819) 2B & Ald 335; 16 ER 389; *R* v *St Mary's Leicester* (1818) 1B & Ald 327; 106 ER 121; and *Aldrich* v *Cooper* (1803) 8 Ves 382, at 388; 32 ER 402, at 405.

look beyond the constitution or statute prescribing the bill of rights. But this is to beg the question. The judges' reasoning may incorporate reference to the broadness of the right itself, the spirit of the constitution or bill of rights, the enduring values of the community recognised in such rights, and the expansive concepts underlying human rights. Those references, however, do not in themselves determine the scope of the particular right, the existence or nature of the enduring values, or the basis of the expansive concepts assertedly underlying the right or value. The scope or content of the right remains undefined until it is judicially declared.

Little in the way of legal theory has been directed at the source of the judges' perception of the actual content of the bill of rights that the constitution or statute presents. But is it natural law? Clearly not; judges and theorists may search the heavens in vain, but they will fail to find a special empyrean category dedicated to human rights. Human rights have no greater natural law pedigree than the natural rights that natural law allegedly sired.

Another more satisfactory, but incomplete, view is that human rights jurisprudence obtains its legitimacy in the universality of the human rights that are recognised. International endorsement can be portrayed as a validating force. But this perception is incomplete in that, while it may explain the pervasiveness and force of the broad rights, it again does not explain the scope and content of those rights in particular situations, or the enduring values recognised by the rights, or the expansive concepts associated with and underlying such rights. For the most part the courts are not proclaiming a right, or value, or concept that has been universally recognised or, indeed, recognised at all. The courts are simply breaking new ground. Take, for example, the Canadian jurisprudence in this area. It cannot be pretended that the law developed by the Supreme Court of Canada in respect of the generally worded constitutional precept of equality, universal or otherwise, existed anywhere awaiting recognition, before it sequestered a majority of that Court. The judges simply forged new principles and made new laws.[56]

Thus, it is to be accepted that human rights jurisprudence constructed from broadly worded constitutional and statutory bills of

---

[56] E.g., *Law* v *Canada (Minister of Employment and Immigration* [1991]*)* SCR 497; *Egan* v *Canada* [1995] 2 SCR 513; *Eaton* v *Brant County Board of Education* [1997] 1 SCR 241; *Benner* v *Canada (Secretary of State)* [1997] 1 SCR 358; *Eldridge* v *British Columbia (Attorney General)* [1997] 3 SCR 624; *Vriend* v *Alberta* [1998] 1 SCR 493; and *M* v *H* [1999] 2 SCR 3.

right over the last two decades is purely judge-made. Ultimately, in the absence of any legislative demarcation, the courts define the boundaries of their own jurisdiction or the reach of judicial power within their jurisdiction.[57]

In the case of human rights, the judges have asserted an unsparing and liberal domain. They have done so for a variety of reasons, many, perhaps, only vaguely perceived and all of them relatively practical and pragmatic. First up must simply be default. In utilising broad language the makers of constitutions and legislators of bills of right have effectively left to the judges the work of deciding the scope and content of those rights in the numerous and varied situations that arise. They have spelt out that the rights are fundamental rights and have used the language of exhortation to command their compliance. But they have not provided the detail. Unless the courts undertake that task, the detail would go by default. Hence, the makers of constitutions and legislators of bills of right have thrust the task upon the judges and they pragmatically accept that they must do their best to discharge it. Commentators may disagree about the way in which the judges discharge that task, and some may be critical of the extent of jurisprudence they have invented, but the present point is that it was never seriously open to the judges to reject the responsibility that has been effectively imposed upon them.

The second reason that may be advanced to explain why the judiciary has assumed an unsparing and liberal jurisdiction in this field is the perceived role of the judiciary to protect the individual and minorities from oppression in a democratic system dominated by majoritarian rule. Again, the pragmatic notion of default creeps in. If the courts do not protect the individual or minorities from the tyranny of the majority, who will? With the entrenchment of constitutions and the enactments of bills of right, judges perceive a mandate to positively pursue the protection of the individual and minorities. In essence, the makers of the constitution and the legislators of bills of right are perceived to have conferred a function, and not just provided a document to be interpreted.

Finally, it must be borne in mind that courts, by their very nature, are oriented to the protection of the individual, either alone or in a congruent grouping, from the excessive exercise and abuse of power. It is the individual or group that is at the centre of the courts' daily business. He or she or they are the plaintiff, or the defendant, or the prosecutor, or the

---

[57] See below, Chapter 10, at 248 and 255–256.

accused, or the appellant, or the respondent. They are the primary focus of the courts' attention and become the focus of the courts' concern.[58] A constitution or bill of rights provides the judge with a new armoury to express that concern.

In the result, any suggestion that the exponential expansion of human rights jurisprudence is indicative of a revival of natural law is to be rejected.

Natural law and parliamentary supremacy

Another area of legal discourse in which there are tell-tale signs of natural law thinking relates to the concept of parliamentary supremacy that prevails in Westminster-type democracies. A new stream of constitutional thought is emerging that would deny absolute and unqualified legislative sovereignty to the legislature. This challenge is portrayed as part of the ongoing development of an unwritten constitution. Just as a written constitution is regarded as a 'living' document that can be interpreted and reinterpreted so as to be relevant to the times so, too, an unwritten constitution must have the fluidity to permit it to be defined and redefined to meet the developments and demands of each generation.

The most recent challenges to the doctrine of parliamentary supremacy have been most forcefully advanced in the extra-judicial writings of Sir John Laws and Sir Stephen Sedley in the United Kingdom. Sir John Laws begins with the role of the courts in judicial review, which he believes is developing to offer an explicit and systematic protection of constitutional rights. Recognising that there are established constitutional norms, some with considerable antiquity, Laws regards the absence of what he calls a sovereign text as meaning that the legal distribution of public power consists ultimately in a dynamic settlement, acceptable to the people, between the different arms of government. That dynamic settlement can change, as history in the last three hundred years shows it can change, without revolution. Thus, Laws

---

[58] This phenomenon can be most plainly seen in the struggle that the victims of crime have endured to be adequately considered by judges in the implementation of the criminal law, particularly sentencing, where the emphasis has historically been on the person charged with the crime or on the prisoner, as the case may be. Improvements in the law, to the extent that there have been improvements, have been largely achieved by statutory reform. No such judicial reticence would have been experienced if the interests of victims had been expressed as a right.

expresses the opinion that the survival and flourishing of a democracy in which basic rights are not only respected but enshrined requires that those who exercise democratic political power must have limits set to what they may do; limits which they are not allowed to overstep. If this is right, he states, it is a function of democratic power itself that it be not absolute.

Balking at what he believes to be an outdated, or perhaps misunderstood, notion of the sovereignty of Parliament, Laws asserts a higher order law by virtue of which fundamental rights possess a status that no government with the necessary majority in Parliament has the right to destroy. For it to be otherwise would mean that the right is not a guaranteed right but exists, in point of law, at least, only because the government chooses to let it exist. If such absolute power is beyond the reach or curtailment of review, fundamental rights are only privileges, and the fact Parliament is an elected body cannot immunise it from playing the tyrant's role. Laws proceeds to extend this perception to democracy itself. It is, he says, a condition of democracy's preservation that the power of a democratically elected government – or Parliament – be not absolute. Ultimate sovereignty therefore rests, not with those who wield governmental power, but in the conditions under which they are permitted to do so. The constitution, not the Parliament, is in this sense sovereign.[59]

Laws' contemporary, Sir Stephen Sedley, perceives in the reassertion of judicial oversight of government, which he rightly describes as having been the greatest achievement of the common law in the 1970s and 1980s, a move to fill the lacunae of legitimacy in the functioning of democratic politics. A 'judicial re-fashioning' has occurred within the organic constitution with popular support sufficient to mute political opposition to it. Still emerging, he argues, is a new constitutional paradigm, no longer of Dicey's supreme Parliament to whose will the rule of law must finally bend, but one of 'a bi-polar sovereignty of the Crown in Parliament and the Crown in its courts, to each of which the Crown's ministers are answerable – politically to Parliament, legally to the courts'. Predicated on the primacy of democracy as a basis for assuming such a jurisdiction, Sedley articulates the problem in these terms: '... how to ensure that as a society we are governed within a law which has internalized the notion of fundamental human rights'. 'If in our society', the distinguished jurist states, 'the rule of law is to mean

---

[59] Sir John Laws, 'Law and Democracy' (1995) Public Law 72, at 81–92.

much, it must as least mean that it is the obligation of the courts to articulate and uphold the ground rules of ethical social existence which we dignify as fundamental human rights, temporary and local though they are in the grand scheme of things'.[60]

It is by virtue of an asserted 'higher order' law that Laws holds that no government with a majority can subvert fundamental rights. Similarly, Sedley earlier suggested that the rule of law can be adopted, if necessary, as a 'higher-order' principle, which, like democracy, is accorded primacy by the social consensus which exists around that concept. Sedley clarified his meaning in the first of his outstanding Hamlyn Lectures.[61] In the end, the learned author suggested, we have to come back to a society's consensus about what is on and what is off limits. He considered that this is not best described as a higher-order law because it has no authoritative source and no forum or means of enforcement. 'It is rather', Sedley decided, 'what we collectively accept is the limit of what is tolerable.'

I have written elsewhere that, in this context, a higher-order law must also be rejected.[62] On a close analysis, both Laws and Sedley's theories rest on a perceived consensus of the people to vest the courts with the capacity, or jurisdiction, to uphold fundamental rights over Parliament's intent. I consider it preferable to leave the debate as to the absoluteness of Parliament's supremacy unresolved. An answer should be deferred until such time as the courts are in fact confronted with legislation that raises a fundamental constitutional issue placing in jeopardy the basis of representative government, the rule of law or the fundamental rights and freedoms that are embedded in these democratic ideals. Much will necessarily depend on the circumstances at that time. Until then, the answer need not be known; it can, as it were, be left up in the constitutional air.

The resulting uncertainty or inconclusiveness serves a valuable constitutional function. A constitution is primarily an instrument to distribute, or the means of distributing, political power and, to paraphrase the words of Lord Russell: 'Every political Constitution in which different bodies share political power is only enabled to exist by the

---

[60] Sir Stephen Sedley, 'Human Rights: A Twenty-First Century Agenda', (1995) Public Law 386, at 389–391.
[61] *The Hamlyn Lectures: Freedom, Law and Justice*, by the Right Hon. Lord Justice Sedley, 'The Free Individual and the Free Society', at 10.
[62] E. W. Thomas, 'The Relationship of Parliament and the Courts: A Tentative Thought or Two for the New Millennium' (2000) 31 VUWLR 5.

forbearance of those among whom this power is distributed.'[63] Uncertainty as to whether the courts will intervene to strike down legislation perceived to undermine representative government and destroy fundamental rights must act as a brake upon Parliament's conception of its omnipotence; and uncertainty as to the legitimacy of jurisdiction to invalidate constitutionally aberrant legislation must act as a curb upon judicial usurpation of power. A balance of power between these two arms of government is more effectively achieved by the unresolved doubt attaching to the question than would be the case if the question were to be resolved affirmatively in either Parliament's or the judiciary's favour. The inconclusiveness begets a cautious forbearance, one of the other.

Conclusion

As long as judges remain under the influence of outdated and discredited theories of law, the judiciary will not escape the opprobrium of 'muddling along'. The common law process is congenitally incremental, and without the guidance that a sound conception of the judicial role can bring, the judiciary will inevitably lurch from case to case without any, or any adequate, direction or purpose. Incrementalism itself demands something more than the application of practical skills. It requires a unifying legal theory or approach.

Society's expectations render the dogmas of the past obsolete. The declaratory theory of law was discredited as befits a fairy tale. Yet, and I have described the problem, judges continue to think and act as if the declaratory theory of law held sway. They continue to shelter behind 'the law' seeking a comfortable immunity from responsibility for their decisions. They continue to develop arguments, adopt reasoning in reaching a decision and write learned judgments as if the judicial exercise were still that of unearthing a pre-existing law. Positivism, including the more modern developments in positivist thought, exacerbates the judge's inclination to behave as if the declaratory theory of law held good. Judicial reasoning is directed to the exercise of assessing the strength of 'recognition' accorded a purported rule instead of determining the merit – or justice and relevance – of the rule. The formalistic propensity to view the law as a system of internally rational or predictable rules

---

[63] Quoted in K. J. Scott, *The New Zealand Constitution* (Oxford University Press, Oxford, 1962), in frontispiece.

becomes a working assumption and any term of reference external to the law itself, other than that of 'recognition', tends to be discarded.

Natural law theory is a sorry mix of superstition and speculation and cannot be vested with some sort of metaphysical dignity. There are no immutable or eternal ideals that constitute an innate property of the law. Human law is the sum total of the law and, while it may be judged by external terms of reference, it is not preceded by or subservient to a higher law, or a higher-order law, of timeless and priceless validity. Natural law cannot therefore be invoked as the foundation of the human rights jurisprudence that has developed over recent years or to sustain the notion of a higher order law to which both Parliament and the courts are subservient.

Discarding discredited and untenable theories as a basis on which to base a sound conception of the judicial role necessitates the deliberate rejection of formalism, or the lingering traces of formalism. Only then will the judiciary have the capacity to adopt the approach or methodology recommended in this book. The denunciation of formalism therefore deserves a chapter in its own right.

3

The 'curse' of formalism

Timur, the barbarian

In the story that follows the reader may find the line between that which is fact and that which is fiction to be somewhat indistinct. There can be absolutely no doubt that the truth does fade into the apocryphal.

Timur, otherwise known as Tamerlane (a corruption of 'Timur-i-lenk', the Persian for 'Timur the Lame', because he limped from a battle wound), was one of the most brutal and aggressive conquerors in all history – at least up to the twentieth and present centuries. He rose from obscurity in a Turko-Mongolian tribe in the fourteenth century to establish an empire stretching from Anatolia to Delhi. His wars of conquest were marked by unbelievable brutality, butchery, carnage and wanton destruction. Timur falsely claimed to be a descendant of Genghis Khan, and openly modelled himself on that infamous conqueror. But Timur outdid his personal afflatus in all aspects of barbaric cruelty.

Timur besieged the City of Sivas – or ancient Sebasteia. For a time the inhabitants resisted. Then the soldiers agreed to surrender to Timur if he would shed no blood. Timur quickly agreed. The soldiers surrendered, and Timur shed no blood. He simply buried them alive![1]

What is the message: that black letter literalism is barbaric? Perhaps, but I must admit that this is not quite the message which I had in mind.

The story continues.

The agreement had been sealed with an exchange of spears, and the representatives of the brave inhabitants and next of kin of the soldiers commenced proceedings against Timur for breach of contract. It was one of those rare cases, no doubt, where the risks of litigation were overshadowed by rather extraordinary extra-legal risks. But those risks became academic. Timur succeeded in the highest civil court in the land.

---

[1] Lord Steyn has a less embellished description in his article 'Contract Law: Fulfilling the Reasonable Expectations of Honest Men' (1997) 113 LQR 433, at 440–441.

The literal meaning of his assurance was clear, and it had not been breached.

Some years later another would-be conqueror sought backing for his war with the firm promise that not one drop of children's blood would be shed in the conquest of their beleaguered country. And not one drop of one child's blood was shed. Those that were not gassed were simply starved.

Seized of the issue, the highest civil court held that it was bound by the precedent in Timur's case. Efforts to distinguish that case on the facts failed. The fact the soldiers had been buried alive was not part of the *ratio decidendi* of that case and the fact the children in the present case had been gassed or starved did not therefore detract from the principle involved. Thus, like must be treated alike. The pleas that, in substance, the bloodless killing rendered the promise nugatory and that, in any event, the promise was in substance a representation that the conqueror would not kill the children were rejected. Finally, argument directed at showing that times had changed and demanded a new and more humane approach fell on deaf ears and, indeed, was rejected as an attempt to persuade the court to indulge in nothing more than a naked piece of judicial activism.

Formalism prevailed. Timur, the reader will agree, has much to answer for. It is remarkable that, even today, judicial opinions that are in substance contrary to plain common sense, and even absurd, will be honoured as being 'legally sound'.

The lingering legacy of formalism

The outward manifestation of the various outdated theories of law that I have discussed is formalism or the residual impact of that discredited approach. I have already indicated that there is no greater solecism in the working of the law than blind unthinking adherence to that creed. As an off-course substitute for a considered conception of the judicial role, formalism is the real and enduring opponent of fairness and relevance in the law.

Essentially, a formalistic approach masks the manifold choices facing the judge in the course of reaching a decision. Judicial reasoning is then diverted into a more or less artificial process in which the reality of choice is ignored or denied, or an explanation as to why a choice is summarily rejected in favour of a nominated rule is denied to others.[2] The distinctive feature of rules, of course, lies in their capacity to be

---

[2] Frederick Schauer, 'Formalism' (1988) 97 Yale LJ, No. 4, 509, at 516–519.

formal. They necessarily exclude from consideration factors whose exclusion has been determined without reference to the particular case at hand. Judicial reasoning is at once stilted in its breadth and its capacity to deliver decisions that are just as between the parties and relevant to the needs of the time.

The object of this chapter is to dispatch the lingering legacy of this judicial creed. Anticipating for a moment what is to come, the final demise of formalism will not mean the law will become an inchoate and shapeless mass subject to every whimsy, caprice and conceit of the individual judge as its surviving partisans fear. Rather, formalism, or the remnants of formalism, will be replaced by a judicial methodology that will be just as effective, if not more so, in curbing aberrant judicial behaviour and preserving the rule of law. Judicial discipline and restraint will no longer be sought, and sought vainly, in the text or content of the law, but will be found in the methodology that is adopted by the judiciary as an integral part of the judicial process.

Formalism will not stay dead

In endeavouring to reconstruct legal formalism in 1988, Professor Weinrib observed that in the last two centuries formalism has been killed again and again, but has always refused to stay dead.[3] Most legal scholarship today, however, would regard its death as irreversible. Edward Rubin observes that ever since legal scholarship dismantled its formalist home it has been traipsing from door to door looking for a methodological refuge.[4] The truth is that, although it has long since been divested of any sound philosophical or jurisprudential foundation, it remains embedded in the judicial consciousness vaguely perceived as being part of the discipline of the law. Thus, all too often, it is practised mechanically after the manner of a conditioned response to the presentation of a stimulus, the stimuli being the choice of tenable alternative premises or propositions open to the judge in any particular case.

Formalism, of course, does not have exactly the same meaning to everyone.[5] But although the term may be used in different ways, the

---

[3] Ernest J. Weinrib, 'Legal Formalism: On the Immanent Rationality of Law', (1998) 97 Yale LJ, No. 6, 949, at 951.
[4] Edward L. Rubin, 'Law and the Mythology of Law' (1997) Wis. LR, No. 3, 521, at 521.
[5] See Duncan Kennedy's answer to the question, 'What is formalism?', *A Critique of Adjudication* (Harvard University Press, Cambridge, Mass., 1998), at 105–107.

notion that it represents decision-making according to rule is common to its usage. 'Rule' in this context implies the language of rule formulation – its literal mandate is to be preferred. As a consequence, the range of factors a judge could or might otherwise take into account are restricted. Deductive reasoning is then necessarily preferred.[6] While this brief description may indicate its methodology, its polestar is a belief that law is intelligible as an internally coherent and rational phenomenon. To the formalist, law has a content that is not imported from without but elaborated from within. It possesses an internal coherence and logic, which makes it decisive for the understanding of juridical relationships. This fundamental article of faith that the law possesses an internal validity underlies the formalist's perception that a more narrow approach to adjudication will promote certainty and predictability. It precedes and sustains the unquestioning acceptance and application of rules to particular cases.

Responding to their critics, adherents of formalism assert a false respectability for their creed by contrasting the rationality of legal analysis with the perceived irrationality of political contests. But it is no answer to assert a pinchbeck rationality or lay claim to a bogus internal intelligibility. Legal analysis cannot divorce itself from policy considerations and politics is not inherently irrational. Nor can formalism find its justification by seeking to be equated with legal method and analysis. No judge, formalist or non-formalist, is free from the adjudicative discipline to which the judiciary is subject. But that adjudicative discipline is properly to be seen as the framework for judicial reasoning, and not a substitute for it. There is nothing intrinsic to legal method and analysis that requires a rule or precedent to be applied without re-evaluating its utility or fairness. What is required is that the process of re-examination be a reasoned process articulated openly by the judge. The fact it must be a reasoned and open process itself operates as a constraint on judicial power in that, to be effective and accepted, the reasoning in the later decision must be superior to that of the rule or precedent.[7] Restrictions, not always easy to define, hedge and circumscribe the judge's action without curbing his or her creative freedom in exercising the choice and without placing the judge outside the proper ambit of legal method and

---

[6] Posner, 'Legal Formalism, Legal Realism and the Interpretation of Statutes and the Constitution', 37 Case W Res LR, 179, at 181–182.
[7] See Chapter 6.

analysis.[8] 'There is', as Cardozo has said, 'a wide gap between the use of the individual sentiment of justice as a substitute for law, and its use as one of the tests or touch-stones in construing or extending law'.[9]

Discredited it may be, but formalism is advanced by some legal theorists today in the guise of, or disguised as, a relatively rigid version of positive theory. The law, they insinuate, fails to fulfil its potential to deliver certainty and predictability because judges fail to enforce the rules. Judges thereby fail to abide by the law – and even their ethical obligations arising out of their judicial oath! The theory is, of course, at the outer edge of flat earth thinking. But its articulation reflects the pressure on judges to conform with 'the law', even though that law may be patently uncertain. All judges would be pleased to abide by the law if it were clear just what the law was in a given case and no question of its fitness was in issue. Between us, my colleagues and I on the Court of Appeal in New Zealand sat on approximately 150 civil appeals each year. The question was never whether or not we should abide by the law but, rather, what was the law or, more particularly, which of two or more competing claims to be the law should be preferred.

Formalism's link with positivism has already been noted.[10] Positivism foments formalism simply because it encourages judges to believe that there is, in any given case, a rule or rules that only have to be identified and applied to resolve the question before the court. The core meaning of formalism mentioned above takes hold: decision-making proceeds more or less according to the literal mandate of a rule or by judges 'hugging' the pre-existing body of rules. The approach comes close to falling prey to the notion that, if there is no clear rule applicable to the question at issue, simply say 'No'. I will describe this negative process in more detail in Chapter 6.

The formalism of 'presumptive positivism'

It follows that I reject Frederick Schauer's theory of 'presumptive positivism'.[11] Schauer advances a theory that he suggests 'may be the most accurate picture of the place of rules within many modern legal

---

[8] Cardozo, *The Nature of the Judicial Process* (Yale University Press, New Haven, 1921), at 114–115. Cardozo himself described formalism as a 'demon'. 'The demon of formalism', he said, 'tempts the intellect with the lure of scientific order', at 66. And so it does.
[9] Ibid., at 140.   [10] See above, Chapter 2, at 33–34.
[11] Frederick Schauer, *Playing by the Rules: A Philosophical Examination of Rule-Based Decision-Making in Law and in Life* (Oxford University Press, Oxford, 1991). See also Schauer, 'Formalism'.

systems'.[12] Many judges and lawyers would agree with this assessment, but it is neither accurate nor desirable, and for that reason it may be productive to deal with Schauer's theory separately.

According to Schauer, rules are binding, unless they produce a clearly unreasonable, and not just suboptimal, result when viewed from the perspective of the wider normative universe. Legal rules that are distinctively recognised as such under accepted rules of recognition or similar 'pedigree' tests obtain presumptive force.[13] The prescriptive force of a rule can be abandoned if the moral, political or practical cost of applying the rule would be too large and unacceptable. Presumptive positivism 'is a way of describing a degree of strong but overridable priority' so that 'decision-makers override a rule ... not when they believe that the rule has produced a suboptimal result in this case ... but instead when, and only when, the reasons for overriding are perceived by the decision-maker to be particularly strong'.[14]

Just as judges are inclined to provide diverse wording to explain a central concept, so too Schauer provides a number of verbal variations of the criteria by which the application of a presumptive legal rule might be overridden. Richard Fallon has collated some of them in a footnote: referring to considerations of 'exceptional strength'; calling for displacement in light of 'particularly exigent reasons'; the 'rule will be set aside when the result it indicates is egregiously at odds with the result that is indicated by [a] larger and more morally acceptable set of values'; and a result indicated by a rule should be reached in the absence of 'a reason of great strength for not reaching [the] result'.[15]

On the face of it, Schauer's presumptive positivism might appear to adhere to what judges actually do in arriving at a decision. In simple terms, a rule is promoted and will be accepted unless other overriding considerations lead the judge to reject the rule. At times, also, it may be convenient to accept a rule if the judge lacks sufficient confidence in his or her judgement, more particularly where the rule encapsulates a range of experience and accumulated wisdom in similar cases.[16] But this description is the description of the approach of a judge of a formalistic

---

[12] Schauer, *Playing by the Rules*, at 206.
[13] Richard H. Fallon, '*Propter Honoris Respectum*: Ruminations on the Work of Frederick Schauer' (1997) 72.2 Notre Dame LR 1391, at 1398.
[14] Schauer, *Playing by the Rules*, at 204.
[15] Fallon, 'Ruminations on the Work of Frederick Schauer', at note 47.
[16] Mark V. Tushnet, 'Playing With the Rules' (1992) 90 Mich. LR 1560, at 1567.

inclination. To such judges, the appeal of the rule can be said to have presumptive potency.

Schauer's presumptive positivism, however, cannot garner support from the judicial methodology and the conception of the judicial role that I develop in this book. In the first place, my judicial experience has undoubtedly conditioned me to reject Schauer's endorsement of a presumption. I have witnessed too many cases where presumptions of one kind or another have distorted the courts' reasoning to happily accept their validity. For example, presumptions in statutory interpretation can be used, and regrettably are at times used, to frustrate the clear intention of the legislature. Legal presumptions are, or should be, on the wane. Lord Mustill admits to reservations about the reliability of generalised presumptions in a statutory context in that they too readily confine the court to a perspective that treats all statutes, and all situations to which they apply, as if they were the same. 'This is misleading', he states, 'for the basis of every rule is no more than simple fairness, which ought to be the basis of every rule.' The application of common sense, he concludes, in words that could be applicable to non-statutory as well as statutory presumptions, 'may be impeded rather than helped by recourse to formulae which do not adapt themselves to individual circumstances, and which tend themselves to become the subject of minute analysis ...'[17]

I allow that it can be argued that Schauer's presumption can be viewed as a description of the legal system and not a presumption of the kind that is from time to time raised in legal argument. But its essential character is not greatly different. It has the effect of conferring presumptive status on all recognised rules; the rule applies subject to defeasibility, and so the process becomes a haven for the formalistic judge. Consider the lines of inquiry: is there a rule; if so, what is the rule; once formulated, does the rule satisfy the rule of recognition or test of 'pedigree'; if so, is there a strong and overwhelming reason why the rule should be displaced or modified? Such a progression is far removed from the process which I advocate in Chapters 11 to 14.

In arguing that a rule applies subject to defeasibility, Schauer's presumptive positivism is irrevocably rule-oriented. It therefore presents an essentially positivist perspective of the law[18] and is subject to the criticisms that

---

[17] *L'Office Cherifien Des Phosphates* v *Yamashita-Shinnhon Steamship Co Ltd* [1994] 1 AC 486, at 524–525.
[18] But see Anthony J. Sebok, '*Propter Honoris Respectum*: Is the Rule of Recognition a Rule?' (1997) 72 Notre Dame LR 1539.

I have mounted in Chapter 2.[19] To some extent it shares the lack of realism of the positivists. The bulk of the cases, certainly at the appellate level, do not turn on the simple question of the applicability of a rule. Rather, the applicable rule or rules will be indeterminate and the struggle for the judge will be to formulate a rule that is suitable to apply in the instant case, or there will be competing and conflicting rules, in which case the judge is faced with the task of reconciling the rules or selecting one over the other in the inevitable balancing exercise that characterises judicial decision-making. How does one give presumptive force to an indeterminate rule, or presumptive priority to two conflicting rules?

Furthermore, it is a mistake to think that Schauer's presumptive positivism would eliminate or significantly reduce judicial discretion. Judicial discretion is simply removed to another time or channelled into a non-substantive framework. Thus, the discretion of the immediate judge may be diminished if he or she more or less mechanically determines whether a rule applies, but the rule that they then apply is the product of a judge's discretion at an earlier time when the rule was developed. If something less than a mechanical application of a rule in the instant case is adopted, the judge must exercise a discretion at each step inquiring whether there is a rule, formulating the rule, and then determining whether there are strong and overwhelming reasons why the rule should be set aside or modified. To meet any of Schauer's formulae, judges must use their discretion when deciding what criteria or considerations to adopt in order to make that determination. In sum, it is doubtful whether the discretion exercised by a judge who vests a rule with presumptive force is less, or significantly less, than the discretion involved when a judge takes a rule and assesses its utility for effecting justice or keeping the law abreast of the times.

These observations indicate another criticism. The criteria or considerations that are to determine whether the prescriptive presumption of a rule should be dispatched or modified are unclear. What are these considerations, and are they specified in the law or are they external to the law?[20] At this point it is likely that a formalistic judge will be flummoxed by the exercise and resort to the rule, not because it has legitimate presumptive force, but because he or she is uncertain as to how to identify the countervailing considerations or, if able to identify those considerations, is unsure as to how to balance their strength, one

---

[19] See above, Chapter 2, at 29–34.
[20] See Fallon, 'Ruminations on the Work of Frederick Schauer', at 1398–1399.

against the other and, ultimately, against the comfortable presumption itself. This criticism is attenuated by the fact that the cases in which a judge will be required to determine whether the presumptive force of the rule should be overridden are likely to be the very cases in which positivists would wish to curb the use of judicial discretion. Social, political and moral judgements are likely to be involved where it is difficult to say that a recognised rule should presumptively apply.

Nor is the validity of Schauer's claim a foregone conclusion that in many, if not most, cases the result indicated by the rule will be the same as the result arrived at by directly applying the rule's background justification. 'Most commonly', he states, 'the application of the rule will be consistent with its justification'.[21] The extent to which this may be so without a discrete examination in each case must be unknown. Schauer is, in effect, introducing an assumption which, certainly in the minds of a number of judges, will be grafted on to the force of the rule. Not only will the rule have presumptive force, but the assumption that it is consistent with the justification of the rule will also be given presumptive force.

These criticisms illustrate the need to re-evaluate any rule that is identified and is said to apply to the particular case without the aid – or the burden – or a prescriptive presumption. The rule may be the starting point for the judge's reasoning, but it should be re-evaluated for its commitment to justice and relevance. In many cases the answer to that question will be immediately obvious and no prolonged inquiry will be required. But it is important that the question be asked at the outset. A rule that is unjust or irrelevant at the outset will either infect the outcome so that it, too, is unjust or irrelevant, or distort the reasoning process as the judge seeks to convert an unjust or out-of-date starting point into a just and relevant decision. But all this is fare for what is to come.

A short portrait of the formalist judge

So it is that a judge who subscribes to formalism will, to a greater or lesser extent, exhibit a number of characteristics. No harm will be done in pausing to catalogue the main characteristics. Treated as a checklist, readers will quickly be able to identify judges who possess these features to a markedly observable degree.

First, the judge will tend to fit the established 'facts' into an existing rule and assume or hope that justice is achieved in the abstract. A close

---

[21] Schauer, *Playing by the Rules*, at 229.

examination of the facts, a process that is essential to adjudication, is likely to be sacrificed to the desire to make the facts fit the law rather than make the law fit the facts.[22]

Secondly, the formalist judge will be inclined, having by definition a penchant for form, to accept form over substance even though this may be at the expense of reality and mean that justice is not done in the particular circumstances.[23]

Thirdly, the judge will have little compunction about proclaiming absolute or near absolute rules. Notwithstanding the lesson of more than two centuries, it is assumed that the dynamic of the common law can be fettered. Treading this formalistic treadmill, the judge will manifest a distrust of judicial discretion and seek to curtail or inhibit it with rules or doctrine. Statutory discretions to do 'as the court thinks fit' will be circumscribed by precedential fiats.[24]

Fourthly, the formalist judge is more than likely to cherish certainty as a goal in adjudication, notwithstanding that he or she may be unable to demonstrate that certainty in the law would be promoted by a particular decision reached on that basis. Hard cases, which may mean cases of real injustice, are to be accepted in the fixed view that this 'hardness' is achieving certainty. Venerating certainty as an end with the same fervour as the Incas worshiped their idols becomes a ritual of judicial thought.[25]

The fifth characteristic is the formalist judge's deference to a relatively strict doctrine of precedent. Lord Steyn has said, '... formalism inculcates an intense respect for the doctrine of *stare decisis* whatever the lessons of experience and the force of better reasoning'.[26] Assuming that the law is rational, judges will not feel inclined to justify the law that they apply. With faith in the inner logic of the law, therefore, their reasoning will often appear mechanical, literal and cramped. In order to support a particular interpretation, for example, an internal 'logic' may be found in an Act of Parliament by punctiliously comparing the precise wording of various sections when it would be a bizarre pretence to think that Parliament, or the law draftsperson, went through the same exercise – or even addressed the point at all.[27]

---

[22] See above, Chapter 2, at 29; and Chapter 11, at 298–299.
[23] See below, Chapter 12, at 312.   [24] See below, Chapter 10, at 266–267.
[25] See Chapter 5, at 128–130.
[26] John Steyn, 'Does Legal Formalism Hold Sway in England?' (1996) 49 II Current Legal Problems, 43, at 46.
[27] E.g., see the argument advanced by Tipping J in *Pacific Coilcoaters Ltd and Ors v Interpress Associates and Ors*, ante n 37, at 61–62.

Sixthly, a formalist judge will possess a compelling inclination to draw distinctions where none should be drawn. The forlorn belief that certainty will be promoted is belied by the confusion which follows. The subsequent reception of the distinction which Lord Hoffmann proclaimed in *MacNiven (Inspector of Taxes)* v *Westmorland Investments Ltd*[28] between a 'legal' concept and a 'commercial' concept in applying the principle in *WT Ramsay Ltd* v *Inland Revenue Commissioners*[29] provides worrying testimony to this formalistic phenomenon. To the detriment of the principle in *Ramsay*, this unhelpful dichotomy has caused bewilderment or dismay, or both, among counsel and judges in each of the later cases in which it has been examined.[30]

Seventhly, faced with the need to change the law, a formalist judge will be predisposed to leave the change to Parliament. Even when the particular law is widely condemned and the change could be readily accomplished by the courts, the judge will wish to leave the matter to the legislature. Such judges may, at times, suggest that Parliament address the issue, and even recommend a particular change, but they are inhibited from going further. More often than not, no reasons for this homage to Parliament and the political process are advanced; it is simply thought that it is not for the courts to make an explicit change in the law.[31] This retiring attitude is in part due to the formalist's strict adherence to the doctrine of precedent in that it presupposes that, once the law is 'declared', it cannot thereafter be changed by the courts.

---

[28] [2003] 1 AC 311, at paras. 58–61.   [29] [1982] AC 300.
[30] It was not difficult to predict the confusion. See my judgment in *Commissioner of Inland Revenue* v *BNZ Investments Ltd* [2002] 1 NZLR 450, at paras. [103]–[112]. The distinction was pressed by counsel on both sides in *DTE Financial Services Ltd* v *Wilson (Inspector of Taxes)* [2001] EWCA Civ 455, [2001] STC 777 but disregarded by the Court. In *Barclays Mercantile Business Finance Ltd* v *Mawson (Inspector of Taxes)* [2002] EWCA Civ 1853, [2003] STC 66, a stoic Peter Gibson LJ took it upon himself to say that it was no doubt due to his own failings that he found the dichotomy a difficult one to apply (para. [44]). Carnwroth LJ also admitted to some difficulty in understanding the distinction, a difficulty that he said had been shared by both leading counsel in the case (paras. [69] and [73]). The Court of Final Appeal of Hong Kong was equally flummoxed. Mr Justice Ribeiro PJ and Lord Millet NPJ (whose judgments were agreed to by Chief Justice Li, Mr Justice Bokhary PJ and Mr Justice Chan PJ) doubted that Lord Hoffmann could really have intended what he said, but were at one in holding that, if he did, the dichotomy formed no part of the law of Hong Kong (paras. [39], [40]–[41], [144] and [145]–[151])! Lord Millet noted that Lord Hoffmann's speech had unfortunate consequences in that it had led to arid debates in an effort to fit the statutory language into one or other of the conceptual categories when the distinction was not clear-cut and yielded an uncertain answer (para. [150]).
[31] See below, Chapter 10, at 254.

In the eighth place, a formalist judge is likely to be committed to deciding no more than is absolutely necessary to resolve the question in issue before the court. This attitude will prevail even where the articulation of general principles at an appellate level would provide the community with valuable guidance in the area and enhance certainty and predictability in the law. Again, it becomes an article of faith. A judge will announce with unfeigned pride that he or she is a 'minimalist', and hold to that commitment even though definitive rulings of principle could assist the resolution of future disputes without resort to the courts.[32]

Ninthly, because it is essentially introspective, formalism tends to inhibit a judge's readiness to refer to and assimilate the learning of other disciplines. The learning of other specializations such as sociology, political science, psychiatry, psychology, economics and the behavioural sciences in general, all of which are part of the real and current world, is at odds with formalism's rule-bound preoccupation with the past. Thus, the formalist judge is reluctant to re-examine existing rules and precedents when they arise against the instruction that advances in other disciplines can convey. He or she remains insensitive to the perceptions that other disciplines bring to the problems that make up the social context in which an issue falls to be decided in the courts.[33]

In the tenth place, again because 'the law' is perceived to have an internal coherence and intelligibility, the community is thought to be served by applying that law without regard to the new and changing needs of society. The rule, rather than the underlying justification or reason for the rule, is likely to be seen as sufficient or more important in the reasoning that is adopted. Unwilling to reassess the justification or reason for the rule, the formalist's ability to respond to change is retarded. In the result, rule-based adjudication is necessarily conservative. It reflects a generally positive view of the status quo and a belief that any radical change from past practice is likely to produce worse rather

[32] Dr James Farmer QC, 'The New Zealand Court of Appeal: Maintaining Quality after the Privy Council' in Rick Bigwood (ed.), *Legal Method in New Zealand* (Butterworths, Wellington, 2001), at 244–245.

[33] A signal example of the judiciary's reticence in keeping abreast of literature in areas relevant to the administration of justice is the failure of many judges to assimilate the extent of the lasting trauma to the victims of rape. See the author, 'Was Eve merely framed; or was she forsaken?' (1994) NZLJ 368. Refer also to the outdated and limited thinking that still persists in respect of the 'recent complaint' rule in relation to sexual offences in *R v Neil* (1994) 12 CRNZ 158, per Eichelbaum CJ at 160; but see the author's observations contra Eichelbaum CJ in *R v H* [1996] 1 NZLR 673, esp at 682–698.

than better outcomes.[34] It follows that the formalist judge, shunning the re-evaluation of rules, is not overly concerned with the rationality of the law either in general or in particular. To quote Lord Steyn again, '... the formalist judge is likely to say that it is not the duty of the court to rationalise the law of England'.[35]

Finally, the formalist judge will frown at the thought of invoking the concept of fairness in judicial reasoning. Fairness is perceived to be incompatible with the rule-bound approach intrinsic to formalism, and it probably is. But where does that leave justice?

A case study: *Sevcon Ltd* v *Lucas CAB Ltd*

There are any number of cases that could be selected to illustrate the points made in this chapter.[36] I propose to take the decision of the House of Lords in *Sevcon Ltd* v *Lucas CAB Ltd*,[37] which, although relating to the interpretation of a statutory provision, provides a stark example of formalism in action.

---

[34] See John Smiley, 'Formalism, Fairness and Efficiency: Civil Adjudication in New Zealand', NZLR, 254, at 255.

[35] Steyn, 'Does Legal Formalism Hold Sway in England?', at 46.

[36] A sharp contrast between a formalistic and more realistic approach is evident from the decision of the Supreme Court of Canada in *Ikea Ltd* v *The Queen* (1988) 98 DTC 6092 and the decision of the Privy Council in *CIA* v *Wattie & Lawrence* [1999] 1 WLR 873. The question in issue in both appeals was whether an inducement payment paid by the landlord to a tenant to enter into a lease was capital or revenue for tax purposes in the hands of the tenant. In both cases the rent fixed in the lease was well in excess of the market rent. In substance, the inducement payment offset the inflated rental. The Supreme Court of Canada declined to ignore the fact that the inducement payment bore directly on the annual rent to be paid and held that it was therefore on revenue account. The Privy Council took the opposite view. The Board assimilated the inducement payment with a premium paid by a tenant to a landlord to obtain a lease (which is on capital account) and therefore held that the inducement payment was capital (a 'negative premium'). In form, there may be a comparison; in substance there certainly is not. The premium paid by a tenant to a landlord provides consideration for the grant of the lease. There is no consideration for an inducement payment paid by the landlord to the tenant where the rent is inflated and the payment is amortised in the rent over the period of the lease. See also *Federal Commissioner of Taxation* v *Montgomery* (1999) 164 ALR 435, where an inducement payment was held by a majority (Gaudron, Gummow, Kirby and Hayne JJ) to be assessable as income of the taxpayer. Note, in particular, the crushing refutation of the Privy Council's notion of a 'negative premium' at 457–458.

[37] *Sevcon* was considered and approved in *Pacific Coilcoaters Ltd and Ors* v *Interpress Associates and Ors* [1998] 2 NZLR 19, per Richardson P, Henry and Tipping JJ (Thomas and Keith JJ dissenting).

The question in issue in that case was whether the sealing of a patent is an integral part of the cause of action for infringements occurring after the date of publication of the complete specification but before the patent is sealed. Section 13(4) of the Patents Act 1949 (UK) reads:

> After the date of the publication of a complete specification and until the sealing of a patent in respect thereof, the applicant shall have the like privileges and rights as if a patent for the invention had been sealed on the date of the publication of the complete specification: Provided that an applicant shall not be entitled to institute any proceedings for infringement until the patent has been sealed.

Two tenable interpretations competed for the support of their Lordships. One was that, as the subsection conferred on an applicant for a patent the like rights and privileges as if the patent had been sealed, the cause of action accrued when those rights are infringed. The proviso merely postponed the applicant's right to take action until the patent had been granted. The alternative argument was that the right to initiate proceedings for infringement was dependent on the grant of the patent to the applicant and that, as a result, unless and until the patent was sealed, the applicant could not assert an essential ingredient of the cause of action. That ingredient is the identification of those claims in the complete specification that remain in force in the patent. The former interpretation prevailed. Their Lordships unanimously held that the cause of action accrued when the acts of infringement were committed and the proviso was merely a procedural bar to commencing an action.

It was common ground that the merits or justice of the case were in Sevcon Ltd's favour. The complete specification had been published in June 1971. Lucas CAB Ltd had then undertaken and pursued opposition proceedings under the Patent Act for ten years, as a result of which the patent was not sealed until 1982. Invoking the limitation period in the Limitation Act 1980 (UK), Lucas then contended that Sevcon could not recover for infringements committed between 1974 and 1977 as its cause of action arose at the date of the infringements and was therefore statute barred. If correct, a patentee who, as the applicant for the patent, had disclosed its invention to the world at large as required by the Act would be prevented from obtaining damages for the infringements of the patent at a time it was not in a position to institute proceedings in respect of those infringements. The injustice might be thought to be aggravated as this situation had been brought about by the protracted opposition proceedings pursued by Lucas. Having obtained the grant of a patent, the patentee was denied the benefit of the grant.

Apart from the choice between these broad competing arguments, their Lordships faced a number of other choices; whether a literal interpretation would in itself resolve the question when a cause of action arose; how the proviso should be read in relation to the body of the subsection; whether and to what extent the purpose or object of the subsection was relevant; whether and to what extent the scheme of the Act should influence the question in issue; whether and to what extent policy questions should be taken into account; whether other sections of the Act were relevant; whether the reasoning in a prior decision of the House of Lords should be adopted, and so on. Their Lordships opted for a narrow and formalistic approach.

The formalistic approach is evident in the pre-emptive ascendancy given the words 'the applicant shall have the like privileges and rights as if a patent for the invention had been sealed' over the proviso. By conferring ascendancy on the body of the subsection, it was thought that the proviso precluding the applicant's right to institute any proceedings for infringement until the patent had been sealed could be relegated to the status of a procedural bar serving only to delay the bringing of the proceeding. In other words, the cause of action had accrued, but the applicant could not sue upon it. The structure of the subsection was allowed to dictate its meaning. But as any numbers of critical commentators have pointed out, there is no inherent reason why the proviso should not be construed as derogating from the existence of the rights rather than merely affecting their exercise.[38]

An interpretation that vests the proviso with substantive effect so as to delimit the rights conferred on the applicant makes good sense and is clearly viable. Indeed, Oliver LJ, in the Court of Appeal, in a judgment agreed to by Mustill LJ, had indicated that, if the matter had been *res integra*, there would be a great deal to be said for the view that, in an action for infringement, it is not possible until the patent is sealed to plead the essential fact upon which the action depends.[39] But notwithstanding the viable choice open to them, the House of Lords chose not to opt for the construction that would have resulted in justice in that and similar cases. Why, then, was a tenable and just argument, which could have been accepted without offending reason or precedent, rejected? The answer can

---

[38] E.g., D. McGee, 'Patent Nonsense' (1986) 49 MLR 650, at 652–653.
[39] *Sevcon Limited* v *Lucas CAB Ltd* [1985] FSR 545, at 549.

only be that the formalistic approach was so firmly entrenched that it took precedence over any desire to do justice.

In pursuing this formalistic approach, their Lordships also had scant regard to the logic of the matter. Their reasoning is flawed in two critical aspects. First, the question whether the sealing of the patent is an integral part of the applicant or patentee's cause of action cannot be resolved by a linguistic or textual analysis of section 13(4). The literal meaning of that section is quite clear; it is that the applicant is to have all the like privileges and rights as if the patent had been sealed from the date the complete specification was published, other than the right to commence any proceedings for infringement until the patent has been sealed. Consequently, the plain meaning in itself simply does not answer the question in issue, that is, whether the proviso derogates from the rights conferred on the applicant or is to be regarded as a procedural barrier to the enforcement of those rights. Secondly, in order to complete the plaintiff's cause of action it is essential that the grant of the patent be pleaded for the very good reason that the grant confirms, not just that the patent has been sealed, but that the claim or claims in the complete specification that the infringer is alleged to have infringed subsist at the time the proceeding is commenced. In other words, the plaintiff must plead and prove the grant of the patent in order to establish that the critical claim or claims that are alleged to have been infringed remain extant. That specific pleading is essential to the cause of action.

Their Lordships were also influenced by a prior decision of the House of Lords. In *General Tire & Rubber Co v Firestone Tyre and Rubber Co Ltd*,[40] the House had held that interest could be awarded under section 3 of the Law Reform (Miscellaneous Provisions) Act 1934 (UK) on damages for infringement from a date before the sealing of the patent pursuant to the statutory prescription reading 'between the date when the cause of action arose and the date of judgment'. Their Lordships considered that, on the true construction of section 13(4), the sealing of the patent was not a condition precedent to the accrual of the cause of action under section 3. As the condition was contained in a different statute from the Limitation Act in the *Sevcon* case, it was not binding on the House, but it clearly had a marked influence on the Law Lords' thinking. Their Lordships did not question the reasoning in that case or seek to re-evaluate it on the grounds of fairness or relevance. Ironically, while the decision in the *General Tire* case may have produced a just

---

[40] [1975] 2 All ER 173.

result in that case, adhering to the same reasoning in *Sevcon* produced an unjust result. One cannot be denied the thought that the law developed on the arbitrary basis of which case happened to come first.

It will be noted that the decision in the *General Tire* case, notwithstanding that it was a decision of the House of Lords, failed to produce 'certainty'. Labouring under a grievance that Lucas' tactics had delayed the sealing of the patent and that, notwithstanding the infringements, it could not initiate proceedings until the patent had been sealed, Sevcon persisted in pressing its case to the House of Lords. Obviously it, or its advisers, considered that the logic and justice of their case would prevail over a decision that, although relevant, was not strictly binding on the House of Lords.[41]

Their Lordships also described as forceful an argument based on the effect of another section of the Patents Act. Section 59(1) provides that, in proceedings for infringement of a patent, damages cannot be awarded if the defendant proves that, as at the date of the infringement, he or she was not aware of, and had no reasonable ground for supposing, that the patent existed. Their Lordships' readiness to give credence to the section is indicative of the formalistic approach. In fact, however, it would be unrealistic to attribute to the legislator an intention to create a cause of action in an applicant pursuant to section 13(4) by virtue of the wording of section 59(1) when, in truth, like Topsy, the provisions 'just growed'. A definitive coherence between the respective provisions would be coincidental in that neither Parliament nor the law draftsperson will have addressed the point. The argument means no more than that the Act may have a lacuna, and it is even then a *non sequitur* in that the lacuna exists irrespective whether the cause of action arises prior to the sealing of the patent or is completed by the sealing of the patent!

A state of dissatisfaction with the outcome seemingly does not take hold in their Lordships' bosom. No dissatisfaction with a literal construction or the reasoning in the *General Tire* case is expressed and no dissatisfaction with the resulting injustice is apparent from a reading of the judgment. Their Lordships were content to adopt a formalistic approach and accept the result as the outcome, not of reason or logic, but of 'the law'.

A judge who has escaped the shackles of formalism would have approached the question in issue in this case quite differently. He or she would have regard to the thrust and object of the subsection. Since

---

[41] Nor did the *Sevcon* case prevent Pacific Coilcoaters instituting proceedings in nearly identical circumstances in New Zealand. See above n. 37.

the applicant was required by the Act to publish details of the invention, the subsection was introduced to protect the applicant's invention pending the grant of the patent. Those who might be inclined to copy or use the invention thereby do so at their own risk knowing that the applicant will be able to recover damages in respect of any infringement if and when the patent is sealed. This object is defeated if the applicant or patentee is ultimately unable to recover damages because of an unavoidable delay in obtaining the grant of the patent. Moreover, reference to the purpose of the subsection confirms that it was not drafted as a limitation provision or for the purpose of limiting the applicant's right to recover damages for any infringement. Neither Parliament nor the draftperson's mind was directed to the question whether, and when, the subsection would confer a cause of action on the applicant or patentee. For the purposes of the Patents Act the subsection says all that it need to say to protect the applicant pending the grant of the patent. Appreciating, therefore, that a literal interpretation does not answer the question as to when a cause of action accrues, the non-formalistic judge would read the section as a whole and vest the proviso with substantive force. It would not be reduced to a procedural right relevant only to the question of enforcement.

The scheme of the Act would also be important. In general terms, the Act vests the patentee with the monopoly rights conferred by the patent. These rights are retrospective. Taking the view that the cause of action does not accrue until the patent is sealed is in accord with this overall scheme. Moreover, regard should be had to section 30, which provided that, once the patent is sealed, a patentee, as the patentee, can retrospectively sue for infringements prior to the sealing of the patent.[42] The prerogative basis of Letters Patent is then fully recognised. Once this is done, it can be seen that the cause of action under section 13(4) accrues to the applicant as applicant. An applicant, once the patent is sealed, can bring proceedings for past infringements, and may wish to do so, for example, where the patent has been assigned to a third party. The non-formalistic judge would acknowledge that monopoly rights in a patent or pending patent have always been highly tradeable, and that section 13(4) would therefore have a substantive function or effect for applicants who assign their rights prior to the sealing of the patent, or assignees of those rights, who do not become the patentees.

---

[42] Keith J makes a most persuasive case for this viewpoint in a dissenting judgment in the *Pacific Coilcoaters* case; above n. 37, at 56–58.

Policy considerations would not be excluded; the patently unjust consequences that follow from holding that the cause of action accrues before the patent is sealed do not reflect well on the law; it is contrary to principle that time should run against a plaintiff at a time when he or she cannot bring the action; it is unsound and contrary to principle to separate the plaintiff's cause of action from the plaintiff's 'right' to bring an action and seek the judgment of the court; the Limitation Act relating to persons under a disability indicates that it is the policy of the legislature to defer the 'right' to bring an action until the plaintiff is in a position to sue; and, finally, by analogy with tort, time should not start to run until the plaintiff is in a position to sue.

Nor would a non-formalist judge have been inhibited in re-examining the *General Tire* case and re-evaluating its validity. The reasoning would, for the same reasons as applied in the *Sevcon* case itself, be found wanting. Not being persuasive, *General Tire* would not be accorded coercive force.

A different outcome seems inevitable once the basic judicial approach is determined. No dissatisfaction with the result emerges when the judge begins to tread the formalistic path. The merits or justice of the case, as well as any wider considerations, do not impinge upon the judge's reasoning. Thus, the possibility of dissatisfaction is effectively excluded from the outset. The judge who adopts a non-formalistic approach, on the other hand, must experience a sense of dissatisfaction almost at the outset having regard to the injustice to the applicant and others in the applicant's situation in holding that the cause of action accrues at a time when he or she cannot sue for its breach and when the reason for that disability is more often than not the delaying tactics pursued by the alleged infringer. Wider terms of reference will at once apply; the subsection will be read as a whole without giving any particular weighting to the structure of the subsection or any particular part of it; substantial regard will be had to the object of the provision; the scheme of the Act will be extremely important; relevant principles and policy considerations will be canvassed and taken into account; the objective of certainty would be taken into account as a consideration having regard to the circumstances of the particular case; and relevant case law would be re-examined and re-evaluated. The underlying criteria would be the fairness and relevance of the law.[43] In all, it is a demonstrably superior approach.

---

[43] I should add that, depending on the composition of the Committee, the issue might possibly fare differently in the House of Lords today. It is more likely that the policy considerations would be addressed. And the demonstratively faulty reasoning evident

Conclusion

There can be no doubt that, although discarded as dead, formalism continues to dog the judicial process. For far too many judges and not a few academics it remains an article of faith quickened by an inchoate fear of a chaotic law. In the result, it is adhered to with greater or lesser strength and commitment, a continuing legacy from the more pure formalism that prevailed at the turn of the twentieth century. It is a legacy that has left the judicial process with a debilitating burden.

The burden is plain to see. First and foremost, formalism inhibits a judge in obtaining a sound conception of the judicial role. An unthinking and convenient adherence to its mandate displaces any desire to become familiar with legal theory and becomes an unarticulated excuse not to question the significance of the form or formal expression of the law that it prescribes. Any inquiry into the purpose or direction of the law becomes redundant, the legal field already being occupied by a ready-made approach that forbids curial inquiry. Without a doubt, formalism, or the remnants of that creed, constitutes the main barrier to the adoption of a contemporary legal methodology in which fairness and relevance command the allegiance of the judicial process.

Further, formalism obscures the reality of the judicial process. In particular, the inherent uncertainty of the law, the pervasiveness of choice in judicial decision-making, and the full scope of judicial autonomy and the extent judges make law and formulate policy in doing so, are skirted rather than confronted. The choices that must be made in judicial decision-making are seemingly ignored or denied or, if acknowledged, the reason for the choice that is made is never fully explained. Much judicial reasoning is still unnecessarily simulated or even mechanical.

I have also pointed out how formalism's commitment to form betrays its positivist leanings. Rules are the stuff of the formal application of the law and it is understandable how a rule-bound approach should become hide-bound. Deductive reasoning inevitably follows. Reference to any term of reference external to the law or to the vast array of considerations that should inform judicial decision-making is largely precluded. A relatively coercive doctrine of precedent becomes imperative to

in the *Sevcon* decision would probably be too much for some of their Lordships to swallow, even given the power of precedent. See the helpful dicta of Lord Bingham relating to the appropriate approach to the interpretation of a statute in *R v Secretary of State for Health, ex parte Quintavalle* [2003] 2 AC 687.

perpetuate the rules. Yet, rules beget more and more particular rules until the law is confused or unknowable. All too often the law's essential principles are overwhelmed.

The belief or assumption underlying the judiciary's continuing penchant for formalism is, of course, the belief or assumption that the law is an internally coherent and rational phenomenon. Thus, the law is vested with an intelligibility that it does not possess and that is inconsistent with its judge-made origin and continuing judge-made incremental development. The judicial process becomes both unduly backward looking and inward looking as judges seek to vest law with a content, purpose and direction elaborated from within rather than, as must be the case, imported from without.

Nor, as I have stressed, is formalism to be equated with legal analysis. Legal analysis is required as part of the adjudicative discipline to which judges are subject. It provides a framework for legal reasoning, and not a substitute for it. Legal analysis is restricted, however, when those of a formalist persuasion seek to impose on the law a doctrinal structure that can be every bit as inhibiting as a rule-bound or precedent-dominated approach. Doctrine, no less than the law, is judge-made, is equally indeterminate and is no less in need of flexibility to allow the law to develop in response to the requirements of justice and relevance. Nothing in the concept of legal analysis, therefore, prevents the law from being re-evaluated for its fairness and utility. Indeed, legal analysis is part of the legal method required to carry out that process of re-examination.

The 'curse' of formalism emerges clearly; first, it is in itself an unsound conception of the judicial role and, secondly, it precludes or inhibits judges developing a sound conception of the judicial role. Yet, it has cast its hex over a sizeable proportion of the legal fraternity and legal academia. Formalism and its known theoretical accomplices succour and sustain a following that at times exhibit all the characteristics of a fundamentalist fervour. Fundamentalism in the law exists as a force and, when forcefully prosecuted, it exerts an influence on judges that can be every bit as telling on their performance of their judicial function as any lack of familiarity with legal theory. So, legal fundamentalism must also be confronted, and that confrontation can make up the subject-matter of the next chapter.

4

Legal fundamentalism

Legal fundamentalism

From time to time I have used the expression 'legal fundamentalists'. They are an extreme lot. Notwithstanding determined self-discipline and the most demanding editing, the phrase has survived all attempts to eliminate it from the text of this book. Persisting with its use reflects the experience or, perhaps, the suffering, of those judges who have sought to bring a viable law into the twenty-first century. They have been met with a brand of legal populism that seeks to deny judges the capacity for choice in administering the law and daunts the judicial instinct to do justice and shape the law to fit the needs of the times. Legal fundamentalism seeks to arrest the common law's essential dynamic. It is this hostile influence on the administration and development of the law that justifies separate reference to the topic. There can be no place for legal fundamentalism in a modern judicial methodology.

Legal fundamentalism encompasses a mode of thought that is essentially simplistic and incomplete. It is best understood as the legal equivalent of religious fundamentalism, being similarly dedicated to the strict maintenance of traditional and historical doctrines and characterised by the extremeness of the positions that are adopted and the evangelical fervency and frequency with which they are expressed.[1] Hence, for example, legal fundamentalists tend to viscerally recoil from anything approaching modernity in the law; are committed to a rigid rule-bound approach and a strict application of the doctrines of precedent and *stare decisis*;[2] have never perceived or accepted the extent of uncertainty in the law, nor fully adjusted to the inevitability of judges making law; believe in the strict separation of

---

[1] See Malise Ruthven, *Fundamentalism: The Search for Meaning* (Oxford University Press, Oxford, 2004). See also Stuart Sim, *Fundamentalist World: The New Dark Age of Dogma* (Icon Books, Thriplow, 2004).

[2] See Jack Hodder, 'Departure from "Wrong" Precedents by Final Appellate Courts: Disagreeing with Professor Harris' [2003] NZLR 161.

powers and the singular omniscience of Parliament; and are vociferously hostile to anything remotely bordering on judicial creativity. To them, past decisions reveal the literal law. It must be said at once that there are many judges, lawyers and legal academics who may nurture thoughts along these lines, but they are not legal fundamentalists. What sets legal fundamentalists apart is their intractable backwardness and the lack of any observable semblance of balance in their perception and expression of the common law or judicial process.

Legal fundamentalism, then, is essentially an ideology marked by what might be called a closed system of thought in which its adherents believe that they are possessed of the absolute and all-encompassing truth. The reality of the legal process must bow to its uncompromising stand, and its simplistic and false thinking become the crutches that both support the creed and provide the means by which disbelievers may be chastised. Supremely confident of its unnerving rightness, it becomes a profound reactionary force. The judge, they may be heard to say, deserves Pound's rebuke when tracing the influence of Puritanism on the law: 'Being a human machine and in consequence tainted with original sin, he [and she] must be allowed no scope for free action.'[3]

Although it is not blasphemous to call such ideologues fundamentalists, it would be profane to call them legal theorists. They are not. Rather, although the peevish contributions of some theorists may suggest a brooding fundamentalism, legal fundamentalists tend to come from the more conservative or far right fringe of the legal profession and academia. Certainly, they may derive some comfort from selected academic legal writings, but much of that literature is misunderstood or mishandled and, certainly, most of it is abridged and simplified. Repeated with frequent fervour, the creed is not always recognised for what it is, a false ideology, and it therefore exerts an influence on the law and judiciary well beyond its due. Its come-uppance is being constantly deferred. Yet, judges must consciously examine and reject its blandishments if they are to deliver justice and relevance in the administration of the law.

It will suffice to touch upon just three of the more common bromides propounded by legal fundamentalists. The first is the challenge to the democratic legitimacy of the judiciary; the second is the use – or misuse – of the appellation, 'judicial activism'; and the third is the perpetuation of the belief that the judicial function is not 'political'.

---

[3] Roscoe Pound, *The Spirit of the Common Law* (Marshall Jones Company, Boston 1931), at 57.

The democratic legitimacy of the judiciary

Judicial independence and impartiality

Resentment or suspicion of the power exercised by the judiciary is widespread. In the case of legal fundamentalists it mounts to outright enmity. The basis of this reproach is the fact that judges are unelected and, allegedly, unaccountable. These unelected and unaccountable judges then make 'political' decisions contrary to the democratic ideal. This thinking is incomplete and simplistic.

The depiction of the judiciary as being somehow elementally undemocratic is a tired and outworn assertion of the so-called 'traditional' role of the judiciary. At base, it is founded on a misunderstanding of the separation of powers and a misplaced faith in majoritarian government to resolve the inevitable disagreements between those in our society who hold power and those who are subject to that power. Thus, it is asserted, the legislature is there to enact laws; the executive or administration is there to administer those laws; and the judiciary is there to interpret and apply those laws. The simplicity of this solemn shibboleth is beguiling, but horribly platitudinous.

Political scientists have long since exposed the strict doctrine of the separation of powers as an illusion. In Westminster-type democracies, in particular, the relationship of the legislature to the executive is anything but separate, and all three branches of government exert powers that can properly be described as legislative, administrative and judicial. This is not to deny, of course, that each branch of government has a core function. The separation of powers doctrine is best diluted to a formula that acknowledges that core functionalism. Feeley and Rubin argue that functionalism in the separation of powers context permits one branch of government to venture into the territory of another so long as it does not interfere with the core functions of that branch.[4] In other words, one branch should not function so as to disable another branch from functioning effectively in its core area of responsibility. If this principle is transgressed, people are denied the advantage and access that the particular branch would otherwise provide.

In respect of the judiciary, however, this perception is best removed from the context of the separation of powers doctrine altogether and

---

[4] Malcolm M. Feeley and Edward L. Rubin, *Judicial Policy Making and the Modern State: How the Court's Reformed America's Prisons* (Cambridge University Press Cambridge, 1998), at 330.

advanced as a critical constitutional doctrine; the independence of the judiciary. For the legislative and executive branches of government to refrain from interfering with the judicial function, they must respect that independence itself and not just the core judicial function. Another way of making the point would be to say that judicial independence is an integral part of the judiciary's core function. But, however the point is made, the level of legislative and executive restraint from interference in the judicial function must be necessarily high if judicial independence is not to be compromised.

A defence of the principle of judicial independence is not required in this book. Generally speaking, however, it is accepted that the courts have the constitutional mandate to reach decisions having binding force on individuals and groups in society without intervention from other governmental bodies. For judges to be elected or to otherwise directly represent any particular individual or group or sectional interest would compromise that independence.

But judicial independence commands a complementary imperative. It is the constitutional price that must be paid for the legislatures and executive's restraint. The judiciary must act impartially. Independence without impartiality is a wayward beast. It is when judicial independence is exercised objectively, without prejudice or favour, that it achieves its real value in a democratic society. That value lies in the ability of the judiciary to resolve issues or disagreements detached from the participants and immune to the relative power, strength and coincident advantages of those participants. Without judicial impartiality, the danger is that the power, strength and coincident advantage of one party will enter into and distort the independence of the judiciary and judicial process.[5]

---

[5] Expedient reference may be made to Lord Hoffmann's participation in the Pinochet saga in the House of Lords. In a judgment delivered on 25 November 1998, by a majority of three to two, the House held that Pinochet was not entitled to immunity and a warrant for his arrest could issue. Lord Hoffmann was a member of the majority ([1998] 4 All ER 897). Amnesty International had earlier been granted leave to appear in the proceedings. Following the decision on 25 November, Pinochet's legal advisers learned that Lord Hoffmann was a Director and Chairperson of Amnesty International Charity Ltd, a registered charity responsible for those aspects of the work of Amnesty International that are charitable under United Kingdom law. Pinochet's legal advisers also learned that Lady Hoffmann had been employed at Amnesty International in various administrative positions. It was not suggested that either Lord Hoffmann or his wife had been involved in the substantive decisions made by Amnesty International in relation to the *Pinochet* case. Not only had Lord Hoffmann not disqualified himself, however, but also he had

It is because the power or 'might' of one party is irrelevant to the merits of a dispute that the legal process and judicial adjudication is particularly appropriate in certain classes of case. The outside domination of power, strength or other temporal advantage is neutralised and the potential for that domination ousted under the umbrella of judicial independence and impartiality. Such a conception is far removed from the neat and tidy 'traditional' understanding of the separation of powers.

To the extent, then, that the phrase the 'legitimacy of the judiciary' must be given currency, it is best restricted to those attributes that mark out the judiciary's role in a democracy, that is, judicial independence and consequential impartiality. It is this impartiality between the government or executive and the citizen and between citizen and citizen that means that the judiciary is indifferent to any disparity between the relative power, strength and coincident advantages of the participants. The forum, which is then available for the resolution of disputes between the government or executive and citizen, or citizen and citizen, provides a process that is deliberative and reflective. Equality before the law is guaranteed in that process. These attributes are not assured by the voluntary assent of the judges only, but by the extensive constraints to which the judiciary is subject. This subjection requires the adoption of a judicial methodology which embodies, protects and promotes those attributes.

The will of the people

Nor can the critics' reliance on the mantra of majoritarian government pass critical muster. In essence, they confuse majority government with democratic governance and equate the periodic electoral return with the will of the people. They would denude democracy of its constitutional foundation or framework.

I allow at the outset that highlighting the imperfections of representative government does not alleviate the imperfections of the judiciary. But that is not the point. The point is that the faith reposed in majoritarian government to represent the popular will obscures certain material factors that

failed to disclose his interest in Amnesty International Charity to counsel. The earlier decision was annulled by the House of Lords on 15 January and the matter referred to another Committee of the House for rehearing. In annulling the tainted hearing, their Lordships held that Lord Hoffmann had been automatically disqualified from hearing the appeal ([2000] 1 AC 119). On the facts as recorded in the judgments, it is difficult to reconcile Lord Hoffmann's decision to sit in the original appeal, or his failure to advise counsel of his interest in Amnesty International Charity, with the standard required to maintain the independence and impartiality of the judiciary.

make the contrast between an elected and accountable legislature and an unelected and allegedly unaccountable judiciary less stark than its adherents claim. Underlying this faith is the assumption that the legislative and executive branches of government represent the will of the people by virtue of the fact that the politicians in the legislature have been elected. But this representative presupposition has been assailed on all sides by modern scholars. As Professor Loughlin, has observed, for example, governments of a modern representative democratic character do not in any strict sense express the popular will.[6] Rather, he states, it would be more accurate to say that the people merely select from amongst the competitors those who will take the political decisions. Representative democracy sanctions a mode of government by elites, subject only to the often inadequate form of retrospective accountability.[7] Quoting B. Mannon, the author points out that representative democracy 'is not a system in which the community governs itself, but a system in which public policies and decisions are made subject to the verdict of the people'.[8]

There is a theoretical tinge to attacks such as these. But there can be little doubt that many factors operate to disturb the comfortable notion that representative government represents the popular will. The first factor I would advert to is the disproportionate influence which certain sectors and special interests in the community exert on the political process. Begin with the outcome of elections. Money counts. Control or dominance in the media counts. Beyond the election, special interest groups lobby for legislative or executive action to protect or promote their special interests and, in the real world of politics, will frequently succeed irrespective that their success may not represent the true will of the people. Compromises are frequently involved which might not withstand specific electoral scrutiny. Finally, but not exhaustively, party discipline can mean that policy decisions are made by a small group of politicians supported by an influential but anonymous public service.[9]

---

[6] Martin Loughlin, 'Rights, Democracy, and Law' in Tom Campbell and K. D. Ewing (eds.), *Special Essays on Human Rights* (Oxford University Press, Oxford 2001), 41, at 51.
[7] Ibid.
[8] *The Principles of Representative Government* (Cambridge University Press, Cambridge, 1997), at 192. See also J. Dunn (ed.) *Democracy: The Unfinished Journey 508 BC to AD 1993* (Oxford University Press, Oxford, 1992), at 247–248.
[9] Sandra Fredman, 'Scepticism Under Scrutiny: Labour Law and Human Rights' in Campbell and Ewing (eds.) *Special Essays*, 197, at 200. See also, Linda deLeon, 'Administrative Reform and Democratic Accountability' in Walter J. M. Kickert (ed.), *Public Management and Administrative Reform in Western Europe*, (Edward Elgar Publishing Ltd, Cheltenham, 1997), at 233–248.

In the second place, and following on from this last statement, the power of the executive and the flaws or shortcomings in the mechanisms designed to ensure that the executive is answerable to the elected legislature may be prudently emphasised. The effectiveness of ministerial responsibility in assessing public accountability has long been questioned.[10] Other mechanisms that have been introduced in modern Parliaments assist, but do not guarantee, the accountability of the administration for all the vast number of decisions made by the executive. Current methods of organisation of the public service further distance the executive from the scope of responsible government.[11] In all, senior unelected officials in the executive exert substantial influence in initiating, shaping and directing, or at times frustrating, governmental policy.

Thirdly, in examining the 'will of the people', the interests of minorities require mention. Save for the situation where a minor political party wields the balance of power in a Parliament or otherwise buttresses a government, minorities lack real political power. Representation of their interests varies from being inadequate to futile. Simplistic appeals to political equality do not come close to resolving the intractable difficulties faced by minorities in the political process.[12] There is, therefore, something slightly askew in speaking of the will of the people when that 'will' can exclude minority groups and interests, especially when those groups and interests are often numerically substantial and able to invoke social justice to support their position or cause. It cannot be said

---

[10] See, e.g., Colin Turpin, 'Ministerial Responsibility: Myth or Reality?' in J. Jowell and D. Oliver (eds.), *The Changing Constitution* (Clarendon Press, Oxford, 1985), at 48–76; Norman Lewis and Diane Longley, 'Ministerial Responsibility: The Next Steps' (1996) Public Law 490; Sir Richard Scott, 'Ministerial Accountability' (1996) Public Law 410; Dawn Oliver, 'Law, Politics and Public Accountability. The Search for a New Equilibrium' (1994) Public Law 238; Diana Woodhouse, 'Analysis Ministerial Responsibility: The Abdication through the Receipt of Legal Advice' (1993) Public Law 412; Diana Woodhouse, 'Ministerial Responsibility: Something Old, Something New' (1997) Public Law 262.

[11] See, e.g., B. Guy Peters and Donald J. Savoie (eds.), *Governance in the Twenty-first Century: Revitalizing the Public Service* (McGill-Queens University Press, Montreal, 2000); Christopher Pollitt and Geert Bouckaert, *Public Management Reform: A Comparative Analysis* (Oxford University Press, Oxford, 2000); Linda deLeon, 'Administrative Reform and Democratic Accountability' in Kickert (ed.), *Public Management and Administrative Reform in Western Europe*, at 233–248; and David Farnham and Sylvia Horton (eds.), *Managing the New Public Services* (2nd edn, Macmillan Press Ltd, London, 1996) esp. the editors, 'Public Service Managerialism: A Review and Evaluation', at 259–276.

[12] Maleiha Malik, 'Minority Protection and Human Rights', in Campbell and Ewing, *Special Essays*, 277, at 293.

that the will of the majority is their will or that the will of the people is complete without the inclusion of, or allowance for, their will. Such a will could only be determined after open and wide-ranging public discussion, undistorted by the media or other powerful influences, and a capacity on the part of people to compromise their own interests. But that discussion is precarious and the capacity of people to compromise their vested or respective interests rickety. In truth, the legal fundamentalists are talking about the will of the majority.[13]

I would reiterate, however, that the shortcomings of representative government should not be overstated. It is to be accepted that, although responsible and representative government may be imperfect, it is still ultimately accountable to the people. Voters hold governments to account by determining who or which party will hold office as the government of the day. Governments must endeavour to explain and justify their actions and policies in election campaigns to avoid the spectre of electoral defeat. Nor is it wholly correct to depict this broad accountability as being a retrospective verdict. Throughout the course of a parliamentary term, governments must adopt certain options and avoid others if they are to avoid electoral retribution.[14] This acknowledgement does not, or course, detract from the fact that many governmental decisions will have been too small, insignificant or selective and affect too few people, to stimulate the interests of electors. Single or dominant issues may carry poorly supported policies in their wake. Then, the voter's interest in holding a government to account for a particular policy or policies may be overwhelmed by the desire to reject alternative parties offering themselves for government. But none of these matters can eclipse the fact that a democratic government is ultimately accountable to the electorate.

---

[13] I also endorse Feeley and Rubin's view that there may be other criteria that could be imposed rather than the reflection of the popular, or majority, will as the sole criterion for a democracy. The authors list such criteria as the principle that a democracy must respect the rights of individuals, or be governed by organic law, or provide opportunities for expression and participation or establish conditions for rational discourse. Even restricting the criteria to a reliance on fair and open elections as the critical determinant, it cannot be said that a democracy is a government in which everyone who makes important decisions is elected or truly answerable to elected officials. *Judicial Policy Making*, at 333.
[14] R. Mulgan and J. Uhr, 'Accountability and Governments' in Glyn Davis (ed.), *Are You Being Served? State, Citizens and Governance* (Allen & Unwin, Sydney, 2001), 152, at 154–155.

The significance of these shortcomings in converting the so-called 'popular will' into legislative and executive action or policy has another important dimension, and it is that dimension which is particularly germane to the question of the legitimacy of the judiciary. The inevitable shortcomings of representative government explain the people's distrust of the democracy. They, the people, have delegated the power of governance to their elected representatives, but they are fearful that the representatives will misuse that power. For evidence of this concern one need look no further than the fact that so many democratic nations have opted to have a written constitution. The people wish their democracy to operate on the foundation and within the framework of a constitution which will, among other things, curb their representatives' misuse of the power that they, or the majority, vest in them. Countries without a written constitution or a full written constitution, such as the United Kingdom and New Zealand, nevertheless accept the force of many constitutional conventions designed to channel the legislature's and executive's power into an acceptable constitutional framework. Both countries have enacted bills of right. Democratic government is required to be both responsible and representative and operate within the bounds of the constitution and the identified rights. Once that qualification is accepted, the need for an independent arbiter to ensure that the democracy remains representative operating within those bounds becomes self-evident.

The judiciary, therefore, is as essential to democracy as is this constitutional framework. At once, the basic democratic legitimacy of the judiciary becomes apparent. The judiciary is an institution performing a democratic function in the context of a constitution, written or unwritten, which stipulates democratic governance. It is part of that governance and a basic component of democratic government.[15] Along with other unelected institutions or major officials, it represents one of a set of institutions integral to the working of a democracy. Further, as disputes are no less inevitable in a democracy than any other form of government, the courts provide an institution which will resolve those disputes with independence and impartiality in a process that is deliberative, reflective and indifferent to the respective power, strength and coincident advantages of the parties. Expressing the function of the judiciary in these terms would seem to put its democratic legitimacy beyond serious question. What, then, are legal fundamentalists driving

---

[15] Feeley and Rubin, *Judicial Policy Making*, at 333–334.

at? Are they really concerned with legitimacy at all? Is that word appropriate to describe their grievance?

What legal fundamentalists are really concerned about, I suggest, is not the legitimacy of the judiciary, as such, but the exercise of judicial autonomy within the bounds of that legitimacy. In other words, they object to judicial creativity or so-called 'judicial activism', which I will touch on shortly. Essentially, their grievance is the extent to which the courts have entered and ruled upon issues which they consider should be the province of the legislature. As such, the complaint is one of degree. It is not that the judiciary or the judicial role is illegitimate, but that the judges, or some judges, go too far. They will not keep within the bounds of what the critic perceives to be the judicial role.

Opinions as to what is 'too far' or properly within the bounds of the judicial role will, of course, vary considerably. It would be absurd to claim that only that judicial activity that the legal fundamentalists and critics accept is on the right side of the line – a line that they have drawn – is legitimate, and that judicial acts going beyond that line are illegitimate, when there is an immense divergence as to where the line should be drawn. Legitimacy would become a sliding and subjective scale. The question what is or is not acceptable necessarily represents a difference of opinion, and it may be that it represents a valid difference of opinion, but it is not a fair challenge to the democratic legitimacy of the judiciary. That term is simply borrowed to support the rhetoric aimed at judicial creativity.

The judge's values!

Allied to this ultra-conservative conception of the judicial role is the legal fundamentalist's resentment of the perceived imposition of judges' values on the community. The question is repeatedly asked; what is superior about a judge's personal values to the values of any other member of the community? Judges are portrayed as a complacent elite, a bevy of philosopher kings and, even, as 'hero judges', with an inflated perception of their own importance and function.[16] Only those judges who are overtly committed to the formalistic orthodoxy escape the fundamentalists' bile, even though the reality is that such judges also bring to their judicial task a set of values every bit as obtrusive as the values of a more progressive judge.

---

[16] See Gava J, 'The Rise of the Hero Judge' (2001) 24 UNSWLJ 747 and the riposte by Hon. Justice Michael Adams, 'Heroes and Heresy: Myth Meets Legal Fundamentalism' (2004) 78 ALJ 587.

Strangely enough, notwithstanding a sociable, if not gregarious, past I have not yet met a judge who considers that the values that he or she brings to judicial decision-making are intrinsically superior to the values of other sections of the community. To most, the exercise of discerning, and then reflecting, the values of the community is a heartfelt duty. But formulating the issue in the terms adopted by the legal fundamentalists is to miss the point. The critical comparison is not between the values of judges and the values of others in the community, but between values which are subject to the judicial process and values which are not subject to that process.

When parties submit their issue or disagreement to the legal process, they are not submitting to the values of the individual judges per se. They are submitting their issue or disagreement to a process. It may well be that, to a greater or lesser extent, the judges' personal values will colour their judgement or their perception of the values immanent in the community, but it is inescapable that those judges are part of and operate within a process, and it is simply not possible to overlook the significance of that process.

I have conceded elsewhere more than once that the legal process has its share of imperfections, but it remains an essentially deliberative and reflective process of decision-making. These features of deliberation and reflection are manifest in a number of respects. The hierarchical structure of the court system, for example, is conducive to close deliberation. At first instance, the facts are exhaustibly established, and form the basis for an appellate process in which argument is equally exhaustively pursued. As the case moves up through the appellate structure, the issues become refined and, generally speaking, every aspect of the issue or disagreement is fully canvassed and considered in the courtroom. Lawyers are assiduous in their determination to leave no stone unturned. The deliberation continues in judicial chambers where, if necessary, judges have the advantage of obtaining further research from their clerks.

Furthermore, by and large, the legal process is not niggardly with time, certainly relative to other processes. Court procedures are for the most part designed to be comprehensive. Ensuring that no one is denied a fair hearing, natural justice is a primary requirement of the system, and one that ultimately overrides all considerations of expedience and efficiency. The comparatively unhurried nature of the process then lends itself to reflection, such reflection being particularly requisite at the appellate level. This deliberation and reflection are essential to the task of balancing the competing considerations and values that vie for ascendancy.

Then, again acknowledging that they are not perfect, judges do not come to the bench without extensive training and experience. Their education and experience continues while they are on the bench. As a body they are, it is fair to say, of reasonable intelligence. Training, experience and intelligence vest the judiciary with an aptitude for judging, which is, of course, the capability to balance one factor against another or to judge where to draw the line or to simply reach reasoned, logical and coherent decisions. The fact that judges may disagree on the outcome does not depreciate their relatively high level of competence.

To these qualities must be added the judicial methodology, including the vast array of judicial constraints discussed in Chapter 10, which both restrain and direct the judiciary. The judiciary operate within an institution and process which is largely unscathed by the pressures and tensions that mark the legislative process. Inequalities in power, strength and collateral advantage, which may exert an influence in determining an outcome within the legislative process, are immaterial in the courtroom. The most humble individual may challenge the most powerful corporation and expect equality before the law. The independence and impartiality of which I have just spoken will, as far as is possible, ensure an objective outcome.

I would reiterate, yet again, that I am not claiming that the legal process is perfect or even near perfect. Far from it. The process cannot help its deficiencies; it is run by human beings. But it is a process that contains strengths and advantages which lend validity to my immediate point; it is impermissible for legal fundamentalists to rail against the imposition of judges' personal values on the community and to then challenge the democratic legitimacy of the judiciary on the basis that those values are not intrinsically superior to the values of anyone else or the populace in general. The argument is a *non sequitur*. Litigants do not submit their cause to the personal values of the judges; they submit it to an independent and impartial process, which, with all its imperfections, is deliberative and reflective. It is a process distinctively designed to minimise the intrusion of the personal values of the decision-maker.

Other considerations

Legal fundamentalists tend to not only construe the question of the judiciary's democratic legitimacy in near absolute terms but also misunderstand or neglect a number of other factors reinforcing the democratic legitimacy of the judiciary.

First and foremost, these critics underestimate the force and effect of the constraints on the judiciary, which are traversed at length in Chapter 10. Those arguments need not be rehearsed now, but in aggregate, as well as individually, they serve to make and keep the judiciary accountable for the way in which the judicial task is performed. In particular, critics tend to underrate the sensitivity of judges to public opinion. Again, I touch upon this subject in Chapter 10, and it will suffice here to refer to the stark example of judicial responsiveness provided by Feeley and Rubin.

In Feeley and Rubin's study of the judiciary's reform of prison administration in the United States it became clear that prison administrators did not represent, or even claim to represent, the will of the people.[17] Indeed, some asserted their independence. A 'gossamer thread of standard political legitimacy' was provided in that prisons were headed by officials who had been appointed by an official who had been appointed by an elected representative. But that gossamer thread did not prevent prisons, especially those in the South, from existing in isolation, unnoticed or ignored by the vast majority of citizens and by the people's representatives. To a greater or lesser extent the prisons enjoyed political autonomy. Feeley and Rubin found that, as a matter of fact, the courts invoked and relied upon popular opinion. Their assumption was that, if citizens were confronted with the realities of prison life, particularly the 'plantation model prisons', they would be repelled and demand reform. The authors believe that the judges were probably correct in their assumption in that, once public attention had become focused on the prisons, many of the extreme practices, such as physical abuse, lack of medical care, bread and water diets, and the use of armed inmates as guards, became impossible to maintain.

Feeley and Rubin's exhaustive study provides hard evidence of the symbiotic relationship between the judiciary and the community. It demonstrates the manner in which judges reflect values immanent in the community and adjust the administration of the law so that it is never out of step, or significantly out of step, with those values.[18]

Secondly, critics who condemn the democratic legitimacy of the judiciary fail to have sufficient regard to the doctrine of the supremacy of

---

[17] Feeley and Rubin, *Judicial Policy Making*, at 331–332.
[18] See also Mark Tushnet, 'Scepticism about Judicial Review: A Perspective from the United States' in Tom Campbell, K. D. Ewing and Adam Tomkins (eds.), *Sceptical Essays on Human Rights* (Oxford University Press, Oxford, 2001), 359, at 365–366.

Parliament, which commands respect in Westminster-type democracies. That doctrine means that Parliament can undo anything that the courts have done. Parliament's legislative supremacy is at one and the same time a political fact, a product of political history, a convention of the constitution and a fundamental principle of the common law.[19] The supremacy of Parliament is thus a day-to-day working reality, and this day-to-day reality means that institution asserts the last word. In a Westminster-style democracy, any perceived shift in power from the legislature to the judiciary is subject to the possibility of a legislative response from Parliament. Moreover, the possibility Parliament will seek to exert its supremacy in this way remains an effective threat. Judges know that they work within a constitutional framework in which the legislature may correct a decision which is seen to be a wayward exercise of judicial power. The possibility totes its own judicial restraint.

Finally, legal fundamentalists cannot accept that the judiciary exercises a 'political' function. Politics is the prerogative of Parliament and, perhaps, the executive. Once the judiciary trespasses into 'political' territory, it is claimed, it loses its legitimacy. As the judicial function is 'political' in a real sense and this 'political' element does not destroy the judiciary's democratic legitimacy, I will deal with this topic separately shortly. But a word in the meantime about so-called 'judicial activism'.

'Judicial activism'

The parable of the activist judge

Let us begin with a parable

A more than usually inquisitive academic set out to unearth the definition of an 'activist judge'. Everyone around him bandied the term about. He, himself, had used it many times over feigning the disdainful turn of the lip to signal unspoken disapproval. But where to start?

He turned to the Great Stephen. The Great Stephen, in his tome on criminal law, you will recall, proclaimed that if A sees B drowning and is able to save him by throwing out a rope, but does nothing, he offends no law. Our inquisitive academic decided to put this thesis to the test and seek to flush out the activist judge.

---

[19] See Philip A. Joseph, *Constitutional and Administrative Law in New Zealand* (2nd edn, Brookers, Wellington, 2001), at 461–512 for a comprehensive discussion of parliamentary sovereignty. And see above, Chapter 2, at 49–52.

Imagine, if you will, a slow-moving river – it has to be slow-moving to allow for the conversations that are about to take place – and in that river struggling for his life is a drowning man. On the bank, conveniently placed, is a coil of sturdy rope.

The first judge to come up to the riverbank is a conservative judge.

'Throw me the rope', cried the drowning man.

'I would like to help', said the conservative judge, 'but my instincts tell me I should leave it to Parliament'.

As the drowning man spluttered and sank he was comforted by the advice from the conservative judge that legislation to require assistance to be given to a drowning person was now Bill No. 127 on the Order Paper.

The second judge to arrive at the river bank was also a conservative judge.

'Please throw me a rope', cried the drowning man.

'That is all very well', said the conservative judge, 'but how do I know you are really drowning, how do I know which end of the rope to throw, and how do I know you will catch it?'

'Obviously', continued the conservative Judge, 'these questions require the attention and research that only the Law Commission can provide'.

'But the process will take months, if not years', wailed the drowning man, 'and then it is likely that the Law Commission's report will gather dust in the Parliamentary basement along with all its other unimplemented reports'.

'Then', admonished the conservative judge, 'you must tread water and be patient.'

The next judge was also a conservative judge.

In response to the drowning man's pleas for help he said, 'I am sorry, but the questions whether your life is worth saving and whether innocent people should put their lives at risk by throwing you a rope involve policy issues, and a judge is ill-equipped to resolve policy issues.'

'If and when you and a number of others have drowned through not being thrown a rope', he added, 'the policy issues will become clearer.'

'In the meantime it is not for me, an unelected judge, to determine a question of policy.'

The fourth judge would have none of this.

'I will not leave it to Parliament, I will not wait for the Law Commission and I accept that judges must address policy issues', he proclaimed.

But, then, alas for the drowning man, he showed his training.

'But can you', he cried out, 'provide me with a precedent for a judge throwing a rope to a drowning man?'

Swallowing water as he spluttered, the drowning man had to concede that there was no precedent directly in point. Nor even indirectly in point. Indeed, the more the drowning man thought about it, the more concerned he became that he would end up being the precedent.

The fifth judge to approach the river bank was a law and economics judge. He decided that the compliance costs of throwing the drowning man a rope would be too high, and concluded that the man's fate should be left to the free flow, not of the river, but of market forces.

The sixth conservative judge to come to the river bank was one of Lord Denning's 'timorous souls'.

'Dear me', he murmured fearfully, 'if I threw you the rope I might slide down this "slippery slope" into the river.'

'Or, the rope might get caught in the mechanism of the dam upstream and "open the floodgates" thereby drowning us all.'

'If that relegates me to the company of "timorous souls",' he said, 'I must face that consequence with such fortitude as I can command.'

The headlines in the newspaper next day read; 'Judge denies he is a wimp.'

At last, to the joy of the inquisitive academic, the seventh and final judge was an activist judge.

'Throw me a rope', cried the drowning man – not for the first time.

At once the activist judge responded. 'Of course it is only fair that I should throw you the rope', he said. 'It will accord', he added, 'with the reasonable expectations of the community.'

But before the activist judge could carry out his noble purpose, a group of legal fundamentalists bearing the standard of their ideology lurched along the river bank from, of course, the right. They selected one of their number to be their spokesperson. 'What is fair?' he demanded.

'And how can you, an unelected judge, know what the reasonable expectations of the community are?'

These inquiries threw the activist judge into utter confusion.

So confused did he become wondering what was 'fair', and how could he, a mere judge, know what was 'fair' and what were 'reasonable expectations', and how could he, even more of a mere judge than when he last asked the question, know how to discern the reasonable expectations of the community, that he began to run around in circles. Alas, as he did so his foot caught in the rope and, as he threw the rope out, he threw himself out with it.

Now, there were two drowning men in the river.

At that point the drowning activist judge looked up and saw the six conservative judges who had preceded him in this parable standing in line on the river bank. 'Save me', he pleaded.

But his plea fell on indifferent ears as one conservative judge metaphorically intoned to his brethren, 'I have always known that if you give an activist judge enough rope, he will drown himself.'

And so, as the activist judge finally sank, the truth, like his life, flashed before his eyes: an activist judge is an orthodox judge surrounded by conservative judges.

The message? It is all relative.

An ersatz concept

The phrase 'judicial activism' is much loved by legal fundamentalists. It trips off their tongues with acidic delicacy. As a distinguished Judge in the United States has said, judicial activism is 'the target of much demagogic bluster'. 'In most cases', the learned jurist states, 'the mindless incantation of this phrase amounts to a political ritual which touches ... the congregation of voters at an emotional level without provoking any reasoned discourse among them.'[20] Further, as the same Judge pointed out, even within the legal profession, defenders and decriers of 'judicial activism' sometimes fail to see the need to explain just what it is that they are debating. All too often, I agree, the epithet 'judicial activism' is employed rhetorically to bolster an ideological position in relation to the judicial role. Equally often, it is used as shorthand for a concealed – or ill-concealed – prejudice.

But I do not discount the wider concern that the repeated use of the expression indicates. The impression or feeling exists in many quarters that judges have tended to run amok during the latter part of the twentieth century. Many persons, both within and without the judiciary, express or nurture the profound misgiving that the courts have become 'little legislators'. Those who harbour this disquiet may not deny that judges make law, for that is undeniable; their concern is that they usurp Parliament's law-making prerogative. Underlying this misgiving is the feeling that the courts have come to exercise a degree of authority over the lives of people, the events of the times, and the direction the country is taking which is unparalleled in history. The power wielded by judges

---

[20] William Wayne Justice, 'The Two Faces of Judicial Activism' (1992) 61 Geo. Wash. LR 1, at 1–2.

in shaping the contours of life is perceived to be excessive and anti-democratic. In a rough and ready way the phrase 'judicial activism' gives vent to this concern.

The point needs to be made, however, that much of this thinking emanates from the United States and the ongoing debate about the Supreme Court's influence in interpreting and applying the Constitution of that country. The fact the Supreme Court annuls legislation held to contravene the rights and freedoms enshrined in the Constitution means that no wider question remains following a decision to that effect. Dissatisfied citizens face the difficult legislative process of seeking a constitutional amendment. In countries that lack this sweeping power, however, such as the United Kingdom and New Zealand, the courts' decisions are not necessarily the end of the matter. The question posed for the judiciary, on the one hand, and the legislature, on the other, is not generally the same question. Describing the former as a more 'legal' question and the latter as a more 'general' question conveys the gist of the divergence. But this divergence is either overlooked or confused. Cases in which it is alleged a statutory provision is discriminatory provide illustrations of the point. The question for the courts will be whether the legislation amounts to discrimination. For the legislature the question is likely to be more wide ranging, with the issue of discrimination one factor only in the debate. Only hardened critics of so-called judicial activism would be prepared to argue that the more 'legal' question, that is, whether a measure constitutes 'discrimination', is a question for final resolution in a popular and partisan legislative assembly.

Certainly, wider public debate may be, and one would hope would be, informed by any determination of the courts. A 'fruitful partnership'[21] or 'dialogue'[22] between the legislature and the judiciary in which each institution addresses the question for which it is most suited becomes possible.[23] Following a deliberative and reflective process the courts may determine whether or not a breach of a fundamental right or freedom exists, but that does not pre-empt legislative action. Outspoken opponents of 'judicial activism' should not be granted the indulgence of merging or confusing the two questions as if the position were the same for all jurisdictions as it is in the United States.

---

[21] See below, Chapter 9, at 237; and Chapter 10, at 263–264.
[22] See s 33 of the Canadian Charter of Rights and Freedoms. See also below Chapter 10, n. 39.
[23] See below, Chapter 10, at 254–265.

Logical thought therefore demands a more competent analysis and a more precise meaning to the phrase 'judicial activism' than just an intuitive dislike of the extent of judicial influence. What then does the phrase mean?

In the first place, the phrase is frequently used to condemn what the courts do, and cannot avoid doing, that is, making law and formulating policy. We have seen that these functions are not only unavoidable, but are also legitimate judicial functions. To describe judicial law-making and policy-making as judicial activism when these functions cannot be avoided is plainly pointless. The proponents of this phrase must be more specific.

In being more specific, as well as more realistic, the proponents must accept that they are speaking of judges who, in their view, make too much law or too much policy and do not leave that law and policy to Parliament. Consequently, it is a matter of degree. Shortly put, these critics would have the judges exercise greater judicial restraint. But even the repeated invocation of this discipline tells us nothing firm about the meaning of judicial activism. All judges endorse judicial restraint; they differ in what they consider the appropriate level of restraint should be. Again, it is a matter of degree. Platitudes about the need for judicial restraint do not advance the debate as to the optimum or appropriate level of restraint.

Once it is accepted the judicial activism is a matter of degree, we can at once perceive that the phrase represents the user's personal perception of the proper performance of the judicial function or role. Legal fundamentalists simply favour a more conservative and orthodox approach against a more liberal and creative approach. Inherent in this preference is a predilection in favour of the values underlying the conservative and orthodox approach. Thus, on analysis, it is those values which are in fact put in issue with the use of the phrase 'judicial activism'. The perceived values of the judges to whom, or courts to which, the label has been directed have, it is believed, departed too far from the allegedly established rules or precedents or strayed too far from the known or ascertainable preferences of the majority that encompass those values.[24]

Proponents of the phrase, therefore, are doing no more than claiming the prerogative of legitimacy for a conservative approach to the administration and development of the law. By branding a more liberal or creative approach as 'judicial activism' they seek to place such approaches outside the boundaries of mainstream jurisprudence and

---

[24] Justice, 'Two Faces of Judicial Activism', at 3.

the judicial process. But, as has already been demonstrated,[25] judicial liberal thinking and creativity have a vital place within the framework of that process and judges of that stamp are equally deferential to the rule of law. The attempt to vest that approach with the taint of illegitimacy is unworthy of serious legal thinkers. It has no greater value than if those of a liberal and creative persuasion were to brand conservative and unimaginative judges with the polemical counterpart; 'judicial passivists'!

Consequently, the phrase 'judicial activism' permits the user to avoid addressing his or her perception of the performance of the judicial role that they are actually pursuing. Their values can remain concealed behind the use of the label. They need not feel obliged to justify with reasons why the conservative approach they favour is, in the particular case, to be preferred to an approach that may be more sensitive to the dictates of justice and to the requirements of the community. The label, in effect, reflects their underlying ideology, and ideology, as already noted, exacts no reasoned defence.

And Lord Denning?

To legal fundamentalists, Lord Denning is the very epitome of a judicial activist. Certainly, he believed in doing justice in the instant case and in keeping the law abreast of the times. Lord Denning's attitude was summed up in *Re Vandervell's Trusts (No. 2)*[26] to the effect that every unjust decision is a reproach to the law or the judge who administers it. He unabashedly pursued what Justice Frankfurter described as 'those canons of decency and fairness which express the notion of justice of English-speaking peoples'.[27]

Ironically, Lord Denning is both revered and reviled. He is at one and the same time accorded a respect approaching reverence for his outstanding contribution to the development of the common law while his approach to the law is treated with disdain. On the one hand, he is extolled as a phenomenon whose impact on the law over the past half century is second to none, and it is accepted that he vastly improved the law. Yet, on the other hand, Lord Denning's approach is not overtly followed by any number of judges, lawyers and academics in a position to practise it. Judges who freely acknowledge his great contribution decline to follow the path that led to that contribution. Lawyers will

---

[25] See above, Chapter 1, at 3–7. See also Chapter 10.   [26] [1974] Ch 269, at 322.
[27] *Adamson v California* 332 U.S. 46, (1947), at 67.

revere him, but are yet scornful of his approach and continue to recite so-called precedents to a weary bench. Academics will extol his style and impact on the law to their students but then raise a snigger with asides about his penchant for the merits and 'fairness'. There is in this paradox between the seemingly genuine admiration for the man and his work and the complacency with which these practitioners of the law then adhere to their orthodoxy an observable feeling of superiority. It is better, it seems, to belong to the priesthood and conform to its rituals than to carry the cross for justice and modernity in the law.

The true legal fundamentalists, however, escape this paradox. They simply refuse to acknowledge that Lord Denning's approach is acceptable. He was a judicial activist and that is that. It is of no moment that, if the law were deprived of Lord Denning's contributions, it would be a far poorer law and the community more poorly served by that law. Ideology admits of no compromise.

There is no question, of course, but that Lord Denning must be accorded the mantle of a progressive judge. But while he would have welcomed this mantle, he appears to have been disinterested in the label of activist judge. To him, the label would have been meaningless. A judge who is aware that the law's dynamic is irreversible simply because the society it serves is forever changing will necessarily develop the law so as to keep it abreast of those changes. Such a conception of the judicial role dictates a creative approach in contrast to the formalist with a mechanical perception of the judicial process who, Lord Denning would have it, simply fails to earn his or her pay.

It is true, too, that Lord Denning was not only sensitive to the iniquities of injustice but also had the creative ability to formulate a solution that would obtain general support, if not immediately, then in the fullness of time. Reaching a state of dissatisfaction with the existing law is one thing; the innovative capacity to perceive the next step is another. This capacity was Lord Denning's great strength. His true boldness lay, not in his sweeping rejection of precedent,[28] but in his ability to proclaim an innovative formula which would, once

---

[28] Not, perhaps, altogether sweeping. In his book, *The Discipline of Law* (Butterworths, London, 1979), at 314, Lord Denning clarified that all he was against in respect of the doctrine of precedent is its too rigid application; a rigidity that insists a bad precedent must necessarily be followed. He would treat the doctrine as a path through the woods. 'You must', he said, 'follow it certainly so as to reach your end. But you must not let the path become overgrown. You must cut out the dead wood and trim the side branches, else you will find yourself lost in thickets and brambles.' Lord Denning's final plea was

pronounced, attract sufficient allegiance to become the law or lay the foundation for the development of the law in the future. If this makes Lord Denning an 'activist judge', so be it.

Notwithstanding his creativity and progressiveness, however, and without detracting from his strengths or contribution to the development of the law, Lord Denning does not neatly fit the conception of the judicial role or approach put forward in this book. He does not appear to have had an articulate theory of law to underpin his notion of justice or a sound conception of the judicial role, and he lacked the commitment to the judicial methodology and discipline outlined in Chapter 10.

One might expect a judge who is pre-eminent in the development of the law to explore and express the theoretical framework for his beliefs. Certainly, Lord Denning briefly toyed with the notion of 'a new equity'. He also posited at one time that the law consisted of deep fundamental principles and suggested that a judge owed allegiance to these principles and not to the mass of illustrative decisions based upon them. But no developed theory ever emerged to support the articles of faith that he so assiduously preached and put into practice. Lord Denning was no Holmes or Cardozo.

To affirm the point that acceptance of the theory of adjudication advanced in this book would not lead to a massive judicial cloning of Lord Denning, it is instructive to compare his approach with that of Cardozo. Certainly, the two shared many similar characteristics. Both emphasised the importance of the facts in the determination of a case;[29] both utilised a raft of literary and stylistic devices to convey their reasoning; and both can on occasion be accused of over-ornate prose and even exaggeration. Then, both Denning and Cardozo were flexible in their approach to precedent; both fully acknowledged the fact of judge-made law; both declined to countenance the notion that the law always possessed a 'right' answer; both were unwilling to separate the law as it is from the law as it should be; and both accepted that the law should achieve justice between the parties and meet the needs of contemporary life.[30]

---

simply to keep the path to justice clear of obstructions which would impede it. See also pp. 297–300.

[29] For example, see Lord Denning's judgments in *Beswick* v *Beswick* [1966] 1 Ch 538, at 549–50 and *The Lloyds Bank* v *Bundy* [1975] QB 326 and Justice Cardozo's judgment in *Palsgraf* v *Long Island Railroad Co*, 162 N.E. 99 (N.W. 1928).

[30] I am indebted to Brady Coleman for an outstanding article comparing the two judges. See 'Lord Denning and Justice Cardozo: the Judge as Poet-Philosopher' (2001) 32 Rutgers LJ 485. Both judges played a major part in the emergence of the doctrine of

In many instances, however, these similar characteristics obscured vastly different theories of adjudication. As Brady Coleman spells out, Denning was strongly influenced by his Christian faith.[31] He believed that justice and truth would emerge from the maintenance of true religion and virtue and not by argument and debate or by reading and thinking.[32] He compressed his trust in God into the notion of what right-minded members of the community would consider to be fair. In the result, Coleman was able to conclude that Denning was neither a forward-looking judge nor a backward-looking judge but rather an inward-looking judge. He did not look forward in a pragmatic or teleological fashion to social policies or overall legal aims. He did not look backward at precedents and the restrictions of established doctrine. Rather, he looked within and decided cases on the basis of his sense of justice, which was strongly influenced by his religious faith;[33] a faith that in turn directed his perception of the moral and cultural values of his time. In essence, Denning's approach was the approach of a natural law lawyer. Frequently, his conviction as to what was right precluded a pragmatic approach that consciously and overtly balanced the relevant considerations, one against the other, in order to arrive at a more disciplined outcome.

Cardozo, on the other hand, was essentially a pragmatist. He believed that 'the juristic philosophy of the common law is at bottom the philosophy of pragmatism. Its truth is relative, not absolute.'[34] He was widely read in pragmatism and often quoted from William James' lectures on pragmatism as a source for his views on judging.[35] Cardozo was also a realist. He was not only influenced by the American Realist Movement but, as we shall see, he in turn exerted a strong influence on that Movement.[36] While, like Denning, he was prepared to reject precedent when the precedent was in conflict with normative values, unlike Denning, he did not believe that acceptable legal decisions derived from an innate sense of justice attributable to a Christian

---

promissory estoppel in the law of contract. For Lord Denning, see *Central London Property Trust Ltd* v *High Trees House Ltd* [1947] KB 130; for Justice Cardozo, see *Allegneny College* v *National Chautauqua County Bank* 159 N.E. 173 (N.Y. 1927). Again, both Judges also developed the law of negligence. For Lord Denning, see *Candler* v *Crane, Christmas & Co* [1951] 1 All ER 426 in which Denning J dissented and sought to permit liability for negligent misstatements. His dissent was subsequently adopted by the House of Lords in *Hedley Byrne & Co* v *Heller & Partners* [1964] AC 465. For Justice Cardozo, see *MacPherson* v *Buick Motor Company* 111 N.E. 1050 (N.W. 1916).

[31] Coleman, 'Lord Denning and Justice Cardozo', at 16.
[32] Lord Denning, 'The Influence of Religion on Law', Thirty-Third Earl Gray Memorial Lecture at Kings College, Newcastle Upon Tyne, 27 May 1953.
[33] Coleman, 'Lord Denning and Justice Cardozo', at 16.
[34] Ibid., at 17.   [35] Ibid.
[36] See below, Chapter 12, at 302–303; and see Chapter 13, at 340–342.

God or from moral absolutes. Bernard Shientag sought to summarise Cardozo's jurisprudential approach in these terms: 'The predominant characteristics of his philosophy are pragmatic – a flexibility, rather than a dogmatic rigidity; a concern with facts and realities and consequences, rather than with abstractions and formal rules and metaphysical subtleties ...'[37] As will become increasingly apparent in later chapters, Cardozo was much closer to the theory of adjudication advanced in this book than Denning by, to use a colloquialism, a country mile.

This lack of any basic jurisprudential theory may also have led Lord Denning to indulge personal prejudices that have no place in judicial decision-making. His patriotic fervour for England and all things English was evident in a number of cases. His judgment in *Attorney General* v *Ortiz*,[38] for example, falls not far short of jingoism. Anyone attempting to thwart the place of cricket in English life would surely become disenchanted with their chances of success after reading *Miller* v *Jackson*.[39] His bias in favour of authority in the form of the defence forces, the police and the interests of national security were also evident.[40] He also believed that England was being 'invaded' by illegal immigrants seeking free welfare. Such people, he said, multiply by increasing their family size. The suggestion that immigration officers are above reproach in his sweeping statement, 'I have never known a case where [immigration officers] have been unfair', is also troubling.[41] Geoffrey Robertson QC's observation in his book, *The Justice Game*,[42] that Lord Denning's 'love of freedom sometimes stops short of extending it to foreigners or dissidents' is undoubtedly pertinent. Lord Denning also seems to have had an all too unhealthy dislike of trade unions. Extra-judicially he described them as the 'robber barons' of modern times. Nor can one ignore the odd touch of sexism in some of his reported comments. Finally, of course, it was his suggestion, bitterly regretted, that certain rioters had been acquitted because the jury contained some coloured people that led to him being described as a racist. It was too much, even for a Judge revered by the 'common people', and he was effectively forced to retire.

---

[37] Bernard L. Shientag, 'The Opinions and Writings of Judge Benjamin N Cardozo' (1930) 30 Colum. LR 597, at 610.
[38] [1984] AC 1.   [39] [1977] QB 966.
[40] R. F. V. Heuston, 'Lord Denning: A Man and His Times' from J. L. Jowell and J. P. W. B. McAuslan (eds.) *Lord Denning: The Judge and the Law* (Sweet & Maxwell, London 1984), 1, at **XX**.
[41] Edmund Heward, *Lord Denning, A Biography* (Barry Rose Law Publishers Ltd., Chichester, 1997), at 230.
[42] (Vintage, London, 1999), at 107.

This bundle of prejudices cannot be described as respectable. Lord Denning is not, of course, necessarily alone. The orthodox judge is able to better conceal his or her prejudices under the less candid cloak of the orthodox legal method. But justice should not have to compete with prejudices of this kind. They blight the purity of the concept of doing justice according to law.

Conservative activism

Finally, it should be pointed out that so-called judicial activism is not, as the legal fundamentalists would have it, the prerogative of the liberal or creative judge. Judicial activism is not consistently liberal and judicial restraint is not consistently conservative. The Supreme Court of the United States provides the best illustration of this disclaimer. Probably no appellate court in the common law world has reversed, modified or reinterpreted more past decisions than the Supreme Court under the leadership of Justice W. Rehnquist. The Court, or the majority of the Court, wish to assert a more conservative approach to the law, and to hold to that approach necessitates reversing, modifying or reinterpreting the law that had developed during the earlier Warren era.[43] The complete story, of course, pre-dates the Rehnquist Court.

During the first half of the twentieth century the conservative Supreme Court of that time invalidated legislation aimed at protecting working people and providing a minimum economic well-being for the general population. In what is usually called the Lochner era, laws limiting the hours of labour were invalidated by the Court as unconstitutional infringements on the rights of employers and employees to enter into contracts. The Court interfered with what it perceived to be legislative intrusions into the economy.[44] Liberals opposed this interference by advocating judicial restraint, conceived as a neutral, independent, universal and overriding principle that transcended

---

[43] I had initially thought to categorise the majority's approach as a wish to 'revert to a less intrusive law', as they would probably describe it, but this description is strained when regard is had to the Court's intrusion into the bedroom (of gay couples), the doctor's consulting room (in the case of pregnant women), and, indeed, into the democratic decision-making process (in cases from affirmative action to gun control to environmental regulation).

[44] *Lochner v New York*, 198 U.S. 45 (1905) invalidating legislation restricting the hours of work in bakeries.

substantive goals or politics.[45] As David Kairys has pointed out, conservatives and liberals have each tended to advocate judicial restraint when they lose control of the courts, typically justified with the lofty stated goal of stopping the courts from interfering with the 'will of the people'.[46]

A conservative Court continued to frustrate President Franklin D. Roosevelt's attempts at liberal reform. A confrontation between the administration and the judiciary was averted because the President was able to appoint more liberal judges as more conservative, older judges retired. But judicial liberalism then found its stride and reached its zenith under Justice Earl Warren. With that Judge's demise, however, judicial retrenchment was not long in coming and has culminated in the ultra-conservative 'Rehnquist Court'. It is not suggested that all landmark decisions of the earlier era have been reversed by this Court. *Brown v Board of Education*[47] and *Roe v Wade*[48] are two examples of seminal and far-reaching decisions, which, while modified at the edges, have otherwise remained relatively intact. Nor is it suggested that this later retrenchment has been out of step with the prevailing public mood.[49] Whether it has sustained the enduring values underlying the law is another question. But irrespective of these questions the degree of judicial revision that has taken place under the Rehnquist Court has, or should have, earned for that Court the sobriquet of being the most activist court in the history of the common law world. The immediate point is that, if so-called judicial activism is illegitimate or wrong in the hands of more progressive judges so, too, is it illegitimate or wrong in the hands of more conservative judges. What is sauce for the liberal goose is sauce for the conservative gander.[50]

---

[45] See Robert L. Stern, 'The Commerce Clause on the National Economy (1933–46)' (1946) 59 Harv. LR 645, at 659–72 for a review of cases during this period.
[46] David Kairys (ed.) in the 'Introduction' to *The Politics of Law* (Basic Books, New York, 1982), at 8. See above at 79–84.
[47] 347 U.S. 483, 493, 98 L. Ed. 873, 74 S. Ct. 686 (1994).   [48] 410 U.S. 113 (1973).
[49] Tushnet in Campbell, Ewing and Tomkins (eds.) *Sceptical Essays*, at 365–366.
[50] For a compelling exposé of the 'activism' of the conservative Judges on the Supreme Court of the United States, see John T. Noonan, *Narrowing the Nation's Power: The Supreme Court Sides with the States* (University of California Press, Berkley, Calif., 2002), at 9–14, in which the author reveals the Court's machinations in relation to the doctrine of sovereign immunity. The conservative majority on the Court has been no less original in their treatment of other aspects of the Constitution.

A 'political' process!

Many judges still prefer the pretence that the judicial process is not political. Politicians who bask in the belief that Parliament is the sole law-making institution certainly consider that the judiciary should be apolitical. They may even fortify the judge's pretence. Legal fundamentalists ram it home. But there can be no doubt that the judicial function involves a 'political' element. It is not 'political' in the sense that Parliament or party politics are political, but it is nonetheless political. When carrying out their judicial tasks and arriving at decisions, judges must make value judgements affecting, not only the parties involved, but also the broader community. Indeed, the intrinsic political character of the judicial role has been manifest ever since it was accepted that judges make law. They are not 'little legislators', as I have already said, but they cannot help being 'political actors' in a social and political system in which the judiciary is the third branch of government.

The notion that the judicial function has a political element is not novel. United States realists in the middle of the last century fully uncovered the political character of judicial activity. Political scientists and sociologists have also confirmed the political function of the judiciary. In examining the justice system in the United States in the 1980s, for example, political scientists shifted the focus from legal rules to actual behaviour and came to depict the judge as a true political actor.[51]

The foolhardiness of denying that the judicial process is 'political' is demonstrated by the ability of the initiated to predict the outcome of a case based on the composition of the court. John Braithwaite has pointed out that the fact a thicket of rules engenders argument in a form that some judges will accept and others will not has produced one kind of very strong predictability in the law.[52] If one knows which judges one will get in a case, one can predict the outcome with a high degree of certainty. He refers to David Robertson's analysis of the decisions of the House of Lords in support.[53] In a multiple discriminate analysis of House of Lords decisions, well over ninety per cent of tax and criminal

---

[51] E.g., Martin Shapiro, *Law and Politics in the Supreme Court: New Approaches to Political Jurisprudence* (The Free Press of Glencoe Collier-Macmillan, London, 1964) postulating a 'new' or 'political' jurisprudence.

[52] John Braithwaite, 'Rules and Principles: A Theory of Legal Certainty' (2002) 27 Aust. Journal of Legal Philosophy 47, at 57.

[53] David Robertson, *Judicial Discretion in the House of Lords* (Clarendon Press, Oxford, 1998), at 48–55.

cases could be correctly predicted (in terms of whether the state or the taxpayer or the accused won) and more than eighty per cent of the public, constitutional and civil cases could be correctly predicted in advance by knowing just one fact about that case. That one fact was which judges would sit on the case.

This capacity to predict the outcome of an appeal on the basis of one's knowledge of the disposition of the judges' temperaments is confirmed by my own experience. For years, having read, at least, the judgment appealed from and counsels' written submissions in advance, I would at my regular early morning sessions with my judge's clerk predict the outcome of the appeal to be heard that day, including whether the decision would be unanimous or be decided by a majority and, if so, by what number and by whom. My recollection, as well as the recollection of my clerks, is that my predictions proved unnervingly correct.

Apart from an assessment based on observation, however, there are many factors which confirm that the judiciary cannot be other than political. As already intimated, few, if any judges, would deny that a value judgement lies at the base of most decisions. As the judge must make a choice between competing values he or she inevitably performs a function of a political character. The decision may create public policy, thus corroborating the political element involved. Of course, the extent of this political element will vary depending on the nature of the case. An appeal relating to the interpretation of a word or phrase in patent legislation or a patent instrument may call for little, if anything, in the nature of a value judgement; an appeal raising an issue of discrimination as, for example, in an appeal involving the validity of same-sex marriages,[54] will necessarily call for a value judgement.

A second significant respect in which the judicial function has a 'political' character is the courts' preparedness to take into account the impact of their decisions. The present judicial readiness to have regard to the consequences of a decision was to some extent forestalled by formalism and is still inhibited by the residual hold of that creed. But because the law exists to serve society it is inevitable that many judges increasingly look beyond any retrospective analysis of the case in hand to the impact that their decision will have on the social, political and

---

[54] E.g., *Quilter v Attorney-General* [1998] 1 NZLR 523; *Halpern v Canada (Attorney General)* [2002] O. J. N. 2714 92002 215 DLR (4th); *Barbeau v British Columbia (A-G)* 2003 BCCA 251; and *Goodridge v Department of Public Health* 440 Mass. 309; 798 N.E. 2d 941 (2003).

economic well-being of that society. It is equally inevitable that they shape their thinking accordingly. For the most part, judges today have an eye for the future, and being divorced from the facts and immediate issues of the instant case, that eye must inescapably have a 'political' cast.

Thirdly, such features as I have already mentioned; the exercise of a value judgement, making law and policy, and having regard to the consequences of a decision are particularly evident in the increasing number of social, political and economic issues that confront the courts in modern times. A wide range of legislation, such as welfare legislation, has been enacted in what is often broad or vague terms or in a manner which leaves it to the court, in its discretion, to implement the objectives of the legislation. Even in legislation regulating commercial activity, the courts may be left to give concrete effect to the broad principles contained in the statute. The courts also strive to make legislation work and to that end will, if necessary, fill in gaps in legislation to promote Parliament's purpose. The enactment of the legislation is obviously political, and giving concrete effect to that legislation means that the judges' supporting activity necessarily shares that political quality, although to a lesser extent.

Fourthly, the courts critical function in supervising the legality of governmental and administrative acts to ensure that citizens live under the rule of law has a birthmark that is intrinsically political. Judicial review, even judicial review conservatively pursued, may influence the formulation and implementation of public policy. The courts' decisions may frustrate government or executive policies on the grounds of illegality, irrationality or unfairness. Judicial review puts the courts in the centre of political activity. In supervising the legality, rationality and fairness of governmental action it is impossible for it to be otherwise.

The fifth significant factor suggesting a political element in the judicial function that may be specifically mentioned is the emphasis on human and civil rights resulting from a constitutional or legislative mandate. A constitution or bill of rights thrusts the courts into the political arena. At times the courts must impose an interpretation on legislation that is consistent with those fundamental rights and freedoms or, even, that the legislation, presumably having the support of a majority of the population, is contrary to those fundamental rights and freedoms. The type of question posed and the factors that must be considered and evaluated in reaching a decision have an unmistakeable political flavour. Indeed, advantage can be taken, and is at times taken, of the process for essentially political purposes. Special interest groups as well as individuals will initiate proceedings in order to further, or seek to further, their cause. Their cause will be in the public domain and their purpose or motivation will be largely or wholly political in nature. Such proceedings seeking the protection of fundamental rights and freedoms require the courts to participate in a process that is an adjunct to the purely political process.

Sixthly, the increasingly, and inevitable, polycentric nature of the judicial process bears on the 'political' character of the judiciary. Fuller made much of the polycentric nature of proceedings.[55] Interests well beyond the immediate interests of the parties to the litigation may present the courts with a complex array of expectations and stakes. These wider interests, and the number sharing in those interests, may be unclear. The judgment of the court will in all probability be effectively binding on all those affected and not just the parties represented in the courtroom. Proceedings relating to the environment, competition law and consumer rights are prime examples of this polycentric process. Other cases arise where those pursuing the cause are unable to obtain redress or a final decision in the conventional political process. Again, the political character of such litigation is self-evident.

The 'political' complexion of the judicial process can be illustrated in many other ways. It is pointless to deny it. But the fact the judiciary is 'political' in this sense does not mean that the judiciary is to be equated with the legislative arm of government or that the judiciary is not beholden to the rule of law. The conditions under which judges may be said to be 'political actors' are different from the conditions that prevail in the political branch of government.[56] That branch and the judiciary operate under a fundamentally different methodology and are subject to a vastly different set of constraints. The methodology and constraints that check and curb judicial heresy and aberrance, as discussed below,[57] also serve to check the 'political' element intrinsic to the judicial function. Judges remain part of a political system exercising a political role, but they are unrelated to that system and perform that function in a manner that is quite unlike that of the conventional political actors.

Conclusion

Perhaps I have been a trifle unfair. Discussing the three topics I have selected; the democratic legitimacy of the judiciary, so-called judicial activism, and the 'political' aspect of the judicial function under the

---

[55] Lon L. Fuller, 'The Forms and Limits of Adjudication', (1978) 92 Harv. LR 353.
[56] See above, at 86.   [57] See Chapter 10.

heading 'legal fundamentalism' is unfair to those persons who entertain genuine and moderate concerns in one or more, or all, of these areas. Laypersons, as well as judges, lawyers and academics, are right to be concerned about the boundaries and nature of judicial power in a democracy. The fact that judges are neither elected nor directly accountable invites close attention. As I have accepted, many persons feel that the courts have come to exercise a degree of authority over the lives of people, events of the times, and the direction their country is taking that is excessive in a democracy. I have no quibble with this misgiving. Indeed, the concern reflects a major problem that I seek to confront in this book. Reasoned and reasonable debate on these issues is imperative.

Legal fundamentalists are singled out, however, because they build on these concerns to construct a creed which is extreme in its expression, generally simplistic and incomplete in its argument and, ultimately, ideological in its force. Yet, the influence that they exert is disproportionate to the substance of their case. By its very nature, populism can obtain considerable popular appeal, and legal populism is no different. Constantly barrelled and hustled, often in publications other than serious law journals or reviews, legal fundamentalism's constant refrain has an undeniable impact on the judiciary. None of this would matter greatly but for its effect on the development of the law and a legal methodology that is appropriate to the times. The fundamentalist creed, however, serves to perpetuate the inadequate and outdated theories that mar the law and thereby shackle the legal process to the past. Judges are denied the capacity for choice in administering the law and stifled in their quest to do justice in the individual case and develop the law to meet the needs and expectations of the times.

Imagine a law today in which the scope for judicial choice and judicial creativity had been restricted, say, from the middle of the last century. Developments in all branches of the law, in particular, in equity, tort law, statutory interpretation and administrative law, would have been seriously retarded. The tinkering reluctantly allowed by some legal fundamentalists would have proved satisfactory to no-one. Injustices would be rife as, for example, the injustice to the person who relies and acts to his or her detriment upon a promise for which there is no consideration, or the injustice to the person who is the victim of a breach of natural justice on the part of a governmental agency, and so on. Clearly, the law would be out of step with a society continuously in a state of flux. With its dynamic stalled, the common law would simply cease to be relevant to society's expectations.

This short musing reveals the wayward assumptions underlying the legal fundamentalists' unrealistic perspective. Either they assume that the common law has arrived at such an advanced state that its further development can be arrested without detriment to the parties or the community, or that society has become strangely changeless and undemanding. Society's expectations, apparently, can be met by the law developed for bygone times or, at most, a 'tinkered' refinement of that law. Yet, it is nonsensical to pretend that the law has reached, or can ever reach, a state of nirvana, or that a society constantly in a state of flux can suddenly become 'fluxless'. Failing to recognise the inherent uncertainty of the law and the necessary exercise of choice involved in judicial decision-making, legal fundamentalists fail to understand the dynamic of the common law and the extent to which the administration of the law would be harsh and unjust and out of step with the reasonable expectations and needs of the community if that dynamic were to be suppressed. Further, they fail to perceive the limitations of the legislative process in changing the law in areas that have been the traditional habitat of the courts or appreciate the positive role of the judiciary as the third branch of government. Notwithstanding the lacuna in the law that their protestations would bring about, their focus is on destroying the judicial creativity innate to the common law rather than seeking to define the boundary between the law-making of the legislature and the legitimate law-making of the courts.

In order to adopt a contemporary judicial methodology, therefore, judges will need to consciously resist the blandishments and bluster of legal fundamentalism. Although unelected and, allegedly, unaccountable, they will need to allay any misgivings they might quarter as to the legitimacy of the judicial role in a democracy. They will also need to accept that judicial creativity is a valid and legitimate judicial function, and recognise that the art is to address and resolve the balance between creativity, on the one hand, and judicial restraint, on the other, within the confines of a judicial methodology along the lines of that to be outlined in Chapters 11 to 14. Both judicial practice and legal theory deserve a more reasoned discourse. Such a discourse will clear the way for judges to develop a sound conception of the judicial role based on a more enlightened understanding of legal theory. An appraisal of this kind is essential to obtaining a better conception of the judicial role. Two particular shibboleths that stand in the way of a better conception must now be deconstructed. Those shibboleths are the judicial compulsion to treat certainty in itself as a paramount goal of adjudication and an overly rigid application of the doctrine of precedent. This deconstruction makes up the content of Chapters 5, 6 and 7. It has not proved possible, however, to draw a hard and fast line between the two topics. They are clearly related. Tolerance is sought in advance for any overlap or repetition which may occur.

5

The idolatry of certainty

A conversation in chambers

(The scene is the Judge's chambers. His two judge's clerks enter. Warm morning greetings are exchanged. The first judge's clerk waxes enthusiastically about a film that he saw the night before. The second judge's clerk is more interested in reviewing a book that she is finding fascinating. The judge interrupts ...)

Judge: Well, I am finding the appeal we are to hear on Monday fascinating. It is conceded that the solicitor's advice to the husband relating to a property investment was hopelessly negligent. But the husband didn't act on it; he made the solicitor's report available to his wife and she made the investment – to her cost. Everyman J at first instance has held that she cannot recover against the solicitor.

1st judge's clerk: It's relevant, Judge, that the solicitor had previously given both the husband and wife investment advice and knew that they invested in properties both jointly and separately. But he hadn't seen the wife for about two years and was undoubtedly acting for the husband on this occasion.

Judge: Yes, but let's sort out the law first before we look at the facts in more detail

2nd judge's clerk: That's not like you Judge. What did you have for breakfast?

Judge: *(Ignoring the sally)* I am aware that in negligent misstatement cases the courts have attempted to create a degree of certainty in the ambit of the duty

	and to counter the danger of indeterminate liability[1] – so, I expect the worse! Let's start with *White v Jones*.[2] I note that in his written submission the appellant's counsel relies heavily on that case. The beneficiaries succeeded against the negligent solicitor, but as I recollect it, only by a majority of three. What was the basis of liability again?
1st judge's clerk:	Take your pick, Judge. Lord Goff was pleased to acknowledge an 'impulse to practical justice' and simply extended the responsibility of the solicitor to the beneficiaries. Lord Browne-Wilkinson thought the case analogous to the *Hedley Byrne* cases[3] and emphasised the similarity between statement-makers and positions occupied by fiduciaries, including solicitors *vis-à-vis* their clients ...
Judge:	So it is the *Hedley Byrne* principle or something akin to that principle? An assumption of responsibility?
2nd judge's clerk:	Not so fast, Judge. Lord Nolan, the third member of the majority, did not base his decision on the *Healey Byrne* principle at all. He held that the three stage test laid down in *Caparo*[4] – foreseeability, proximity, and fairness, justice and relevance – had been satisfied.
Judge:	So, no assumption of responsibility is involved on that approach?
1st judge's clerk:	No, no, no. Lord Nolan thought that duties in such cases were derived from an assumption of responsibility in embarking upon potentially harmful activity.
Judge:	Well, where does that leave us – apart from the appeal of doing 'practical justice'?
2nd judge's clerk:	Judge, I would plump for the *Caparo* approach.

---

[1] See Stephen Todd (gen. ed.), *The Law of Torts in New Zealand* (3rd edn, Brookers, Wellington, 2001), at 222.
[2] [1995] 2 AC 207.
[3] *Hedley Byrne and Co. Ltd* v *Heller & Partners* [1964] AC 465.
[4] *Caparo Industries plc* v *Dickman* [1990] 2 AC 605.

1st judge's clerk:	Not me. I would go back to *Hedley Byrne*.
Judge:	It looks as though we could get a different answer depending on which approach you persuade me to adopt. Let's take *Caparo* first.
2nd judge's clerk:	Proximity becomes the main issue. In *Caparo*, the Law Lords held that proximity will only exist where the defendant knew that his statement would be communicated to the plaintiff, or someone in the plaintiff's class, specifically in connection with a particular transaction. The plaintiff also had to rely on that statement.
1st judge's clerk:	More than that; a statement cannot be used for a purpose other than the purpose for which it was given. There was no match in *Caparo*. There is a decision of the High Court of Australia, the name of which I can't remember at the moment, to much the same effect.[5]
Judge:	(*Somewhat smugly*) It was the *Esanda* case. Anyway, counsel claim that the two appeals heard at the same time by the House of Lords in the *Smith* v *Bush* case[6] categorically establish that an assumption of responsibility is not a prerequisite.
2nd judge's clerk:	Its not that easy. In *Henderson* v *Merrett*[7] the House of Lords stressed that an assumption of responsibility is central to liability under the *Hedley Byrne* principle.
1st judge's clerk:	Although Lord Goff did seem to suggest that concept might be inadequate as a test for proximity in some kinds of *Hedley Byrne* cases. And Lords Oliver and Roskill in *Caparo* and the Australian High Court in your *Esanda* case said the phrase means no more than the existence of circumstances in which liability will be imposed, or words to that effect.[8]

---

[5] *Esanda Finance Corporation Ltd* v *Peat Marwick Hungerfords* (1996–1997) 188 CLR 241.
[6] *Smith* v *Eric S Bush*; *Harris* v *Wyre Forest District Council* [1990] 1 AC 831.
[7] *Henderson* v *Merrett Syndicates Ltd* [1995] 2 AC 145.
[8] Above n. 4, per Lord Roskill at 628–629 and per Lord Oliver at 638–642; and above n. 5, at 263–264.

Judge:	So, we do not have to look at the defendant's intention to see whether he or she has assumed responsibility?
2nd judge's clerk:	That's not entirely clear. In *Hedley Byrne*, four of their Lordships opted for an objective approach in that it can be said the defendant's obligation is imposed by the courts. But Lord Devlin adhered to the subjective approach. Subsequent cases appear to favour the objective approach, but there are still a significant number of cases and any amount of dicta which do not – if Your Honour wants to go that way. And Lord Steyn in the *Williams Natural Foods* case,[9] while emphasising that the test should be objective, also said that the inquiry was whether the defendant conveyed to the plaintiff, directly or indirectly, that he or she was assuming personal responsibility.
Judge:	I see what you mean. That inquiry would seem to be directed at the defendant's subjective intention – or possibly the plaintiff's belief! No, that cannot be.
1st judge's clerk:	The position is further complicated, Judge, by the fact that the courts are not at one on whether the assumption of responsibility must be *voluntarily* undertaken by the defendant.
Judge:	Voluntariness surely suggests a subjective approach? How can the courts impose a *voluntary* assumption?
2nd judge's clerk:	You asked for the law, Judge, and the phrase, voluntary assumption of responsibility, is commonly used. Anyway, some sort of 'special relationship' has to be shown.
1st judge's clerk:	In *Hedley Byrne* Lord Devlin emphasised the need for the relationship between the parties to be 'equivalent to contract'.[10]

---

[9] *Williams v Natural Life Foods* [1998] 2 All ER 577, at 582–583.
[10] Above n. 3, at 528–529.

Judge:	I find that difficult. There must be many cases where the defendant doesn't communicate with the plaintiff and nothing in the circumstances would suggest anything equivalent to contract. And, in any event, surely the law of negligence should be concerned with the relationship or proximity that comes about, not some antecedent relationship? That is, focus on the actions of the maker of the statement rather than his or her relationship with the plaintiff?
2nd judge's clerk:	That may be so, but the cases don't spell that out. Some sort of mutuality would seem to be required. The House of Lords expressly said so in the *Williams Natural Food* case.
Judge:	But why should there be a requirement of mutuality simply because the damage is economic?
2nd judge's clerk:	Don't ask me, Judge. The judges are scared of opening liability for economic loss up so that it is altogether too indeterminate.
Judge:	The law couldn't be much more indeterminate than it is.
1st judge's clerk:	Excuse me, Judge, but you just confused indeterminate liability with indeterminacy in the law.
Judge:	*(Gives his clerk a hard look, but knows better than to try and defend his slip).*
2nd judge's clerk:	In any event, I don't agree that it has yet been established that mutuality is a necessary element of liability. Where, for example, was mutuality in *White* v *Jones*?
Judge:	Where indeed? I see that the appellant's counsel cites a number of cases to the effect that it is sufficient to establish reliance for the cause of action to be made out. Are the cases at one in making reliance a decisive element in *Hedley Byrne*-type liability?
1st judge's clerk:	Nope. *Henderson* v *Merritt* and *White* v *Jones* utterly undermine that concept.
Judge:	Suits me. I have difficulty seeing why the actions of a third-party plaintiff should determine the liability of the defendant. Liability in negligence must surely be directed at the actions of the defendant and reliance relevant only

	to the causal link between the statement and the economic loss.
2nd judge's clerk:	Lord Goff may have beaten you to that one Judge.[11] But I don't quite agree with my colleague. Lord Bridge in *Caparo*[12] regarded reliance as an essential ingredient in establishing proximity. The defendant must know, among other things, that the plaintiff would be very likely to rely on his statement.
Judge:	Why, then, don't we simply apply *Donoghue* v *Stevenson*?[13] Yes, yes, I know, because we are frightened of indeterminate liability. Well, assuming that the *Hedley Byrne* principles are made out, we do not have to go further and determine whether a duty of care arose and liability would be 'fair, just and reasonable', do we? I think that there is a judgment of this Court to that effect.
2nd judge's clerk:	Not quite, Judge. Your judgment was to that effect, but it was a dissenting judgment. The majority held that it was necessary to determine that question.[14]
Judge:	I am bound by that decision, then.
2nd judge's clerk:	Not if you don't want to be Judge. You could prefer the reasoning in *Henderson* v *Merritt*. The House of Lords held that once a case is identified as falling within the *Hedley Byrne* principles there should be no need to embark upon an inquiry whether it is 'fair, just and reasonable' to impose liability.[15] Although toying with the wording a little, Lord

---

[11] Above n. 7, at 180.
[12] Above n. 4, at 621. See also Lord Steyn in the *Williams Natural Life Food* case (above n. 9), at 583–584.
[13] [1932] AC 56.
[14] *R M Turton & Co Ltd (In Liquidation)* v *Kerslake & Partners* [2000] 3 NZLR 406, Henry and Keith JJ; Thomas J dissenting. For a trenchant criticism of the majority's judgment, see Todd, above n. 1, at 233–234.
[15] Above n. 7, at 181.

	Steyn said the same in the *Williams Natural Life Foods* case.[16]
Judge:	Well, how did the majority in our Court justify departing from the principle so clearly laid down in those cases?
2nd judge's clerk:	They seem to have simply ignored them.
Judge:	Really! Okay, then, but lets assume the 'fair, just and reasonable' requirement is out, when do we get the opportunity to go into policy considerations?
1st judge's clerk:	Only covertly – or if you branch out on your own. Notions of assumption of liability, reliance, proximity, mutuality, acceptance of a relationship, voluntarily undertaking a service, undertaking a duty, and so on and so on contain policy concerns but they have tended to be perceived but dimly through a heavy curtain of dicta.
Judge:	Yet, I do not doubt that it is nevertheless those policy concerns that have directed the imposition of liability. Dear me, is there no certainty in the law? You have certainly enlarged the adage that the only things that are certain in life are death and taxes. It should be that the only things that are certain in life are death, taxes and uncertainty itself.
1st judge's clerk:	Don't go overboard, Judge. One thing is absolutely certain; it is exactly eleven working days since you took us out to coffee.
Judge:	(*Pausing resignedly before standing*) C'mon then.[17]

---

[16] Above n. 9, at 581, denying the need for a further inquiry in respect of the 'extended' *Hedley Byrne* principle.

[17] The above conversation is apocryphal in unlimited respects. For some serious discussions searching for coherence in this area of the law, see Christian Witting, 'Justifying Liability to Third Parties for Negligent Misstatements' (2000) OJLS 20; Kit Barker, 'Unreliable Assumptions in the Modern Law of Negligence' (1993) 109 LQR 461; J. Stapleton, 'Duty of Care and Economic Loss: A Wider Agenda' (1991) 107 LQR 249; and Bob Hepple, 'The Search for Coherence' (1997) 50 Current Legal Problems, 67.

An uncertain world

Philosophers, humanists and sociologists all agree that the daily world in which we live is incorrigibly uncertain.[18] Yet, we crave certainty. We think of certainty as our protection against superstition, prejudice and ignorance. To be certain is to be free of these deficiencies. But our desire for certainty blinds us to the reality that, all about us, our social life is uncertain. With human failings we respond by preferring the illusion of certainty. We do not want to hear, as Rohinton Mistry puts it, that we 'cannot draw lines and compartments and refuse to budge beyond them'.[19]

Small wonder that the law, as a social institution, reflects this craving for certainty. In an uncertain world it provides the hope that certainty, and with it truth and stability, will exist, if not as the cornerstone of society, as something other than an illusion. The reality is that the law is as uncertain as the socio-economic aspects of the society from which it emanated and to which it continues to owe its allegiance.

The law is inherently uncertain

The fact the law is inherently uncertain is a reflection of our uncertain world. The law has always been uncertain and it always will be uncertain. This uncertainty is the reality. Cardozo recognised this truth eight decades ago. Pause to share that great jurist's eloquent description of his disillusionment and subsequent enlightenment:

> I was much troubled in spirit, in my first years upon the bench, to find how trackless was the ocean on which I had embarked. I sought for certainty. I was oppressed and disheartened when I found that the quest for it was futile. I was trying to reach land, the solid land of fixed and settled rules, the paradise of a justice that would declare itself by tokens plainer and more commanding than its pale and glimmering refractions in my own vacillating found 'with the voyagers in Browning's "Paracelsus" that the real heaven was always beyond'. As the years have gone by, and as I have reflected more and more upon the nature of the judicial process, I have become reconciled to the uncertainty, because I have grown to see it as inevitable. I have grown to see that the process in its highest reaches is not discovery, but creation: that the doubts and

---

[18] E.g., John Ralston Saul, *On Equilibrium* (Penguin Books, Toronto, 2001), at 7–16.
[19] Quoted in Saul, Ibid, at 15.

misgivings, the hope and fears, are part of the travail of the mind, the pangs of death and the pangs of birth, in which principles that have served their day expire, and new principles are born.[20]

Yet, Cardozo's perceived truth continues to elude so many in the legal community. Why? One of the greatest mysteries of legal practice is why and how so many intelligent men and women can continue to delude themselves into believing that the law is certain or can be made certain. After over two centuries of striving, during which the law has become more and not less indeterminate, too many continue to proclaim this delusion as an article of faith. In the result, certainty is treated as the paramount goal of adjudication. It is the Pole Star of much appellate decision-making. Far too many judges, lawyers and academics still worship it with an almost blind and superstitious veneration.

Consequently, there is, in the practice of the law, a perpetual drive for absolute rules and precise commands and an almost compulsive search for finite formulas and doctrines that will eliminate judicial discretion and reduce to a minimum the need for judicial creativity. What is the source of this drive? Clearly it is potent. How else could intelligent men and women be persuaded that simply because a rule is embodied in one decision, the application of the rule to future cases is justified by that very act of embodiment, and that no further appeal to the social reasons or ethical precepts which inspired the rule in the first place is necessary? A distinctly legal reason then exists for the perpetuation of the rule independently of the social and moral relevance to the community it purports to serve.[21] Notwithstanding that the most conservative of jurists have felt constrained to question the application of the strict doctrine of precedent,[22] it continues to command profound fidelity on the basis that it provides greater certainty in the law.

An inquiry into the source of this drive for certainty will or should put it into better perspective. As a goal it is legitimate only to the extent that it can be perceived in rational terms. Further, if the certainty that is found to be legitimate is not served by the doctrine of precedent, close adherence to that doctrine cannot be justified. In the course of the inquiry it will also be helpful to evaluate the extent to which a more

---

[20] Cardozo, *The Judicial Process*, at 166–167.
[21] K. A. Warner, 'Judicial Reasoning and Precedent: Negligently Inflicted Psychological Injuries' (1990) 10 Legal Studies 63.
[22] Lord Devlin, *The Judge* (Oxford University Press, Oxford, 1979), at 13; 90; 95; 179; 184–185; 194–195; and 201.

principle-oriented approach would promote the attainment of certainty.

Of course, people want to know where they stand so they can order their affairs in advance. Commercial men and women, in particular, crave to sit across the desk from their lawyer and be told what the law is, not what it may be or what it probably is or is not. Positive advice, perhaps it is thought, will more acceptably justify the fee. Predictability is seen as the hallmark of a successful legal system, and this expectation is cemented in place by any number of lawyers and commentators who adhere to a simplistic view of the law and legal process.

The public's expectation that there is, in advance, a general law which can be predictably applied to particular circumstances is understandable as it derives from the factors that I have already alluded to; centuries of legal scholarship from the natural law theorists to the positivists, and the diehard attitude of many modern day practitioners of the law, whether lawyers, judges or academics, who decline to forego the remnants of the discredited declaratory theory of law and opt for a crude version of positivism. In the result, the community continues to be beguiled into believing that certainty and predictability is achievable to an extent that is clearly impossible. I am not saying that predictability is unimportant, but rather that it is not achieved by pretending that the law is or can be certain, or more certain than is actually possible. Because the law is not a science, certainty will never be achieved with scientific precision, but it can be furthered by having regard to the range of factors traversed in this book, only one of which is the extent to which the law may be regarded as settled.

It is indisputable that uncertainty is inherent in the process of reducing the general to the particular. Reducing the general to the particular is a process that unavoidably involves an act of discretion on the part of the judge. Moreover, the historical perception that the process is one of applying the general to the particular has become an oversimplification. The general principle has tended to vanish in a mass of particulars,[23] many of which conflict or compete one with the other for application in any given case.

The notion of providing certainty in the law is at times overtly professed in the reasoning advanced by a judge in the course of a

---

[23] Notable examples of cases in which a general rule has been effectively overwhelmed by exceptions are *Foss* v *Harbottle* (1843) 2 Hare 261; 67 ER 189, and *Addis* v *Gramophone Co Limited* [1909] AC 488.

judgment. More often than not in practice, however, the consideration is an unspoken postulate. A judge will reject an otherwise tenable proposition because it is thought that its acceptance might foment uncertainty in the law. He or she possesses a deeply felt foreboding that it is safer to adhere as closely as possible to more or less applicable rules and precedents than directly confront the question of the law's fairness and relevance to contemporary conditions. In the result, an unarticulated presumption is raised against the application of a more general rule or principle to the case irrespective of, or despite, the merits or justice of that case.

Apart from the possibilities of injustice in the instant case, what is the outcome of this judicial reticence? A particular decision simply serves to modify or qualify the general rule. It becomes less general and more particular, and each particular, whether appearing to add to or subtract from the general rule, gives rise to scope for argument as to whether the rule applies. Certainty becomes even more elusive and predictability fares no better. For the purposes of argument it can be accepted that predictability follows from a decision to treat all instances falling within some accessible category in the same way.[24] But when that accessible category is so heavily particularised as to generate argument whether any particular case falls within its increasingly ragged bounds, the application of the rule to the next and inevitably different factual situation that arises for adjudication will be uncertain.

Many eminent jurists and commentators have gone so far as to represent certainty as an illusion or myth. Jeremy Bentham even compared the law to astrology. If one wanted to know the content of law, he advised, too often 'as well grounded a guess might be had of an astrologer for five shillings as of counsel for twice or thrice as many guineas.'[25] Rampant inflation and ever larger legal fees since that eminent jurist's day may give this advice added force. One of the leading scholars in the Critical Legal Studies Movement, Professor Unger, has referred to the 'incorrigible indeterminacy' of the law.[26] More and more modern scholars have accepted and emphasised that the law is commonly vague so that the requirements of the law are frequently indeterminate.

---

[24] Frederick Schauer, 'Formalism' (1988) 97 Yale LJ, No. 4, 509, at 539.
[25] See J. Bowring (ed.), *The Works of Jeremy Bentham* (Tait, Edinburgh, 1843), Vol. 2, at 306.
[26] R. M. Unger, 'The Critical Legal Studies Movement' (1983) 96 Harv. LR 561, at 578–579.

Vagueness, and the resultant indeterminacies, are seen to be essential features of the law.[27] I confess to feeling that some of these descriptions suggest an element of hyperbole in that they approach the question in absolute terms. I acknowledge later in Chapter 9 that there is a considerable body of law that may be said to be relatively well established and that is more than likely to be re-endorsed if put in issue in the courts. As Professor Cross has observed, a very great deal of judge-made law is settled beyond the possibility of serious controversy.[28] But I do not disavow the claim that the law is inherently uncertain.

If Judge Learned Hand's description of the common law as a monument slowly raised like a coral reef from the minute accretions of past individuals is correct,[29] the reef should get larger and larger. On this view, each case that clarifies or extends a precedent would leave behind it a greater area of law that is certain. But that does not follow. The fact the coral reef of the law gets larger does not automatically mean that the law gets more certain. I have in the past myself adopted what I thought was a better metaphor to describe certainty – or uncertainty – in the law. Imagine a circle. Within the circle is the settled law. Around its circumference, not unlike the profile of the sun when its bulk is shut out, is a seething perimeter of uncertainty as the general is reduced to the particular, or is extracted from a multiplicity of particulars, or one particular conflicts with another particular, or the like. As more and more cases are decided, the circle expands. The size of the circle of settled law increases. But, necessarily, so too does the perimeter of uncertain law.

Tempting though such metaphors are, we know instinctively, if not from hard experience, that they are not accurate. Neither the so-called settled law within the reef nor that within the circle is beyond challenge. Perhaps in some fields of law the residual body of ostensibly settled rules may expand, but in others the most fundamental of concepts seem susceptible to continuing doubt. Contract is one example. Who, today, can assert with confidence that consideration is a prerequisite to the enforcement of a promise? Or who can claim, without fear of challenge, that the principle of privity of contract precludes a third party from suing on the contract? Can anyone assert with certitude that the

---

[27] Timothy A. O. Endicott, *Vagueness in Law* (Oxford University Press, Oxford, 2000), at 1.
[28] R. Cross, *Precedent in English Law* (2nd edn, Clarendon Press, Oxford, 1968), at 29.
[29] Learned Hand reviewing Cardozo's 'The Nature of the Judicial Process' (1932) 35 Harv. LR 479.

law in England, Australia and New Zealand is not on the verge of admitting the concept of good faith that is common to all or most other jurisdictions? Who can say with any degree of assuredness that the whole of the conventional law of contract and tort is not yielding to a wider concept of liability based on a general concept of obligations? Who can preclude the possibility that developing areas of the law such as fiduciary obligations, constructive trusts, or other equitable principles may not unhinge these long-established branches of the law? Who can foretell, with the intermingling of law and equity, that the 'basket of remedies' approach will not gather force, thus dislocating any number of established legal premises? When so many traditional legal concepts are at large, the comfortable notion that there is an expanding body of certain law beyond serious challenge is, at least, questionable.

It is in this sense that I speak of the law as inherently uncertain or vague. No law, it seems, is so definitive as to be beyond challenge. Rules, or few rules, can be stated with total finality as they depend for their endorsement on their 'interpretation' or 'reinterpretation' in the next case. Life has the habit of throwing up circumstances that call for a reappraisal of the law if it is to be just and relevant to the needs of the times. It is this infinite capacity to be challenged, and every so often to be challenged successfully, that makes the law inherently uncertain. Of course, at any given time there may be particular rules that are relatively settled, but that fact does not impair the validity of the general observation that, because it is open to challenge on all fronts, the law is inherently uncertain.

An assumption is evident in the thinking of some to the effect that the law would be more certain if judges would only apply rules and precedents with greater rigidity. Legal fundamentalists brand this alleged failure a lack of 'intellectual rigour'. The assumption is false. Experience suggests that it is much easier to discern the merits and justice of the particular case and predict the outcome based on that discernment than it is to predict the law. As Professor Atiyah has said; 'it is sometimes suggested that it is actually easier to predict discretionary decisions than rule-bound decisions, which is only to say that it is often simpler and clearer to identify (and agree upon) the justice of a case than the law.'[30] In other words, untrammelled by an overly strict rule-bound approach or adherence to precedent, judges are free to revert to fundamental

---

[30] P. S. Atiyah, *Law and Modern Society* (Oxford University Press, Oxford and New York, 1983), at 95.

principles and, still within the discipline of the law, arrive at a conclusion that is consonant with their sense of justice and perception of the needs and expectations of the community. In practice, that sense and perception are easier to predict.

Nevertheless, many argue that, notwithstanding the inherent uncertainty of the law, the present system provides a greater measure of predictability than would a system in which a rule-bound approach and the doctrine of precedent are relaxed. I believe that the judicial approach advanced in this book could be achieved without any significant loss of predictability in the law, and there may even be a gain in certainty in comparison with the present rule-bound and precedent-directed regime. The main reasons may be conveniently recapitulated here. First, dissension and doubt arising from the question of which of two competing particulars would be favoured must recede if it is known that the court will most certainly resort to the general principle underlying the particular rules. Secondly, the disputation that is quite common as to whether or not a precedent precludes a claim or a defence would be overtaken by the fact that precedents do not automatically command coercive force. Thirdly, there is the point made by Professor Atiyah and referred to in the preceding paragraph, that it is often easier to predict the exercise of a discretion than the outcome of a disputed question of law. The merits and justice of the case will obtain greater prominence. Fourthly, while not eliminating the inevitable differences between judges, the emphasis on the constraints, and the introduction of the structured constraints discussed in Chapter 10, would be likely to provide a greater measure of common ground within narrower and more closely defined boundaries. In short, the tensions in the formalistic approach that give rise to uncertainty, such as the continuing tension between form and substance, between precedent and principle, between certainty and justice, and the like, will largely disappear. The uncertainty that presently arises, which can fairly be described as unproductive, would be significantly diminished.

Ultimately, however, much more is at stake than just achieving a balance between certainty and fairness. It is important that the judicial system should be realistic and authentic. It is equally essential that the law should be coherent and capable of developing to meet the ever-changing needs of the community. The conclusion reached in this book is that these aims can best be achieved by adopting an approach in which practical reasoning, including a principle-oriented approach, and not precedent, is dominant.

Acknowledged causes of uncertainty

Many elements have been identified that contribute to uncertainty even though the courts may be pursuing a relatively strict doctrine of precedent. Those elements that might be said to be recognised causes of uncertainty may be referred to first.

The uncertainty of the facts

The initial factor relates to the facts of the case. The finding of facts is a formidably problematic exercise. Uncertainty is rife within the judicial exercise of finding the facts. It will be convenient to deal with this subject in more detail in Chapter 13. In short, it is rare for the facts of one case to be exactly the same as those in another case. Judges then have a multiplicity of choices open to them. They may conclude that the facts are sufficiently similar to come within the broad rule embodied in a precedent; they may decide that notwithstanding a difference in the facts the rule should nevertheless be applied; they may decide that, as the facts are different, the case should be distinguished; they may decide to simply ignore the difference and treat the facts as being the same; they may decide to restate the relevant facts for the purpose of the rule or precedent and thereby reduce or increase the generality of the rule; they may decide that it is not possible to extract the relevant facts which support the rule from the reasoning in the prior case; or they may decide that even though the facts cannot be distinguished, the precedent should not be followed for any number of other reasons.[31]

The marked extent to which differences between the parties as to the facts creates uncertainty in adjudication is not always appreciated. Until the facts are determined, for example, it cannot be known which of the competing versions of the law will be applicable. Even on appeal, the expression of a different view of the law by the appellate court may simply obscure what is in fact a different perception of the facts or a covert shift in the findings of fact. Consequently, in the adjudication of a dispute, the facts are frequently all-important and the court's finding of fact often decisive. But the facts do not often leap up to greet the judge. They must be probed, discerned, extracted and weighed from a mass of evidence, at times poorly organised. This inquiry is also part of a

---

[31] See R. W. M. Dias, *Jurisprudence* (5th edn, Butterworths, London, 1985), at 157; and C. G. Weeramantry, *The Law in Crisis* (Capemoss, London, 1975), at 85.

discretionary process in that the judge exercises a choice of facts to accept or reject. Notwithstanding the objective of seeking to find the facts so that they accord as closely as possible with the true facts, whatever they might be, the exercise of choice is inevitable.[32]

The uncertainty in defining the legal dispute

It is only if the dispute is not resolved as a result of the judge's findings of fact that a legal dispute is likely to arise.[33] One or other of the parties, or both, will claim the advantage of proximity to an established rule or precedent and produce an authority or, more likely, volumes of authorities, to support their claims. It is here that uncertainty becomes certain. The judge must make a choice between the conflicting legal contentions. That choice will at once depend on the judge's personal perception of the judicial role in adjudication and, in particular, the extent to which he or she inclines to a formalistic or anti-formalistic exemplar.

Once the issue has been framed, the element of uncertainty in relation to the question in issue does not miraculously disappear. The fact that the issue has been formulated in certain terms in one case does not mean that it will be formulated in the same terms by another court. The other court may be either a higher court on appeal in the same case or another court in another case that examines the issue afresh.

The uncertainty of the ratio

With the facts settled, and the legal dispute defined, and presumably, authorities cited in support, the judge must determine the true *ratio decidendi* of any authority, for it is that *ratio* that he or she may feel bound to follow pursuant to the doctrines of precedent and *stare decisis*. The exercise is again fraught with difficulty and doubt.[34] The *ratio* may be genuinely difficult to discern. It may be that the earlier case never really had a *ratio* at all. There may be a number of *ratios*, even as many as

---

[32] Jerome Frank, *Courts on Trial* (New Jersey Princeton University Press, Princeton, 1973), at 15, 23, 55, 70 and 318. See below, Chapter 13, at 321–327.
[33] See above, Chapter 13, at 327–329.
[34] See below, at 131–132. Julius Stone has described the notion of '*ratio*' as one of his 'categories of illusory reference' and as 'a category of indeterminate reference'. See Stone, *Legal Systems and Lawyers' Reasonings* (Stanford University Press, Stanford, 1964), at 263–270. See also Stone, *Precedent and Law* (Butterworths, Sydney, 1985), at 123–128.

the number of judges giving separate judgments. Nor, if the *ratio* is clearly stated, can it be known for sure whether the later judge will accept that rationale. He or she may decide to reconstruct the *ratio decidendi* in the earlier case in somewhat different terms. The problem of ascertaining the correct rule to apply is exacerbated when not one, but a multiplicity of rules, compete for the allegiance of the adjudicating court. Finally, a splendid rule pressed upon the court may be debased by being branded an *obiter dictum*. In all, it must be accepted, the concept of *ratio decidendi* is elementally controversial.

The uncertainty of exceptions

Another cause of uncertainty follows from the law's tendency to make rules absolute. What is wanted, Lord Devlin said, are general rules for standard cases, which can be readily departed from in exceptional circumstances.[35] 'Exceptional circumstances' are said to arise when there is a need to do justice in the individual case or to adapt the rule to meet changing circumstances. An exception is then made to the rule. Of course, Lord Devlin was wrong to perceive the point in terms of 'exceptional circumstances'. More often than not it is simply the next set of circumstances. Be that as it may, some rules have been bedevilled by exceptions, some are eventually undermined by exceptions, and some ultimately prevail so that the exception becomes the rule.[36] No-one can ever know for certain whether the judge will apply the rule or an exception to it, make an exception to the rule or to an exception to it, or declare that the exception constitutes the rule. What is certain is that any worthy claimant faced with an inflexible rule will at once contend that his or her claim is an exception to that rule.

The uncertainty as to what other jurisdictions are up to

A host of other reasons may be added that make predictability in the law at best an adventurous art. For example, with so many sturdy and diverse common law jurisdictions, it is inevitable that different trends in the law will develop. The pendulum in judicial thinking and attitudes will not swing in different countries in perfect harmony. While reference to the authoritative decisions of other countries is desirable, a further element of uncertainty is at once introduced. For example, although in

---

[35] Devlin, *The Judge*, at 184–185, but see 195–196.   [36] See above n. 23.

the past the deference which judges in post-colonial countries, such as New Zealand, paid to decisions in the United Kingdom was frequently excessive,[37] it cannot now be known for certain whether the decisions in that jurisdiction will be preferred ahead of the decisions in more recently established common law jurisdictions. The latter may often manifest a different approach.

The uncertainty arising from an abundance of riches

A final practical point has been acknowledged as a further cause of uncertainty in the law. With the advent of the computer age the capacity for lawyers to search for and find all relevant – and many irrelevant – authorities has been enlarged exponentially. With the modern appreciation that no one country has a monopoly of judicial wisdom, the search is extended to most developed jurisdictions. Further, the boundaries between the common law and civil law are increasingly rejected. In the result, the number of reported and unreported decisions available to counsel imposes a formidable burden on the doctrines of precedent and *stare decisis*. The doctrines may yet become logistically unworkable.

The immediate point, however, is that, as the number of cases escalates, uncertainty must increase rather than decrease for no-one can ever be certain that every relevant case has been found until the search has worked its way to its exhausting end. Moreover, there is always the possibility that an apparently authoritative decision may be weakened by assiduous counsel discovering another decision, or other decisions, which were not cited to the deciding court. Authoritative cases will, of course, fall by the wayside as they are distinguished or replaced, but the overall increase in case law is incontestable. The risk with this exponential explosion of easily ascertainable case law is that principles will be obscured and lost and the general will be submerged in a mass of particulars.

Some underlying causes of uncertainty

The imprecision of language

There are other more underlying causes of uncertainty in the law. The first is the imprecision of language and our deficiencies in

---

[37] *McPhee v Wright, Stephenson & Co* (1900) 19 NZLR 321, at 331, cited in *White v The New Zealand Stock Exchange & Ors* 162/00, 16 October 2000 (CA), and referred to in *Nimmo v Westpac Banking Corporation* [1994] 1 NZLR 472, at 475.

understanding language. Our whole experience is bound by words, and they have proven an inexact tool to convey a certain meaning.[38] Linguistic indeterminacy, says Professor Endicott, seems pervasive and obdurate.[39]

Having said that, however, I would sound a caution against the trend to press the indeterminacy of language too far. We are far removed from a state of linguistic anarchy. While examples of the confusion that the use of language causes abound, the occasions when meaning is accurately conveyed are probably the norm. It is enough to accept that the indeterminacy of language is a recurring and unavoidable cause of uncertainty or vagueness in the law without purporting to portray chaos.

The need for finality in judicial adjudication

The second underlying cause of uncertainty in the law that I would identify is the irredeemable compulsion on the courts to reach a decision. For the good of the community as well as the immediate parties there must be an end to disputes. Finality in adjudication is a functional imperative of the legal process, and seemingly unique to that process. The legislature may shelve or obfuscate a difficult issue. Administrators may consign a problem to the 'too hard' basket. Both may equivocate and temporise. Those indulgent options are not open to judges. Like it or not, they must reach a decision in the instant case.[40]

Dworkin has argued that the requirement that a court provide a determinate outcome supports his claim that the law is itself

---

[38] Andrew Halpin, *Reasoning with Law* (Hart Publishing, Oxford and Portland, Oregon, 2001), esp. Chapter 6 at 103 *et seq.*
[39] Endicott, *Vagueness in Law*, at 7, and see esp. Chapters 2 and 3.
[40] Courts may, of course, decline to resolve a particular issue definitively by relying on or resorting to a more amenable test or principle. Thus, the Court of Appeal of New Zealand has successively declined to be drawn on the question of what constitutes an invalid search under s. 21 of the New Zealand Bill of Rights Act 1990, and resolved the cases coming before it on the basis whether the search was 'reasonable' or not for the purposes of that section. Although the issue may remain unresolved and uncertain, the individual cases are nevertheless decided. Appellate courts may also effectively defer and leave undecided an issue where appellants must obtain leave to appeal. It has been the practice of the Supeme Court of the United States, for example, to defer leave in cases raising certain issues and allow divergent approaches to be taken in lower courts until the 'right' case arises for that issue to be reviewed. This practice may be justified, and I think it is, but it must also necessarily detract from the formalist's emphasis on the objective of certainty in the administration of the law.

determinate. It provides a reason to reject indeterminacy. Any argument that the law is indeterminate about some issue, he says, must recognise the consequences of that being true, and take those consequences into account.[41] But as Endicott has pointed out,[42] the need for a decision cannot support an argument that the requirements of the law are determinate. A duty to decide is a reason to give a decision, but it is not a reason to conclude that there is only one right decision. Neither the plaintiff, the defendant, the appellant, nor the respondent obtains an advantage simply because the court must arrive at a decision.

Again, I favour a more realistic appraisal. Contrary to Dworkin's perception, the tendency arising out of the need for finality in adjudication is to foster uncertainty. Finality is thought to require a definiteness which the judge may not necessarily feel but feels obliged to express. Comments in the course of a judicial conference following a hearing to the effect that the decision could go either way are not generally repeated in the judgments in that case. I am not, of course, suggesting for one moment that the requirement that there be finality in adjudication should be abandoned. Rather, I am suggesting that this requirement tends to create a judicial environment and attitude in which there is no room for the appearance of indecisiveness. Not having the luxury of saying that the point in issue is open to doubt and leaving it at that, the judge must make up his or her mind one way or the other. Having made up his or her mind, the judge must then justify the decision so that it will be accepted as an authoritative solution to the dispute in issue.

This approach can be observed in two respects each, ironically, leading to greater uncertainty. In the first place, the judge, in seeking to justify his or her decision as an authoritative finding of the law, is likely to think deductive reasoning more condign. He or she will seek to show that the particular decision they reach is deduced from a rule. But, as already pointed out, the decision will necessarily modify or qualify that rule. In the second place, concerned to reach a final decision that will be accepted by the parties and the legal community as authoritative, the judge will seek to bolster his or her decision by reference to precedent. As stated earlier,[43] this practice itself generates uncertainty. Adherence to the doctrine, in short, results in every step in the evolution of a principle being open to challenge, irrespective of the merits or justice of the individual case. In

---

[41] Dworkin 'Objectivity and Truth: You'd Better Believe it' (1996) 25 Collosvian Philosophy and Public Affairs 87, at 137.
[42] Endicott, *Vagueness in Law*, at 167.   [43] See above at 126.

striving to produce a decision to justify the finality with which it will be vested the judge launches upon an exercise which leads to ongoing uncertainty as more and more cases have to be distinguished or reinterpreted.

The 'status' of justice

The third underlying cause of uncertainty that I would proffer is the uncertain status of justice in legal reasoning. This topic will also be pursued in Chapter 11. No maxim seems to beat more strongly in the hearts of lawyers than the principle that like cases should be treated alike. Justice is done, it is thought, when that axiom is implemented from case to case. A judge will reject an otherwise tenable proposition because it is thought its acceptance would or might represent a departure from this basic principle. Judges possess a deeply felt foreboding that it is safer to adhere as closely as possible to more or less applicable rules or precedents than directly confront the question of the law's fairness or relevance to current conditions. In the result, an unarticulated presumption is raised against the application of a rule or principle to a particular case if its application would appear to depart from the recognised body of rules or precedents irrespective of, or despite, the merits or justice of that case.

Justice, if justice is to be served at all, it is claimed, is to be served in a broader systemic sense, that is, the so-called justice to be found in adherence to a system. In short, it is assumed at some point that justice in the individual case can yield to justice in the abstract and, then, that the application of the abstract can yield justice in the individual case. The concept of treating like alike is fundamental to this perception. Justice lies in the implementation of that concept and not in the particular circumstances of the individual case. Also basic to this perception is an optimistic view of the possibility of achieving certainty in the law. Like cannot be readily treated alike if the existing law cannot be ascertained with sufficient certainty to enable that comparison to be made.

There is no more barren and sterile concept of justice than this stilted perception. It is, in fact, a recipe for injustice. In the first place, it is essentially unrealistic. Of course, a person in an identical or substantially similar position to another person will feel aggrieved if he or she is denied the same advantageous outcome. Treating like alike is then a valid consideration. But as I have already pointed out,[44] the reality is

---

[44] See above at 122–123.

that the circumstances of different cases are seldom alike. Life, and commercial activity, is much more complex and cases can be, and are, frequently distinguished simply because they are in fact distinguishable. The legal process copes with facts and circumstances that are infinite in their variety. Nor is it sound to accept that a comparison of cases to determine whether they are 'like' should be restricted to a comparison of the facts. Other factors, such as other developments in the law, may necessarily bear upon that comparison.[45] Further, of course, the high level of certainty required in the law to enable it to be said that a person has been treated like another person at an earlier time is simply not achievable.[46] There will almost invariably be argument as to how the first 'like' was in fact treated.

Most importantly, in the second place, the notion of systemic justice is basically flawed in that it assumes that justice is internal to the law rather than being imported from without the law. The justice of an earlier case is the justice that the judge at that time vested in his or her decision, and there can be no valid warranty for a system which proclaims that a decision which would be widely condemned as unjust today is in fact a just decision because it follows that earlier unjust decision. The notion only has to be spelt out to be self-evidently silly. A mature concept of justice must necessarily reflect values that are immanent in the community at any given time and not some artificial justice that is the creation of a formalistic and precedent-driven system.

Nevertheless, some judges will consistently favour the abstract or systemic perception of justice while others will prefer to do justice in the individual case. The latter will not be prepared to sacrifice justice in the interests of achieving some perceived consistency in the application of the law. They will regard the sacrifice as a bogus sacrifice sheltering, yet again, beneath the cloak of formalistic reasoning.

The pursuit of justice in this abstract sense is ineffective in ensuring certainty. No matter how many times the perception of justice in the individual case is made to yield to justice in the abstract, citizens will continue to approach the courts to redress a grievance felt to be unjust. A person with little or no knowledge of the law who suffers some loss or detriment and feels a sense of grievance believes that the law should provide them with a remedy. The belief, rightly or wrongly, is founded upon the same community values that eventually shape the law. That

---

[45] See below, Chapter 8, at 187.
[46] See below at 131–132; and Chapter 6, at 146.

person consults a lawyer who will be sympathetic to commencing a legal claim if it offends the same set of values. In such circumstances, the party's expectation that the law will provide a remedy is likely to reflect the community's expectation that this should be so. Because of the richness and diversity of the law and legal principles it is highly probable, if not inevitable, that a tenable argument to support the claim will be shortly developed. Equally assuredly, however, that tenable argument will be met with a tenable counter-argument. The parties are likely to differ, not only on the relevant facts, but also on the law applicable to the facts. At that point, and notwithstanding that the highest and most precise authority may proclaim that the law does not provide a cause of action or remedy, the law is uncertain.

There are, therefore, two particular deficiencies detectable in the approach of judges who adhere to the notion of systemic justice. The first is that they think that this search for justice to right particular grievances suffered by citizens can be suppressed by persisting with a regime of doing justice in the abstract. Centuries of direct experience reveals that this is a foolhardy thought incapable of realisation. Justice in the abstract service of some wider goal is likely to be seen as a rank injustice if it does not accord with a community's sense of justice in the circumstances of the particular case. The second deficiency, which assails judges inclined to do justice in the systemic sense, is that they forgo any notion of doing justice in the particular case, even where justice in the abstract sense would not be impaired. In their quest to serve the greater good they become indifferent to the injustice, or the prospect of injustice, and the suffering that injustice may wreak in the instant case. Justice in the sense of the Justinian precept of rendering to every person his or her due is inadvertently thrown out the courthouse window.

Two critical consequences

The inherent uncertainty in the law that results from the above factors has a number of unfortunate consequences, the two most important of which may be briefly touched upon. The first is that the community continues to be cozened into believing that certainty and predictability are achievable to an extent that is clearly impossible. This subterfuge is damaging to the operation and integrity of the law. It is by far preferable that the community be given a realistic understanding of the extent of indeterminacy in the law, and that citizens understand that uncertainty is inherent in the law. In this way their expectations of the law will be based on a realistic appreciation of the law and the legal process. The gap between the community's expectations of the law and the law that is delivered will be reduced.

The second concern is that the goal of certainty becomes an excuse in the hands of the formalist judge to avoid the hard exercise of an available judicial discretion. As already pointed out, the full reality of judicial choice is denied and judicial reasoning is diverted into a mechanical process that excludes the rich and diverse considerations that make up the law. Formalism thrives on such excuses.

Certainty and precedent

The doctrine of precedent is dealt with in the next chapter, and I do not wish to pre-empt its thrust. Those who proclaim certainty as a goal of judicial adjudication, however, look to the doctrines of precedent and *stare decisis* to achieve that certainty. It is therefore permissible in the present context to question whether the law will lose anything in certainty and predictability if precedent and *stare decisis* were to be harnessed to a more pragmatic approach. In other words, to what extent does precedent promote certainty and predictability in the law in actual practice? A number of factors already mentioned may be briefly reconsidered in this particular context.

The first element that calls for comment arises from the nature of precedent itself, and creates an inherent uncertainty in the application of the doctrine. What is binding in a precedent is the *ratio decidendi*; nothing more nor nothing less than the core holding in that case. As touched upon already, however, the *ratio* must be located and identified. It would do a mischief to experience to claim that the *ratio* of any case necessarily jumps out and hits its readers between the eyes with the speed and force of the proverbial upturned rake. With justification, Sir Anthony Mason declined to explore 'the arcane mysteries of divining the *ratio*',[47] and so will I. The immediate point to make is that in many cases the *ratio* or holding that constitutes the binding precedent must be discerned and declared by the later court considering the earlier case. Lawyers and commentators may proffer their opinion as to what the *ratio* of a case is, but until it has been defined by a later court, their

---

[47] Hon. Sir Anthony Mason, 'The Use and Abuse of Precedent' (1988) Aust. Bar Rev. 93, at 103.

opinion is necessarily provisional. The *ratio decidendi* is what the reviewing court holds the *ratio decidendi* to be.

In this process judicial choices cannot be avoided. Thus, the judge must choose which of the competing precedents, if more than one, to prefer. He or she must, from that case, choose the facts that they consider pertinent. They can call a fact irrelevant that the prior judge considered critical, or vice versa. They can 'make a legal molehill' out of what a prior judge called a 'mountain',[48] or vice versa. They must then choose the facts in the current case that they consider germane and compare them with the facts of the previous case – an exercise that again involves choice. They must then choose which of the contending *ratios* vying for acceptance is the true *ratio* in the prior decision and, in doing so, must analyse and define that holding. They must then decide to what extent, if any, and how, the *ratio* they have discerned and defined applies to the facts of the case under consideration. The meaning of precedents, then, will only emerge as judges analyse, compare and use them in subsequent cases – and the outcome can seldom be predicted with assured confidence.

Reference to the importance of the facts of the prior case brings out a second point bearing on the certainty arising from precedent. As already asserted, the facts of disputed cases are seldom similar, and never identical. It was the realist's school of thought that first emphasised that no two cases are ever exactly alike. There will always be some difference in the multitude of facts in the respective cases.[49] Yet, until the facts are determined, it cannot be known which competing precedents will be applicable. Even on appeal, as I have suggested, the expression of a different view of the law by the appellate court may simply obscure what is in fact a different perception of the facts, or a covert shift in the findings of fact.[50]

In practice, if judges want to find a difference in the facts of the instant case from the facts of the precedent, it is generally not difficult for them to do so. A close examination or analysis of the facts is not necessary to achieve that simple end. Indeed, the danger is that a judge who wishes to distinguish an awkward precedent will strain to find a difference in the facts of two cases and thereby distort the facts of one or the other of them

---

[48] Lief H. Carter, *Reason in Law* (Longman, New York, 1998), at 25–26.
[49] E. Mensch, 'The History of Mainstream Legal Thought', in David Kairys (ed.) *The Politics of Law* (Basic Boolis, New York, 1982), at 34.
[50] See above at 122–123.

in the process. The uncertainty in a process that begins with a comparison of the facts is readily apparent.

In the third place we must confront the uncertainty arising from the application of precedent as a conscious or unconscious response to its coercive or binding effect. One commentator has referred to this phenomenon as 'the inherent tendency of judges to manipulate the doctrine politically'.[51] But judges have been equally frank. Lord Reid, for one, in a statement quoted with approval by Sir Anthony Mason,[52] has pointed out that rigid adherence to precedent has promoted uncertainty in that it has forced courts to distinguish on inadequate grounds decisions of which they disapprove. Artificial distinctions of this kind have led to a general inability to predict in advance whether, in a particular case, a court would follow its previous decision.[53] As to be expected, Lord Denning has taken candour to an exceptional extreme. Binding it may be, he states, but there are always ways and means of getting around a previous decision that is wrong. It may be distinguished by finding some minor distinction on the facts or on the law, which, although minor, will 'serve its turn'. Another means is by 'pouring cold water' on the reasoning in the previous case; for example, by saying that it was unnecessary for the decision of the case, that it was too widely stated, or that the judges cannot have had such cases as this in mind. Or, Lord Denning concludes, one can depart from a previous decision by simply saying that things are different now that equity and law are fused![54]

To some extent, all judges indulge in these gambits, those of a formalist inclination more so than others. The indulgence may be unconscious, being absorbed in the judge's perception of legal method or consciously assumed in an effort to persuade others of the validity of the judge's reasoning. One galling technique is for a judge to 'explain' what another judge meant, especially as the judge doing the explaining may be motivated to reformulate what the earlier judge said so that he or she can purport to follow it.[55] Judicial reasoning in general, however, is

---

[51] C. P. Banks, 'Reversals of Precedent and Judicial Policy-Making: How Judicial Conceptions of *Stare Decisis* in the US Supreme Court Influence Social Change' (1999) 32 Akron LR 233, at 235.
[52] Mason, 'The Use and Abuse of Precedent', at 100.
[53] *Jones v Secretary of State for Social Services* [1972] AC 944, per Lord Reid at 966.
[54] Lord Denning, *The Discipline of Law* (Butterworths, London, 1979), at 297. And see above, Chapter 4, at 94–99.
[55] This was the fate of the minority in the Privy Council, Lord Reid and Lord Morris of Borth-y-Gest, in *Mutual Life & Citizens Assurance Co. Ltd v Evatt* [1971] AC 793 when

sufficiently elastic to introduce an element of intrinsic uncertainty into the doctrine of precedent – an element that becomes all the stronger the more coercive the doctrine. No precedent is necessarily immune from the artifice inherent in a system that purports to compel judges to accept decisions that they may not like and are asked not to question, or question too closely.

Fourthly, the doctrine also creates uncertainty in that every step in the evolution of a principle is open to challenge, irrespective of the justice or contemporary needs of the individual case. The plaintiff will claim a remedy, or the defendant will resist liability, on the basis of a decided case or cases when reference to principle, policy, reason or plain common sense would suggest they must fail. A defendant, for example, may resist the plaintiff's claim on the ground that it is outside the principle evidenced by an authority or line of authority on which the defendant seeks to rely. He or she, or his or her legal advisors, understandably press that contention in litigation believing that, irrespective of the merits, the court will or should dutifully apply the precedent. The more realistic perception of the working of precedent in practice would make that assumption nervously unsafe. But for the defendant's overly optimistic expectation of what the doctrine of precedent will deliver, the case might never have been litigated.

Fifthly, the growing instability of precedent in the computer age to which I have referred earlier should not be overlooked. Indeed, it may be that this growing instability preceded the computer age and that age has simply escalated the instability. Cardozo observed that the fecundity of case law would make Malthus stand aghast. He added: 'So vast a brood includes the defective and the helpless. An avalanche of decisions by tribunals great and small is producing a situation where citation of precedent is tending to count for less, and appeal for an informing principle is tending to count for more.'[56] The great judge may have been speaking of his own court or, perhaps, just being optimistic. Experience in the intervening years suggests that he was over-optimistic. But, if the advent of the computer results in precedent counting for less, and an appeal to an informing principle counting for more, technology will have won for the human race an unexpected boon.

Lord Diplock explained how the speeches of each of the two in *Hedley Byrne & Co. Ltd* v *Heller & Partners Ltd* [1964] AC 465 were to be understood.

[56] Cardozo, quoted in C. G. Weeramantry, *The Law in Crisis: Bridges of Understanding* (Capemoss, London, 1975), at 82.

Finally, the idea that the law only changes if and when the courts decline to follow a precedent, or if and when they skirt an unfavourable precedent by one or other of the judicial techniques mentioned above, is also a fugitive from reality. The law may change dramatically when, due to a change in the composition of a court, the later court adopts a different approach or different perception of the judicial role from that of its predecessor without any assault on precedent at all. The same rule or principle is simply applied differently. Dramatic change of this kind occurs with the swing of the judicial pendulum reflecting the make-up of an appellate court at any given time. Compare, for example, the jurisprudence of the Court of Appeal of New Zealand in administrative law at a time when the President was Sir Robin Cooke (now Lord Cooke of Thorndon) and when the President was his successor, Sir Ivor Richardson. It is fair to say that the 'Cooke Court' developed administrative law in New Zealand to a point where many observers, not excluding the Privy Council,[57] considered judicial supervision of governmental activity to be excessively obtrusive. A few short years later the 'Richardson Court's' commitment to maintaining the vitality of the court's traditional supervisory role was being questioned.[58] The basic rules or legal principles had not been overtly changed. All that had happened was that the composition of the Court had changed, and with that change, the approach of the Court had changed. The same basic rules or principles were being applied, but being applied more conservatively. Thus, uncertainty in the law is not necessarily whether or not precedents will be followed; it may be uncertainty as to how the changing composition of the court will influence the 'swing of the pendulum'.[59]

Certainty as a relevant consideration

Once its pretension as a primary goal of adjudication is discarded, certainty can be allowed to achieve acceptance as a valid consideration, but a consideration only, in the particular case. I acknowledge that not much would turn on certainty being called a 'goal' of adjudication if it is

---

[57] E.g. *Petrocorp v Minister of Energy* [1991] 1 NZLR 641, at 655–656.

[58] J. A. Farmer QC, 'The New Zealand Court of Appeal: Maintaining Quality After the Privy Council' in Rick Bigwood (ed.), *Legal Method in New Zealand* (Butterworths, Wellington, 2001), at 237.

[59] See *Waitakere City Council v Lovelock* [1997] NZAR 492, at 505–506, adverting to the remarks of Lord Wilberforce in the foreword to Michael Taggart (ed.), *Judicial Review of Administrative Action in the 1980s: Problems and Prospects* (Oxford University Press in association with the Legal Research Foundation, New York and Auckland 1986), at ix.

perceived in this more limited light. Nothing turns on a label. I prefer to call it a 'consideration', however, in order to contrast certainty's proper function with the judicial thinking that is presently under fire. I take the view that the impact of a decision on the community's ability to order its affairs should be taken into consideration in the context of the particular case and not applied in a blanket sense as a general goal of adjudication. Certainty, in other words, must be given particular relevance to the case in hand.

Those who pursue certainty as if it were a general, abstract goal of judicial adjudication do the law a disservice. Assume for a moment that complete certainty was achieved, individual justice would be sacrificed and, because it would be static, the law would cease to serve the needs and expectations of the community. The law would forfeit the concept of justice and abandon its social utility. Certainty is not therefore an ideal, as justice is an ideal. Nor is it a justification, as social utility is a justification. Rather, it is a concept designed to serve these ends. Its rationale lies in its ability to promote justice and to serve the needs and expectations of the community. As such, it is an important and ever-present consideration in the administration of the law. But its relevance and applicability needs to be demonstrated in the particular case. Consigning certainty to this particularised role prevents it from assuming an elevated and dominant appointment in the process of judicial adjudication without depriving the law of its advantage where that advantage can be demonstrated.

Whether certainty is a valid consideration in a particular case will therefore need to be expressly addressed by the court. It will cease to be an unspoken mantra. Judges will need to set out reasons in their judgments for holding that certainty is a valid consideration in the context of the instant case or that the need for certainty in the law requires a particular outcome.

The first inquiry must necessarily be directed at the question whether the existing law can be considered settled. If the law is in doubt it cannot promote certainty in the law to pretend that it is not in doubt. Thus, if judges, lawyers, academics or other commentators have expressed such a measure of dissatisfaction with an authority that a sensible person would know better than to regard it as settled, certainty should not be a relevant or overriding consideration.

In some cases it may not be enough that the law in issue is settled or relatively settled. The litigant should be required to show that he or she, or other members of the community in a similar position, have relied and acted upon the allegedly settled law. If they have not, the claim that the particular law should be applied on the basis that it will promote certainty and predictability loses much of its force. The court can in such cases have closer regard to the fairness of its decision and the relevance of its decision to contemporary requirements.

The nature of the allegedly settled law will also be relevant to consider. If the law relates to property and contractual interests, the court will be much less inclined to make changes in the law that might adversely affect those interests. It is particularly relevant that the law should not develop in a way that might deprive people of vested rights that have accrued to them, particularly in commercial transactions.

In other cases, it may be that the law has been settled for so long that it is preferable to leave the change to Parliament. The considerations germane to this course are dealt with at greater length in Chapter 10.

There might, of course, be other aspects of the case in hand that are relevant to the question whether the notion of certainty is a valid or dominant consideration in the particular case. What must be made clear is that it would not be the end of the matter if it is held that certainty is in fact a relevant consideration. A balancing exercise would still be required to determine whether that factor outweighs other considerations, such as the justice of the case or the relevance of the law to modern conditions. The important point is that the issue would be openly addressed in the judgment, and that discussion would in all probability indicate the true basis of the judges' decision.

Conclusion

Obtaining certainty in the law is a valid aspiration. That aspiration has not been challenged. What has been challenged is the absolutism that has infected that aspiration so that certainty in the law has become a paramount goal of the legal process. It has assumed a predominant status in the thinking of the formalist judge. It deserves a more realistic and rationale appraisal.

For the reasons I have given, it is to be accepted that the law is inherently uncertain in the sense that no law is so definitive as to be beyond challenge. Vague laws are a reality. Acknowledging this reality does not mean that the law becomes any less predictable than is now the case. Indeed, as I have sought to show, there is a strong argument to suggest that certainty and predictability would be improved if the formalistic rule-bound approach were abandoned and the doctrine of precedent were relaxed. Although no absolute assertion is possible, as whatever approach is adopted the law will remain inherently uncertain, a better understanding of the legal process and the judicial methodology adopted should enhance predictability.

Certainty, therefore, should not be discarded as an aspiration of the adjudicative process, but should be deliberately displaced from its elevated perch as a paramount goal. In line with the pragmatic approach commended in this book, certainty would be treated as a consideration to be taken into account in the circumstances of an appropriate case. Whether or not it would prevail over other considerations must depend on those circumstances. At all times, however, it is to be borne in mind that its rationale rests in its ability to promote justice and to serve the needs and expectations of the community.

6

The piety of precedent

A foolish consistency ...

I have previously been pleased to quote, roughly in context, the saying of Ralph Waldo Emerson:

> A foolish consistency is the hobgoblin of little minds.[1]

Regrettably, it has to be said, there are judges and lawyers who deserve the implied rebuke. They are seemingly obsessed with precedent. With a dedication born of faith, they turn to precedent to reveal the law. The past, it is somehow thought, has predicted the future. Keeping faith with that past is the accepted wisdom. Do not such judges and lawyers portray a 'littleness' of mind? Surely, the notion that it is better to be consistent with a past decision and, at the same time, to be foolish in preferring that consistency, is indefensible?

Those judges and lawyers, and not a few academics, who still think of the common law as a body of immutable law, a legacy from the past to be cherished, nurtured and preserved as far as humanly possible in its inherited state, dent the administration of the law. The thinking of some past era, perhaps appropriate to its time and place, is forever being introduced to deal with the problems of today. The law's ability to cope with the fast-moving changes of the modern world is forever shackled by a 'wisdom' that belongs to the past. Of course, the experience of history has its value, but it should not be exaggerated beyond what it is – the experience and thinking of the past. Roscoe Pound has truly pointed out how '... legal machinery may defeat its own ends when one age conceives it has said the final word and assumes to prescribe unalterable rules for time to come.'[2]

---

[1] Quoted by the author in Rick Bigwood (ed.), *Legal Method in New Zealand* (Butterworths, Wellington, 2001), at 141.
[2] Roscoe Pound, *The Spirit of the Common Law* (Marshall Jones Company, Boston, 1931), at 105–106.

With this precedent-oriented attitude prevalent, the law progresses fitfully with only furtive reference to the community values that the judges consciously or unconsciously reflect. Even when a change in the law occurs, it may happen surreptitiously, obscured by a purported adherence to precedent. The change may not be acknowledged or may be downplayed in a judicial romp of reinterpretation and rationalisation through the authorities. Certainty, stability and continuity in the law are purportedly achieved because the formal or formalised presentation of the change in the law does not admit of any change or the extent of the change. The outcome, it is claimed, has been extracted from precedents. In the result, the legal record becomes opaque. As pointed out in the previous chapter, judicial initiative and innovation are sacrificed to the false idol of certainty in the law. At the very least, the creativity necessary to ensure justice in the individual case and to keep the law in step with contemporary requirements is diverted into the futile exercise of seeking to distinguish unwelcome arguments allegedly backed by authority or to otherwise rationalise a decision within the present rule-driven framework.

In the hands of a formalist judge, precedent becomes the famously articulated principle: 'Never do anything for a first time.'[3] If the law has not addressed or covered the situation before, do nothing. In this way precedent comes to exert a negative influence. It matters not that the judges who made the law in the first place had no truck with such a notion when they made the law for the first time. Nor does it matter that it may be purely fortuitous that the question in issue has not been before the courts before. It is enough that there is no law to apply. In this way, never doing anything for a first time becomes a recipe for injustice in the individual case and stagnancy in the law generally. Rigidity in judicial thinking becomes a virus.

The judge who adopts this unmerited adherence to precedent fails to perceive the law as a process or continuum, as will be emphasised in Chapter 9. The judge's perception is necessarily a perception of the law in cross-section at a particular time, for the precedent can only validly represent the law at that time. No precedent can represent the law in transition, as it ought to be, or as it will be in the next case.[4] The judge's horizons are forever confined by an essentially static view of the law.

---

[3] See the Rt. Hon. Sir Stephen Sedley, 'On Never Doing Anything For the First Time', The 16th Atkin Lecture, The Reform Club, 6 November 2001.
[4] See below, Chapter 9, at 218–219, and 224–225.

Another way of making this point is to frankly acknowledge that the rigid application of precedent limits judicial autonomy. Judges of a precedent-oriented bent do not have the independence or freedom to ensure that justice is done in the instant case or that the law is developed to meet society's needs and expectations. Conversely, judges who are not hide-bound by precedent can seek to give effect to the sense of fairness or sentiment of justice rooted in the community. To the best of their ability, judges can endeavour to convert the abstract notion of justice with no specific content into the stuff that will shape their value judgement in a particular case. Having eschewed undue adherence to precedent, they are not impeded in an undertaking, which is vital if the law is to command the respect and confidence of the community which it serves.

Much rhetoric is expended extolling the concept of justice. Justice for the individual is portrayed as a glorious concept taking pride of place in the common law. It is then aberrant to utilise that same common law to suppress justice in the individual case. Nor can judges make a satisfactory contribution to the community's problems if they are constantly charged with the task of following cases from the past. The conceptions of justice and relevance which are involved must surely be current conceptions.

Truly, a foolish consistency is the hobgoblin of little minds.

The doctrine of precedent

One can only wonder at the undeserved praise precedent attracts. C. K. Allen, for example, has described precedent as the 'life-blood of every legal system'.[5] Yet another commentator has said that, compared to precedent, the concept of due process is a superficial notion and the presumption of innocence a passing fancy![6] Such praise, it should be said, is to some extent offset by the censure the doctrine of precedent has also evoked, especially when linked to *stare decisis*. Precedent has been variously condemned as fortuitous, striking 'with all the predictability of a lightning bolt',[7] as a 'backwater of the law';[8] as 'a mask hiding other considerations';[9] and as a 'doctrine of

---

[5] C. K. Allen, *Law in the Making* (7th edn, Clarendon Press, Oxford, 1964), at 243.
[6] A. H. Knight, *Life of the Law*, (Crown Publishers, New York, 1996), at 41.
[7] H. P. Monaghan, 'Our Perfect Constitution' (1981) 56 NYULR 353, at 390.
[8] F. H. Easterbrook, 'Stability and Reliability in Judicial Decisions' (1988) 73 Cornell LR 422, at 422.
[9] H. P. Monaghan, '*Stare Decisis* and Constitutional Adjudication' (1988) 83 Colum. LR 723, at 743.

convenience to both conservatives and liberals' whose 'friends are determined by the needs of the moment'.[10]

These competing epigrams notwithstanding, precedent is inevitable. It is part of every legal system assured of its role by the fundamental precept of justice that like cases should be decided alike.[11] Consistency in decision-making is a self-evident virtue.

Shortly stated in these general terms, the case for precedent is seemingly irrefutable. Precedent is not a uniform doctrine, however, and it is not applied uniformly. The strength with which it is formulated and applied varies from one jurisdiction to another, from one court to another, and from one judge to another. Without doing damage to the precept that like cases should be treated alike, adherence to precedent may range from an inclination to provide consistency in the law where that consistency is seen to be merited to a positive obligation to follow a previous decision other than in exceptional or circumscribed circumstances.

The English doctrine of precedent, with its overlay of *stare decisis*, accords with this latter perception. It possesses a coercive element peculiar to English law. Precedent is said to be 'binding'. Decided cases are vested with the quality of 'law' and given the status of 'rules', and must be followed if they are not distinguishable or cannot be distinguished.[12] It is this rule-making or 'rulish' character of the doctrine of precedent that I contend must be eradicated.

In contrast, precedent is a much more flexible concept in legal systems based on Roman Law. A judge in France, for example, does not regard him or herself as bound by the decision of any court in a single previous instance. The judge will seek instead to ascertain the trend of recent decisions relating to the issue in question.[13] The point has been made in these terms: 'The practice of the Courts does not become a source of law

---

[10] C. J. Cooper, '*Stare Decisis*: Precedent and Principle in Constitutional Adjudication' (1988) 73 Cornell LR 401, at 402. This disposition has been noted by Michael Gerhardt in relation to the Supreme Court of the United States, although there is no reason to think that the phenomenon is not universal. 'Conservatives criticize the Warren Court's disregard for precedent, but not the Rehnquist Court's assault on liberal precedents', while 'liberals denounce the Rehnquist Court's attacks on their icons, but not the Warren and Burger Courts' overrulings of conservative precedents'. See M. Gerhardt, 'The Role of Precedent in Constitutional Decision-Making and Theory' (1991) 60 Geo. Wash. LR 68, at 72.

[11] R. Cross and J. W. Harris, *Precedent and the English Law* (4th edn, Oxford University Press, Oxford, 1991), at 3.

[12] R. W. M. Dias, *Jurisprudence* (5th edn, Butterworths, London, 1985), at 56.

[13] Cross and Harris, *Precedent*, at 11.

until it is definitely fixed by the repetition of precedents which are in agreement on a single point.'[14]

The coercive element in the common law perception of precedent rests on the theory of *stare decisis*. *Black's Law Dictionary* translates the phrase: 'To adhere to precedents, and not to unsettle things which are established.'[15] But the latitude that the reference to 'established' law must necessarily permit has been rejected. Parke B's expression of the classical conception of the doctrine of precedent in 1833 exemplifies and exalts this rejection:

> Our common law system consists in the applying to new combinations of circumstances those rules of law which we derive from legal principles and judicial precedents; and for the sake of attaining uniformity, consistency and certainty, we must apply those rules, where they are not plainly unreasonable and inconvenient, to all cases which arise; and we are not at liberty to reject them, and to abandon all analogy to them, in those to which they have not yet been judicially applied, because we think that the rules are not as convenient and reasonable as we ourselves could have devised.[16]

It would be comforting to be able to say that this approach or, at least, the 'absolutism' of this approach, is long since dead. Such a claim, however, must invite much the same response as that proffered by a very much alive Mark Twain when his obituary was published: 'The reports of my death are greatly exaggerated!' Indeed, a modern counterpart to Parke B's classical conception can be found in an article by Justice Kenneth Hayne of the High Court of Australia.[17] The Judge opines that the faithful application of the doctrine of precedent is at the heart of the judicial task, which is to do justice according to law, and that a judge, particularly a judge at first instance, 'is not free to recast the law at will,

---

[14] E. L. Lambert and M. J. Wasserman, 'The Case Method in Canada and the Possibilities of its Adaption to the Civil Law' (1929) 39 Yale LJ 1, at 15. See also the Hon. Mr Justice Lockhart, 'The Doctrine of Precedent – Today and Tomorrow' (1987) 3 Aust. Bar Rev. 1, at 10–11.

[15] *Black's Law Dictionary* (6th edn, West Pub. Co., St. Paul, Minn., 1990), at 1406 ('*stare decisis et non quieta movere*').

[16] *Mirehouse v Rennell* (1833) 1 Cl & F 527, at 546: 6 ER 1015, at 1023.

[17] 'Letting Justice Be Done Without the Heavens Falling' (2001) 27 Monash Univ. LR 12, esp. at 17. An even more extreme position is to found in the address by J. D. Heydon (now Justice Heydon of the High Court of Australia) 'Judicial activism and the death of the rule of law', Quadrant Address reproduced in (2003) 23 Aust. Bar Rev. 110; (2004) Otago LR 493; an unabashed exercise in determined legal fundamentalism.

whatever he or she may think of it'. Of course, a judge is not free to recast the law at will, but faced with a contentious law the judge must make what he or she will of it. More often than not judges will be able to reach differing views, each or all claiming the benediction of 'precedent'.

It would therefore be an exaggeration to assert that the classical conception of *stare decisis* does not continue to have an allure to judges, lawyers and academics. It continues to nurture a headstrong authority in the practice of the law.[18] It is that authority that I examine in this chapter.

Before turning to such an examination, however, I must reiterate that I do not decry a broad doctrine of precedent. As already noted, some sort of system of precedent is common to all legal systems. Reference to earlier cases is inevitable, and frequently valuable, and there is and will continue to be many occasions when it would be inappropriate not to follow a precedent or line of authority. Long-standing and respected precedents can reflect the wisdom of the court as an 'institution transcending the moment'.[19] Moreover, the incremental approach of the common law, and the analogical reasoning that is part of that approach, is in large measure dependent on adherence to precedent.[20] I do not therefore seek to eradicate precedent. Rather, I wish to expose the gulf between theory and reality, and to recommend a conscious relaxation of the coercive element in the doctrine and, in particular, the dissolution of the 'attitude of mind' engendered by it.

The perceived value of precedent unmasked

The various reasons why precedent should be adhered to have been spelt out many times over. Lawyers are familiar with the list: assuring stability in society by promoting certainty and predictability in the law; protecting the interests of those who have relied on existing case law; maintaining the legitimacy of the law and public confidence in the courts;

---

[18] Those judges and lawyers today who steadfastly uphold and apply a strict doctrine of precedent should be aware that they cannot claim the support of history. Contrary to conventional thought the doctrine is a relatively modern phenomenon. See E. W. Thomas, 'A Return to Principle in Judicial Reasoning and an Acclamation of Judicial Autonomy' 4 (1993) VUWLR Mono. 5, at 14–15.

[19] *Welch* v *The State Department of Highways and Public Transport* 403 U.S. 468, at 479 (1987), quoting *Green* v *United States* 355 U.S. 184, 215 (1957). For a full discussion, see the Note 'Constitutional *Stare Decisis*' (1990) 103 Harv. LR 1344.

[20] Hon. Sir Anthony Mason, 'The Use and Abuse of Precedent' (1998) 94 Aust. Bar Rev. 93, at 93.

ensuring that the courts do not usurp the law-making prerogative of the people's elected representatives; and achieving greater judicial efficiency.

Stability

Stability is advanced as the principal rationale of the doctrine of precedent. By eliminating inconsistency in the legal system, it is thought, certainty and predictability will be promoted, and the perception that the law is stable and relatively unchanging will be sustained. People can order their affairs and commit their resources with confidence. Able to rely upon 'the law', disputes can be settled without recourse to the courts. Assuring certainty and predictability in commercial dealings is particularly important. Taking the argument to its extreme, it is said that the frequent overruling of decisions 'tend[s] to bring adjudications ... into the same class as a restricted rail-road ticket, good for this day and train only'.[21]

Without doubt, there are many circumstances in which people rely on past court decisions. People make decisions and commit their resources on the basis that the 'case law' will remain the law. Their actions reflect a valid expectation that those actions will be upheld by the courts. People's desire for stability also extends beyond the private affairs of citizens to a concern for the stability of social and political institutions. Yet, the need for stability cannot oust the need for flexibility.[22] As change is inevitable, and legal rules need to adapt to change to deliver the law's ultimate rationale of serving the community, the law cannot be permitted to be static. As Dean Pound observed: 'Law must be stable and yet it cannot stand still.'[23]

It is evident that adherence to precedent for reasons relating to stability owes its force to the norm of equality. The principle that like cases are to be treated alike means that persons in similar situations should be treated equally. The axiom involves a host of admirable notions. Consistency and uniformity underlie the concept. Justice is itself at stake, and a person who is treated less favourably or differently than any other person in a like position can complain to have been treated unfairly. But as a justification for the doctrine of precedent, the norm of equality suffers from a basic

---

[21] *Smith v Allwright* 321 U.S. 649, at 669 (1942), per Roberts J dissenting.
[22] T. N. Benditt, 'The Rule of Precedent' in L. Goldstein (ed.), *Precedent in Law* (Clarendon Press, Oxford, 1987), at 91–93.
[23] L. H. Carter, *Reason in Law* (Longman, New York, 1998), at 104, quoting Dean Pound's opening sentence in *Interpretations of Legal History* (The University Press Cambridge, 1923), at 1.

fallacy. If two similar cases are not treated alike, the principle does not determine which of the two cases is in error. It may be the first, it may be the last. Precedent goes further, however, and stipulates that it is the later case that will be mistaken. Certainty in the law may then be perceived as certainty of injustice. This notion must be a repugnant prospect for all but those incurably addicted to *stare decisis*.

Nor, as I have outlined above,[24] does the reference to the principle that like cases are to be treated alike define what it is that makes cases 'alike'. Conventional wisdom looks to the similarity of the facts. But there can be no immediate assumption that the 'likeness' must begin and end with the facts. Before the requirement that like should be treated alike can be said to be breached, more than just the facts must be the same. The standards, needs and expectations of the community would need to be the same, developments in other areas of the law would need to be the same, all the external sources that would bear on the decision would need to be the same, and so on. Where any of these factors vary, it cannot be said that it jars any conventional notion of consistency if the later case is not dealt with in the same way as the first. Indeed, it may be unjust to treat the two cases the same simply because the facts are identical when the community's perception of the facts, and the values associated with such facts, have changed. These differences in perceptions and values are as important to the one litigant as are the similarities of the facts to the other.

Jerome Frank, a United States Federal Judge and writer, asks us to assume that a judge-made rule embodies a court's past view of policy. Why, he asks, should a view of policy once expressed by a court be beyond recall by that same court? Why should the policy be frozen? Why should the judicial power to formulate a policy be exhausted by an erroneous exercise of that power? Frank concludes that the judicial practice of adhering to a rule embodying an unjust policy seems itself to be a policy – a policy of doing injustice.[25]

Candour is also required before departing from the topic, and again there is none better than Frank to provide it. This foremost judicial realist observed that it must be accepted that in general terms some acceptance of precedent stems from an 'inevitable inertia'. He accepted that it is probably a truism that in all aspects of life, individual or social, there is resistance to change. There seems to be, he said, a deep-lying physiological and psychological basis for hostility to change. Adopting a

---

[24] See above, Chapter 5, at 131–132.
[25] Jerome Frank, *Courts on Trial* (Princeton University Press, Princeton, 1973), at 270.

metaphor, Frank points out that people do not necessarily substitute a new track, even though it is shorter and more suitable, for the usual one. As long as the known track is not unpleasant, one preserves that track fearful of what might happen with a new one. Is it not the wisest course, he asks, to pass with the utmost care by the places that everyone has already passed? Frank concludes: 'Fear, then, seems to play a role in adherence to precedents.'[26] It surely cannot be said that truckling to this human condition contributes to genuine stability and is a sound foundation for a doctrine of precedent.

Nothing that has been said, however, negates the fact that stability in the law is desirable to the extent that it can be sensibly achieved. Thus, the need for stability is a factor to be included, where appropriate and relevant, in the balancing exercise that can only be sensibly done in the individual case.

A variant of the stability rationale for precedent, at times articulated as a constitutional principle, is the desire to promote the stability of social and political institutions. According to this view, it is accepted that over time change is inevitable, even in respect of principles that are regarded as fundamental and of constitutional significance. Indeed, it is the certain prospect of change, or the ever-present threat of change, which is seen to give the doctrine of precedent its value. As the doctrine is commonly known and accepted it provides a community facing constant change with a sense of security. This sense of security is seen to be important for the stability of the social framework and order. On this conservative view, it is said, it matters not that the doctrine in reality contributes little to the achievement of certainty in the law; it is the perceived stability of the system that is important. People know, or think they know, where they are and where they stand, and society is all the more stable for it.

This reason for continuing to subscribe to a strict doctrine of precedent, however, is more rhetoric than reality. People in fact know, and expect, that the law will adapt to change. Furthermore, it is unsound to seek to sustain the stability of society on a bogus claim. To some, perhaps, the doctrine, or the existence of the doctrine, may provide some sort of security blanket,[27] but this is a childhood fantasy that is to be discarded with maturity. In all, there is no reason to think that a pragmatic and principle-oriented approach would lead to instability or

---

[26] Ibid., at 272.
[27] Cf. Frank's concept of the 'father-symbol' in *Law and the Modern Mind* (Peter Smith, Gloucester, 1930), at 21–22.

disquiet in the community any more than it did when the judges of old demanded that a precedent be justified, or when the judges of today exercise the wide discretionary powers that the people's parliamentary representatives vest in them by statute.

Reliance

Another venerated reason for rigidly adhering to *stare decisis* and a strict doctrine of precedent is the importance of preserving existing proprietary or contractual rights.[28] Indeed, invoking a reliance interest, *stare decisis* has been called a rule of property.[29] Citizens, particularly members of the commercial community, enter into transactions on the basis of the existing case law and the security of those transactions, including the vested rights that have accrued under them, would be prejudiced if 'the law' was not followed.[30]

The reliance argument in support of a strict doctrine of precedent is at times given a moral imperative of keeping faith with those who have relied upon previous decisions, or relied upon the system of *stare decisis* itself.[31] David Lyons has advanced the argument in these terms:

> ... when such a precedent has claims to be respected, that would seem to be because the original decision *constituted a commitment*, made to others, that future decisions in similar cases shall be made similarly. It is not that the commitment *follows from* a general requirement to go as before ... but rather that the commitment to go as before *accounts* for the requirement to do so.[32]

The apparent appeal of this argument is undeniable. A court that departs from an established line of cases is one that seemingly betrays all those who relied or acted upon the earlier decisions. As a reason in support of the strict doctrine of precedent, however, it begs the question. People rely upon the earlier decision because of *stare decisis*; the need to keep faith with them therefore also arises because of *stare decisis*.

---

[28] Lockhart, 'The Doctrine of Precedent', at 4.
[29] C. P. Banks, 'Reversals of Precedent and Judicial Policy-Making: How Judicial Conceptions of *Stare Decisis* in the US Supreme Court Influence Social Change' (1999) 32 Akron LR 233, at 239.
[30] Mason, 'The Use and Abuse of Precedent', at 106.
[31] J. Evans, 'Precedent in the Nineteenth Century' in Goldstein (ed.), *Precedent in Law*, at 37.
[32] D. Lyons, 'Formal Justice, Moral Commitment, and Judicial Precedent' (1984) 81 Journal of Philosophy 580, at 585.

Without a strict principle of precedent there can be no justification for a claim to have been betrayed if a later decision reverses an earlier authority. In other words, the only reason why the original decision should constitute a moral commitment to decide similar cases the same way in the future is the doctrine of precedent, backed by *stare decisis*, itself. Remove that element and the moral force of the argument is dissipated.

Realism must be again permitted to intrude. Although case law is frequently uncertain, where it is relatively certain, it is highly unlikely that there will be litigation by those persons who have ordered their affairs on the basis of that certain case law. They will not be prejudiced. Where the law is uncertain, however, the person has no option but to act on his or her perception, or their lawyer's opinion, as to what the law is – or what it will be if the matter is litigated. Such a state of affairs is unavoidable, and as common as the typical case where both parties contend for a different view of the law and claim to have ordered their affairs on the basis of their respective views.

Two qualifications then emerge in respect of this 'reliance interest' as a foundation for *stare decisis*. The first is that the legal rule on which the person acts must be certain or, at the very least, relatively certain. There is no reason why litigants should be able to claim the decisive benefit of precedent if they have ordered their affairs on the basis of a misconception or dubious view of the 'certainty' of the legal rule that is said to be applicable. The second qualification is that litigants should have actually relied on the rule encompassed in the precedent. Litigants should not be able to persuade the court to follow an unwise or unjust decision if they, and possibly others, have not in fact relied upon the decision in a material manner.[33]

Yet again, both these qualifications require the question whether the prior decision should be followed to be dealt with in the context of the instant case. Where the legal rule is certain, or relatively certain, and the litigant actually changed his or her position in reliance upon it, the courts will be markedly reluctant to avoid rejecting the precedent. This reluctance will, of course, stem in large part from the injustice involved in changing the rule to the detriment of the person who has relied upon it. In such cases, this factor is unlikely to be outweighed by competing considerations. But, again, it is no more than a factor to be taken into account in the individual case.

---

[33] Frank, *Courts on Trial*, at 270.

Legitimacy

Stare decisis, it is claimed, supports the courts' legitimacy and maintains public confidence and respect for the law.[34] It not only ensures equality in the administration of justice but also projects to the public the impression that the courts administer justice equally.[35] This argument carries overtones of a particular perception of the rule of law. To permit courts to change the law by overruling precedents, it is argued, is to usurp the function of Parliament. The act of overruling is a legislative act. This thinking is most pronounced in decisions relating to the construction of statutes. Where the courts have ruled on the meaning of a statutory provision, it is thought, that meaning should be adhered to other than in exceptional circumstances. Not only will citizens have acted on the basis of that interpretation, but Parliament has apparently not seen fit to reverse the effect of the decision. Thus, it is claimed, changes in the law should be left to Parliament. That institution may then pass amendments that will have prospective effect only.

The argument that the legitimacy of the legal system depends on the courts refusing to change the law once it has been declared in a prior decision must be rejected out of hand. As already observed, no one today believes the fairy tale that judges do not make law. For this reason, the suggestion that only Parliament can or should make the law is totally untenable today. Because it is untenable, the argument for *stare decisis* based on preserving the legitimacy of the legal system on this basis must also be rejected. Increasingly, judges, lawyers and academics protest the view that a plaintiff should not be denied a remedy by an out-of-date rule of law on the footing that it is the sole province of Parliament to alter the law so that future plaintiffs may succeed.[36] To the contrary, rigid adherence to precedent destroys, or at least inevitably delays, the development and application of fundamental principles. Emerging principles are forced back into the judicial chest lest their release impair the appearance that the court is controlled by the doctrine of precedent.

Nor, to the extent that the legitimacy of the legal system rests upon public confidence in the courts, can it any longer be said that the doctrine of precedent should be pursued in order to create an impression of equality

---

[34] T. R. Lee, '*Stare decisis* in Historical Perspective: From the Founding Era to the Rehnquist Court' (1999) 52 Vanderbilt LR 647, at 652–655.
[35] Carter, *Reason in Law*, at 30.
[36] Mason, 'The Use and Abuse of Precedent', at 95.

when that impression is divorced from reality. It has been correctly said that the courts should not be placed in the position of going through the 'charade' of distinguishing prior decisions on insufficient grounds.[37] Sir Anthony Mason has also pointed out that when judges acknowledge the binding nature of a decision of which they do not approve, but then formulate a distinction without a difference, thereby outflanking the old decision, they deprive the law of its rationality and its intellectual integrity.[38] Do we not sell the public, and certainly the perceptive public, short when we presume that they do not see the techniques used to avoid unfavourable precedents for what they are – a sentacious judicial pageant? If that is so, it cannot enhance the public image of the courts as an institution dedicated to contemporary justice. Public confidence in the courts will be diminished if the courts are not prepared to use the past to resolve the issues of the present with perceptive discrimination.

Judicial craftsmanship and so on

A variation of the legitimacy argument is the belief that the 'method of logical form' adopted by the courts is essential to command public acceptance.[39] Proceeding step by step from a proposition that case law has yielded is seen to be the stuff of judgments. The judge appears removed and impersonal, expanding and applying pre-existing law.[40] But, as has been said, this is a fiction and, in fact, the embodiment of the justification for formalism. Again, it cannot be desirable to preserve a fiction in the administration of the law in order to achieve public acceptance of the courts' decisions. Strict adherence to the doctrine of precedent is, of course, an integral part of this fable, and it suffers a setback once it is appreciated that the preservation of a fiction is both unnecessary and unwise to maintain public respect. In truth, the method of logical form commands the acceptance of lawyers steeped in the tradition of precedent, but members of the community who are untroubled by that outlook are unimpressed by its perceived pretence.

---

[37] Lockhart, 'The Doctrine of Precedent'; and see the dicta of Lord Reid in *Jones v Secretary of State for Social Services* [1972] AC 944, at 966.
[38] Mason, 'The Use and Abuse of Precedent', at 94.
[39] C. G. Weeramantry, 'Judicial Reasoning and the Common Law' (Papers of the Ninth Commonwealth Law Conference, 1990), at 84.
[40] This rationale is only a slight refinement of Lord Radcliffe's overt endorsement of a grand deceit in the law. See above, Chapter 2, at 26–27.

Yet, another similar argument to justify a close adherence to precedent is advanced, but it is one which does not embrace the accompanying exhortation to necessarily follow the precedent or precedents cited. In this argument, it is accepted that judges distinguish, reinterpret and make exceptions to prior cases so as to achieve justice in the instant case. Consequently, it does not matter, it is said, whether the precedent is rejected or even undermined; the result is the same in both cases. The court is saying: 'The King is dead, long live the King.' Thus, the proper handling of precedent is seen as 'part of judicial craftsmanship; the judge must learn how to use it and in particular how to identify the rare occasions when it is necessary to say that what judges have put together they can also put asunder.'[41]

This argument is again an appeal to formalism, yet one that would appear to allow the application of the doctrine a measure of flexibility. But the sting is in the tail. The expectation is that, if the judicial craftsmanship is of the requisite standard, the occasions when it is necessary to reverse or modify a precedent will be few and far between. The craftsmanship will capture and overwhelm the judge's creativity. Yet again, what price artifice? Professor Benditt has commented on the similarity of law to foreign policy in this regard in that it is considered desirable to avoid acknowledging what is actually happening.[42] Yet again, a fiction exists in the disparity between the actual decision and the stated rationalisation for it.

Even where the precedent is distinguished or reinterpreted, judicial rationalisation can hamper the true exercise of judicial autonomy in a subtle manner. This impediment occurs when the precedent, although ultimately rejected, nevertheless determines the structure or direction of the judge's reasoning. The precedent may effectively define the issues in the instant case; influence the selection of facts; suggest what is important or not important; and identify the feature or features in the case which are regarded as relevant. In such cases, although it may suffer the ignominy of being spurned, the precedent may nevertheless have been critical in determining the framework of the judge's reasoning. Yet, there is no necessary reason why it should be the correct framework for that particular case. In the absence of precedent, the judge might well have defined the issues differently, selected or included as relevant

---

[41] Lord Devlin, *The Judge* (Oxford University Press, Oxford, 1979), at 201.
[42] Benditt, 'The Rule of Precedent' in Goldstein (ed.), *Precedent in Law*, at 100.

different facts, and determined that different features of the case were important to achieve a just or contemporary outcome.

Efficiency

It has been claimed that, to some extent, the court's workload itself dictates its adherence to precedent. That workload would become intolerable if every proposition advanced in the course of argument had to be reconsidered. Judicial economy dictates adherance to precedent in order to avoid the wasteful use of resources that would be involved in reinventing the wheel in each case.[43] As Cardozo said, '... the labour of judges would be increased almost to the breaking point if every past decision could be reopened in every case, and one could not lay one's own course of bricks on the secure foundation of the courses laid by others who had gone before him.'[44] Courts must be able to ease the burden by relying on what judges have done in similar cases.

Of course, it would be foolhardy for the court to 're-examine every possible issue presented in every case ...' But the efficiency argument begs the critical question. That question is not whether the court *may* rely on precedent in any case, but whether it *must* do so when it considers the previous court in error, or where conditions have changed, or where a rank injustice would result in the case before the court if the precedent were to be followed. No-one contests the fact that judicial decision-making begins with a premise. The premise may be a rule or precedent or it may be a pre-existing corpus of rules or a line of precedents, and it will provide the starting point for the reasoning that follows. It is not suggested that this starting point should be reinvented in every case, and any argument seeking to justify a strict doctrine of precedent on this basis is patently a make-weight argument.

'Non-binding' precedents?

A brief word about the impact of non-binding precedents in judicial reasoning is not out of place. I will refer, in the first place, to so-called persuasive precedents and, in the second place, to what may be described as 'famous dicta'.

---

[43] Lee, '*Stare Decisis* in Historical Perspective', at 654.
[44] Benjamin N. Cardozo, *The Nature of the Judicial Process* (Yale University Press, New Haven, 1921), at 149.

Persuasive precedents

Overwhelmed by the strict doctrine of precedent, the courts are far too inclined to vest persuasive precedents with something akin to binding force. Certainly, an observer listening to legal argument would be unlikely to be able to detect which cases being referred to in argument were binding and which were persuasive only. All cases that are known to counsel and are possibly relevant are cited and dealt with at length for the purpose of supporting an argument or distinguishing the instant case. Cases are likely to be mentioned in the judgment and, although only persuasive, examined in detail, before being approved or disapproved, as the case may be.

Yet, if the decision is persuasive only it is frequently pointless to examine it at such great length for the purpose of distinguishing it from the instant case. Refer to the decision for its intrinsic reasoning, if any, but why cite a persuasive precedent for the purpose of distinguishing it if it is not binding? At times, of course, this exercise has a point. Persuasive precedents may be used in an effort to extend or confine the ambit of a binding precedent or to reduce the judge's reluctance to depart from a precedent by showing that he or she is not breaking new judicial ground.

Apart from instances such as this, however, it should only be necessary to examine and deal with precedents that are of persuasive force if they in fact persuade. In other words, the reasoning in the precedent should be capable of making a positive contribution to the reasoning of the decision in the instant case. Judges can in such circumstances be assisted as much by the 'wisdom' of past persuasive precedents as they can by the 'wisdom' of so-called binding precedents.

'Famous dicta'

Another legal phenomenon, which should not be accorded more than persuasive value, if even that, are the well-known dicta expressing a particular principle or rule. Repeated in textbooks, articles and in decision after decision these dicta eventually assume a status that seemingly places them beyond the questioning of mere mortals. Such judicial pronouncements are accorded something akin to the respect and force of statute law.[45]

---

[45] For example Lord Selbourne's statement of the liability of third parties to a trust in *Barnes* v *Addy* [1874] 9 Ch App 244, at 251–252. See the comments of Ungoed-Thomas J in *Selangor United Rubber Estates Limited* v *Cradock (No. 3)* [1968] 1 WLR 1555, at 1591, relating to Lord Selbourne's phrase, 'dishonest and fraudulent design'.

Nothing probably demonstrates the debilitating impression of our close adherence to precedent more than this slavish attitude to judicial dicta. It is immature. Cardozo exclaimed that it was a mystery to him how judges, 'of all the persons in the world, should put their faith in dicta'.[46] He correctly identified the need to separate the accidental and the nonessential from the essential and the inherent.

Of course, the dicta may aptly encapsulate a legal principle. That possibility is not challenged. It is the tendency to treat a dictum as if it were equivalent to statute law that is irksome. Nor, generally speaking, should any dictum ever be read apart from the context of the case in which it appears. The famous dictum will be part only of the judge's reasoning. Nor should it be necessarily thought that the judge concerned was essaying a comprehensive and definitive statement of the rule or principle in that dictum. Purporting to speak for his or her times, they would not begrudge the judges today the opportunity to speak for their times.

Separate from famous dicta is a library of ordinary dicta. Such dicta add little or nothing to an argument. Lawyers, it seems, have a penchant to quote the words of someone else, however humble and undistinguished, whenever it is possible to do so in making a point rather than using their own words. The active quotation, it is apparently assumed, adds a lustre to the argument in that it suggests that it is not a novel argument, that the judge need not be fearful or suspicious of it, and that it has a sort of pedigree or authority, however modest, which the same point made by counsel in his or her own words could not feign. Unnecessary quotations of this kind are again a by-product of an undue dedication to legal argument rooted in the doctrine of precedent.

Relevance and justice

A number of judges have expressed scepticism as to the ability of precedent to cope with change and deliver justice. Sir Stephen Sedley is one who has done so in the United Kingdom.[47] Commenting on Lord Bingham's description of precedent as 'a guide, not a cage', Sedley observes in a delightful paper that guides can take one horribly astray – and that a cage did not keep Hannibal Lecter in for very long! What keeps law on the boil, he states, is that neither experience nor logic stands still.[48] Justice Lockhart in Australia has voiced the view that large

---

[46] Cardozo, *The Judicial Process*, at 29. [47] Sedley, 'On Never Doing Anything', at 6.
[48] Ibid., at 11.

and rapid social reform, the existence of law reform commissions, and the constant stream of new legislation all raise a real query as to the capacity of the traditional doctrine of precedent and *stare decisis* to cope with society's future needs.[49] Sir Anthony Mason has expressed similar sentiments. Precedent brings in its train a mode of argumentation that appears to be excessively formal because it is preoccupied with past decisions and dicta, and is unable to respond to the need for change. Examination of past authorities, he suggests, dominates the process of legal reasoning.[50] The learned jurist also observes that the attention lavished on the discussion of decided cases is often disproportionate to discussion of the inherent considerations that might influence an outcome one way rather than another. This characteristic of legal reasoning conveys the impression that the law superimposes its own standards on the process of reason.[51]

Sir Anthony Mason adds that in bygone days the law's inability to adapt to the need for change did not matter. The pace of economic and social change was slow, sometimes imperceptible, so that the common law's incapacity for change was not seen as a disability. The pace of change has itself changed dramatically, however, and brought the doctrine of precedent into critical focus. It has inevitably generated pressure on the courts to take an active part in updating the law.[52] Similarly, the common law will have lost is vitality and usefulness, and have become doctrinaire, if it cannot render to every person his or her due in the individual case. Indeed, when precedent produces injustice and lack of rationality, it defeats the very objectives that it was originally designed to accomplish.[53]

This question bears further reflection. I have already asserted that there is no more outdated and repugnant notion than the stricture that justice in the particular case must be subverted to the goal of certainty in the law. This proposition is a disturbing anomaly in a system ostensibly devoted to justice. The anomaly is all the greater in that its impact extends beyond the single, unjust decision. As pointed out by Christopher Peters, its effects can be cumulative; a single erroneous court decision, if followed, becomes two erroneous decisions, then three, and soon a 'line' of cases. In this way *stare decisis* has the potential to import injustice irremediably into the law.[54]

---

[49] Lockhart, 'The Doctrine of Precedent', at 20.
[50] Mason, 'The Use and Abuse of Precedent', at 94.
[51] Ibid., at 94.   [52] Ibid., at 94–95.   [53] Ibid., at 94.
[54] C. J. Peters, 'Foolish Consistency: On Equality, Integrity and Justice in *Stare Decisis*' (1996) 105 Yale LJ 2031, at 2033–2034.

Unyielding adherence to precedent increases the difficulty of escape as precedent builds upon precedent.[55]

Frank has collected together numerous judicial statements in which judges acknowledge that they were inflicting injustices while claiming an inability to do anything about it because of a higher duty to follow precedent. Similar statements can be found on the other side of the Atlantic and on the under-side of the world. Frank branded this process 'a proud and dignified cruelty'.[56] Pious statements by judges claiming a higher duty to follow precedent notwithstanding their perception of where the justice of the case lies are, of course, heard less frequently today, but the danger nevertheless remains that judges fail to perceive the injustice, or remain indifferent to its harsh toll, for no other reason than their perceived or felt obligation to precedent. Institutional consistency can seldom if ever be permitted to outflank a consistent commitment to justice.

The 'attitude of mind'

Reference has already been made to Sir Anthony Mason's trenchant observation that, despite the relaxation of a strict doctrine of precedent as espoused by Cardozo as long ago as 1921, precedent has continued to exercise a constraining influence on the development of the law. As noted, Sir Anthony admits to the impression that sometimes precedent is transformed from a judicial policy into an 'attitude of mind'. He observes that at times there has been a tendency to apply non-binding decisions and dicta without making any attempt to analyse their worth – a tendency he perceives to be an abdication of the judicial function. It is, he states, one thing to apply a judicial opinion on a matter of law when the opinion has been accepted after consideration in a later case and in learned writing; it is another thing to blindly apply such an opinion when it has not been considered critically.[57]

I unhesitatingly concur in this perception. The danger and damage of precedent today is not the scope of the doctrine, as such, but the judicial attitude of mind it continues to engender. It is an attitude that walks hand in hand with formalism. This 'attitude of mind' extends to a judge's

---

[55] The Hon. Mr Justice C. S. C. Sheller, 'Pride and Precedent: Economic Loss – The Search for a New Bright Line' [1995] LMCLQ 203, at 203.
[56] Frank, *Courts on Trial*, at 266–267.
[57] Mason, 'The Use and Abuse of Precedent', at 106.

perception of the principle that underlies the cases cited in argument. In most instances, the principle may be drawn in narrow or in general terms. Precedent-minded judges will tend to define the principle narrowly. They will not wish to depart further than is absolutely necessary from the starting point provided by the existing body of rules. Because precedent tends to be fact-based, general principles are unappealing to such judges, and the principle that is extracted is unlikely to be released from the particular factual setting of the precedents that have been cited. It is true that there is a growing consensus among judges today that what is important is not precedents, as such, but the 'informing principle' that emerges from them. This growing consensus cannot result in a uniform approach, however, when the perception or definition of the relevant principle will vary depending on the attitude of the particular judge.

Concrete manifestations of this attitude of mind are readily evident. Judges with the commitment to precedent of which I speak are likely to perceive the absence of a direct precedent as fatal to a novel claim. The question to counsel is still heard from the bench during oral argument with the expectation that a negative answer will lead to its rejection: 'Mr or Ms So-and-so, can you cite an authority for that proposition?' The absence of a direct authority seems to dictate the law and thereby can tend to deflect the court from the principles or policy considerations in issue. To succumb to this approach, of course, reflects the 'never do anything for a first time' syndrome, and would allow the law to become unacceptably unresponsive to the demands and expectations of the community.

This negativity works most harshly on would-be plaintiffs. Plaintiffs are not required to point to a specific ruling authorising their cause of action in order to sustain a proceeding. They need only point to a general principle and seek to argue that the cause of action falls within its proper scope. In determining whether a cause of action should apply to apparently new circumstances, therefore, a judge whose unarticulated inclination is to adhere to the nearest proximate precedent as the only acceptable legal method will have a built-in resistance to extending a cause of action to a new set of facts. This built-in reluctance may prevail even though the facts may on any objective analysis give rise to the same principle.

Take, next, the influence of the doctrine of precedent on the attitude of a judge imbued with precedent when making a decision that they perceive may have precedential effect. Judges, particularly appellate judges, arrive at their decision in many cases in the knowledge that it will or may be treated as a precedent in the future. In this sense the doctrine of precedent operates prospectively. Present decisions are influenced by as yet undecided future cases. The way in which the rule in the present case is articulated is therefore likely to be defined or limited having regard to the judge's perception of the impact that the court's decision will have in the future. The judge will not wish to be responsible for an awkward or dangerous precedent or to open the door to a perceived undesirable trend.

This phenomenon is best illustrated by the not uncommon cases where it is necessary for the judge to 'draw the line', that is, to determine that a rule goes so far and no further. Justice Holmes has said: '[W]here to draw the line ... is the question in pretty much everything worth arguing in the law.'[58] The resulting closer definition or limitation of a rule arises because the decision-makers fear that it may be applied in circumstances that they have not contemplated. At a baser level, the present judges may distrust those who follow to contain the rule in the manner that they would like. It may be felt that their court, with all its wisdom, should not depend on that wisdom being perpetuated in a differently constituted court!

Two adverse consequences follow upon this reaction. The first is that judges may not 'draw the line' where it should be drawn so as to do justice in the instant case for fear of the wider unforeseen impact of the resulting rule. Better to confine the rule, it will be thought, than unleash an unpredictable beast. The second disadvantage is that, even if judges adapt the rule to suit the instant case, they will nevertheless over-define or unnecessarily restrict its stated scope for fear of its future impact. Subsequent judges are then confronted with a precedent that is narrower than it need be and one that may be difficult to apply to the facts of a later deserving case. With a more flexible system of precedent, a judge would know that later judges will not be unduly perturbed should his or her judgment not find enduring favour. It will be re-evaluated for its validity in the context of the later case.

Finally, the doctrine of precedent resulting in this attitude of mind will at times claim a subtle allegiance, even where the precedent is distinguished, explained or reinterpreted. As has been explained,[59] this influence occurs when the precedent, although ultimately rejected, nevertheless determines the structure or direction of the judge's reasoning. The issues, the selection of facts, what is important or not important, and the feature or features regarded as relevant may all be effectively defined by the discarded precedent.

---

[58] *Irwin v Gavit* 268 U.S. 161, at 168 (1925).   [59] See above at 152–153.

The immediate advantage of a more flexible use of precedent would be its indirect impact on judicial thinking and methodology. Rather than being unnecessarily coercive, or exerting its influence in engendering the attitude of mind of which I speak, precedent would be treated pragmatically on a case-by-case basis. Respect for the wisdom that may be garnered from past decisions would supplant a doctrine of precedent that proclaims a false wisdom for itself. Where one or other of the reasons that provide the rationale for *stare decisis* exists in the particular case, it would be given due weight. Thus, for example, a precedent would be likely to hold sway where a litigant had acted in reliance on a precedent or line of authority. Even then, however, that interest would be weighed against the requirements of contemporary conditions and the need to do justice in the instant case. In all cases the needs of stability, reliance interests and legitimacy would be balanced against the need to keep the rule relevant to contemporary requirements and community expectations and responsive to the demands of justice in the individual case.

The outcome of such a weakening in the lure of precedent would be significant. Precedent's close companion, formalism, or the lingering residue of formalism, would diminish and conceivably at long last disappear. Form would seldom, if ever, prevail over substance because a precedent would not prevail over reality. Absolute or near absolute rules embodied in a precedent would be shunned in preference for broad principles that could be applied without being retarded by the attitude based on unthinking deference to precedent. Case law would no longer be perceived to have its own coherence and intelligibility. The application of a precedent would be able to be approached pragmatically, so that the community's ability to order its affairs would be fully taken into consideration in the context of a particular case. But no precedent would be applied without regard to its merit and relevance.[60]

A desirable adjunct to this relaxation of precedent would be the need for judges to deliberately and consciously express the real reasons for their decisions. An extensive review of all the remotely relevant case law would be redundant and judicial transparency would be required

---

[60] See for a most refreshing article, B. V. Harris, 'Final Courts Overruling their Own "Wrong" Precedents: the Ongoing Search for Principle' [2002] 118 LQR 408. Harris concludes that a court should overrule its own precedent if it considers the precedent to be wrong unless the retention of the precedent can be justified by overriding *stare decisis* values. For a predictably purist, but essentially unrealistic and outdated response, see Jack Hodder, 'Departure from "Wrong" Precedents by Final Appellate Courts: Disagreeing with Professor Harris' [2003] NZLR 161.

whenever a prior decision is in point. The considerations that provide the rationale of *stare decisis*, and the factors that weigh against it, would be considered and the court's choice to favour or reject the decision explained. If an earlier decision is followed or applied, it would be necessary to clarify why it was considered relevant and valid in modern times. If a prior decision is not followed, it would be necessary to explain what had changed to bring about an alteration in the court's thinking. To be effective, the reasoning of the later decision will need to be superior to that of the precedent. In all respects, the judges would seek to consciously elaborate the actual reasons which led them to their decision and articulate the value judgement underlying that decision. In this way, the judiciary would be more accountable, and the judicial process would gain in integrity and legitimacy.

Conclusion

If the foregoing examination demonstrates anything, it demonstrates that Emerson got it right: 'A foolish consistency is the hobgoblin of little minds.' The notion that it is a superior judicial virtue to be consistent with a past decision and yet, at the same time, to be foolish in preferring that consistency is plain malarkey. I have acknowledged that it is through precedent that the bedrock principles propounded in the law are preserved, and that the process therefore confirms the presumption that the law is founded upon principles and not the proclivities of individuals.[61] But the doctrine of precedent, including *stare decisis*, is applied to cases well beyond those embracing bedrock principles. It serves to perpetuate the false presumption that there is an impersonal law. To adhere to precedent in all cases, therefore, is to transform *stare decisis* into what may be termed an 'imprisonment of reason'.[62]

I have not decried a role for precedent. Reference to past decisions can be immensely helpful. What is being challenged is the rigidity or effect of the coercive element in the doctrines of precedent and *stare decisis*. A legal process can garner the wisdom and experience of the past without committing itself to the perpetuation of the past. Stability in the law; protecting the interests of persons who have relied on existing case law; maintaining the legitimacy of the law and public confidence in the courts; safeguarding Parliament's legislative supremacy; and achieving

---

[61] *Vasquez v Hillery* 474 U.S. 254, at 265–266 (1986).
[62] *United States v International Boxing Club* 348 U.S. 236, at 249 (1955).

judicial efficiency, can all be realised without recourse to the coercive element in precedent presently peculiar to English law.

It is surprising that so many judges, lawyers and legal academics continue to discuss the validity and application of the doctrine of precedent as if the courts were constantly being confronted with authorities that were directly in point in the case in hand. Such a situation seldom arises. Perhaps the misconception has gained ground because at least one side's counsel will be disappointed at the outcome of the litigation and it is easier on the soul, and more compatible with client relations, to blame the court for not following the authorities that they had so diligently cited in argument than accept that they 'blew it'! In fact, of course, the analogical use of past cases is much more common. Rather than rely on a particular precedent, counsel endeavour to persuade the court that their argument accords with the pre-existing body of law as indicated in any number of cases.

Consequently, the major problem with the doctrine of precedent is not the direct application of a prior decision. I have utilised Sir Anthony Mason's phrase to identify that major problem; the doctrine has been transformed from a judicial policy into an 'attitude of mind'. In the language I have used in earlier chapters, this attitude of mind could equally have been described as a judicial preconception or predilection or, even, a prejudice. Irrespective of its label, the attitude means that, in the absence of a direct precedent, judges subject to this attitude are inclined to adhere as closely as possible to what is perceived to be the pre-existing body of law. They are prone to consciously or unconsciously 'never do anything for a first time'.[63] In the result, the development of the law is crimped and the aims of justice and relevance are relegated to an inferior role.

The major advantage of a more flexible use of precedent, therefore, would be its indirect impact on judicial thinking and methodology. It would come to be accepted that precedents need to be treated pragmatically on a case-by-case basis. A relevant authority would be reviewed and re-evaluated for its compatibility with justice and the current requirements of the community. It would have to 'earn its spurs', as it were. With the relaxation of the doctrine of precedent, formalism, or the lingering residue of formalism, would suffer a setback, and one that could conceivably be fatal. Principles rather than precedent would predominate in legal discourse and judicial reasoning.

---

[63] See above at 140.

Furthermore, the need to re-establish the validity and relevance of a precedent would require judges to deliberately and consciously express the real reasons for their decisions. The underlying value judgements would not be readily obscured by reference to and reliance upon a purportedly binding precedent or a strained interpretation of the existing law. Judicial transparency would be advanced and, with that transparency, judicial accountability would be improved. For the court's decision to be effective the reasoning adopted in that decision would need to be superior to that of the precedent. The integrity and legitimacy of the judicial process would be earned by the judiciary rather than conferred by an approach which, after all, was never more than a policy of the judiciary's own making.

7

The foibles of precedent – a case study

Lewis v Attorney-General of Jamaica

In *Lewis* v *Attorney-General of Jamaica*,[1] the Privy Council overruled five of its previous decisions in respect of three different issues. All but one of these decisions had been decided in the previous five years. *Lewis* v *Attorney-General of Jamaica* is, therefore, a suitable decision to discuss in the light of the points made, and the thesis advanced, in the previous chapter.

Consolidated appeals were brought before the Privy Council on behalf of six death row prisoners in Jamaica. Five other death row prisoners in Belize, and the Attorney-General of Trinidad and the Bahamas, were given leave to intervene.

The first of the three issues was whether the Jamaican Privy Council, which is obliged by section 91 of the Constitution to advise the Governor-General on the prerogative of mercy, is required to disclose to the prisoner the information it has received pursuant to that section and to hear representations from the prisoner. These questions had been decided in the negative in *Reckley* v *Minister of Public Safety and Immigration (No. 2)*,[2] when the Board followed and applied its previous decision in *de Freitas* v *Benny*.[3] The second issue was whether it would be lawful to execute a sentence of death while a petition that the prisoner was lawfully permitted to make to the Inter-American Commission on Human Rights (IACHR) of the Organization of American States and the United Nations Human Rights Committee (UNHRC) remained under consideration. The Privy Council had decided in *Fisher* v *Minister of Public Safety and Immigration (No. 2)*,[4] and more recently in *Higgs* v *Minister of National Security*,[5] by majorities of three to two in each case, that the execution could proceed notwithstanding that the IACHR's

---

[1] [2001] 2 AC 50. [2] [1996] AC 527. [3] [1976] AC 239.
[4] [2000] 1 AC 434. [5] [2000] 2 AC 228.

determination of a petition to it from the prisoner had not been received. The third issue was whether the execution of the sentence of death is unlawful when the prisoner, while in detention, had been subjected to treatment that was unlawful or unconstitutional. It had been decided in *Thomas v Baptiste*,[6] and in *Higgs v Minister of National Security*, that, save in exceptional circumstances, prison conditions amounting to cruel and unusual treatment in violation of a prisoner's constitutional rights would not make the sentences imposed upon the prisoner unconstitutional.

For the purposes of discussion, my focus will be on the first two issues. Common to both issues is the question whether or not the procedure set out in the Constitutions of the various American Island States preceding the exercise of the prerogative of mercy is justiciable or reviewable by a court of law. Both issues depend on whether or not the precepts of fairness and natural justice apply to that constitutional procedure. If they do, then the argument is compelling that the advisory bodies reporting to the Governors-General of those States must make information they have received available to the prisoners, and then receive and consider representations from the prisoners. So, too, the requirement that the execution process be delayed pending the receipt of reports of the international bodies would seem inevitable. *Stare decisis* undoubtedly posed an obstacle to the reconsideration of this basic question.

A majority of the Board comprising Lords Slynn, Nicholls, Steyn and Hutton accepted that they should not depart from the Board's earlier decisions unless they were satisfied that the earlier cases had been wrongly decided. Lord Slynn, speaking for the majority, stated that the 'need for legal certainty demands that they [the Board] should be very reluctant to depart from recent fully reasoned decisions unless there are strong grounds to do so'.[7] 'But', he added, 'no less should they be prepared to do so when a man's life is at stake, where the death penalty is involved, if they are satisfied that the earlier cases adopted a wrong approach'. 'In such a case', he said, 'rigid adherence to a rule of *stare decisis* is not justified.'[8] Lord Hoffmann, who had been a member of the unanimous Board in *Reckley*, a member of the majority of three in *Fisher*, and the author of the judgment of the majority of three in *Higgs*, delivered a strong dissenting judgment essentially based on the principle of *stare decisis*. 'The fact', he said, 'that the Board has the power to depart from earlier decisions does not mean that there are no

[6] [2000] 2 AC 1.   [7] Above n. 1, at 75.   [8] Ibid.

principles which should guide it in deciding whether to do so.'[9] He complained that, if the Board felt able to depart from a previous decision simply because its members on a given occasion have a 'doctrinal disposition to come out differently, the rule of law itself would be damaged and there will be no stability in the administration of justice in the Caribbean.'[10] Lord Hoffmann postulated that the decision in *Lewis* could be reversed by a differently constituted Board in a future case.

Does this mean that the majority in *Lewis* were precluded from departing from the earlier precedents? Obviously, it is asking a lot of *stare decisis* to expect a judge to adhere to the decided cases in a matter involving the life or death of eleven persons if that judge genuinely believes that the earlier cases were wrongly decided. I shall, however, defer for the moment an examination of the reasoning of the Board to make a preliminary point.

Lewis demonstrates that the legal process can be insatiably fortuitous. In *Lewis*, the lives of eleven prisoners sentenced to death were spared because the majority were prepared to eschew a legalistic approach and depart from precedent. With a differently constituted Board, however, the decision could well have been different, and the prisoners would have been expeditiously put to their death. The earlier case of *Higgs* provides a concrete example of the importance of the court's make-up in any given appeal. The majority in *Higgs* comprised Lords Hoffmann and Hobhouse and Henry J from New Zealand. The minority were Lords Steyn and Cooke. I regard the reasoning of the minority Law Lords as markedly superior. Consequently, had I been sitting on the Privy Council in the place of Henry J,[11] Mr Higgs would not have been executed.

In ultimately determining the procedure or rules by which the death penalty is administered in the American Island States, the death penalty is perceived as receiving the sanction of one of the most developed civilisations in the world. Many persons would consider it bad enough that the death penalty should receive the apparent imprimatur of the United Kingdom, without that imprimatur being so patently dependent on the particular composition of the Board hearing an appeal. In such circumstances, at least, the relevance and application of the doctrine of precedent needed to be thoroughly rethought.

But this preliminary point skirts the real issue, namely, whether it was open to the majority of the Board in *Lewis* to overrule the previous

---

[9] Ibid., at 89.   [10] Ibid., at 90.
[11] The author has been a member of the Privy Council since 19 November 1996.

decisions without impairing the doctrine of precedent. Because I contend for a less rigid application of precedent, I believe that it was open to them to do so. Reference to the earlier decisions reveals that the reasoning in those decisions was unduly legalistic. This undue legalism is not evident in the reasoning of the minority in *Fisher*, *Higgs* and the majority in *Lewis*. What emerges is a different approach reflecting a different methodology; the one a more legalistic and case-bound formalism, the other a more principled approach fully alert to the fundamental human rights involved.

Consequently, to limit the discussion of precedent to *Lewis* would be incomplete. *Lewis* was the culmination of the earlier cases representing an inevitable change in the direction of the Privy Council's thinking. Precedent had led the Board astray well before counsel for the prisoners stood up in *Lewis* and sought to persuade their Lordships to depart from the earlier decisions. The wayward path started with *de Freitas v Benny*.

de Freitas was decided in 1975. The prisoner's appeal caused no difficulty to the Board. Indeed, their Lordships did not trouble respondent's counsel to address them. Lord Diplock, delivering the decision of the Board, held[12] that the exercise of the royal prerogative of mercy in Trinidad and Tobago remained the same as it was in England at common law. At common law, the prerogative had always been a matter that lay solely in the discretion of the sovereign. So would it be in Trinidad and Tobago. In an aphorism, which was eventually to be rejected in *Lewis*, Lord Diplock stated: 'Mercy is not the subject of legal rights. It begins where legal rights end.' Under the Constitution of those countries, the Governor-General was required to exercise his prerogative on the advice of a Minister. The Advisory Committee set up for that purpose remained a purely consultative body without any decision-making power. Their Lordships held that its functions were, in their nature, purely discretionary and not capable of being converted 'into functions that are in any sense quasi-judicial'.[13]

The decision was applied in *Reckley*, twenty-one years later. The prisoner's counsel[14] made a strong plea that *de Freitas* was no longer good law and that the prerogative of mercy was by then justiciable. Counsel submitted that the constitutional prerogative power of mercy was subject to the constraints of fairness, and that a condemned man must have, at least, the right to procedural fairness in relation to the way

---

[12] Above n. 3, at 247–248. [13] Ibid., at 248. [14] Above n. 2, at 530–531.

in which the prerogative was exercised. Consequently, the Minister and the Advisory Committee must weigh all the information.

Lord Goff, speaking for the Board, observed that these submissions immediately faced the difficulty that they were contrary to the decision of the Privy Council in *de Freitas*.[15] The Board affirmed that the prerogative of mercy was not justiciable. Lord Diplock's aphorism in *de Freitas*, that mercy is not the subject of legal rights but begins where legal rights end, was expressly endorsed.[16] In the course of its decision, the Board referred[17] to the 'valuable views' of Cooke P to the opposite effect in relation to the exercise of the power of pardon in *Burt v Governor-General*.[18] These valuable views were dismissed by the Board[19] on the basis that they were obiter, that they were tentatively expressed, that the legislation was different, and that they were not directly concerned with the reviewability of the exercise of the prerogative of mercy in a death sentence case. As we have seen, making such points as these to banish an unwanted decision is a standard judicial technique, but it should not be overlooked that it is a technique that enabled the Board to avoid confronting Cooke P's reasoning. The proverbial man, or woman, from Mars with the advantage of objectivity would surely think that the Board's points, particularly in the context of a case involving life and death, bordered on the frivolous. 'What games,' the Martian would say, 'these earthly judges play.'

Of the decisions under consideration, the Board's judgment in *Reckley* is the most disappointing. Their Lordships' thinking was undoubtedly confined by the decision in *de Freitas*. Much of their reasoning is a defence and repetition of that decision. Precedent obviously held sway. Administrative law, however, had advanced markedly in the intervening twenty-one years. The classification of powers into judicial, quasi-judicial, and administrative had fallen into disuse, the overriding requirement being that a power must be exercised fairly and in accordance with the principles of natural justice. The notion that there are some areas of discretionary decision-making that are non-justiciable was in retreat. In particular, the House of Lords had held in *Council of Civil Service Unions v Minister for the Civil Service*[20] that the exercise of a prerogative power was not immune from judicial review. Thus, the issues in *de Freitas* needed to be reconsidered in accordance with current and developing principles of administrative law. Instead, the 'attitude of mind'

---

[15] Ibid., at 537.   [16] Ibid., at 540.   [17] Ibid., at 541.   [18] [1992] 3 NZLR 672.
[19] Above n. 2, at 541.   [20] [1985] AC 374.

generated by the doctrine of precedent and *stare decisis* prevailed. A bad decision, which was possibly explicable in terms of the principles of administrative law that had pertained at the time, was cemented into the law by a decision out of step with the current tenets and direction of administrative law and the emerging importance of human rights.

Fisher was decided in 1998. Lords Lloyd, Hoffmann and Hutton constituted the majority. Argument focused on Articles 16 and 17 of the Bahamas' Constitution, which provided that no person was to be deprived intentionally of his or her life, save in execution of the sentence of the Court on conviction for a criminal offence, or subjected to 'inhuman or degrading treatment or punishment'. It was not in dispute that the prisoner had the right to petition the IACHR, and that the Government accepted that it had a responsibility to consider the recommendations of that international body. The majority of the Law Lords in *Fisher* held, however, that there was no express provision in the Constitution that a person had a right to life pending the determination of a petition to the IACHR, and that no such right should be implied. To imply a constitutional right to obtain the IACHR's report before carrying out the death sentence, they considered,[21] would be to give direct domestic effect to an international treaty that had not been incorporated in domestic law by legislation. In arriving at this finding, the majority followed *R v Secretary of State for the Home Department, ex parte Brind*,[22] which had held that the right to petition the IACHR could not be enforced by a prisoner facing execution.

Lords Slynn and Hope dissented. Their Lordships pointed out that for the government to carry out the death sentence while still awaiting a recommendation that might, when considered, lead to its commutation to a sentence of life imprisonment would seem in itself to be an obvious violation of the prisoner's right to life.[23] Moreover, the prisoner had spent a further nine months in a condemned cell for no other purpose than to await the recommendation of the IACHR. As such, to be executed prior to the recommendation being received would constitute 'inhuman treatment'. Their Lordships asserted that it was hard to imagine a more obvious denial of human rights than to execute a man, after many months of waiting for the result, while his case was still under legitimate consideration by an international human rights body. They concluded that a 'legalistic' interpretation should give way to

---

[21] Above n. 4, at 445.   [22] [1991] 1 AC 696.   [23] Above n. 4, at 452.

an interpretation that protects the individual from such treatment and respects his human rights.[24]

Although counsel for the prisoner had requested the Board 'as a last resort' to reconsider *Reckley*,[25] the majority cited that decision without disapproval.[26] Even the minority's argument was restricted to the interpretation of the relevant articles in the Constitution. Precedent had, it seemed, set the bounds of tenable argument.

Thomas v *Baptiste* followed in 1999. Section 4(a) of the Constitution of Trinidad and Tobago included a due process clause that precluded a person's life being taken without that person being accorded procedural fairness. The Board held[27] that due process required access to the IACHR and, while it would be lawful for the Government to provide an overall time limit for the completion of such international processes, the measures that had been adopted in that case curtailed the prisoner's right not to have the legal process pre-empted by executive action.

To reach this decision the Board had to confront and circumvent the decision in *Brind*. It did so by arguing[28] that the prisoners were not seeking directly to enforce the right to petition the IACHR, but rather a 'general right accorded to all litigants not to have the outcome of any pending appellate or other legal process pre-empted by executive action.'[29] That right, it said, did not derive from the treaty in issue, but it was a right accorded by the common law and affirmed by section 4(a) of the Constitution. The majority noted that a similar argument had been rejected in *Fisher*. In the time-honoured fashion of precedent, however, their Lordships chose to distinguish that case on the narrow ground that the Constitution of the Bahamas under consideration in *Fisher* did not include a due process clause similar to that contained in section 4(a) of the Constitution of Trinidad and Tobago. It was, of course, an artificial argument designed to avoid treating *Fisher* as a direct precedent. It was a distinction without a difference destined to be rejected in both *Higgs* and *Lewis* – but for quite different reasons.

Fisher was, however, applied in *Higgs*. *Higgs*, decided in the same year, again on the question whether the execution was required to be stayed until the finding, report and recommendations from the IACHR were available. Lord Hoffmann said[30] that the majority could find nothing that materially distinguished the case from *Fisher*. The scope of *Thomas* v *Baptiste* on this point was then restricted on the basis that

---

[24] Ibid.   [25] Ibid., at 441.   [26] Ibid., at 447.   [27] Above n. 6, at 20–21 and 23–24.
[28] Ibid., at 23.   [29] Ibid.   [30] Above n. 5, at 243.

the due process clause in the Constitution of Trinidad and Tobago gave the Crown power to accept an international jurisdiction as part of the domestic criminal justice system. 'It is not for their Lordships to say whether this was right or wrong', said Lord Hoffmann.[31] But it was, he said, not possible without throwing the law on the subject into a state of total uncertainty to do otherwise than apply the distinction that the Board had drawn in *Fisher*. Moreover, it was a very recent decision of the Board and was precisely in point. Their Lordships did not think it would be right to reopen it unless they were obliged to do so by precedent or unless they were satisfied that it was wrong. Further, the majority declined to accept[32] that the Constitution prohibited the infliction of treatment or punishment in addition to the penalty of death unless the abuses in prison 'were connected with the sentence of death' and objectively aggravated that sentence.

In a dissenting judgment, Lord Steyn expressed the compassionate view[33] that locking prisoners up for seventy-two hours every weekend, week after week, without any opportunity to exercise, was inhuman treatment. *Thomas* v *Baptiste* then had to be distinguished on this point. Working within accepted methodology the distinguished Law Lord pointed out[34] that the dicta to the contrary in that case had not been made with the express approval of three members of the Board; that, in any event, Trinidad and Tobago had a differently worded constitutional guarantee, namely, one directed against torture and cruel and unusual punishment; and that the important decision in *Conjwayo* v *Minister of Justice, Legal and Parliamentary Affairs*,[35] a decision of the Constitutional Court of South Africa, had not been cited to the Board in that case.

Also dissenting, Lord Cooke took a broader view seeking to acknowledge the reality of appeals in death penalty cases.[36] The right of every human being not to be subjected to inhuman treatment was a right inherent in the concept of civilisation recognised rather than created in any number of international human rights instruments. Whenever a violation of such a right is in issue the court will not fulfil its function without a careful examination of the facts of each individual case and a global assessment of the treatment in question. Commonly, Lord Cooke said, decisions in this field are findings of fact and degree, not expositions of law. If more than one assessment is open, the choice made is not

---

[31] Ibid., at 246.   [32] Ibid., at 247–248.   [33] Ibid., at 259.   [34] Ibid., at 257.
[35] 1992 (2) SA 56.   [36] Above n. 5, at 260–261.

one of law or legal principle but one of evaluation. The learned Law Lord observed that, although the decision might properly have some influence on a later court faced with somewhat similar facts and anxious to achieve consistency of results, it could not be a binding precedent. He stated: 'To subscribe to a contrary doctrine of precedent would be to insist on the "austerity of tabulated legalism".'

Lord Cooke concluded by observing[37] that majorities and responses to broadly similar factual situations vary in the Judicial Committee as in other appellate courts. There were, he pointed out, no small number of members of the Privy Council who, over the years and not always in majority judgments, had taken a view of what humanity requires in capital punishment cases. Lord Cooke hoped his opinion conformed to that spirit. In the end result, Lord Cooke predicted, it would prevail.

Ultimately, of course, that spirit did prevail in *Lewis*. The majority of the law Lords in *Lewis* held[38] that the prerogative should, in the light of Jamaica's international obligations, be exercised by procedures that are fair and proper and amenable to judicial review. They further held that, in considering what natural justice required, it is relevant to have regard to international human rights norms laid down in treaties to which Jamaica is a party, despite the fact that they might not be independently enforceable in domestic law. Secondly, the majority held[39] that, where the State assented to treaties that allowed individuals to petition international human rights bodies, the protection of the law conferred by the Constitution entitled a prisoner to complete that procedure, and to obtain the reports of such bodies for consideration by the Jamaican Privy Council before the application for mercy is determined.

Lord Slynn reaffirmed[40] the proposition that the merits of the exercise of the prerogative of mercy are not for the court to review. He noted that the insistence by the courts on the observance of the rules of natural justice – of 'fair play in action' – had in recent years been marked even before, but particularly since, decisions such as *Council of Civil Service Unions v Minister for the Civil Service*.[41] There is no clear-cut distinction as to procedural matters between mercy and legal rights that Lord Diplock's aphorism (that mercy begins where legal rights end) might indicate. Moreover, Lord Slynn continued, there are many areas in which the exercise of the prerogative is subject to judicial review.[42] His Lordship then moved to the essence of the majority's thinking. It was

---

[37] Ibid., at 263.   [38] Above n. 1, at 75–80.   [39] Ibid., at 84–85.   [40] Ibid., at 75.
[41] Above n. 20.   [42] Above n. 11, at 75–79.

their Lordships' view that 'the act of clemency is to be seen as part of the whole constitutional process of conviction, sentence and the carrying out of the sentence.'[43] Their Lordships noted that the penalty of death was mandatory in capital cases, the sentencing judge having no discretion.[44] The clemency process allowed the fixed penalty to be dispensed with, and the punishment modified, in order to deal with the facts of a particular case so as to provide an acceptable and just result.

With respect to the question whether the Governor-General should be obliged to wait for the report and recommendations of the IACHR, the majority had to confront the argument that a positive answer would be inconsistent with *Fisher* and *Higgs*, and an extension of *Thomas v Baptiste*. Again, the majority declined to take a narrow or legalistic view. Section 13 of the Constitution of Jamaica provides that every person in that country is entitled to the fundamental right, without discrimination, to 'the protection of the law'. Their Lordships held that the phrase, 'the protection of the law', covered the same ground as the entitlement to 'due process' in *Fisher*.[45] Thus, when Jamaica acceded to the American Convention and the International Covenant and allowed individual petitions, prisoners became entitled under the protection of section 13 to complete the human rights petition procedure and to obtain the reports of the human rights bodies for the Jamaican Privy Council to consider before it dealt with the application for mercy. The execution was to be stayed until those reports had been received and considered.

An assessment, a rebuke and a note of optimism

The basic perception that carried the majority to the conclusion that the principles of natural justice applied to the function of the Jamaican Privy Council is compelling. This perception is that the prerogative of mercy has a firm basis and role in the Constitution. Clemency is the final step in the constitutional process that begins with the conviction of the accused and ends with the mandatory death sentence. Indeed, I would suggest that, to the extent that the prerogative of mercy is a constitutional safeguard, it is the final step in a process that begins with the arrest of the prisoner and ends with the execution of the sentence. Procedural fairness must apply to that entire constitutional process, including the procedure provided in relation to the exercise of the prerogative of mercy. It is this core perception that is lacking in *Rickley*, *Fisher*, and

---

[43] Ibid., at 77.   [44] Ibid., at 78.   [45] Ibid., at 48–49.

Higgs. In these circumstances, and for the reasons to which I have adverted, it was not necessary for the Board in *Lewis* to follow the earlier cases. As Lord Cooke said, to insist on adherence to precedent would be to insist on the 'austerity of tabulated legalism'. Indeed, it would have made a parody of precedent as a respectable judicial doctrine.

I would, however, base my conclusion that the Board in *Lewis* was entitled to review the earlier cases and overrule them on more than the fact that the death penalty was involved and that a number of persons' lives were at stake. In the first place, it is telling that the majority in *Lewis* were seized of a compelling perception of the constitutional process relating to the execution of the death sentence, concluding with the prerogative of mercy, that had seemingly escaped the Board in the previous cases. That perception cannot properly be subjugated to precedent. Secondly, I would emphasise that the restricted view of procedural fairness underlying the previous decisions could no longer be regarded as sufficient to meet the universally endorsed expectations of fundamental human rights. If human rights are to mean anything, precedents set prior to that universal endorsement must be subject to review. Thirdly, I would focus on the Board's decision in *Reckley*. It is not good enough to look at *Lewis* alone and, in the name of precedent and *stare decisis* cry 'foul'. The true 'foul' occurred in *Reckley* when the Board failed to reconsider the issue in *de Freitas* afresh having regard to the significant developments that had taken place in administrative law. There must be a point at which an appellate court is entitled, and even obliged, to ensure that a bad precedent is not perpetuated in the law. Fourthly, I would frankly acknowledge the different judicial methodology. The reasoning of the majority in *Lewis* evidences an approach different from that evidenced by the reasoning of the Board or the majorities in the previous cases. The more legalistic approach in those cases had to defer at some stage to the inexorable trend away from formalism. That trend cannot at times be securely advanced without departing from precedent. In other words, a discernible and acknowledged trend must be permitted to outweigh the coercive element in the doctrine of precedent.

Finally, I would endorse the insight of Lord Cooke in *Higgs*. It is unwise and unproductive to seek to reduce every issue to an exposition of law. What is required is a close examination of the facts of each case and a 'global assessment' to resolve what is essentially a question of fact and degree. As Lord Cooke has pointed out, the choice, where there is a choice, is not one of law or legal principle but one of evaluation.

A mature system of law cannot deny the need for such evaluation. When made, as made by Lords Steyn and Cooke in *Higgs*, the decision can be informed by the spirit of what humanity requires in capital punishment cases. Again, precedent must give way to the inexorable march of that spirit.

Incontrovertibly, the cases from *de Freitas* v *Benny* to *Lewis* make up a sorry saga demonstrating at one stage or another most of the shortcomings of precedent. In *de Freitas*, existing authorities were all too quickly applied to the Constitution in issue when a more fundamental examination of the critical function of the prerogative of mercy in the scheme of that Constitution was required. As a precedent it was overtaken by other developments in administrative law but was nonetheless followed and applied in *Reckley*. Judicial rationalisation is plain to see, made necessary because the process lacked the flexibility to be relevant. A bad decision was cemented into the law. The penury of the approach of the House of Lords in this case may be contrasted with the approach of the Supreme Court of Canada in *United States* v *Burns* in which the Court revisited a number of earlier decisions and expressly referred to evolving international attitudes to the death penalty.[46] Precedent then allowed the majority in *Fisher* to adopt a 'legalistic' approach that seemingly impaired their ability to have regard to the impact of universally recognised human rights. *Reckley* was not questioned. Precedent set the bounds of the Board's reasoning. With a differently constituted Board, *Thomas* v *Baptiste* represented a departure, although limited, from the enduring premise that legal rights did not attach to the exercise of the prerogative of mercy or the constitutional procedure provided for its exercise. The Board, however, had to 'distinguish' *Fisher* on narrow and artificial grounds that were ultimately to prove unsustainable. *Fisher* was then firmly reinstated by the majority in *Higgs*. They sought to interpret – or reinterpret – what the Board said in *Thomas* v *Baptiste* to avoid any precedential force that decision might have had.

Throughout this process, the hallmarks of the traditional approach to precedent or *stare decisis* are readily apparent. A tendency to adopt formalistic or legalistic reasoning; interpreting and reinterpreting prior decisions so as to 'distinguish' them; adverting to what must seem to any outsider to be peripheral points in order to circumvent earlier decisions that are in the way; blindly and unrealistically appealing to the notion that following precedents without questioning their validity and relevance somehow achieves certainty and predictability in the law;

---

[46] [2001] SCC 7.

and time and time again demonstrating thinking confined within boundaries set by the earlier cases. All of this judicial rationalisation and obfuscation served to obscure the essential issue in those cases.

This sorry saga does not flatter the Privy Council and the senior Law Lords who occupy that tenure. Their Lordships are jurists of notable intellect. Why, then, did they surrender to a discipline that, objectively viewed, proved to be anything but a discipline? They did so for a very simple reason. They strained to work within the bounds of the doctrine of precedent and *stare decisis* and were, as a consequence, diverted from squarely considering and addressing the critical question as to the function of the prerogative of mercy in the Constitutions of the American Island States. Their logic was the perverse logic of formalism incorporating, as it does, an excessively strict doctrine of precedent. The approach which the Law Lords exhibited until *Lewis* was the very 'attitude of mind' that I have sought to demonstrate is generated by precedent. It continues to possess a coercive element that will from time to time disfigure the law.

But all is not bleak. After all, the majority in *Lewis* did resist the siren call of precedent. The disfiguring attitude of mind was arrested, and the enlightened approach which was adopted gives some cause for optimism that the formalistic approach, although not routed, is in retreat.

Postscript; don't speak too soon!

After the manuscript of this book had been submitted to the publisher, the Privy Council delivered three related decisions in which the constitutional validity of the mandatory death penalty for murder in three of the American Island States was challenged.[47] The Board to hear the appeals was enlarged to nine members. In the two appeals, which it is necessary to touch upon, *Charles Matthew v The State of Trinidad and Tobago*[48] and *Lennox Ricardo Boyce and Jeffrey Joseph v The State of Barbados*,[49] a majority of five upheld the constitutional validity of the mandatory death penalty.[50] Although the issue therefore differed from the question in issue in *Lewis*, it is apparent that the enlightened and

---

[47] In the interim, a case note by the author based on the text of this Postscript has been published; (2005) 121 LQR, 175.
[48] Privy Council Appeal No. 12 of 2004.
[49] Privy Council Appeal No. 99 of 2002.
[50] The third appeal was *Lambert Watson v The State of Jamaica*, Privy Council Appeal No. 36 of 2003. Because of the particular wording of the Constitution, the appeal was allowed.

forward-looking spirit that permeated the majority judgments in that case has taken a setback in these more recent appeals.

The majority comprised Lords Hoffmann, Hope, Scott and Rodger and Mr Justice Zacca, a retired Chief Justice of Jamaica. The minority comprised Lords Bingham, Nicholls, Steyn and Walker. Lord Hoffmann delivered the judgments of the majority in both cases. The joint judgment of the minority in *Matthew* was supported by a strongly worded separate judgment by Lord Nicholls. Addressing the judgments is made marginally awkward by virtue of the fact that the majority delivered their main judgment in *Boyce* and the minority their main dissenting judgment in *Matthew*. It is convenient, however, to refer to the Constitution and provisions that were pertinent in the latter judgment and only refer to dicta in the former should that prove helpful.

It is not possible, however, to examine the decision in detail. In essence, the Constitution of Trinidad and Tobago provided that Parliament could not impose or authorise the imposition of cruel and unusual treatment or punishment.[51] Existing laws were protected from invalidation.[52] But section 5(1) of the Constitution of the Republic of Trinidad and Tobago Act 1976, which gave effect to the Constitution and to which the Constitution was appended as a schedule, provided that existing laws 'shall be construed with such modification, qualifications, adaptations and exceptions as may be necessary to bring them into conformity with this Act.'[53] The law proscribing the mandatory death penalty which was under challenge was an existing law.

It was common ground that the arbitrary nature of a mandatory sentence of death rendered it cruel and unusual punishment contrary to the Constitution. Again, it was agreed that the power in section 5(1) to modify an existing law was a wide power permitting the courts to effectively rectify a defect in a statutory provision so as to make it conform to the Constitution. It was also acknowledged that the law proscribing the mandatory death penalty placed the States in breach of a number of obligations contained in international covenants to which they were signatories. The Universal Declaration of Human Rights and the International Covenant for Civil and Political Rights were two such instruments.

In his judgment for the majority, Lord Hoffmann adopted the traditional approach to statutory interpretation and declined to apply section

---

[51] Section 5(2)(b) of the Constitution.   [52] Section 6(1) of the Constitution.
[53] Section 5(1) of the Constitution of the Republic of Trinidad and Tobago Act 1976.

5(1) and so modify the law to make it conform to the constitutional right to be protected from cruel or unusual punishment. No such interpretation, it was held, could have been intended by Parliament. Section 5(1) was not part of the supreme law contained in the Constitution and was necessarily subservient to the constitutional provision placing existing laws beyond challenge. If section 5(1) were to be invoked as sought by the appellant, an impugned provision would be saved where a modification was possible but not where the wording would not permit such a modification. The majority rejected the notion that the framers of the Constitution could have wished to install such an 'arbitrarily incomplete mechanism' for securing conformity between existing laws and the Constitution.[54] The contrary interpretation, ultimately accepted by the minority, was denounced in many terms, but relaying one will suffice to convey the chasm between the two encampments; the interpretation was described as 'unreasonable to the point of being perverse'.[55]

The minority replied with equal vigour clearly viewing the majority's approach as legalistic and over-literal and evidencing 'the austerity of tabulated legalism'.[56] They accepted that the majority's interpretation was a possible reading of the Constitution, but preferred an approach that would give full recognition to the guarantee of human rights that the people had intended to embed in their Constitution.[57] To this end, their Lordships made a point of reading section 5(1) together with the relevant provisions of the Constitution. The Constitution is approached as a 'living tree'[58] and, in effect if not so many words, the same living dynamic is attributed to section 5(1). The minority were therefore able to conclude that the provision providing the mandatory death penalty could be modified, or rectified, so as to confer a discretion on the sentencing judge to decide whether or not to impose the death penalty.

The different judicial approaches could not be more marked. The one inclines to a more legalistic, literal and conservative approach; the other to a more expansive and creative approach informed by a conscious

---

[54] Paragraph 38 in *Boyce*.
[55] Paragraph 54 in *Boyce*. Lord Hoffman's observation in *Boyce* (at para. 59) in defending the majority's approach that if it 'provokes accusations of literalism, originalism and similar heresies, their Lordships must bear them as best they can' has about it an unchallengeable and unsettling certitude, as well as shades of Asquith LJ's famous rebuke to Lord Denning, the Master of the Rolls, in *Candler v Crane, Christmas* & *Co* [1951] 2 KB 164, at 195. But, of course, Lord Asquith was right in projecting himself as a 'timorous soul'; see *Hedley Byrne & Co Ltd v Heller & Palmer Ltd* [1964] AC 465.
[56] Paragraph 34 in *Matthew*.   [57] Paragraph 78 in *Boyce*.   [58] Paragraph 42 in *Matthew*.

perception of the value of fundamental human rights and human dignity and the courts' responsibility to ensure the protection of those rights and that dignity. It is essentially a difference reflecting the difference between a formalistic and non-formalistic approach, and it is that basic difference that underlies and ultimately determines the outcome of their Lordships' alignment on the question in issue.

A less doctrinaire approach than that taken by the majority is required. Section 5(1) of the 1976 Act may not be included in the Constitution itself but it is not alien to it. It is contained in the Act giving effect to the Constitution and, in substance, it bears upon the rights and freedoms of vulnerable human beings and the measure to which those rights and freedoms are secured. Although not in the Constitution itself, section 5(1) is undoubtedly vested with constitutional significance.

The true status or function of section 5(1) can be tested by assuming for a moment that the section appeared in the Constitution itself (as is the case in some of the Constitutions of other American Island States). There can be little doubt that the minority's opinion would then prevail. The provision in the Constitution providing that an existing law shall not be invalidated could not be interpreted and reconciled with a section worded as section 5(1) is worded, but having the status of supreme law, in any other way. The same asserted 'irrationality' or 'arbitrariness' stressed at length throughout the judgment of the majority would still be present. But it is unthinkable that an overt provision of the Constitution providing a power of modification designed to ensure the protection of fundamental human rights and freedoms would or could be effectively read out of existence. Existing laws would, to use Lord Hoffmann's term, still be 'immunised' from constitutional challenge on the ground that they were unconstitutional, but the power to modify any existing law to ensure conformity with the Constitution would need to be given effect. The only reconciliation possible would be the interpretation contended for by their Lordships in the minority.

Consequently, having regard to the fact that a basic human right, the right to life, and a basic prohibition, the right not to be subject to cruel and unusual punishment, was at stake, it would seem but a modest step to read section 5(1) together with the pertinent provisions of the Constitution. Put another way, the refusal to invoke section 5(1), essentially because it is in the Act giving effect to the Constitution rather than the Constitution itself, would seem to be a mean-spirited response to the grave responsibility inherent in the constitutional task confronting the Board.

It is to be noted that the only legislative intention relating to section 5(1) that could be posited was a presumed or purported intention. In enacting section 5(1) the Parliament of Trinidad and Tobago must necessarily have contemplated that there would be occasions when it would be appropriate to modify existing laws so that they would conform to the Constitution. That much is certain. It is doubtful, however, that the Parliament ever directed its mind to whether section 5(1) should be utilised to rectify any specific law, including the mandatory death penalty. Even if it had, values had changed with time. In 1976 when the Constitution was given effect, the mandatory death penalty was not generally regarded as cruel or unusual punishment, certainly in the American Island States. The Parliament of Trinidad and Tobago, therefore, never had to direct its mind to the situation where that punishment might be considered cruel and inhumane and its imposition a breach of a fundamental right. Yet, it was accepted by the majority, as well as the minority, that the arbitrary death penalty was cruel and unusual punishment and contrary to the Constitution. This changed perception of the death penalty had come about as a result of a widespread change in human values and the treatment of a constitution as a 'living instrument' to reflect those changing values. Not only, therefore, should the same 'living' dynamic be accorded a provision such as section 5(1), but it should also be fully appreciated that the 'intention' to be attributed to the legislature in relation to the status or function of section 5(1) is necessarily a judicial construct. There is no sound reason why the majority should not have started from the basis that the modern and unchallenged view of what constitutes cruel and unusual punishment had rendered Parliament's 'intention' in relation to section 5(1) largely otiose and that, in those circumstances, it was incumbent upon the Board to exercise the power of modification contained in that section to bring the offending provision into line with the fundamental rights and freedoms protected, and intended to be protected, in the Constitution.

Before their Lordships in the majority adopted what was essentially a conventional interpretative approach, the standard precepts and principles of statutory interpretation required overt re-examination in the context of the interpretation of constitutions.[59] No magic can be attached to the notion that the courts' task is one of 'interpretation' when the protection

---

[59] To some extent the same may be said of the interpretation of bills of right, but it is prudent to adhere to the constitutional context of the cases under discussion where an

of the fundamental rights guaranteed citizens in a constitution requires, at the very least, what Professors MacCormick and Summers have described as 'interpretation of a far reaching kind'.[60] Where fundamental human rights are involved, it is no longer sufficient to look for an ambiguity in the language before being prepared to adopt a meaning which is consistent with the protection of those rights and freedoms. The outcome should not turn on the draftperson's competence or incompetence in expressing Parliament's intention or otherwise avoiding ambiguities. Nor, where Parliament cannot be said to have had any ascertainable intention in the circumstances which have arisen or in the light of changed values in the community, is it satisfactory to impose a purported or presumed intention on that Parliament. In such circumstances, the judicial compunction to search for the legislature's intention in the wording of the statute when the lives of people and their fundamental rights are at stake is deficient. Rather than focusing on the intention of Parliament in respect of the impugned provision, the focus should be on the antecedent intention manifest in the provisions of the constitution itself. That overpowering intention reflects the citizens' insistence on being secure in the enjoyment of the fundamental rights and freedoms enshrined in the constitution.

Nor was it appropriate for the majority to bring to the task of interpreting the provisions in issue the judicial habits born of long allegiance to the doctrine of parliamentary supremacy. After all, how true to that doctrine is a court that constructs a presumed or purported intention when there was no parliamentary intention relating to the circumstances in issue or where the original intention has been overtaken by changes in the values of the community? A majority in the House of Lords had declined to adopt such a stilted approach in *Ghaidan* v *Godin-Mendoza (FC)*[61] and extended language in the Rent Act 1977 applicable to a 'wife or husband' to a couple living in a stable and homosexual relationship. The spirit that pervades the judgments of the majority in that case is lacking in Lord Hoffmann's judgment for the majority in these cases, notwithstanding that the latter involved a question of life and death. In the present cases, the express power to modify a statutory provision so as to bring it into conformity with the Constitution was

---

express power to 'modify' a statutory provision that did not comply with the Constitution was in issue.
[60] *Interpreting Precedents: A Comparative Study* (Ashgate, Dartmouth, 1997), at 550.
[61] [2004] UKHL 30.

vested in the courts by Parliament and necessarily meant that the doctrine of parliamentary supremacy required some refinement to accommodate the primacy of the fundamental rights and freedoms protected in that Constitution.

The final aspect of these decisions that calls for comment relates to the majority's decision to overrule the Privy Council's earlier decision in *Roodal* v *The State of Trinidad and Tobago*.[62] In *Roodal* the Privy Council had held, by a majority of three to two, that the mandatory death penalty provision was to be modified by vesting the sentencing judge with a discretion whether or not to impose that sentence in the individual case. As a precedent it stood as a road block to the majority's decision. So it was overruled. In this regard, it is fitting to recall Lord Hoffmann's plea in *Lewis* when his Lordship was a minority of one. Lord Hoffman then said the fact the Board has the power to depart from earlier decisions does not mean that there are no principles that should guide it in deciding whether or not to do so.[63] He quoted with approval dicta to the effect that a decision to overrule a case should rest on some special reason over and above the belief that the prior case was 'wrongly decided'. It will be recollected that his Lordship observed that, if the Board felt able to depart from a previous decision simply because its members on a given occasion have a 'doctrinal disposition to come out differently, the rule of law itself would be damaged and there would be no stability in the administration of justice in the Caribbean.'[64] Yet, the requisite 'principles' do not emerge from the majority's judgments in the present appeals. Nor are any of the principles which Lord Hoffmann carefully garnered from various past cases referred to in these cases. A majority, not of four as in *Lewis* but of one, simply reversed *Roodal* on the ground they considered that case had been wrongly decided.

Nevertheless, it is in fact this emphasis on the doctrines of precedent and *stare decisis* that is misplaced. If, to be effective, constitutions are to be approached as 'living instruments', the doctrine of precedent needs to be sufficiently flexible to permit the constitution to 'live'. Undue adherence to precedent can only stifle the certain development and recognition of values underpinning human rights and freedoms. Judges, then, it might be thought, should cease to pay such boundless homage to the doctrine and instead spell out and defend their 'doctrinal disposition' rather than merely seeking by orthodox theory to capture the numbers necessary to constitute a majority. In any event, it is asking a lot of the

---

[62] [2004] 2 WLR 652.   [63] See above at 166, n. 9.   [64] See above at 166, n. 10.

doctrines of precedent and *stare decisis* to ask a judge to apply a decision because it is a 'precedent' when the judge believes the decision amounts to a denial of the citizen's basic rights and will result in one or more persons being put to their death.

Recall, too, Lord Hoffmann's warning in *Lewis* that the decision could be reversed by a differently constituted Board having a different 'doctrinal disposition' in a future case.[65] That difference in 'doctrinal disposition' is clearly evident in these two appeals; the majority had a 'doctrinal disposition' to adhere to a legalistic and literal interpretation; the minority a 'doctrinal disposition' to adopt an expansive approach to the interpretation of the Constitution and its related provision. This basic difference in the doctrinal dispositions of the two encampments will not be resolved unless and until their Lordships, in the context of constitutional interpretation, overtly and transparently address the question whether they must restrict their 'interpretation' to what might reasonably be attributed to Parliament or whether they may adopt a 'meaning' that, while it may not accord with Parliament's intention or a presumed or purported intention, will safeguard the fundamental rights and freedoms enshrined in the constitution.

Until that core question is resolved, the outcome in cases such as *Matthew* and *Boyce*, and, indeed, *Ghaidan* and *Lewis*, will depend on the composition of the Board that sits on any given appeal. Such a random outcome dependent on the composition of the Board will not surprise readers who have come this far, but where the lives of vulnerable people and the rights they have acquired under the Constitution of the State of which they are citizens is involved it is highly unsatisfactory. People in jeopardy of death and the fundamental rights that they invoke become the playthings – the ping pong balls – of judicial doctrinal competition. This unseemly state of affairs will persist unless and until the issues raised above are more squarely and openly confronted and the remnants of formalistic thinking are reversed.

Delayed though it may have been by this Postscript, it is now timely to turn to the task of constructing the promised new judicial methodology. That task must begin by emphasising that there is no impersonal law.

---

[65] Ibid.

8

There is no impersonal law

A shout from the rooftops

Let it be shouted from the rooftops; there is no impersonal law distinct from the law that judges have made and will yet make. Once it is accepted that there is no impersonal law it must also be accepted that there is no 'right' answer. As there is no impersonal law it is immature for judges to keep thinking and behaving as if there were such an impersonal law. Similarly, as there is no 'right' answer, it is equally immature to keep thinking and behaving as if there were a 'right' answer. Judges can do no more than harness and manage their intelligence and capabilities so as to provide the best answer possible in the circumstances of the case. As an increasing number of judges obtain a sound conception of the judicial role, the best answer, I believe, will be one that seeks to render justice in the individual case and meet the contemporary needs and expectations of society.

The notion that there is an impersonal law crumbles once it is accepted that there is no law hovering in the heavens waiting to be declared and that, in fact, judges constantly make and remake law. As society is in a constant state of flux so, too, the law is constantly in motion as judges, or some judges, strive to keep abreast of society's needs and expectations. This process, as already observed, represents the irrevocable dynamic of the common law. Judges have no option but to cope with the inherent uncertainty of the law when making a decision. A plethora of choices is involved. In a real sense, the exercise of those choices, one way or another, makes a decision personal to the judge. They cannot evade responsibility for the resulting decision. Judges may bury themselves in the discipline of the law, or in a particular methodology, but they still cannot escape responsibility for the choices that they choose to make. They are their choices. If a decision is unjust, that injustice is not necessarily the fault of the law or legal system – it is the responsibility of the individual judge. If a decision is harsh, the suffering and distress it causes is not necessarily due to the mandate of the law, but is likely to reflect the indifference or limited vision or horizons of the individual judge. If a decision fails to meet contemporary needs and circumstances or to fulfil the reasonable expectations of the community, it is again not necessarily the law or system that is outmoded but the individual judge who has failed to be sufficiently creative to keep the law abreast of the times.

Certainly, some judges will be more creative than others in this process, but all judges possess the autonomy to translate the needs and expectations of the community into legal rules or principles that will determine the outcome of their reasoning. It is because there is no impersonal law that judges have the freedom, independence and capacity to consciously undertake that task. In the process, it is inevitable that, subject to the constraints, disciplines and influences which preclude arbitrary or capricious lawmaking, the judges' personal and subjective perceptions of the values and norms of the community will intrude upon the decision-making process. For the moment, however, the point is that this judicial autonomy is incompatible with an impersonal law. Judicial autonomy exists simply because there is no impersonal law.

For many, the fact reality dictates that judicial autonomy must be accepted as an irrevocable part of the adjudicative process and that this autonomy will embrace the personal and subjective perceptions of the individual judge is a bitter pill to swallow. Working within definite constraints, judges are doing nothing other than shaping the legal materials available to them to express that opinion which best serves their intelligence and wisdom and best meets their conception of the judicial role. It is the methodology that is adopted and not any impersonal law that sets the outer boundaries for that opinion.

Judicial autonomy is apparent whenever two or more judges approach a legal problem. No two judges think alike. Compare Lord Denning, undeniably creative, with Viscount Simonds, undeniably conservative. If all the judges over the past fifty years had been clones of Lord Denning the law would be vastly different today. So, too, if all judges had been determinably cast in the mould of Viscount Simonds the law would also be immensely different.[1] Yet, in both cases, it would still be 'the law'. The difference would reflect the different approaches of the judges who

---

[1] For an interesting discussion of the Law Lords in action see, Alan Paterson, *The Law Lords* (Macmillan, London, 1982), at 170–189 and 190–212.

had been at work moulding the common law. In this milieu of judicial humanity, the notion of an impersonal law becomes a banality.

An internal logic and coherence?

More sophisticated judges, lawyers and theorists are prepared to abandon the idea of an impersonal law, as such, but still claim that 'the law' possesses an internal logic and coherence, and that it is this internal logic and coherence that is impersonal to the individual judge. This claim is, of course, the basic creed of the formalist judge.

I imagine that one does not have to dispel this assumption, but I must confess to having often struggled as a judge to find an internal logic and coherence in various branches of the law. Inconsistencies, anomalies and legal fictions abound, and the relationship of one rule to another is frequently plainly illogical and incoherent. I cannot gainsay Feeley and Rubin's description of contract in this context. They acknowledge that it can be argued that contract law consists of rules clustered around basic elements such as offer, acceptance, performance, breach and damages. Because these elements are logically connected, and the rules that govern them derive from the concept of contract in general, they constrain the judge and preclude the expression of personal prejudice or political preference. But the authors perceive that the difficulty with this argument is that it fails to indicate what counts as logic. Precisely, they ask, what is the internal relationship among a set of rules that would satisfy this criterion? In fact, the authors saltily observe, the logic of contract is approximately equivalent to the logic of a lasagne recipe![2]

Apart from the need to be sceptical of the claim to logic and coherence, however, the notion that the law is an internally logical and coherent phenomenon cannot be sustained in theory. To accept such a proposition is to accept that the law is an end in itself. Developments in the law would be directed by the law's internal logic and coherence and not by the changing needs and expectations of the society which the law exists to serve. The law would have an internal rather than an external term of reference. Yet, experience confirms that it is society's needs and expectations that generate changes in the law and those changes regularly defy a logical and coherent footing in the law. The formalists' claim

---

[2] Malcolm M. Feeley and Edward L. Rubin, *Judicial Policy Making and the Modern State: How the Courts Reformed America's Prisons* (Cambridge University Press, Cambridge, 1998), at 252.

to a distinct internal logic and coherence for the law becomes nothing more than an unwarranted pretension.

Certainly, logic and coherence – or reason – are, or should be, the hallmarks of legal decision-making. Logic in a broad sense, as Lord Steyn has said, plays an essential role in legal reasoning.[3] Judges seek to bring logic and coherence to bear on the question in issue. But this feature does not dictate the conclusion that logic and coherence are intrinsic to the law itself any more than it could be pretended that these qualities are exclusive to the law or legal reasoning.

Of course, consistency is an undoubted virtue. But consistency with what? There is no logic or coherence in seeking consistency with past rules or cases that may be outdated or irrelevant to contemporary requirements. Consistency in its most pure form is an attribute of logic, and like logic, it can be harnessed to achieve the objective of enhancing legal reasoning. But let us not pretend that it is innate to the law. Judges introduce it from outside the law and its induction into legal rules and principles cannot make it an innate property.

Furthermore, why seek to peg the need for consistency to adherence to past rules or precedents? Why prefer consistency with past rules and precedents ahead of consistency with their underlying principles? Why attach consistency to past rules and cases rather than consistency with public policy that may, for example, be evident from legislative enactments? Indeed, consistency may exist in a vast array of factors apart from rules and precedents, such as, developments in the applicable law or in other areas of the law, the purpose of the law, the policy of the law, sociomoral norms, and the standards, needs and expectations of the community. Consistency is not the prerogative of rules or precedents.

This point can be illustrated by referring to Professor Weinrib's last ditch attempt to resuscitate a respectable theoretical foundation for formalism. Weinrib attributes to the law an 'immanent intelligibility', which extends to its content and regards the notion of form as the way to draw out that intelligibility. The intelligibility it yields is one which is internal to judicial relations and those relations are to be understood by reference to themselves and not by reference to something else.[4] It is to be noted that Weinrib does not seek to vaunt certainty as a consequence

---

[3] John Steyn, 'Does Legal Formalism Hold Sway in England?' (1996) 49 II Current Legal Problems, 43, at 46.
[4] Ernest J. Weinrib, 'Legal Formalism: On the Immanent Rationality of Law' (1998) 97 Yale LJ, No. 6, at 963–966.

of this process. He accepts that indeterminacy, as the critics understand it, follows from formalism's conception of the relationship between the general and the particular.[5] The distinctive feature of form, in his theory, is that it denies the primacy of the particular by claiming that particulars are intelligible only through their conceptual categories. Particulars, considered directly on their own as particulars, are regarded as unknowable – forms of the general patterns through which these particulars are understood as juridically coherent.

But what is this immanent intelligibility? It cannot be anything other than the law as made by judges in the past. If a conceptual category or general pattern has emerged through which particulars can be understood, it is because judges of an earlier time have perceived that category or pattern from the myriad of factors of which they have been cognisant, many or most of which have been external to the law. There can be no basis for suggesting that the law at some magical or mystical time obtained an immanent quality of intelligibility separate and distinct from the logic and coherence that judges vested in it. Nor can there be any basis for describing the process of applying the general rules to the particular circumstances as formalism when that process must occur irrespective whether the law has an immanent intelligibility or not. Moreover, Weinrib's theory of legal formalism suffers the inevitable flaw of formalism generally. It ignores the justification underlying the rule or the underlying community value which prompted the rule. It proceeds on the false assumption that internal coherence or intelligibility is superior to other values.[6]

The doyen – Ronald Dworkin

The legal theorist who has probably done more than any other to sustain the notion that there is an impersonal law is undoubtedly Ronald Dworkin. His influence on contemporary jurisprudence has been pervasive and, it seems, any serious venture into legal theory which did not refer to his work would be regarded as incomplete, or even defective. I do not want that. But my sustained criticism of several aspects of Dworkin's theory in the remainder of this chapter is intended to serve a wider purpose than to simply demonstrate the error of Dworkin's

---

[5] Ibid., at 1008–1012.
[6] Dennis Patterson, 'Why Should the Law be Immune from Superior or Possibly Superior Values?' *Law and Truth* (Oxford University Press, Oxford, 1996), at 22–42.

ways. The arguments mustered in rebuttal form an essential part of the judicial methodology recommended in this book. Thus, it is to be accepted that there is no 'right' answer; that the law cannot be neatly divided into categories of principles and rules, or of principles and policies; that judges exercise a vast degree of discretion in making the choices innate to judicial decision-making; and any attempt to 'formalise' a doctrine of precedent is counter-productive. Overall, no better means of emphasising the reality of judicial adjudication is available than a study of the unreality of much of Dworkin's theory.

This is not to say that Dworkin's entire theory is untenable. Many aspects are of value. For example, I accept without reservation Dworkin's perception that law is much more than a system of rules. 'Principles, policies and other sorts of standards' that do not operate as rules but that nevertheless command a critical 'legal' function[7] provide a superior perspective of the law and legal process to that of the positivist's simplistic analysis. Dworkin's most enduring contribution to jurisprudence has undoubtedly been the promotion of a concept of law that expanded and elevated principles to a position of dominance in the legal order.

The aspects of Dworkin's theory that invite, if not provoke, critical comment are his contention that the process of legal reasoning presupposes, not just a determinate answer, but as a matter of law a 'right' answer that supports decisively and authoritatively one of the parties' claims; that the legitimacy of the legal process is dependent on determining that answer; that the law is so diverse and rich with principles that even the hardest case can be resolved without recourse to making law; and his resulting unshakeable conviction that judges have no discretion in the process of adjudication. These aspects are all implausible. Carried to this extreme, Dworkin's theory ultimately becomes a sophisticated version of the declaratory theory of law[8] or a refined rendition of natural law imaginings.[9]

While the thesis offered in this work proceeds on the basis that principles are of paramount importance in judicial reasoning, the notion that cases are predetermined, if not by settled rules, then by the weight and complex interaction of the relevant principles is rejected.

---

[7] R. Dworkin, 'Is Law a System of Rules?' in Robert S. Summers (ed.), *Essays in Legal Philosophy* (Basil Blackwell, Oxford, 1970), at 34.
[8] H. Lucke, 'The Common Law: Judicial Impartiality and Judge-Made Law' (1982) 98 LQR 29, at 35.
[9] See R. M. Unger, 'The Critical Legal Studies Movement' (1983) 96 Harv. LR 561, at 575.

Legal principles are neither so abundant nor fruitful as to constitute a law which is complete and determinate. They do not represent an underlying moral order that is then utilised to justify a system of individual rights or entitlements.[10] No unseen hand directs the judges to a predetermined conclusion.

Basically, Dworkin is committed to the ideal that each citizen has equal value. Fairness, to Dworkin, requires an equal concern for the individual's welfare and an equal respect for the individual as a person. To realise this ideal it is necessary to have regard to past decisions and rules, not so much because of what they might say in themselves, but because they embody legal principles which respect this ideal. Dworkin's ideal therefore leads him to articulate a rights model of the law. Individuals have rights and duties with respect to one another and political rights against the state as a whole. He insists that these rights must be recognised in positive law so that they may be enforced 'upon the demand of individual citizens' through courts or other judicial institutions. These rights are captured in rules and represented in legal principles.[11]

For Dworkin, therefore, law embraces moral and political rights as well as strictly legal rights. In addition to the rights and duties created by statute, precedent and custom, and standards having a moral dimension, law consists of the rights that are implicit in the entire legal system itself. 'A principle is a principle of law if it figures in the soundest theory of law that can be provided as a justification for the explicit, substantive and institutional rules of the jurisdiction in question.'[12]

While using the term 'principles' generically to refer to principles, policies and other sorts of standards as distinct from rules, however, Dworkin draws a distinction between principles and policies. 'Policy', he defines as 'that kind of standard that sets out a goal to be reached, generally an improvement in some economic, political or social feature of the community.'[13] This distinction, it may be thought, is conveniently drawn simply to avoid the inevitable conclusion that judges at times

---

[10] Ibid.
[11] R. Dworkin, 'Political Judges and the Rule at Law', Proceeding British Academy, London (1978) Vol. LXJV 259, at 262.
[12] R. Dworkin, 'Social Rules and Legal Theory' (1972) 81 Yale LJ 855, at 876. See also David Pannick, 'A Note on Dworkin and Precedent' (1980) 43 MLR 30; and E. P. Soper, 'Legal Theory and the Obligation of a Judge; the Hart/Dworkin Dispute' (1977) 75 Mich. LR 473, at 501, *et seq.*
[13] R. Dworkin, 'Is Law a System of Rules?' in Summers, *Essays in Legal Philosophy*, at 34–35.

exercise a quasi-legislative function, a conclusion that would follow if policies were to rank as principles for the purpose of Dworkin's thesis.

Rules and principles, however, are quite different. Rules are applicable in an 'all or nothing fashion'. If the facts a rule stipulates exist, the rule is either valid, in which case its answer must be accepted, or it is not valid, in which case, in Dworkin's view, it contributes nothing to the decision.[14]

Whether or not a rule is 'valid' is ultimately determined by reference to the relevant legal principles, that is, principles that judges must take into account as a consideration which inclines the decision in one direction or another. Dworkin then advances his inflationary definition of principles: 'If we tried actually to list all the principles in force we would fail. They are controversial, their weight is all-important, they are numberless, and they shift and change so fast that the start of our list would be obsolete before we reached the middle.'[15] Principles, therefore, have an important dimension lacking in rules; that is the dimension of weight or importance. When these principles intersect the conflict is resolved by the judge taking into account the relative weight of each.[16] Unlike rules, which must be deemed to have been abandoned or changed when a contrary result is reached, principles that have not been applied survive intact.[17]

Dworkin's theory of adjudication therefore appears to invoke a progression of steps in judicial reasoning. If the facts are covered by a settled rule, that rule must be applied and that is the end of the matter. If the rule does not point to a single result, or two rules are in conflict, the case is to be determined by reference to the relevant principle or principles implicit in the particular rule or rules. If the principle or principles point in one direction, the judge is bound to recognise their force and decide the case accordingly. Legal obligations can thus be established by 'a constellation of principles as well as an established rule'.[18] If they point in different directions, then the judge will weigh them one against the other and, because they will not be of equal weight, will be able to reach the right decision. If this process still does not provide an answer, the case becomes a 'hard case' and the judge must revert to the political and moral theory that best explains and justifies the existing legal material and then apply the principle that is consonant with that theory. This, of course, is to return to Dworkin's soundest theory of law.

---

[14] Ibid., at 37. [15] Ibid., at 58. [16] Ibid., at 39. [17] Ibid., at 49. [18] Ibid., at 59.

In Dworkin's writing, a superhuman judge, Hercules, is charged with this task. Fortuitously, Hercules J is already imbued with Dworkin's concept of the ideal of fairness. But, if, at the end of the day, the mortal judge does not arrive at the same answer as Hercules J, he or she has simply made a mistake. As the law is a 'seamless web', complete, consistent and determinant, capable of providing a uniquely correct solution, the law cannot be uncertain. The only uncertainty is not in the law itself, but in the mortal judge's capacity to unearth that correct solution. His or her failure may be due to an inability to identify the question, a defect in reasoning or a faulty assessment of the weight to be accorded the various relevant principles, but not to any ambiguity in the law or incompatibility between the rights of the litigants.[19]

While Dworkin's jurisprudence provides a welcome departure from the more rule-based theories of law and adjudication, much of it is clearly misconceived. Not all the blemishes or excesses that might preclude it from acceptance as a realistic and tenable theory need be traversed here. For present purposes, it is relevant and will suffice to touch upon four aspects; first, Dworkin's distinction between rules and principles; secondly, his distinction between principles and policy; thirdly, his rejection of judicial discretion and his commitment to a concept of law which is determinant of cases; and, finally, his justification of precedent. All these aspects are unrealistic and strained, and ultimately, implausible.

Dworkin's implausible distinction between principles and rules

It is to be recollected that, in Dworkin's perception, if a rule applies it is dispositive of the case. Dworkin must maintain this for the purpose of his theory because, if a rule is applicable but not dispositive of the case, his sharp distinction between rules and principles is lost or meaningless. In fact, it is just that. The rigid distinction is not recognised in practice and, as to be expected with a theory that fails to accord with reality, cannot be sustained in theory. The way in which a judge formulates a rule is critical in determining the decision he or she will reach, and a rule, particularly a rule contained in a precedent, may be vested with a variety of formulations. What the judge is doing is making that formulation which accords with his or her basic value judgement.

---

[19] See Pannick, 'A Note on Dworkin', at 36–38, for a valid criticism of Dworkin's theory in this regard.

Dworkin never confronts the fact that in real terms his rules operate as if they were principles. Yet, if rules are the function of, and are subservient to, principles it seems pointless to maintain the hard and fast distinction between rules and principles insisted upon by Dworkin. At some point a principle manifests itself with sufficient clarity and firmness to be called a rule. But the rule is still dependent on the principle for its validity. If the principle changes or is discarded, the rule should change or be discarded. Again, the point in making the distinction is lost.

Once the search is abandoned for a legal concept of rules that will give rise to binding obligations or entitlements divorced from the fact that those rules are subject to verification in the next decision, the distinction between rules and principles becomes even more blurred. Rules that dictate obdurately merge into principles that guide but do not dictate. They form a continuum, at one end precisely worded rules permitting of little flexibility and, at the other end, loosely framed principles allowing considerable elasticity in their definition and application. In other words, concepts at one end of the continuum are relatively firm and settled and may qualify for the description of rules; concepts at the other end are relatively vague or controversial and may barely qualify for the title of principles.[20]

This point is reinforced by reference to the numerous rules to which there are exceptions. As, to Dworkin, an exception is part of the rule, he requires a full statement of the rule to include all the exceptions.[21] Inevitably, this must require reference to the relevant principles in order to determine the scope and extent of the exceptions so that the distinction between rules and principles is yet again lost.[22]

The tautologous nature of Dworkin's theory may be illustrated in yet another way. Ultimately, rules are the issue of those principles identified by reference to the soundest theory of law. The soundest theory is ascertained, in turn, by reference to the body of settled rules. But those rules are themselves the function of the very same principles.[23] To put what Dworkin is saying succinctly, rules are the manifestation of

---

[20] Yet another continuum, or an extension of the continuum between rules and principles – it does not matter – is that between principles and policies. See below at 195–201.
[21] Dworkin, 'Is Law a System of Rules?' in Summers, *Essays in Legal Philosophy*, at 37.
[22] See A.C. Hutchinson and J.N. Wakefield, 'A Hard Look at "Hard Cases"; The Nightmare of a Noble Dreamer' (1982) 2 OJLS 86, at 107–108; and J. Raz, 'Professor Dworkin's Theory of Rights' (1978) 26 Pol. Stud. 123, at 132–137.
[23] Hutchinson and Wakefield, ibid., at 108–109.

principles that are identified by reference to other rules and principles dressed up as the soundest theory of law. Dworkin's error lies in endeavouring to avoid a term of reference external to the law itself. He demonstrates the folly of seeking to turn the law in upon itself. He has the dog chasing its tail with a vengeance.

Dworkin also refers to rules that incorporate words such as 'reasonable', 'negligent', 'unjust' and 'significant'. Each of these terms makes the application of the rule that contains it depend to some extent on principles or policies lying beyond the rule and, in this way, makes the 'rule itself more like a principle'.[24] According to Dworkin, however, words of this kind do not turn the rule into a principle, because even the broadest of these terms nevertheless restricts the kind of other principles and policies on which the rule depends. But it is difficult to see why the use of a descriptive word in itself should have this inhibiting effect. Of course, covenants that are an unreasonable restraint of trade cannot be enforced (other than by legislation) and to that extent the range of principles or policies that might be considered are curtailed, but that does not logically provide the concept with the imprint of a rule. Many principles similarly exclude the converse to what they permit or prohibit.

Moreover, it is impossible to consider the application of the rule in the light of principles made relevant by the rule without appealing to non-relevant principles.[25] Evaluation of relevance must embrace a consideration and rejection of that which is not relevant. As has been observed in this context, Dworkin's 'rule–principle' distinction seems useful only after the fact. It provides a label for the conclusion reached after the event that certain standards alone were relevant in deciding a case.[26]

The same point also demonstrates that Dworkin is guilty of looking at the law in cross-section. As rules are dependent for their validity on their underlying principles and ultimately on their consonance with the soundest theory of law, the rules represent those principles and that theory at any given time. The principles constantly change with the result that, also at any given time, there will be a number of rules which do not accurately reflect the prevailing principles. Not only will these rules distort the soundest theory of law which in turn will distort the principles which are identified by reference to that theory, but the dispositive nature of the rules is undermined. It can never be known

---

[24] Dworkin, 'Social Rules', at 41.   [25] Soper, 'Legal Theory', at 481–482.
[26] Ibid., at 482.

without inquiring into the background principles whether a particular rule is valid or not.

Dworkin's implausible distinction between principles and policy

Dworkin distinguishes principles, which are about a person's rights, and policy, which is about community goals. It is essential to touch upon this facet of Dworkin's theory because it is an integral part of his commitment to the notion that judges can arrive at a right answer. In 'hard cases' judges must refer to principles. At no time may they consider policy. The distinction therefore becomes necessary for, if judges are to entertain policy considerations, the structured edifice by which they may arrive at the right answer is undermined. Considerations outside that edifice and divorced from Dworkin's focus on individual rights would enter the judicial domain.

It is also important to touch upon this distinction for three specific reasons. First, Dworkin claims that the distinction is largely descriptive of the distinction between principles and policy made by lawyers in practice. Certainly, lawyers will at times differentiate between principles and policy, but they do not do so in the emphatic form insisted upon by Dworkin. Secondly, by making principles central to judicial adjudication, Dworkin requires judges to follow an organicist conception of law; it is to be developed from within. The reality is that it is external forces that give the law its dynamic for change and that prevent it becoming a closed and cloistered institution removed from the real world. Thirdly, the distinction enables Dworkin to demarcate between the legitimate function of the judiciary, that is, being bound by principles, and that which would be an illegitimate excursion into legislative power, that is, dealing with policy. Regrettably, if this is the basis for the legitimacy of the judiciary and the integrity of the law, the judiciary is wholly illegitimate and the law utterly lacking in integrity!

Dworkin calls a principle a standard that is to be observed, not because it will advance or secure an economic, political or social situation deemed desirable, but because it is a requirement of justice or fairness or some other dimension of morality. He calls a policy that kind of standard that sets out a goal to be reached, generally an improvement in some economic, political or social feature of the community. Arguments of principle are arguments intended to establish an individual right; arguments of policy are arguments intended to establish a collective goal. In short, principles are propositions that describe rights;

policies are propositions that describe goals.[27] Consequently, judges are required to arrive at their decisions on grounds of principle and not policy. They must demonstrate that the parties had the legal rights and duties that their decision embodies at the time the parties acted or at some other pertinent time in the past.[28] Dworkin accepts that the text which the judge is required to interpret may have been influenced by policy arguments, but policy will not figure in his or her judgment. Where case law is involved the judge will decide which of the parties has the stronger right and take no accord of community goals.

The distinction Dworkin makes fails the test of reality. First, the distinction is not largely descriptive of what lawyers and judges do in practice. A number of theorists have lamented the fact that lawyers are not especially concerned to distinguish principles from policies.[29] Certainly, lawyers do at times differentiate between principles and policies, but the differentiation is motivated by one side's desire to brand a consideration a 'policy' so as to generate resistance, if not hostility, to that consideration from the bench. The other side is likely to claim that the same consideration is a legitimate, if possibly broad, legal principle in order to gain readier access to the attention of the court. The differentiation is at least in part due to the insistence of theorists, not just Dworkin, but also Hart and Sachs to name but two, who have sought to maintain a sharp distinction that cannot be, and is not, maintained in practice.

The second point is that no sharp distinction is permissible in theory. There is, of course, a distinction between a policy designed to further the general welfare of the public, or section of the public, and a principle already embedded in the law. But they are opposite ends of a spectrum. Some policies are so plainly 'political' in character that they must be left to the goings on of the legislature. Some principles are so wholly legal in character that they would be inappropriate or unhelpful to a legislative body. Between these extremes there are a significant number of policies and principles that do not clearly bear the stamp of one or the other or that could reasonably be categorised as both. Further, a principle may be

---

[27] Ronald Dworkin, *Taking Rights Seriously* (Duckworth, London, 1977), at 90–93.
[28] Ronald Dworkin, *Law's Empire* (Hart Publishing, Oxford, 1998), at 244. For a masterly summary and critique of *Law's Empire*, see George C. Christie's book review, 'Dworkin's Empire' (1987) Duke LJ 157, in which Christie is clearly striving to make some sense of the lack of realism in Dworkin's thesis.
[29] E.g., Harry H. Wellington, 'Common Law Rules and Constitutional Double Standards: Some notes on Adjudication' (1973) Yale LJ 83, at 222.

the genesis of a policy, and a policy may become implanted in the adjudicative process and so become a principle recognised in the law. A further reason no firm demarcation is possible is simply that principles are, as they must be, frequently defined in terms of goals. Goals are not the sole prerogative of policy, and principles without purpose would be an odd phenomenon indeed.

Thirdly, and most importantly, as I have repeatedly stressed, judges do consider policy. Nuisance is regularly given as an example. A benefit to the community from an activity alleged to be a nuisance is taken into account before a decision is made whether to prohibit the activity or not. But policy is much more widespread than this. Policy is directly relevant to most areas of the law, particularly tort and administrative law. It is increasingly referred to openly.[30] Policy considerations are then often decisive. Professor Hart has pointed out that Dworkin's view that a judge who steps into the area of policy, as distinct from principles determining individual rights, is treading forbidden ground reserved for the elected legislature is only possible because for him the law is a gapless system. Indeed, not only is it a gapless system but it is a gapless system of rights or entitlements determining what people are entitled to have as a matter of distributive justice, not what they should have because it is in the public advantage that they should have it. Hart then concludes; 'This exclusion of "policy considerations" will, I think, again run counter to the convictions of many lawyers that it is perfectly proper and indeed at times necessary for judges to take account of the impact of their decisions on the general community welfare.'[31]

It is difficult to deny that judges do not become policy-minded every time they have regard to the consequences of various rulings open to them. Yet, such regard is commonplace. As Neil MacCormick points out, decisions are commonly determined by consequentialist considerations.[32] To dip into the law reports, MacCormick says, is to be confronted at every turn with such arguments, and the learned author gives a number of examples of such an approach.[33] He concludes by adverting to the extrajudicial testimony of Lord Reid who includes in the process of justification common sense, one's sense of justice, legal principles and

---

[30] See above, Chapter 1, at 5.
[31] H. L. A. Hart, *Essays in Jurisprudence and Philosophy* (Clarendon Press, Oxford, 1983), at 141.
[32] *Legal Reasoning and Legal Theory* (Oxford University Press, 1978), at 149.
[33] Ibid., Chapter VI, at 129–151.

'public policy'.[34] As MacCormick says, what it comes down to is that laws must be conceived of as having rational objectives concerned with securing social goods or averting social evils in a manner consistent with justice between individuals.[35] Policy is inveterate.

John Umana unveils Dworkin's dilemma most persuasively when he takes various kinds of cases that had been suggested by Kent Greenawalt.[36] Umana shows that it simply conflicts with 'common sense intuition' to suggest that judges characteristically are, and ought to be, oblivious to social policies.[37] Some legal standards, such as 'unreasonable search' and 'nuisance' appear to build in notions of competing costs and benefits. In such instances a judge is properly weighing competing social interests in deciding cases. Judges also take account of social consequences 'in the sense of administrability and likely effectiveness of proposed rules'. When the court knows that 'the legislature will not soon address a small problem within a large area covered by legislation' it is difficult, claims Umana, to argue that the court should then refuse to take into account considerations that would be important for the legislative body.

Umana explores three kinds of cases in which judicial consideration of policy seems particularly appropriate. He reaches the conclusion that Dworkin is able to accommodate these apparent 'counter-examples' in his rights thesis only by engaging in a conceptual 'gerrymandering' that abandons the original formulations of the principle and policy distinction.

Learned Hand's formula for negligence provides Dworkin with a counter-example. He repeats Hand's economic test: whether the defendant could have avoided the accident at less cost to himself than the plaintiff was likely to suffer if the accident occurred, discounted by the improbability of the accident. The formula would seem to be laden with policy considerations. Dworkin accepts that it may be said that this test provides an argument of policy rather than principle, because it makes the decision turn on whether the collective welfare would have been advanced more by allowing the accident to take place or by spending what was necessary to avoid it.[38] But he argues that Hand's test is not a

---

[34] Lord Reid, 'The Judge as Lawmaker' (1972) 12 JSPTL 22, at 26.
[35] J. W. Harris, *Legal Philosophies* (2nd edn, Butterworths, London, 1980), at 149.
[36] Greenawalt, 'Discretion in Judicial Decision' (1975) 75 Colum. LR 359.
[37] Note: 'Dworkins Rights Thesis' (1976) Vol. 74, No. 6, Mich. LR 1167, at 1179–1183. The author of the Note is not identified, but other sources suggest that it is John Umana.
[38] Ronald Dworkin, 'Hard Cases' (1975) 88 Harv. LR 1057.

simple cost-benefit formula at all but, rather, a method of compromising competing rights.[39] Thus, a judge who appeals to an apparent policy goal as a ground for limiting some right must be understood as appealing to the competing rights of those who would be affected. The judge's argument is an argument of principle if it observes the restriction that the weight of a competing principle may be less than the weight of the appropriate parallel policy.[40]

Umana rightly condemns the sophistication of this argument. He points out that, on one hand, Dworkin wishes to maintain the position that judges should not adjudicate on the basis of policy arguments. Yet, on the other hand, he is forced to concede that much of what looks like adjudication by policy arguments is quite appropriate after all. Dworkin's attempt to reconcile these two views by suggesting that ostensible policy considerations are actually appeals to competing rights must fail. If policy considerations can be understood as an appeal to competing rights, what force remains behind Dworkin's original distinction between principles and policies? When is an ostensible policy consideration to count as a 'hard-core' policy consideration and when not?[41]

Umana also refers to the situations where a judge is called upon to weigh social policies when the legislature leaves some area in a statute largely open for subsequent development by the courts. Under such circumstances, judges must calculate social consequences in much the same way as do legislatures. Dworkin's response is to argue that the issue remains an argument in principle because the judge uses policy to determine what rights the legislature has already created. In other words, the judge is not simply weighing policies *ab initio*. Instead, he must determine '[w]hich arguments of principle and policy might properly have persuaded the legislature to enact just that statute' in light of the legislature's general duty to pursue collective goals defining the public welfare. But this reappraisal still leaves judges considerable discretion in choosing which policies to include in their calculations and in determining how they should be balanced. Calculation of social policies is more than a peripheral task of a judge engaged in statutory interpretation, particularly when the language is of a very general nature.[42] A statute requiring interpretation necessitates not only an assimilation of the legislature's policy but a policy-driven approach on

---

[39] Ibid., at 1077. I have omitted Dworkin's further distinction between 'abstract' and 'concrete' rights.
[40] Ibid. [41] Above (Umana) n. 37, at 1181. [42] Ibid., at 1182–1183.

the part of the court. Judges cannot be expected to turn this approach on and off depending on whether they are dealing with the common law or statutory interpretation.

Dworkin's refinements can be looked at from another perspective. If what the courts are really doing when they appear to be having regard to community goals is weighing the rights of some claimants against the rights of others, they will go wrong, if they go wrong, not because they take into account arguments of policy rather than principles, but because in weighing the rights embodied in the various principles they misinterpret the particular rights or balance them wrongly.[43] Professor Harris correctly observes that, if the argument that a judge's decision that appears, on its face, to be based on considerations of public policy ought really to be understood as an appeal to the rights of individual members of the public were the only argument for understanding references to policies as references to rights, it would have little force. If the 'public good' has a certain weight, how can the 'good to each and every member of the public' have less weight?[44]

To these criticisms I would add a further substantive consideration. If rights are trumps that override the general welfare or public good their pre-eminence must be justified. If there is no justification, a policy elevating the right over the general welfare has been implicitly established. A balancing exercise on the part of the court is therefore inevitable to determine whether the right should have that priority or not. N. E. Simmonds takes the example of the interests of an individual in freedom of speech, and asks why that interest should take priority over the general welfare.[45] The effect of saying that free speech is a right, Simmonds states, is to place the interest in free speech above the social balance of one interest against another. The author shares my concern that any interest should be given that type of priority. Why should the law confer an inbuilt priority or weighting for any particular interests or values? Bills of right may be of great value in spelling out the protection required for individuals and minorities in a representative democracy, but it is to be constantly borne in mind that it is the interest or value underlying the particular right that must be weighed in the inevitable judicial balancing exercise. A priority or weighting will or may distort that process, and this is so whether the priority or weighting takes place

---

[43] Harris, *Legal Philosophies*, 180.   [44] Ibid., at 181.
[45] N. E. Simmonds, *Central Issues in Jurisprudence: Justice, Law and Rights* (Sweet & Maxwell, London, 1986), at 149.

when weighing a principle against a principle, a principle against a policy, or a principle against, in Dworkin's terms, an ostensible policy consideration.

The sooner theorists cease endeavouring to categorise and place labels on individual and group interests and values and accept that the courts must look to the substance of those interests and values in determining which shall prevail, the better it will be for the administration of justice. The legal system will be that much more responsive when the balancing exercise is carried out having substantive regard to the competing interests or values. That exercise is something judges can best do in the deliberative environs of the courthouse in a concrete case untrammelled by inhibiting labels or formulae.

A closing comment is called for. The distinction Dworkin seeks to draw between principles and policy is ultimately put beyond acceptance because it is too absolute in its terms. Law-making by the legislature and by the courts will necessarily have some elements in common. But like it or not, it is law-making in both cases. Having regard to policy considerations when making law is one such element. But there will almost invariably be marked differences in the extent to which policy is taken into account or, in broad terms, the kind of policy that is taken into account, and the way in which it is treated by the two institutions. As I have already emphasised, the legislative process and the judicial process are incontrovertibly different. The legal process is a deliberative and reflective process in which an independent and impartial judiciary is subject to a methodology that includes extensive constraints. Policy considerations, when in issue, will be considered in the exercise of that methodology and discipline. An early nineteenth-century judge may well have protested against entering too strongly upon public policy with the sally that it is 'a very unruly horse, and once you get astride it you never know where it will carry you.'[46] But in fact the unruly horse has long since been broken in. Today the steed is kept under tight rein.

---

[46] *Richardson* v *Mellish* 1824 to Bing. 229, per Burrough J at 303. But the judge revealed his die-hard formalism by saying in the next sentence; 'It may lead you from the sound law.' Then, perhaps, the judge protested too strongly. With the fluid aplomb of so many judges, having protested against the heterodoxy he succumbed to it himself expressly holding that there was no public policy against entering into the contract in issue in that case.

Dworkin's implausible rejection of judicial discretion

Under Dworkin's theory, judges have no measure of judicial autonomy. Any judicial creativity beyond that required to implement the process of adjudication is simply a mistake, for judges do not make law. Able to avoid such a mistake, Hercules J arrives at the conclusion predetermined by the law, and if we are to imagine a court comprising three or five or more Hercules JJ, presumably they would all agree and arrive at the same conclusion! The theory confounds all observable experience.

In this book I have chosen to speak of the vast range of choices open to a judge in reaching a decision, but I could equally have referred to judicial discretion. When a judge makes a choice he or she effectively exercises a discretion and, as the dilemma of choice permeates the adjudicative process, discretion can be seen to be as boundless as the law. No factual situation, no rule and no principle is immune from judicial discretion. But Dworkin says otherwise.

Dworkin is at his weakest when seeking to exclude judicial discretion. He endeavours to meet the positivist's view that, if a case is not able to be resolved by an established rule, it is a 'hard' case and the judge must decide it by exercising a discretion, with a semantic examination of the respects in which the word 'discretion' is used.[47] Judges, he argues, never exercise discretion except in the 'weak sense' of applying the law as found in rules and principles. They do not have discretion in the 'strong sense' of being able to arrive at decisions that make new law or change existing laws.[48] But it is neither of great interest nor productive to examine the different senses in which Dworkin claims the word discretion is used. Essentially, discretion is absent in Dworkin's view because the judge is bound to follow the rules or principles if they apply. It is almost cavalier to say that, if they do not, the judge has simply made a mistake. Possibly, it may be open to Dworkin to advance this theory as a normative concept of the law, but as a descriptive theory it is wide of the mark. To save some semblance of plausibility he would have to contend that, while judges might think they are exercising a discretion and, at times, making law, they are not in fact doing so. Properly informed with the soundest theory of law, they are guided by the unseen hand through the range of diverse and rich principles to the correct answer. The claim

---

[47] Dworkin, 'Is Law a System of Rules?' in Summers (ed.), *Essays in Legal Philosophy*, at 44–54.
[48] Dworkin, 'The Model of Rules' (1967) 35 Univ. of Chic. LR, 14, at 32–33.

is as improbable as it is likely that all judges share the same size shoes as the former Lord Chancellor.

There is also an element of incongruity in Dworkin's description of principles and his denial of judicial discretion. If, as he claims, principles are controversial, numberless, and shift and change so fast as to render any attempt to list them futile, and if they have the dominant characteristic of being able to be weighed, it would seem to follow that the exercise of a judicial discretion in applying those principles is inevitable. Dworkin is not eliminating discretion when he says that a judge who believes that those principles he or she is bound to recognise point in one direction and the principles pointing in the other direction, if any, are not of equal weight, must then reach a decision in favour of the principles having greatest weight, just as he must follow what he believes to be a binding rule.[49] Having been at pains to distinguish the two, Dworkin is simply equating the effect of principles with the effect of rules to exclude judicial discretion. Yet, the exercise of discretion will be present at many points; in determining the facts, in ascertaining whether or not there is an applicable rule and whether it is dispositive on the case; in determining whether it is necessary to refer to principles; in deciding which principles are relevant and which are not; and in the important process of assessing the weight of the respective principles and establishing, if necessary, what is the soundest theory of law. The scope for the judge to exercise a choice between alternatives is self-evidently vast. Merely to assert that the judge must follow that alternative that he 'believes' is right does not succeed in eliminating the discretion inherent in the process of determining what it is that the judge will choose to believe.

Moreover, principles do not just 'shift and change', they are also made, and the act of making a principle (or rule) is incontestably discretionary. Dworkin meets or avoids this point, of course, with his inflationary definition of principles. Whatever considerations serve to found the creation of the 'new' principle, they are already embraced within the definition of 'principles, policies and other sorts of standards'. Quite remarkably, therefore, there cannot be such a thing as an entirely new principle. Hercules J is always able to decide an issue in accordance with existing principles. But even Hercules J must decide whether it is necessary to forge a 'new' principle out of the old or not.

---

[49] Dworkin, 'Is Law a System of Rules?' in Summers (ed.), *Essays in Legal Philosophy*, at 49.

The claim that no discretion is involved is therefore essentially semantic. It is lacking in 'horse sense'.[50]

An even more fundamental objection to the logic of Dworkin's theory is his inability to ultimately embrace the external standards, needs and expectations of the community that influence the value judgements judges make in deciding cases. The notion of a value judgement that is determinative of a case is alien to his thinking. But he is singularly unsuccessful in the attempt to eliminate the necessity for a judge to have recourse to values outside the law.

The first point which can be made in this regard relates to Dworkin's account of 'hard cases'. Easy cases are quickly dispatched with the application of a rule. Hard cases require the examination and weighing of the relevant principles. But how does a judge identify the hard case? It is probably simple enough for an observer to analyse a case as a hard case *after* the event, for it can then be seen that the judge has rejected any rule as being dispositive of the case and explored the underlying principles involved. At the point a judge is confronted with an argument that a rule is applicable and a counter-argument that it is not, however, Dworkin's theory provides no means by which the judge may decide that a case is a hard case, certainly without exercising a discretion.

This circularity in Dworkin's reasoning has attracted comment.[51] In short, the initial process of classifying a case into a hard case can only be decided by reference to underlying principles and, ultimately, by preferring those principles which are justified by the soundest theory of law. Once the judge has made that decision, however, he or she is then required to go through the motion of applying precisely the same principles they have already resorted to in deciding that it is a hard case. In a later work, Dworkin defended his position by refusing to accept that there are distinct stages to the process of judicial adjudication in dealing with rules.[52] In short, he collapsed the initial question whether a rule is applicable and the subsequent issue whether that rule

---

[50] The phrase is Llewellyn's, *Law in Our Society* (unpublished manuscript), referred to by W. Twining, *Karl Llewellyn and the Realist Movement* (Weidenfeld and Nicholson, London, 1973), at 503.

[51] Hutchinson and Wakefield, 'Legal Philosophies', at 100. The authors suggest that, if Dworkin is to maintain any degree of consistency or coherence, he must treat all cases as 'hard cases'. Yet to do so would effectively destroy Dworkin's imperative distinction between rules and principles.

[52] R. S. Bell, 'Understanding the Model of Rules: Toward a Reconciliation of Dworkin and Positivism' (1972) 81 Yale LJ 912, at 917.

ought to dispose of the case into one and the same inquiry. This modification may be accepted, but the point remains that the decision whether or not the rule disposes of the case anticipates an appeal to the very principles that will be considered if it is decided that the rule is not dispositive of the case.

Dworkin's implausible justification for precedent

Dworkin's justification of precedent in principled adjudication must be addressed at this point. The theorist's theory of precedent is part of his larger thesis that litigants have rights that they are entitled to enforce and that give rise to one 'right' answer. Rather than accepting that precedent impedes the judge's capacity to weigh principles and determine rights, Dworkin incorporates the doctrine of precedent into his theory. He insists upon a role for precedent and 'institutional history' in the determination of hard cases.[53] Of course, Dworkin is again virtually bound to adopt this approach. It would be incongruous if a theory of law committed to judicial predetermination failed to recognise the force of precedent.

Dworkin develops his position by contending that an argument from principle can supply a justification for a particular decision only if it can be shown to be consistent with decisions not recanted.[54] Precedent or institutional history therefore acts, not as a constraint upon the political judgement of judges, but as an ingredient of that judgement, because it is part of the background that any plausible judgment about the rights of an individual must accommodate.[55] Even where a judge may disapprove of a line of precedents, Dworkin's doctrine of articulate consistency nevertheless requires the judge to 'allow his argument to be affected by them'.[56]

Dworkin confers two types of precedential force on prior judicial decisions. One is 'enactment force'. This force vests the decision with something akin to a statutory rule and is limited to its exact words. The other is 'gravitational force', and it is this more genial genus that is the basis of Dworkin's theory of precedent. It requires judges to extend the force of a precedent beyond the linguistic limits of a particular phrase[57] and is explained by appealing, not to the wisdom of enforcing enactments, but to the fairness of treating like cases alike.[58] Applying the precedent, the judge must limit the gravitational force of the earlier decisions to the extension of the arguments of principle necessary to

---

[53] Dworkin, *Taking Rights Seriously*, at 89. [54] Ibid., at 88. [55] Ibid., at 87.
[56] Ibid., at 89. [57] Ibid., at 111. [58] Ibid., at 112–113.

justify those decisions. If an earlier decision was based on some argument of policy, it would have no gravitational force and could be ignored.[59] So, in defining the gravitational force of a particular precedent, the judge must take into account only the arguments of principle that justify the precedent.

It will at once be observed that Dworkin's theory still falls far short of a defence of a strict doctrine of precedent. Few decisions would possess enactment force and only those that can be justified by arguments of principle would have gravitational force. The judge in the later case is therefore obliged to look behind the decision at the principle on which it is based, and it is those principles rather than the decision itself that would appear to give the precedent its force. In broad terms, Dworkin's theory could be said to require judges to respect past well-founded decisions and to accommodate them in their reasoning in the instant case. Such a flexible theory is unobjectionable and approximates what I have said about precedent in Chapter 6.

In the context of Dworkin's larger thesis that litigants have rights that they are entitled to enforce and that give rise to one correct decision, however, precedent is unnecessary and must distort the adjudicative process.[60] It is unnecessary because, if the judge believes that an earlier decision was correct, he will apply its reasoning and its conclusion to the instant case pursuant to his task of enforcing rights and arriving at the right decision. He will not be forced to do so by the gravitational – or enactment force – of a precedent.[61]

Nor do concepts such as enactment force and gravitational force have any place in a worthwhile analysis of the role of precedent in the adjudicative process. They are not two distinct species. The 'force' of a precedent, using that word in Dworkin's sense, is to be measured by reference to the proximity of the instant case to the language of the precedent. At one end of the spectrum, therefore, is enactment force and at the other end gravitational force. The further the facts of the instant case move away from the earlier decision the more the force of that decision diminishes.[62] But if this is what Dworkin is saying, it is to state a platitude. Self-evidently a precedent will have less force the less similar it is to the instant case. Measuring the force of a precedent in this way is

---

[59] Ibid., at 113.
[60] For a telling criticism of Dworkin's theory of precedent see Pannick, 'A Note on Dworkin'. See above at 190, n. 12.
[61] Pannick, ibid., at 37–38.   [62] Ibid., at 41.

unsound. Obviously, a 'precedent' that is not on all fours with the particular case will lack 'force' in that sense. The true pull or appeal of a precedent must reside in what it says; the quality of its reasoning, its foundation in basic legal principle, and its consonance with the standards, needs and expectations of the times in which it is being applied. Precedent, to survive, must face a substantive test and not just some formal criterion of 'likeness'.

Further, Dworkin's insistence on precedent distorts his adjudicative process in two distinct respects. In the first place, it requires the judge to 'allow his argument to be affected' by a prior decision that may be misguided. Once it is accepted that a judge's decision may be different in a given case depending on whether there is an earlier precedent, the corrupting effect of a bad precedent on the determinative outcome is apparent. In the second place, if, as Dworkin claims, recognition of precedent is necessary to ensure fairness, that is, that like cases are treated alike, he is vesting one or other of the parties in the later case with a right or entitlement arising out of the precedent. In other words, fairness will only be secured if the precedent is followed, for only then has like been treated alike. But assessed against any other standard, including Dworkin's own commitment to the recognition of the rights of citizens, the decision may be anything but fair. His thinking involves the assumption that the earlier case is fair. Dworkin must either accept that the ability of the present judge to weigh the relevant principles or entitlements has, at least in part, been displaced by the same exercise carried out by the earlier judge, or has been selective in defining what earlier decisions the later judge is obliged to regard as precedent.

Enough has been said to illustrate the problems of endeavouring to incorporate the doctrine of precedent into a viable theory of law that promotes principled decision-making. It is logically inescapable that the doctrine confers on the precedent a force that is independent of the principle on which it is based. Placing principles ahead of precedent, as I urge, restricts the latter's force to its merits. Its persuasive or directive force is to be 'found either in the events that made it what it is, or in some principle which enables us to say of it that it is what it ought to be.'[63] It means that before being accepted and applied, a precedent must be justified as reasoned, relevant and responsive to current standards and needs. Earlier decisions must demonstrate their utility and

---

[63] Cardozo, *The Judicial Process*, at 52.

timeliness in the circumstances of the given case before being accorded the benediction of authority.

Trigwell's case: Hercules J confronts Athena J

The implausibility of these aspects of Dworkin's theory can be illustrated by reference to the decision of the High Court of Australia in *State Government Insurance Commissioner* v *Trigwell and Ors*.[64] I select this case because it has been the subject of an article by Max Atkinson,[65] in which the author invokes Dworkin's legal thesis to demonstrate that the High Court was in error.

The High Court applied the House of Lords decision in *Searle* v *Wallbank*.[66] In that case the House of Lords held that a landowner owed no duty of care to avoid injury caused by his or her animals wandering on to a public highway. Notwithstanding that the decision had been widely criticised, the High Court (Murphy J dissenting) considered that it represented a 'settled rule of the common law', and that the desirability of departing from it 'should be left to Parliament'.[67]

The Court of Appeal in New Zealand had reached much the same conclusion for much the same reasons nine years earlier in *Ross* v *McCarthy*.[68] *Searle* v *Wallbank* was earnestly applied amidst declarations to the effect that, if the rule in that case was to be amended, the amendment was not a matter for the courts, but *par excellence* a matter for the legislature.[69] To the Judges, the issue was so straightforward that they did not call upon counsel for the respondent, and delivered oral judgments on the spot. Assuming that the passing of each year confers some measure of enlightenment, possibly all that can be said is that, if a

---

[64] (1979) 26 ALR 67.
[65] M. Atkinson, 'Trigwell in the High Court: Judicial Opinion v Legal Principle: A Case of Bad Law from Bad Philosophy' (1979–1982) 9 Syd. LR 541.
[66] [1947] AC 341.
[67] Ibid., at 78 (per Mason J, with whom Barwick CJ, Gibbs, Stephen and Aickin JJ agreed). In his lone dissenting judgment, Murphy J fully recognised that 'one of the virtues of the common law is its flexibility, that it is capable of changing with the times and adapting its principles to new conditions', at 87–88.
[68] [1970] NZLR 449.
[69] Ibid., at 456 (per Turner J). See also at 457 (per McCarthy J). The rule was duly amended in 1989; see s. 5 Animals Law Reform Act 1989. It may be noted that Turner J took a much more robust view in respect of the law of evidence ('Judge-made Law') a year before in *Jorgonson* v *News Media Limited* [1969] NZLR 961, at 990.

court is going to be wrong it is better to be completely wrong, and then completely wrong earlier rather than later.

Atkinson is undoubtedly correct in suggesting that *Trigwell* was wrongly decided. As he points out, no attempt was made to analyse *Searle* v *Wallbank*, and assess the 'quality of the reasoning'.[70] The doctrine of precedent was accepted with no more than a token discussion of its merits. Nor did the High Court allow for the fact that, following the 1966 Practice Statement, the House of Lords might have itself reversed *Searle* v *Wallbank* but for the fact that it had already been negated by legislation in 1971. The Court also brushed aside the 'apparent illogicality' of the rule in relation to the well-settled liability for damage done by animals wandering on to the property of neighbours.[71] Further, the High Court failed to have regard to the vastly different conditions pertaining to stock allowed to wander on to modern high-speed highways compared with the danger they represented in 1916 when the rule had its historical inception.[72]

Atkinson's principle criticism, however, is that the High Court failed to adopt Dworkin's so-called principled approach. First, the Court failed to reconsider *Searle* v *Wallbank* in the light of the principle of liability for negligence stated and applied by Lord Atkin in *Donoghue* v *Stevenson*[73] in 1932 and subsequently enforced by numerous decisions of the House of Lords, Privy Council, and the High Court, itself, since that time. Secondly, it failed to justify adequately the case for an exception to that principle of law. Had the Court adopted this so-called principled approach and tested *Searle* v *Wallbank* against *Donoghue* v *Stevenson*, Atkinson argues, the Court would have been led to the conclusion that liability did not depend on some nineteenth-century precedent but the fact that the defendant had created a significant risk of harm.[74] The general legal principle in *Donoghue* v *Stevenson*, Atkinson complains, was given no precedent force of its own.[75]

If the thrust of my thesis is accepted, *Trigwell* is a model of what a decision should not be in all these respects. What is of present interest, however, is that Atkinson invokes Dworkin's legal philosophy to provide a 'principled' solution to *Trigwell*. Obliged to view rules in terms of the principles they embody and the rights those principles support, the

---

[70] Atkinson, 'Trigwell', at 542. [71] Atkinson, 'Trigwell', at 77.
[72] *Heath's Garage Limited* v *Hodges* [1916] 2 KB 370. See also *Hughes* v *Williams* [1943] KB 574.
[73] [1932] AC 56. [74] Atkinson, 'Trigwell', at 552. [75] Ibid., at 553.

Court would not have been entitled to ignore the general principle which imposes a duty to be careful where risk of injury to others is attendant on one's conduct or enterprise.[76] Mainly by reference to changed circumstances, Atkinson concludes that, had it done so, it is hardly conceivable that the Court would have concluded that an exception to the general principle was justified in 1979.

Atkinson's application of Dworkin's legal philosophy, however, merely serves to demonstrate the flaws in his philosophical warrior's theory of adjudication. In fact, the majority simply held that the rule in *Searle* v *Wallbank* was dispositive of the case, just as Dworkin would have the courts do where a settled rule is clearly applicable. The circuitous nature of this reasoning has already been mentioned above.[77] In comparison, the approach recommended in this book would simply require the rule in *Searle* v *Wallbank* to be reconsidered in the light of all the considerations referred to by Atkinson. Its quality and value as a precedent would have to be re-established before it was applied as a precedent.

Atkinson makes the point that the High Court could have adhered to a principled approach and yet remained free of the charge of 'judicial law-making as a discretionary pursuit of selected social goals'.[78] The judges' commitment, in other words, is to 'respect and apply principles which have determined past claims of right'.[79] It is certainly true that the High Court would have reached a preferable result by applying the principle in *Donoghue* v *Stevenson*, but I do not accept that the Court should have ignored 'arguments of general welfare and social policy'.[80] On the approach endorsed in this book, these considerations would have been regarded as highly relevant. Indeed, it is consistent with more recent authority to inquire whether there is any policy reason which would negate the application of the principle.

The same point can be made by referring back to the decision in *Donoghue* v *Stevenson* itself. There was then no prior principle for Lord Atkin to apply. Indeed, most of the precedents were unfavourable to the development of such a principle. In essence, and apart from a comparative reference to the United States' decision in *MacPherson* v *Buick Motor Company*,[81] Lord Atkin articulated the principle by reference to the 'love thy neighbour' precept. If, therefore, we value a system of law that can inspire a case such as *Donoghue* v *Stevenson*, reference to concepts

---

[76] Ibid., at 562. [77] See above at 193–194. [78] Atkinson, 'Trigwell', at 561.
[79] Ibid., at 563. [80] Ibid. [81] 217 NY 382.

beyond the law itself remains essential. The so-called principled approach devised by Dworkin cannot be restricted to principles which have determined 'past claims of right'.

Consequently, there is a marked difference in the way Dworkin's epitome of the superhuman judge, Hercules J, and a judge acting in accordance with the thesis of this book would have decided *Trigwell*, although both would have unhesitatingly rejected the approach of the majority in the High Court. As it is open to Hercules J to weigh a principle against another principle but not a principle against a rule, Hercules J would initially have to decide whether the precedent of the House of Lords in *Searle* v *Wallbank* laid down a rule or applied a principle. Hercules J, as an honest superhuman judge, might feel obliged to find that *Searle* v *Wallbank* established a rule. It is stated as a rule; a landowner owes no duty of care to avert injury from animals wandering on to the highway. Even if it is perceived as an exception to a broader concept of liability for negligence, it becomes part of that rule and is equally binding. Nor does the rule as stated admit any exception. If he was forced to accept the rule, Hercules J would then need to only examine whether it was applicable.

The question whether a rule is applicable depends on whether the facts the rule stipulates are given, and the absence of a rule to the contrary. Here the required facts exist and there is no rule to the contrary. Hercules J, therefore, would hold that the rule in *Searle* v *Wallbank* applied and find for the defendant.

We know from our reading of Dworkin, however, that this is not what he expects of his heroic judge. Hercules J would undoubtedly find that it is a 'hard' case. What rationalisation he would adopt to reach the conclusion that *Searle* v *Wallbank* did not advance the rule, or that the rule was not applicable, is not clear. Possibly, Hercules J would resort to Dworkin's distinction between statutory law and case law or, at least, cases that do not contain a canonical form of words[82] but, whatever the basis, it has to be assumed that Hercules J would reject the rule, discard syllogistic reasoning and adopt a principled approach.

At this point Hercules J would have regard to the array of factors and standards discussed by Atkinson and briefly mentioned above. Undoubtedly, he would hold that the principle of liability established in *Donoghue* v *Stevenson* must prevail over the rule in *Searle* v *Wallbank*. He would no doubt do this on the basis that, as a rule derives its validity

---

[82] Dworkin, *Taking Rights Seriously*, at 110–115.

from the legal principles it embodies, the rule in *Searle* v *Wallbank* is invalid. But Hercules J's omnipotence notwithstanding, *Searle* v *Wallbank* does not, of course, embody the principle in *Donoghue* v *Stevenson* at all; just the opposite. It is based on a 'principle' of non-liability founded on the notion that it would be unfair to hold owners of straying stock liable for any injury caused by their beasts when they did not represent a danger on the road in the circumstances that existed at the time. Weighed against the established general principle of responsibility for negligent conduct, however, and having regard to the changed circumstances on the road, Hercules J would undoubtedly find for the plaintiff. But, he would not purport to have made new law. The relevant principles, when weighed correctly, would have pointed inescapably in the right direction.

Whether or not Hercules J would expressly renounce any consideration of social goals or policies or just ignore them is not certain. What is certain is that he would not purport to embrace such considerations in his thinking. To do so would be to assert the existence of a discretion to decide what the law should be and to intrude upon the prerogative of Parliament. Apparently, however, he would not blush at the fact that the decision giving rise to the principle that he held to be predominant did just that.

To a judge imbued with the thinking set out in this book, *Trigwell's* case would pose no difficulty. We will call the Judge Athena J.[83] Athena J would initially examine the facts in considerable detail. From this close examination of the facts she would probably express an expectation that the plaintiff should have a remedy in law. Unfettered by any strict doctrine of precedent, Athena J would not be unduly concerned about *Searle* v *Wallbank*. Whether or not it represented a rule or principle would be of little concern to her. Rather, her overriding interest would be whether *Searle* v *Wallbank* reflected contemporary standards, needs and expectations. Athena J would at once perceive that in today's circumstances the exclusion of the owner's liability for harm resulting from straying stock should be re-examined. She would proceed to do so. The changed circumstances on the road between 1916, when the rule was conceived, and the present day

---

[83] Athena was one of the twelve Greek Olympian Gods, the Goddess of wisdom and a few other things besides. She was the embodiment of wisdom, reason and purity, the champion of justice and the civil law, and only bore arms when threatened or attacked or when coming to the aid of heroes. She was often called upon to settle disputes between the Gods and various mortals, and was lauded for her superb intellect and logic. She was regarded as strong, independent, fair and merciful. It need not spoil the story line that she was the half-sister of the mortal Hercules.

would be shortly, but illuminatingly, described. No-one would be left in doubt that straying stock on modern roads represented an unacceptable hazard to innocent and careful users of public highways. *Searle v Wallbank* would therefore be perceived as obsolete.

Next, Athena J would refer to developments in the law of negligence, beginning with *Donoghue v Stevenson* and articulate the inconsistency of *Searle v Wallbank* with the general principle of liability for negligent conduct. Falling for decision fifteen years after *Donoghue v Stevenson*, it would become apparent in Athena J's judgment that *Searle v Wallbank* had been poorly reasoned. Reference would be made to the unacceptable illogicality of having one rule of liability for the owners of stock straying on to a highway and another for the owners of stock straying on to a neighbour's farm. Moreover, the learned Judge would acknowledge the possibility that, if *Searle v Wallbank* had not been overtaken by remedial legislation, it might well have been subsequently overruled by the House of Lords itself. She might well observe in passing that, in any event, there was no reason why, sitting in the High Court of Australia, she should treat a decision of the House of Lords as either binding or persuasive.

Nor would Athena J be swayed by an argument that the farming community had relied and acted upon the precedent of *Searle v Wallbank* for many years. It is likely that our worthy Judge would caustically inquire whether this reliance meant that farmers had directed more of their resources into securing the boundary fences adjoining their neighbours, to whom they would be liable for harm caused by their straying stock, than to roadside fences where they would not be liable for injury to the passing public. She would hold, in any event, that ensuring certainty and predictability in the law in this case was far outweighed by the other considerations to which she had adverted.

Finally, unlike Hercules J, Athena J would not exclude social goals and policies from consideration. The social and economic impact of exempting stock owners from liability would be considered, as would the social and economic effect, particularly upon the farming community, of abandoning the immunity. Policy questions of cost allocation and the incidents of insurance would require to be taken into account. The outcome would be a decision that best achieved justice in the instant case and brought the law into the closest possible harmony with the needs of the community. In expressing that decision, Athena J would not be diffident about accepting that her decision represented a change in the law. Nor would she be hesitant about spelling out the standards and values of the community, as she perceived them, which motivated her thinking and led to her judgment. Athena J's value judgement, her choices and her reasoning would be transparent. Being a wise judge, she would also know that, if the legislature did not like her decision, it could reverse it by legislative fiat.

Conclusion

The thinking of those who persist in believing that there is an impersonal law distinct from the law that judges have made in the past and will yet make in the future is ultimately impenetrable. The death knell of the declaratory school of law alone should have put an end to the persistence of this myth. It is an inescapable reality that judges effectively make law every time they exercise a choice, and that judicial decision-making is fraught with choices. Choices are exercised, and law is made, irrespective of whether the resulting decision advances or entrenches a rule or principle of law.[84] It is because there is no impersonal law that judicial autonomy is a fact of judicial life. Judges cannot therefore shelter behind an impersonal law. The law is what they make of it.

A strong current of realism runs through this chapter. Take, for example, the reality of any case giving rise to an arguable issue. One court may find the facts and define the issue in such a way as to attract a allegedly binding precedent, and hold itself bound by that precedent; another court may find the facts or define the issue in different terms so that the precedent is not binding; yet another court may agree that the precedent is in point but distinguish it by either stating the *ratio decidendi* of the precedent in narrow terms or defining the issue in the instant case in different terms; the next court may hold that the *ratio* of the precedent is in point and decline to distinguish it, but nevertheless refuse to follow it for one or more of a variety of reasons, such as the fact that it has been overtaken by a contrary indication of legislative policy or developments in other areas of the law; and yet another court may simply overrule, decline to follow or disregard the precedent in favour of a consequentialist or policy-oriented argument.

Can any judge in any of the above cases claim that his or her view represents 'the law'? Of course, they cannot sensibly do so. The most that they can claim is that the view they have expressed is their opinion of the law, or more accurately, their view as to what they think the law should be. Yet, every judge who has put pen to paper or two fingers to a

---

[84] See above, Chapter 1, at 3–4.

computer keyboard to write a judgment in any of the above cases will purport to proclaim the law. This trait amounts to no more than a claim that 'it is the law because I say it is the law'. The conceit in such a posture may be overlooked, but the assumption that there is in fact a law that coincides with their view cannot. When so many choices are available, a judge's notion that it has been given to him of her, either alone or in conjunction with like-minded colleagues, to discern some transcendental law assumes a prescience of mind or infallibility that judges simply do not possess. The notion that the law at some magical and mystical time attained an immanent or impersonal quality separate and distinct from the logic and coherence that judges vested in it is painfully feeble; one could say, even pantomimic.

In the result, there is no 'right' answer. Working to a sound conception of the judicial role and within a well-founded legal methodology, including the constraints of judicial discipline, the judge must simply strive to arrive at the best solution which his or her intelligence and capabilities permit.

On analysis, Dworkin's theory that there is a 'right' answer becomes wholly implausible. The fundamental failure of Dworkin's theory is simply that it does not accord with the reality of judicial decision-making. It can only be sustained by the impossible prospect of positing an impersonal law. When judges finally discard this notion they will have a more realistic appreciation of the actual process of judicial decision-making than does Dworkin. They will have the basis for the development of a sound conception of the judicial role.

The four-pronged challenge to Dworkin undertaken in this chapter seems out of proportion to my respect for this theorist. I would reiterate that there is much of great value in Dworkin's writings; his refutation of positivism, his elevation of principles to their rightful place of pre-eminence in the legal order, his cathartic perception of the boundless nature of considerations that influence judicial decision-making; and his recognition of the close nexus between judges and the moral values that judicial adjudication reflects. Irrespective whether I agree or disagree with aspects of Dworkin's theory, the potted summaries I have given do not do justice to the force of his exposition.

I continue to entertain a hunch, akin no doubt to the renowned judicial 'hunch', that, if Dworkin were to abandon his basic commitment to the notion that there is a 'right' answer in the law and replace it with a pragmatic judicial quest for the best answer possible in the circumstances of the case, the implausible excursions he has been led to undertake would become unnecessary and vain; exercises better left to students of legal history. It is a woeful wrong to jurisprudence that a theory that began with such realistic aims and insights was driven by the force of this basic premise to eventually become inconsolably unrealistic. But, nonetheless, such is my regard for this philosopher I can truthfully say that, should my family and friends who have gathered to bid me a final farewell replace the customary wreath of white lilies on my casket with a copy of *Law's Empire*, I will not bat an eyelid.

I appreciate that it is not enough to dismantle the notion of an impersonal law without constructing an alternative view of what constitutes law. The phrase, 'the law', is used too often, including being used regularly in this book, for me to avoid advancing a description which is devoid of any metaphysical content. I explore that description in the next chapter.

9

So, what is the law?

'The law' is essentially a process

The fact that there is no impersonal law does not denude the phrase, 'the law', of all meaning. Usage alone requires that it be given a meaning. But this is not to say that the question; 'What is the law?' is anything other than congenitally ambiguous. What lawyers will mean by the word 'law' in the concept, the 'rule of law' will be one thing, what they mean by the word 'law' in the judicial oath requiring the judge to do right 'according to law' will be another. Laypersons will use the words 'the law' to signify those statutes and rules that must be obeyed or that will attract a penalty if not complied with. The fact the meaning of some statutes and rules may be a trifle vague so that it is not known exactly what it is to be obeyed or complied with does not detract from this meaning. Legal theorists may need to adopt different meanings depending on what particular theory they are seeking to propound. As William Twining has pointed out, a common error in contemporary jurisprudence arises from the tendency to treat all 'legal theories' as if they were attempts to answer the same question or set of questions. Jurisprudence is not a single-question subject.[1] A meaning can be taken down from the jurisprudential shelf and dusted off for any particular theory.

Depending on the purpose and topic, a great number of things may be included in 'the law'. It may include institutions, legal processes, rules, the source of rules, principles, standards, the source of principles, the source of standards, the contribution of other disciplines, the impact of international treaties and human rights covenants, and the norms and expectations of the community that underlie the rules, principles or standards. Ultimately, the meaning of the 'the law' in this multiplicity of facets depends on how one orders those facets and where one then draws

---

[1] W. Twining, *Karl Llewellyn and the Realist Movement* (Weiderfeld and Nicholson, London, 1973), at 3.

the line, above which is 'the law' and below which is not, or what one includes within a circle labelled 'the law' and what one excludes, as best fitting one's perception of what constitutes 'the law'.

It is more helpful to identify and describe the qualities that characterise one's perception of 'the law'.

As will be evident from what I have already said in previous chapters, I rank the fact that the law is the product of judicial law-making a primary quality. Custom and usage from time immemorial provide its mainspring. The judges extracted and evolved the law from sources outside the law. In this sense the common law represented a process by which the customs and usages which the community had evolved to meet its needs and expectations became the law of the land. The momentum for the law to continue to evolve to meet the changing needs and expectations has never been subverted. It is this perception of the law as a process that has sadly waned. When, for example, positivists claim that it is the duty of a judge to abide by the law, they must accept that they are talking about a law which some other and earlier judge made. When that earlier judge did so there was no 'law' for him or her to abide by.

Once the law is clearly perceived as a continuum, which is constantly being refined to meet current standards and needs, the value judgements made by judges on a case-by-case basis explains its creativity. The law's ability to develop in accordance with these standards and needs will be only as good as the judges' perception of those standards and needs and their ability to reflect those standards and needs. As, in this process, the question of what law 'is' cannot be separated from what it 'ought to be', the judges may be regarded as the means by which the 'ought' element is introduced into the law in a concrete and continuing fashion.

The phrase 'legal system' itself implies continuity. As a system that is part of a functioning society of institutions and relationships, its continuity is readily apparent. Yet, viewing law in cross-section at any given point of time obscures this essential characteristic. Professor Dias draws an attractive parallel between the concepts of a 'motor car' and 'motoring'. The latter means more than just a 'car'; it includes use, technique, road sense, destination and the like. So, too, with the legal system; any concept of it that excludes its motivating force and the factors that keep it in being is incomplete.[2] The judges, as the 'drivers', are responsible for ensuring that the motoring is directed to a social purpose and

---

[2] R. W. M. Dias, *Jurisprudence* (5th edn, Butterworths, London, 1985), at 503.

serves its social function. No automaton at the wheel can achieve that objective. Nor can a formalist.

The perception of the law as a continuum can be illustrated by a hypothesis; that of postulating exactly the same case arising three times over, say, two decades apart in each case. While the actual outcome may or may not vary, it is highly improbable that the cases would be decided in an identical fashion. Even the same judge, if it were possible, would not decide the three cases in the same way. Ignoring for the purposes of the hypothesis the bearing that the earlier cases would have on the later cases, the standards, needs and aspirations of the community will have changed and, with those changes, the values which the judges will reflect in their thinking will have changed. At any given time the law is in transition from one decision to the next. It would therefore be illusory to describe the law at any given time by reference to just one of these three hypothetical cases. Rather, it can only properly be described by reference to the progression of judicial thinking and reasoning extending through the three cases – and beyond. The difference between the situation at the beginning and the outcome at the end would be both the measure and the product of the judicial autonomy involved.

Is 'the law' what the courts ultimately decide?

Viewing the law as a process or continuum facilitates the perception that the law is what the courts ultimately decide. Writing in the period when Justice Holmes described the prophesies of what the courts will do in fact, and nothing more pretentious, is what is meant by the law, John Gray sought to restrict law to the decisions of the courts. He drew a distinction between law and the source of law; law is what judges decide and everything else, including statutes, are only sources of law until interpreted by a court.[3] Professor Dias promptly pointed out that, if this theory is pushed to its logical conclusion, it must mean that even a judicial decision is 'law' only for the parties to the dispute in question as the decision at once becomes a 'source of law' depending on the interpretation put upon it in a later decision.[4] In the result 'law never is but is always about to be. It is reached only when embodied in a judgment, and in being realised expires.'[5]

---

[3] Gray, *The Nature and Sources of the Law* (Macmillan, New York, 1921), at 123.
[4] Dias, *Jurisprudence*, at 449.
[5] Benjamin N. Cardozo, *The Nature of Judicial Process* (Yale University Press, New Haven, 1921), at 126, speaking critically of this perception.

A similar theory was advanced by Frank. Frank met Dias' criticism by opining that law is either 'actual law' made up of a specific past decision in a given situation or 'probable law' being an informed prediction as to a specific future decision.[6]

I think Gray's perception too extreme, Dias' criticism of it unduly technical, and Frank's revision too shaky. Both Gray and Frank try too hard to formulate a firm concept of law which would nevertheless embrace the inherent non-firmness – or uncertainty – of the law. Although ardent realists, they allow themselves to become too entangled in a linguistic and theoretical exercise. Gray's perception is too extreme in excluding the notion that there is a body of law that is so settled that it is artificial to suggest that it does not form part of the law of the land. Much law is safely predictable. Accepting, as I do, however, that there is no law which is so absolute or definitive as to be beyond challenge, this settled law remains subject to reinterpretation by the courts. But the fact this relatively settled law is subject to review does not mean that it is to be excluded from the definition of law. To exclude it because it may yet be revised would be to effectively exclude the whole of the known common law from the definition. A more fluid perception is required, one that embraces both the fact that there is at any given time a body of rules that can be regarded as relatively well settled in the sense that they are predictable, that is, likely to be applied by the courts, and the process by which those rules may be reinterpreted by the courts.

I agree that the distinction between the law and sources of law can be helpful in demonstrating the range of diverse factors that influence the content of the law or influence the courts in determining that content. I am not certain, however, that the distinction is of much value in determining what we mean by 'the law'. Law, viewed as a process, can fairly include the sources of law. Nor is it possible to draw a sharp distinction between the two. In Gray's terms, a court may decide in a particular case what it considers the law to be, but in doing so may rely on what would ordinarily be thought of as a source of law. Endorsed in that way the source of law would be law. It is impossible to escape from the notion that 'the law' is essentially a process and must be viewed as such.

Professor Dias' criticism shows the paucity of the distinction between law and sources of law for the purpose of determining what is law. But it is a technical point. To suggest that a ruling of the court immediately loses its identity as law and becomes a source of law for the next case and

---

[6] Jerome Frank, *Law and the Modern Mind* (Peter Smith, Gloucester, 1930), at 50–55.

so on *ad infinitum* is in itself plainly perverse. Again, the better view is to regard 'the law' as being principally a process operating within a relatively strict methodology or discipline. On its face, such a notion may seem to exclude rules and precedents, or the content of rules and precedents, even when widely accepted, from being included in the concept of 'the law'. But it is the place of these rules and precedents within the concept rather than their existence that is an issue. They do not in themselves make up the totality of 'the law'. Rather, they are part of the process, and cannot be divorced from that process. In short, the process has primacy.

Specific rules and precedents are therefore to be viewed as 'tools' that the judges use to determine what 'the law' is or ought to be at the date of their determination. Many other 'tools' are at hand; the source of rules, principles, standards, the source of principles and standards, the contributions of other disciplines, the social and economic consequences, public policy, such as public policy legislatively indicated by Parliament, and all the other manifold considerations which may be taken into account by judges in arriving at a decision. This is not to say that rules and precedents may not possess greater weight than these other considerations. Relatively firm rules and precedents will obviously enjoy greater prominence in the decision-making process. Nevertheless, they remain tools which the judges use – or decline to use – to shape and reshape 'the law'.

Take a twenty-year-old precedent as an example. The precedent is only the law if one adopts the limited and incomplete cross-section approach which I have already condemned. In that twenty years there will have been other developments or changes and, as at the date the issue is before the court, 'the law' will have developed or changed accordingly. The judge's task is to ascertain what 'the law' is as at the time the issue is in court. He or she may accept and apply the precedent. But assume, for example, that Parliament has in the meantime passed a statute which indicates that the judicial policy underlying the precedent is not the policy that Parliament supports. The judge may reject the precedent. The precedent may have stood for twenty years, but it is in the end no more than a tool that is part of the process of determining 'the law' at a given time. Not just the courts, but also lawyers advising their clients, will use the precedent in this sense. Lawyers astute enough to anticipate that the court will decline to follow a precedent because of the parliamentary signpost as to public policy will advise their clients that the precedent is not the law or, at least, not necessarily the law. Law, therefore, is ultimately a process in which rules and precedents will play an important role in determining the outcome, irrespective of the fact that they do not obtain presumptive or coercive force but are treated as tools available to the judges in the performance of that process.

It is therefore better to accept the reality that there is a vast body of law, some of which is relatively settled and some of which is highly uncertain, but all of which may at any time be revised if put in issue in the courts. The law can be both law that is relatively firm and predictable and law that is relatively vague and unpredictable. The whole spectrum is part of the law. Which brings me back to Frank.

Frank's theory dividing the law into 'actual law' and 'probable law' followed a vigorous attack on the notion that certainty could be achieved through rules. That much can be agreed. It is not necessary, however, to go further and seek to impose a less than sensible classification on the law to account for that phenomenon. Reduced to its essentials, the theory is no more than an attempt to categorise law as sufficiently certain to be called 'actual' or sufficiently problematic to be called 'probable'. That assessment can only be subjective. So what is actual law to one person may be doubtful law to another and what is probable law to one may be improbable to another. Furthermore, eventually the classification must break down. A specific decision in a given situation decision may be the 'actual law,' but at the same time the opposite view to that reached by the court may be the 'probable law' when it can be reasonably predicted that the decision will not stand. This cannot be.

A more fluid concept

Consequently, I prefer a more fluid concept, one that does not detract from the critical significance of court decisions in determining the content of the law, but one that does not exclude the reality that at any given time there is a body of law that is unlikely to be questioned. For the parties who have received a final determination, it is 'law' that can be enforced. For the community, it is 'law' that in the same or similar situation may be enforced. It is 'law' captured at different points of the process. To cast 'the law' as being in a state of perpetual evolution, and therefore somewhere between the last decision and the next, is simply to recognise the dynamic of the common law. The art is to predict the point 'the law' has reached at any given time. The courts will then determine whether one's art is secure.

Up to that time there may be competing versions as to what the law is, but those competing versions relate to the content of the law and do not detract from its status as law. In truth, providing the law is not elevated to the status of predetermined rules or edicts waiting to be declared or to commands requiring blind adherence and automatic application by judges, it does not matter how the content of the law is classified. The law will still exist notwithstanding that its overall boundaries, or the boundaries of its constituent concepts, cannot be fixed with any degree of precision. It exists because it is essentially part of a process.

To be fair to Gray and Frank, for whom I have the utmost respect, neither went so far as to exclude rules from their concept of law altogether.[7] Their views represented a sharp reaction to the belief that rules provide certainty and uniformity in the law. But it would have been incongruous for realists to have rejected rules entirely having regard to the pre-eminence attributed to them by so many participants in the legal system. The danger that Gray and Frank stressed was the danger of making legal rules the sole or main focus of attention. With that sentiment I am in full agreement.

I therefore adhere to what is essentially a realist's perception of law. Rules exist, some of greater persuasion than others, as part of the institution of the law. They are utilised by judges, lawyers, teachers and textbook writers as part of the armoury of the law. They provide a guide for the conduct of human affairs and the basis for seeking to determine the existence of enforceable rights, including obligations or powers.[8] But they remain part of a process that predominates and that is the gist of what we can sensibly describe as 'the law'. The fact that this process will be paramount in determining the existence and scope of a rule, is not to deny the existence of rules. Uncertain rules can still be tangible.

Further, as I expand in Chapter 13, when confronted with a legal issue, the judge must obviously start with some premise. It may be a rule. The rule may eventually be rejected or modified, but it is still the starting point and cannot be excluded from the concept of the law or the legal process.

---

[7] Dias, *Jurisprudence*, at 451–453; Frank, *Law and the Modern Mind*, at 329.
[8] See Twining, *Karl Llewellyn*, at 488–489 for a clear exposition of Llewellyn's description of rules.

The 'as is' and 'ought to be' distinction dissimulated

The approach I have adopted precludes the notion that the law 'as it is' must be kept separate from the law 'as it ought to be.' Bentham, Austin, Hume, Kelsen, Hart, and now, Joseph Raz, form a long line of brilliant theorists who have, to a greater or lesser extent, sought to keep the two poles separate. But it is not difficult for a practising judge to perceive that they are in error. Even the temporary divorce of 'is' and 'ought' favoured by the realists for the purpose of study[9] is out of place, for the 'ought' always infects what 'is'. As Fuller observed; '... in the moving world of law, the is and the ought are inseparably linked.'[10]

A decision may define a particular rule or principle but, because the law is to be seen as a continuum, that rule or principle is at once affected by what it ought to be. At any given time, therefore, the law is not just what the decision purports to be, but what the decision purports to be modified by considerations of what it ought to be to keep pace with the changing standards, needs and perceptions of the community. Even if these standards, needs and perceptions have not changed over time, the rule or principle identified in the decision is informed by the thinking that it ought to remain the same. Once the values around which the law and the legal system revolve have changed it is the judges' autonomy that ensures that the change in values will prove fatal to the continuance of a law at odds with those values. Clearly, unmerited adherence to precedent is inimical to this perception for the precedent can only represent the law at a given time. It cannot represent the law in transition – as it ought to be or will be in the next case.

I am here, therefore, in sympathy with the likes of Finnis and Dworkin who reject the idea that the social institution of law can simply be described 'as it is'. The law, as it is, cannot be adequately portrayed as law without taking account of the basic function of the law. Where I differ is that I do not see the function of law in some esoteric moral sense of 'forms of human flourishing', as does Finnis, or in a particular perception, arbitrarily proclaimed, of the law's capacity to justify collective governmental force, as Dworkin holds. Nor do I embed the function itself in the law in the sense that such theorists do. I take the

---

[9] K. Llewellyn, *Jurisprudence: Realism in Theory and Practice* (University of Chicago Press, Chicago, 1962), at 55–57.

[10] Quoted in Neil Duxbury, *Patterns of American Jurisprudence* (Clarendon Press, Oxford, 1995), at 224.

more pragmatic stance that the irredeemable function of the law is to serve society and that, as a social institution, the law may be judged good or bad, or legitimate or illegitimate, or valid or invalid, or as having integrity or not having integrity or by any number of such criteria. But it is unhelpful to insist that these criteria are necessarily part of the law.

The fact that I have no truck with the positivists' persistence in viewing the law more or less as a static cross-section of what in reality is a process or continuum may be reiterated in this context. Viewing the law in cross-section, and not as a process, contributes to their penchant to vest the law with a certainty it does not have and which it is incapable of ever obtaining. But without that certainty it is impossible to maintain the distinction between the law 'as it is' and the law 'as it ought to be'.

The view that the law is to be seen as a process or continuum makes judicial methodology all important. As it is part of the process by which the law is made and re-made, that methodology is to be included within the concept of law. It is the methodology which will decide the extent to which the judge's preconceptions or predilections will be curbed or will affect his or her decision-making; which will influence the decisions made and the content of the rules and principles; and which will import the constraints which inhibit judicial waywardness. All these factors are an integral part of the law. It is what makes the process a discipline, and necessitates an examination of the 'rule of law'.

The rule of law in the scheme of things

The rule of law is a nebulous concept, at least at its margins. To seek to vest it with a firm meaning is like trying to fix a cloud with a uniform and fixed description. Seldom will it hold its form. In large part, however, this difficulty in describing the rule of law is due to the misplaced orthodoxy that governmental action and judicial decision-making can function as an interpretative process bereft of discretion, or anything more than a minimal recourse to discretion.[11] Such a view survives on the unrealistic belief that law can be reduced to rules which are fixed and certain and therefore able to be reasonably predicted in advance. Only then, it is thought, will people be governed by laws and not by the whim of men or women and only then will governance avoid being arbitrary

---

[11] Malcolm M. Feeley and Edward L. Rubin, *Judicial Policy Making and the Modern State: How the Courts Reformed America's Prisons* (Cambridge University Press, Cambridge, 1998), at 207–210 and 241–246.

and capricious. Only then, it is not going too far to say, will society bilk mobocracy!

Plainly put, we need a perception of the rule of law which accords with reality. The rule of law simply cannot be equated with a law of rules, as Justice Scalia would have it.[12] Lord Steyn has rightly described such a version an 'impoverished concept'.[13]

As George Fletcher points out, there are two versions of the rule of law; a modest version of adhering to rules, and a loftier ideal that incorporates criteria of justice.[14] I am here concerned with the modest version. My aim is to replace the 'impoverished concept' with a perception firmly founded in the reality of judicial adjudication. Judicial behaviour is constrained, I will argue, not by the text of the law, that is, by certain, predictable and known rules, but by the judicial methodology and discipline that make up the legal process. The constraint required by the rule of law is to be found in that process.

We are here, of course, concerned with the application of the rule of law to judicial decision-making. Irrespective of the more fluid concept of 'the law' that I have advanced, rules may provide guidance to governmental agencies, and those rules may be more or less certain, but my focus is on the institution that ultimately determines the common law, the judiciary. It can be observed, however, that other commentators have pointed out that governmental administration requires the use of discretion and that, rather than being regarded as a necessary evil, discretion is often a desirable adjunct of good governance.[15] As the law is inherently uncertain and judicial discretion or autonomy is an inevitable part of the judicial process, the same approach needs to be applied to the rule of law in its application to the judiciary. A revised perception of the principle may become a desirable adjunct to the judicial process.

First, however, the present orthodox perception of the rule of law in relation to the judiciary needs to be more fully examined with a view to discerning the essence of that perception. As already noted, the orthodox perception seeks to restrict the judicial function to an interpretative function thus limiting the use of discretion. Its adherents look to the text

---

[12] Antonin Scalia, 'The Rule of Law as a Law of Rules' (1989) 56 Univ. of Chic. LR 1175.
[13] Lord Steyn, 'Democracy Through Law', Occasional Paper No. 12, at 6–7.
[14] George P. Fletcher, *Basic Concepts of Legal Thought* (Oxford University Press, Oxford 1996), at 11.
[15] See, e.g., Timothy A. O. Endicott, *Vagueness in Law* (Oxford University Press, Oxford, 2000), at 188–203.

of the law to control the judge's discretion, which is why fixed and certain rules are regarded as being so important. The more uncertain the rules, it is contended, the larger the discretion and the further removed the judicial process is from being governed by a rule of laws as distinct from the whim of men and women. Cognisant, perhaps, of the difficulty of providing a text of sufficient certainty to make the theory credible, the orthodox perception is at times extended to 'legal doctrine'. In other words, where the text of the law is indeterminate, judges must or should adhere to legal doctrine. Notwithstanding that these doctrines will have been created by judges in the past, they are perceived to operate as a restraint on the discretion of judges in the present.

The open intent of such a framework is to reduce the scope for the judiciary to make law or promulgate new legal doctrine. Judicial policy making is contrary to its mandate; judicial discretion or judicial autonomy is alien to its dictates; and judicial creativity is to be spurned. The notion of an impersonal law is a virtual prerequisite. Yet, if this more orthodox perception is correct judges are regularly violating the rule of law. The notion of the third branch of government with the constitutional responsibility of upholding the law being in regular and unavoidable violation of the rule of law is patently unacceptable.

The core element that underlies this orthodox perception is that judicial decision-making should be constrained. It is this constraint that limits the scope for judicial whim, arbitrariness or aberrancy resulting in inconsistency and unpredictability. The mistake is to think that the constraint can be found in the text of the law or legal doctrine. As I have elaborated earlier,[16] rules and legal doctrine may be important tools in the judicial armoury, and to that extent they may have a restraining influence on judicial behaviour, but they are not the decisive factor in ensuring adherence to the rule of law. The decisive constraint is to be found in the judicial methodology that is adopted, including the numerous constraints that I traverse in Chapter 10. Thus, the rule of law is preserved because judges are subject to constraint, but the constraint is primarily the product of the judicial process and not of the text of the law as such.

In his outstanding work, *Vagueness in Law*, Timothy Endicott, has demonstrated that the indeterminacy of the law does not threaten the pursuit of the rule of law.[17] Endicott realistically entertains no doubt

---

[16] See above at 221–222. See also Chapter 13, at 346; Chapter 14, at 353; Chapter 15, at 363 and 393–394.
[17] Endicott, *Vagueness in Law*, at 197–203; or, it may be said, the pursuit of justice.

that indeterminacy in the law is pervasive and obdurate. Vagueness is an essential feature of law.[18] Law is necessarily vague.[19] As vague language cannot be eliminated from the law, non-linguistic indeterminacies arise because life and legal systems are complicated.[20] When judges are called upon to resolve disputes for which the law provides no resolution, the law as such does not constrain the will of the judge with respect to such disputes. Lawyers, Endicott continues, think that applying the law and treating like cases alike are the heart and soul of the judges' task but, because of the vagueness of the law, that expectation cannot always be realised. The rule of law then seems unattainable. In the result, Endicott states: 'An impossible ideal seems romantic at best, and at worse absurd.'[21]

Not surprisingly, Endicott sets about reconstructing the ideal. He argues that a vague law does not necessarily represent 'a deficit' in the rule of law. Consequently, replacing a vague law with a precise law does not necessarily bring a community closer to the ideal of the rule of law. Such a step, he suggests, might even increase uncertainty and he gives the English Statute of Frauds as an example of how precisely formulated laws stimulated the interpretative ingenuity of lawyers and judges and led to extravagant pragmatic vagueness being given to precisely formulated laws.[22] Noting that precise laws can lead to arbitrariness in the sense that the requirements of the law will not reflect the reasons on which such a law ought to be based, Endicott concludes that increasing precision can in fact increase arbitrariness. I agree. The absence of flexibility or discretion in a law, or how a law is to be applied, can lead to arbitrary consequences in the circumstances of a particular case, and even result in like being treated unlike. Legislatures incline to give judges broad discretionary powers to implement their statutory requirements precisely to avoid such arbitrary outcomes. Discretion permits a power or rule to be adapted to suit the manifold different, diffuse and complex circumstances that will inevitably arise.

Endicott also rejects the notion that changes in the law are contrary to the rule of law. He finds a legal system with no rule of change inconceivable. A legal system, to be in good shape, needs not only rules of change, but also active law-makers.[23] If the law did not provide for its own change, Endicott states, it would commit itself to increasing irrationality by refusing to respond when existing regulations or forms of

---

[18] Ibid., at 7 and 190. [19] Ibid., at 189. [20] Ibid., at 7. [21] Ibid., at 188.
[22] Ibid., at 191–192. [23] Ibid., at 192–193.

regulation are seen to be or to become pointless, and when new regulations and forms of regulation are needed, that is, when the reason of the law demands a change in the law.

Taking the organising principle of the rule of law as being that the law must be capable of guiding behaviour, Endicott points out that this principle does not require that the law's guidance never change. Rather, it requires that the prospect of change should not make it impossible to use the existing law as a guide. Thus the author distinguishes between using the law as a guide and using the law to dictate an outcome in every possible case.[24] I would add that the prospect of change does not make it impossible to use the existing law as a guide once a contemporary judicial methodology is adopted. Precedents may still provide a guide if they are treated as tools of the judicial trade and considered or reconsidered in the light of other relevant factors that are part of the community of considerations that I describe in Chapter 13.

The insight in Endicott's thesis which I most applaud is his appreciation that the rule of law can be identified in the law's capacity to provide for the resolution of its own indeterminacies.[25] As noted elsewhere, it is an innate characteristic of the legal system that there is finality in adjudication.[26] Hence, Endicott is able to claim that the law provides for its own indeterminacies, just as it provides for its own identification, and its own change, and its own enforcement. These are all senses in which, as Kelsen said, the law regulates its own creation.[27] Endicott argues that, to make sense of the ideal of the rule of law, therefore, it is necessary to accept that, in addition to the forensic role of fact-finding and the watchdog role of ensuring compliance, the role of the courts includes the creative role of resolving unresolved disputes about the requirements of the law. Consequently, there is no escaping the rule of people. The necessary creative role of judges means that 'the rule of laws, not of men' is a rhetorical figure for 'the rule of laws *free from abuse* by men'.[28] In this way, Endicott continues, the duty of judges to enforce a final resolution in a dispute becomes a basic requirement of the rule of law in that the law possesses the capacity to resolve its own indeterminacies.

---

[24] Ibid., at 203. [25] Ibid., at 197. [26] See above, Chapter 5, at 126–128.
[27] Hans Kelsen, *General Theory of Norms* (translated by Michael Hartney Clarendon Press, Oxford, 1991), at 124, 126, and 132 *et seq.*
[28] Endicott, *Vagueness in Law*, at 197–199.

I fully accept that the capacity and responsibility of judges to impose a final resolution is an essential element of their legitimacy. In this respect, judicial review provides a prime example of the rule of law in action. The rule of law does not exist in having precise rules controlling administrative action available in all circumstances, for that is impossible. Rather, in general terms, the courts will intervene if governmental action is illegal, irrational or unfair. The certainty required by the rule of law does not therefore exist in exact rules of public law, but in the certainty that the courts will provide a remedy if minimum standards of substantive rationality and procedural fairness are not met. The standards may be vague and indeterminate, but the rule of law is nevertheless met if the expectation of citizens that there are standards that will be proclaimed and enforced by the courts is realised. Ironically, conservative judges who decline to judicially review an administrative decision because of the indeterminacy of the law, do the rule of law a disservice if it can fairly be said that the administrator has not acted with fidelity to his or her governing statute.

I will now return, however, to my basic contention that judicial behaviour is constrained, not by the text of the law, but by the judicial methodology and discipline that make up the legal process, and that it is this constraint that satisfies the rule of law. Not unexpectedly, I return to Feeley and Rubin's research for support.

The authors acknowledge that the rule of law demands that judges be subject to external constraints that are general, clear, well accepted and congruent with the legal order. They are firm in holding that, although the judges in the cases that they studied broke new ground, and at times radically so, they operated within the framework of law.[29] In formulating policy, the judges were not guided by any text, because there was no text to guide them, but the authors did not get the impression that this was so. Feeley and Rubin suggest that the judges seemed to be groping towards some image of a just, efficient prison system rather than expressing their desire or exercising their own will. Their impression was that the judges were the same judges who decide contract cases and construe the Securities Exchange Act, and that they felt the same sense of constraint as they do in those more traditional activities.[30]

Feeley and Rubin argue that the judicial policy-making they identified in the prison reform cases were limited, like other judicial decisions, by the rule of law. They acknowledged at once, however, as I

---

[29] Feeley and Rubin, *Judicial Policy Making*, at 208–209. [30] Ibid., at 241–242.

have acknowledged, that this version is precluded in advance if it is asserted that only judicial fact finding and interpretation satisfy that doctrine. Rejecting this assertion as unsustainable, Feeley and Rubin refer back to their perception that the law functions as both a framework that engenders judicial decision-making and a constraint that disciplines it. Thus, the process is inherently constrained. Judges engaged in the process do not feel unconstrained at all, but feel subject to powerful forces limiting their range of action. The methods they use to create legal policy are simultaneously a framework or conceptual process that empowers them to do so and a set of constraints that guide their actions.[31] A modern version of the rule of law, therefore, incorporates the concept of constraint, but jettisons the idea that the constraint must necessarily consist of fixed, pre-established rules.

In my own terms, the hundreds of judges involved in deliberating the far-reaching decisions in the prison reform cases were subject to an effective constraint that ensured the paramountcy of the rule of law. That constraint existed in the judicial methodology and discipline that prevailed, not in the text of the law. Judicial constraints of the kind to be described in Chapter 10 prevented the judges exercising any unrestrained personal whim or will. Thus, the rule of law is inherent or indwelling within the legal process itself.

Rechtsstaat or *justizstaat*?

At the conclusion of their book, *Interpreting Precedents: A Comparative Study*,[32] the editors, Professors MacCormick and Summers, conclude with some general reflections and conclusions. Under the heading, '*Rechtsstaat* or *Justizstaat*', they express some concern at the formidable power of courts and judges in contemporary society and raise the question whether the rule of law is nothing better than the rule of judges rather than parliamentarians.

MacCormick and Summers observe that concern about 'judge-made' law in countries that purport to have constitutional and democratic government, with law-making power primarily vested in the people or their representatives in a parliament, is enhanced wherever democratic

---

[31] Ibid., at 210 and 241–242.
[32] D. Neil MacCormick and Robert S. Summers (eds.), *Interpreting Precedents: A Comparative Study* (Ashgate, Dartmouth, 1997), MacCormick and Summers, 'Further general reflections and conclusions', 531, at 549.

institutions are held to presuppose an entrenchment of basic human rights to guarantee the security and dignity of every person. They point out that, if entrenched rights are not justiciable, or are freely alterable by the decision of parliamentary assemblies or popular referenda, they may prove ineffectual, that is, mere paper guarantees. On the other hand, the authors say, if they are justiciable, the judges necessarily exercise formidable powers, powers in certain matters to second-guess the ordinary democratic process.

To draw this distinction out, MacCormick and Summers utilise the concepts of *rechtsstaat* and *justizstaat*. The German notion of *rechtsstaat* captures the vision of a state based on the ideal law, that is, law in the 'higher sense'.[33] It presupposes an ordering of state authority in which the independence of the judiciary is an essential component.[34] Thus, interference in the rights of citizens is permissible only if the interference is sanctioned by statute, and the protection of the citizens whose rights are refused can only be achieved by permitting 'victims' to have recourse to the courts. Consequently, the *rechtsstaat* imports the justiciability of a concept of the bill of rights.[35] MacCormick and Summers then present readers with a paradox. If the idea of the state under law, the 'law state' or the *rechtsstaat*, is to be taken as entailing, not only a governance of state officials under the rule of law, but also the justiciable guaranteeing of a bill or charter of rights, must the *rechtsstaat* turn into a *justizstaat*? Will the law state turn into a justiciary state and is the rule of law nothing better than the rule of judges rather than parliamentarians?[36]

MacCormick and Summers do not seek to answer this question. Nonetheless, they unreservedly endorse the notion of legal and constitutional stability and accept that this stability cannot be achieved without a trusted judiciary genuinely independent of partisan involvement and political favour.[37] For this purpose they allow that the judiciary 'must have interpretive power of a far-reaching kind'.[38]

I do not disagree with this sage observation. As my previous discussions indicate, my thesis is that these objectives can be more effectively achieved by the adoption of the judicial methodology advanced in this book. Without abandoning precedent, which would be a valuable tool at

---

[33] Fletcher, *Basic Concepts of Legal Thought*, at 12.
[34] Johan d. van der Vyver, 'Sovereignty in Human Rights in Constitutional and International Law' (1991) Emery International LR, 321, at 385–386.
[35] Ibid.   [36] MacCormick and Summers, *Interpreting Precedent*, at 549.
[37] Ibid., at 550.   [38] Ibid.

the judge's disposal, principles rather than precedent should provide the legal and constitutional stability which the authors seek. 'Consistency of decisions over time' to use their phrase,[39] is more likely to be obtained if it is based on practical reasoning dominated by principles as traversed in Chapter 13.

This qualification apart, however, still leaves MacCormick and Summers' question open in relation to the conception of the rule of law advanced above. Does that conception mean that we move from a system of *rechtsstaat* to *justizstaat*? In other words, in seeking to find and establish the constraints on judicial power necessary to retain a viable conception of the rule of law within the judicial process itself, are we moving from a state governed by enacted law to a state ultimately governed by judicial decree?

The terms *rechtsstaat* and *justizstaat* may be convenient terms with which to portray the balance between the law-making powers exercised by the legislature, on the one hand, and the judiciary, on the other. The above revision of the rule of law, however, does not impinge on this dichotomy. Limited to judicial decision-making, it does no more than assert that the essence of the rule of law exists in the constraints upon the judiciary and it attempts to define the constraints on judicial power in terms of judicial methodology and discipline rather than the text of the law. The argument is that the process provides a more effective constraint than the traditional 'constraint' provided by an uncertain and vague law and the fiction that judges do no more than declare or interpret the law. A judge purporting to 'interpret' an uncertain law is exercising as much, if not more, discretion than a judge working within the confines of an articulated and transparent judicial methodology. Consequently, acceptance of the proposed revision of the rule of law would not in itself move the judiciary towards *justizstaat*. Indeed, if the constraint on the exercise of errant or aberrant judicial behaviour is more effective, the corollary must be that the rule of law would be that much more effective.

Nevertheless, a realistic appraisal of the judicial process reveals a development that needs to be addressed. It is a development which gives some substance to the notion that the judge is at times more than a herald, and can become 'a king'.[40] The exercise of kingly sovereignty is evident where a constitution empowers the courts to annul an enactment of a legislative assembly, as in the United States. In countries where this is not the case, however, such as the United Kingdom and

---

[39] Ibid.   [40] Halpin uses this analogy in *Reasoning with Law*, at 58.

New Zealand, the courts are struggling to determine the limits of the powers vested in them as 'guardians' of fundamental human rights and freedoms. It is in the context of acknowledging that there cannot be legal and constitutional stability without a trusted judiciary genuinely independent of partisan involvement and political favour, that MacCormick and Summers state the judiciary 'must have interpretative power of a far-reaching kind'.[41]

The question becomes more acute when the 'interpretative power' assumed by the courts cannot be said to be an 'interpretative power' without adopting an extremely artificial and forced meaning of that phrase. When fundamental rights and freedoms can be assured by an interpretation of the statute in issue, even where that interpretation may be said to be expansive, the judiciary is seen to be fulfilling the constitutional function vested in it by the legislature.[42] Such an approach relies upon what has been called 'the malleability of language'.[43] Irrespective whether Parliament has addressed the question at all or, if it has, whether it has made its meaning clear, the courts can adopt an expansive approach and vest the statutory provision with a meaning that would presumably accord, or that they presume would accord, with Parliament's intent.[44] The problem arises when the possible 'interpretation' cannot be said to have been within the intention of the legislature. Can the courts, to frame the point as a question, adopt a construction of the statute in issue consistent with the human rights protected by a constitution or bill of rights that is plainly outside the legislature's intention? Can the courts adopt a 'meaning' consistent with basic human rights and freedoms when that 'meaning' could not have been arrived at through the application, even an expansive application, of conventional interpretative precepts and principles?

The decision of the House of Lords in *Ghaidan* v *Godin-Mendoza (FC)*[45] provides a good example of this development and the problem that goes with it. Section 2(1) of the Rent Act 1977 provides that the surviving spouse of an original tenant residing in the dwelling house immediately before the death of that tenant shall, after the death, be the

---

[41] MacCormick and Summers, *Interpreting Precedent*, at 550.
[42] Section 3 of the Human Rights Act 1998; sections 4 and 6 of the New Zealand Bill of Rights Act 1990.
[43] Andrew Butler, 'Strengthening the Bill of Rights' (2000) 31 VUWLR 129, at 133.
[44] For the author's observations on this subject, since largely recanted, see *R v Poumako*, below n. 50, at paras. [80]–[84].
[45] [2004] UKHL 30.

statutory tenant. Subsection (2) then states that a person who was living with the original tenant as 'his or her wife or husband' shall be treated as the 'spouse' of the original tenant. The question before their Lordships was whether the survivor of a close and stable homosexual relationship was entitled to be a statutory tenant under these provisions. Clearly, the words 'as his or her wife or husband shall be treated as the spouse ...' indicate a heterosexual relationship. Indeed, the clarity of the language was sufficient for Lord Millet, and he declined to join the majority in dismissing the appeal.

The majority, Lords Nicholls, Steyn and Rodger and Baroness Hale, turned to the Human Rights Act 1998. Section 14 of that Act prohibits discrimination on the ground, *inter alia*, of 'gender'. Section 3 then became the key provision. That section provides that legislation must be read and given effect to in a way which is compatible with the rights set out in the European Convention 'so far as it is possible to do so'. Considerable argument turned on the interpretation of the word 'possible'. That word could be confined so as to allow for the resolution of ambiguities or it could be construed in a much stronger sense and permit the courts to depart from the evident intention of Parliament. Lord Nicholls framed the problem in these terms:

> Section 3 may require the court to depart from this legislative intention, that is, depart from the intention of the Parliament which enacted the legislation. The question of difficulty is how far, and in what circumstances, section 3 requires the court to depart from the intention of the enacting Parliament.[46]

Attributing the stronger meaning to Parliament, the majority held that it was 'possible' to construe section 2(2) of the Rent Act so as to treat the survivor of a close and stable homosexual relationship as being within the scope of the section. No ambiguity was required to reach this conclusion. It was accepted that the right to a house and to have one's housing problems solved was a matter for the state but, it was held, if the state makes a legislative provision, that legislation cannot be discriminatory. The evils of discrimination were stressed and legislation denying a homosexual couple in a close and stable relationship equal protection and the same security as heterosexual couples was held to be discriminatory. The court's power is limited only by what is 'possible', and in determining that question the meaning imported by section 3 must be one which is 'compatible with the underlying thrust of the legislation'.[47]

[46] Paragraph 30.   [47] Paragraph 33.

Words implied must 'go with the grain of the legislation'.[48] It is only when the proposed meaning is inconsistent with the scheme of the legislation, or with its essential principles as disclosed in its provisions, that the meaning would fall on the wrong side of the boundary between 'interpretation' and amendment of a statute.[49] In this respect, the social policy providing security of tenure to the survivors of couples living together as husband and wife was held to be equally applicable to the survivors of homosexual couples living together in a close and stable relationship.

As will be observed, their Lordships in the majority regarded the exercise that they undertook as being within the framework of interpretation, albeit that they dispensed with the standard precepts and principles associated with statutory interpretation. This approach may qualify for MacCormick and Summers' description of an 'interpretative power of a far-reaching kind'. Debating whether the approach can properly be called interpretation or not, however, would be to miss the point. It is the fact that, in the process, however it is described, the courts can depart from the acknowledged intention of Parliament that attracts, and will continue to attract, the sombre shadow of *justizstaat*.

The same division of opinion arose in New Zealand. In two successive decisions the Court of Appeal demonstrated that there is more than one way of standing a court on its head in an effort to avoid giving criminal legislation retrospective effect when that effect undeniably represented Parliament's intent.[50] Parliament was denied its undoubted objective, some Judges adopting 'an interpretation of a far-reaching kind' and yet others attributing a meaning to the statutory provisions which, it must be acknowledged, went beyond that more benign description.[51]

---

[48] Paragraphs 33 and 121.   [49] Paragraph 121.
[50] See *R v Poumako* [2000] 2 NZLR 695; and *R v Pora* [2001] 2 NZLR 37.
[51] See esp., Elias CJ and Tipping J at paras. [17]–[56] and the author at paras. [130]–[170] in *R v Pora*, above n. 50. See also the decisions of the Privy Council dealt with in the Postscript to Chapter 7. In the cases noted, the majority of their Lordships declined to apply a provision conferring on the courts a power of 'modification' to ensure the compliance of existing laws to the rights contained in the Constitutions in question on the basis that the exercise of that power would have been outside any 'reasonable intention' that could be ascribed to Parliament. The minority were not deterred by this consideration. The fact the provision vested the court with what was effectively a power of rectification enabled them to prefer a 'meaning' consistent with the fundamental rights and freedoms protected by the Constitutions. Their focus was on a meaning which would serve that purpose rather than ascertaining what might or might not have been the legislatures' intention.

It is not my present purpose, however, to endeavour to explain the source of this judicial division of opinion or seek to resolve the difference of approach one way or another. One set of judges is unable to break out of the square of the traditional precepts and principles of interpretation and recognise an 'interpretation' that is not reasonably tenable on the face of the statute. The other, thinking outside the square, hold to a different and enlarged 'interpretative' approach in which Parliament's immediate intention may be subverted to the prior and ultimate intention apparent in the enactment of a supreme law or charter of rights.[52] For present purposes it is only necessary to reiterate that this excursion into *justizstaat*, if that is what it is, does not undermine the concept of the rule of law that I have advanced above.

Outside the special area of protecting fundamental human rights and freedoms, a dichotomy which contrasts the power of the legislature and the powers of the judiciary in absolute terms is somewhat misplaced, even in the context of the rule of law. Holding to the view that the legislature and the courts represent a 'fruitful partnership' in the law-making business together,[53] both institutions must necessarily contribute to the rule of law. The legislature makes its contribution by enacting laws which conform to the rule of law, more particularly the 'ideal' of the rule of law referred to earlier. The judiciary can be said to serve the same goal when enforcing fundamental human rights and freedoms or, possibly, when ensuring on review that governmental agencies act with fidelity to their governing statutes. At a more modest level, judges simply serve the rule of law by working within the constraints imposed by the legal process. None of this makes the rule of law the rule of judges or rule by judicial decree in any sensible sense.

The reality is that judges are different things at different times. When adjudicating a dispute in which the applicable rule or principle is relatively well settled, judges can be said to be 'interpreting' and applying the law in the traditional sense; when required to shape the law to do justice in the particular case or to develop the law to meet contemporary circumstances judges are advancing the common law as law-makers; when curbing the use or abuse of governmental power pursuant to the courts' supervisory jurisdiction, the judges are ensuring that the

---

[52] See below, Chapter 10, at 263–265. My thinking is indicated in the Postscript to Chapter 7.
[53] I have already suggested that the question whether the courts may declare particular legislation invalid in a system in which the doctrine of parliament supremacy prevails should be 'left up in the constitutional air'. See above, Chapter 2, at 51.

administration of government adheres to the basic precepts of the 'ideal' of the rule of law; and when applying general and abstract statements of fundamental human rights and freedoms to concrete situations, the judges are effectively legislating the detail of those rights and freedoms. In all these tasks it is the judicial methodology and discipline that will provide the most effective constraint on the judiciary for the purposes of a viable and contemporary rule of law.

The judicial oath

It is convenient to briefly touch upon the judicial oath all judges are obliged to swear. If judicial methodology is not part of the law, judges are in trouble with the traditional oath because they swear or affirm to do justice 'according to law'.[54] But accepting the reality of the judicial process, what can this oath mean? Judges make law. Is the oath therefore to be understood as an obligation on the judge to do justice according to law that he or she may then make, or to do justice in accordance with the law that some other judge has made and that may not be just? That other judge, of course, being the first in line, presumably did justice according to a law that he or she made – in breach of the judicial oath! Further, as the inherent uncertainty of the law cannot be denied, is the oath to be construed as requiring the judge to do justice according to law that is inherently uncertain? These formulations are nonsense. Yet, if the reality is that there is no law to be declared, how can sense be made of the oath? The answer can only be to recognise that it refers to the legal process and judicial methodology, including the constraints that the process or methodology embraces.[55]

I have always found the unquestioning adoption of the judicial oath by judges disappointing. To give the words 'according to law' meaning, justice, or the obligation to do justice, seems to take a back seat. The oath, as often applied in practice, it seems, could be better worded '... to apply the law according to the law', and if this tautology were not

---

[54] The historical form of the judicial oath reads in part: 'I [the Judge] swear that ... I will do right to all manner of people after the laws and usages of [the country] without fear or favour, affection or ill will'. The word 'usages' is omitted in some jurisdictions.
[55] In the context of cases in which judicial bias, more particularly actual bias, is alleged the significance of the judicial oath is regarded as 'an important protection' but not as 'a sufficient guarantee to exclude all doubt'. See *Starrs* v *Ruxton* [2000] JC 208, at 253; [2000] SLT 42, at 72, affirmed in *Davidson, Petitioner* [2004] SLT 805, per Lord Bingham at para. [18].

enough the word 'law' is then construed to mean 'the law as I [the judge] perceive it to be'! In particular, conservative judges who embrace formalism may be heard to proclaim from time to time that they have been true to their judicial oath with a disturbing degree of self-satisfaction, seemingly oblivious to the fact that the law was either uncertain or nonexistent on the point in issue before their decision, and that they themselves formulated the law to which they then so complacently adhered. The superficiality of their approach, of course, reflects the deeper philosophical malaise that I described in Chapter 1.

Conclusion

Different definitions of what is meant by 'the law' will undoubtedly persist. The fact different descriptions are used may not matter much providing that the definition that is adopted accords with the reality of the judicial process and does not have a distorting effect on that process. Much turns on that perennial question of where to draw the line or what one chooses to include within the descriptive title of 'the law'.

In essence, providing that 'the law' is not defined as predetermined rules or principles virtually having the force of edicts waiting to be recognised and the outmoded theoretical language that supports such a perception is abandoned, I am somewhat sceptical of the need to provide a precise definition of what is meant by 'the law'. The phrase can be given different meanings for different purposes and, for that reason, its boundaries do not need to be defined with precision. I prefer a fluid concept that can accept that there is a body of relatively well-established rules which, in the event of a dispute, will be more than likely adopted by the courts. But their adoption will be due to their current utility and not to the fact they have acquired the status of 'the law'. Consequently, while there may be a substantial body of 'law' that can be securely predicted and used as a guide to conduct, there are no rules or principles that cannot be questioned or that may not be challenged as new or different circumstances arise. What the law is will then be determined by the court at the time. Even 'law' which is admittedly uncertain can still provide a guide, but not an edict or directive, once it is appreciated that 'the law' is somewhere between the last decision and the next. It is inevitably in a state of evolution.

For these reasons, the perennial question 'what is the law?' is best answered by giving paramountcy to the legal process itself. Rules exist but are ultimately subservient to a process that permits them to continue, or modifies them, or destroys them. But this does not mean that the rule of law no longer prevails. Judicial behaviour is constrained, not by an uncertain and vague text, but by the judicial methodology and discipline that make up the legal process. The constraints, both present and quiescent, which form part of that methodology and discipline are examined in the next chapter.

10

The constraints on the judiciary

The significance of judicial constraints

Democratic imperatives require the power of the three arms of government to be constrained. Indeed, the constraints are the essence of the constitutional framework of a democracy and the rule of law. In broad terms, the legislative branch is constrained by elections and such structures as Parliament puts in place to permit it to monitor the legislative process. The executive branch is not elected, but is constrained by the terms and purpose of its empowering statutes, parliamentary supervision, internal control mechanisms and judicial review in the courts.[1] Judges are neither elected nor supervised, judicial independence being a fundamental tenet of the constitution. But to conclude from this apparent freedom that the judiciary is unconstrained is misleading. Judges are subject to a wide range of effective constraints. The depiction of the errant or aberrant judge kicking over the traces and subverting the democratic process or the rule of law is indicative of an obsessional fear of judicial discretion or judicial autonomy.

Critics of judicial autonomy, of course, seek to do more than curb the errant or aberrant judge. They seek to eliminate judicial initiative and creativity and thus confine the judge's law-making power to the barest minimum. The constraints do not achieve this objective. Nor should they. There must be room in the law for the bold and the timorous, the progressive and the cautious, the liberal and the conservative, and a host in-between. In sum total, the sweep of the law nets a balance, diversity and fullness greater than its component parts. But no part must be

---

[1] In some jurisdictions, of course, the executive could be said to be elected in that, as in the United States, the head of the administration is elected by popular vote. In yet another sense, the executive is 'elected' when voters generally know who will be the prime minister and who are likely to constitute the cabinet when voting for a particular candidate or party. But in broad terms, which is all I seek to say, the executive is not elected.

debarred lest the vital spark that provides the dynamic of the common law is extinguished.[2]

Let me specifically clarify that I accept that it is open to such cavillers to condemn judicial law or policy-making or, if they wish, to rail against judicial liberalism. My immediate point is that it is wrong to suggest that the judges who are being so condemned are exercising an unfettered will and imposing their own personal opinion on the law. In the first place, such so-called opinions reflect or are reducible to value judgements, and value judgements are common to all judges – conservative and liberal alike. Once the presence and influence of value judgements is accepted as a reality of judicial decision-making, it adds nothing to seek to relabel the phenomenon as 'personal opinions'. In the second place, any such 'opinions' are subject to a judicial methodology and discipline. They are the outcome of a deliberately deliberative and reflective process. Certainly, the opinion (or value judgement) must be that of the individual judge, but it is an institutionalised 'opinion' in the sense that it is fashioned and confined by the vast range of constraints bearing upon the judiciary.[3]

Once it is accepted that the proper purpose of judicial constraints is to impose a brake on the errant or aberrant judge and not to enforce a particular perception of the judicial role, the topic probably loses much of its popular interest. But it is an important topic nonetheless. It is important because it is through the constraints on the judiciary, both imposed and self-imposed that, not only is the law spared an errant or aberrant judiciary, but also the law and legal process obtains coordination, coherence and direction. A judicial methodology without this discipline is not so much dangerous as incomplete.

Admitting that the values that are applied in the judicial process are the values as perceived by the individual judge and that various judges' perceptions may differ is not inconsistent with the view that they are channelled into a form which is acceptable to the community and consonant with the values of the community. A plethora of factors operate to curb any arbitrary element in the judge's appreciation when

---

[2] I am not, of course, suggesting that there is room in the law for the formalist judge as well as the non-formalist judge. My attack on the residual influence of formalism is too strong to permit such a lapse. A judge of, say, a conservative frame of mind can be 'conservative' without embracing formalism or a formalistic approach.

[3] See below, at 243–249.

arriving at a decision. As I stated earlier,[4] these factors are not to be found in the text of the law, as such, or in the 'rigour' of legal doctrine, but in the adjudicative discipline to which the judiciary is subject.

The point of an expansive excursion into the constraints that bear upon the judiciary, therefore, is to demonstrate that the adoption of a pragmatic and principle-oriented approach does not mean that judges operate as free-ranging, idiosyncratic spooks imposing their unfettered will on hapless litigants and an equally hapless community. Even without the abandonment of the residual influence of formalism and the obsolete or unrealistic theories on which it is founded, the demotion of certainty from a goal of adjudication to a consideration to be taken into account in appropriate cases, and the wilful adjustment of the doctrine of precedent so as to challenge, whenever required, the validity of a precedent, the constraints on the judiciary are sufficiently potent to confine the judicial law-making power within bounds that are constitutionally sound. The constraints, certainly taken together, yield decisions that are every bit as 'principled' as decisions overtly following a formalistic pattern, and they permit a perception of the role of the judiciary that falls within any rational perception of the rule of law.

I turn first to the external constraints, that is, those constraints that impinge on the judge by virtue of his or her judicial office.

The external constraints

To the forefront of these external constraints, of course, is the structure of the legal system. Judges do not and cannot operate alone. The judgments of a judge at first instance, for example, face the examination inherent in the appellate process. It is highly improbable that a decision which represents the personal aberration of a judge who is subject to the appeal process will be shared by three to five, or more, other judges. Furthermore, the language of the appeal court's judgment or judgments may, politely or not so politely, imply that the judge has fallen short of an expected standard. Judges, or some judges, may not be unduly concerned in writing their judgments whether or not they will be reversed on appeal, but no judge wishes to be reversed on a regular

---

[4] See above, at 221 *et seq.*

basis or reversed in a way which reflects on his or her capacity to judge. Such treatment goes to their self-esteem.

Even on an appellate court, the presence of other members of the court exerts a constraining effect on a judge who might be prone to aberrant or idiosyncratic decisions. Present at the hearing, the judge will obtain the benefit of the interchange between counsel and other members of the court and will, if he or she ventures a fatuous point, be likely to be corrected by counsel or enlightened by another judge. Then, the case will be subject to whatever procedures an appeal court chooses to adopt to arrive at a decision. Conferences and the circulation of draft judgments are commonplace. All these factors necessarily exert a correcting influence on the judge who might be disposed to 'go off the rails'. They will not prevent the judge reaching a different opinion from his or her colleagues, but they will inhibit the much-feared wayward judge.

Secondly, the administration of the common law requires judges to give reasons for their decisions. This requirement is not just a tradition; it is an intrinsic element in the common law method in which a decision is perceived to have a starting point from which it restricts, extends or departs from what has gone before. Decisions must therefore be justified to the parties, to their counsel, to the judges' colleagues, to the judiciary generally, to the legal profession, to legal academics, and to the public at large. Judges cannot escape laying out their purported reasoning. Using a technique that is intrinsic to the process, therefore, judges cannot do otherwise than seek to couch their reasons in terms that will appeal to others, including those who may or may not share the value judgement on which the decision is based. Reasons, then, are inimical to arbitrary decision-making. Aberrant reasoning will be readily discerned and simply prove counter-productive.

Feeley and Rubin have pointed out[5] that the legal process becomes powerfully self-reinforcing, not only because judges like to do things the way their predecessors did, but also because the process of development in law, as in so many other fields, is 'path dependent'.[6] The process of incremental, step-by-step development, with each step being fully realised or complete, resembles 'punctuated evolution'. In the absence of codification, no judge has the time or means to reconstitute or 'smooth out' the collection of ideas that have gone before. Consequently, the law retains the imprint of its generative process, and strongly encourages

---

[5] *Judicial Policy Making*, at 234–235.
[6] See W. Brian Arthur, 'Competing Technologies, Increasing Returns, and Lock-In by Historical Events' (1989) 99 Econ. J 116.

that process to continue. No judge can escape that imprint. Judges may, as I urge, evaluate particular rules or precedents to ensure that they remain just and relevant before applying them, but the judges are nevertheless creatures of their time and place in a process that is indubitably larger than them.

The third external constraint is that which no judge can escape; legal education and training and, probably, the best part of a lifetime of practising or working in and with the law. Education and experience obviously leave their mark. The lawyer who is appointed a judge is not an automaton, certainly when it comes to the confident formation of opinions, but he or she has been conditioned in such a way as to virtually preclude the possibility of stepping outside the bounds of legitimate judicial reasoning.

Fourthly, judges cannot escape comment or criticism. Their judgments will attract the evaluation of independent-minded and highly motivated lawyers and the critical appraisal of the academic community. A deviant decision is certain to be strongly criticised by counsel in later cases and robustly condemned by academic commentators in a prolific number of articles and case-notes. Of course, judges learn to be stoic about criticism. Stoicism, as well as criticism, comes with the turf. Perhaps it is the case that more judges tend to respond positively to endorsement or praise, if given, than to criticism, however well founded! But show me a judge who is not to a greater or lesser extent sensitive to criticism and I will show you a Pharisee. Criticism, whether its impact is acknowledged or not, can have a chastening effect and undoubtedly sets broad boundaries that no judge will wilfully cross.

Ultimately, of course, a judge's performance must meet the broad but at times vigorous scrutiny of the community itself. If a decision jars the community's sense of values it is not likely to survive for very long. So, too, if a judge were to express personal opinions that were at variance with the prevailing values of the community, his or her departure from acceptable limits to judicial dissension would quickly become a target for commentators. This climate of legitimacy will not prevent genuine differences among judges, but it does curb any loitering tendency towards extremism.

'Internalised' constraints

The above constraints are external to the judges. They are there whether they like it or not. But there are another set of constraints, equally real, which are self-imposed or self-generated. These constraints are 'internalised' by virtue of a judge's membership of an institution. The judiciary as an institution is constrained, and along with that constraint, although enjoying considerable discretion, the individual judge is constrained.

The overriding constraint is the judge's own sense of the proper judicial role. No judge is without such a sense, whether his or her perception is formalistic or pragmatic or something else again. An inevitable part of that perception is the fact that judges cannot do otherwise than perceive themselves to be part of an institution and an ongoing legal process that began well before them and that will continue long after they have gone. Unless within bounds acceptable to the institution, any contribution they might seek to make will be wasted, and it may be taken as a given that it is foreign to a judge's fibre to be irrelevant.

There are a further set of constraints which may be said to be also internal to judges. They fall under the heading of judicial restraint. I touched upon the more important factors in my Monograph,[7] but the phenomenon has been comprehensively elaborated by Feeley and Rubin.[8] The phenomenon may be summed up as the individual judge's sense of institutional propriety. The fact that this sense is particular to the individual judge does not mean that it is not an effective constraint against wilful or aberrant judicial reasoning. Indeed, it provides a potent curb on any tendency to resort to extreme views or actions.

Persons appointed judges come to the bench bearing their own expectations of themselves and aware of the expectations of them held by others. They become a member of an institution with a role to play and that role attracts a broad perception which subverts the idiosyncratic to the institution. The judge will wish to be a worthwhile member of that institution and fulfil the expected institutional role. As a matter of social conditioning, he or she will wish to live up to their own and other's expectations and, in most cases, will strive hard to do so. No judge is an island, whatever his or her background, and he or she will consciously or unconsciously respond to the expectations of a raft people. They will not want to let them down or disillusion them. A greater or lesser measure of conformity with the role prescription is inevitable.

Judges are also required to swear an oath of office when accepting appointment. I would not pretend that the oath they have sworn constantly throbs in the forefront of their minds as they administer the law.

---

[7] E. W. Thomas, *A Return to Principle in Judicial Reasoning and an Acclamation of Judicial Autonomy* 4 (1993) VUWLR Mono.5 ('Monograph'), at 54–56.
[8] Feeley and Rubin, *Judicial Policy Making*, esp. at 214–228, 236–243 and 353–355.

But it does signify a commitment to the institution of which they have become a member. That commitment, of course, runs even deeper than the oath. Judges will have effectively committed their lives to the law, and will not lightly sully that commitment by acting inconsistently with it. A judge may be branded a 'judicial activist', or worse, but it is doubtful that his or her love of the law could be seriously questioned. This basic commitment drives judges to coordinate or integrate their efforts with the work of others equally dedicated to the law and the legal process.

Judicial self-restraint also follows from judges' appreciation of the function of the law. They know that the law must at once seek to provide stability and continuity and yet develop to meet the requirements and expectations of the changing times. They are well aware of the tension between these two objectives. They know that the tension can only be resolved within certain parameters, and realise that for a judge to step outside those parameters will be counter-productive. Feeley and Rubin have accurately described the process by which a judge coordinates his or her opinion into the totality of the law.[9] To be effective, the judge's opinion, however creative or imaginative it might be, must be integrated into a legal context, and that context, as distinct from the opinion itself, will generally be one that is acceptable to most, if not all, members of the judiciary. Of necessity, if the opinion is to be acceptable to the judge's colleagues it must fall within the tolerance of their own perception of the judicial role and the limits of the role expectations for a member of the institution.

It is for this reason that a judge will constantly seek to coordinate or integrate his or her contribution into the context provided by the law in a manner that will persuade and appeal to, or at least not affront, their judicial colleagues, the legal profession and legal academics. Even if the opinion is creative or imaginative and expresses a minority viewpoint, it must seek to maintain some sort of continuity with the existing body of law if it is to be received as credible. It must 'stretch it without snapping it'.[10] The judge may hold that the rule or principle claimed to be the existing law is incomplete or wrong, but he or she must nevertheless place it in context and demonstrate that the continuity of the law or legal process remains intact. If the judge's effort does not comply in that respect it will count for nothing. The judge may as well flap his or her tongue in the breeze. In short, to avoid futility, which no judge would want, the opinion must be capable of being implemented by the institution, then or in the future, as part of the law and in harmony with the

---

[9] Ibid., esp. at 227–229 and 353–355. [10] Ibid., at 355.

direction of the law. As Feeley and Rubin say, a judge cannot concoct a new rule on the basis of his own predilections; not only would it be reversed by a higher court, or distinguished by lower ones, but the judge himself would end up looking like an idiot.[11] There is an appealing reality to that observation.

Judges are also constrained by their adherence to the rule of law, however that concept might be defined. The concept does not have to be external to judges to provide a constraint on judicial errancy or aberrance. It is locked into judges' judicial being and forms an integral part of their conception of the judicial role. They will consciously strive to reach a decision which is acceptable within the bounds of that concept rather than to self-indulgently impose their own will or ideal.[12] Admittedly, a judge's concept of the rule of law may abandon the old notion of firm, known and prospective rules and incorporate the concept of constraints as an internal phenomenon.[13]

Similarly, certainly under a Westminster system, judges are constrained by their perception of the relationship between Parliament and the courts. They consciously strive to work within the bounds of the principle of the legislative supremacy of Parliament. This striving represents a self-imposed restraint that is also integral to the judges' conception of the judicial role and becomes an innate property of their judicial personality. Furthermore, judges know that if they step beyond the bounds of what the peoples' elected representatives will accept, their decisions, or the wider effect of their decisions, are likely to be nullified by legislative decree. I have pointed out elsewhere that this knowledge imposes a tangible constraint.[14]

Internalised constraints and constraints of this kind do not stand alone. The judges' adherence to an acceptable perception of the judicial role, or to the rule of law, or to any other feature of a constitutional democracy, becomes institutional. A judge who does not share in these perceptions and crosses the line will be reversed on appeal, have his or her decision disapproved by other members of the judiciary, have their

---

[11] Ibid., at 353.
[12] No-one has ever put the judicial perception of self-constraint better than Cardozo. See Benjamin N. Cardozo, *The Nature of the Judicial Process* (Yale University Press, New Haven, 1921), esp. at 115–119 and 140–141.
[13] Feeley and Rubin, *Judicial Policy Making*, at 350. As explained in Chapter 9, at 225–231. The emphasis has shifted from adherence to fixed, pre-established rules to a self-regulating process in order that it may accord with the reality of judicial adjudication.
[14] See above, chapter 4, 87–88.

reasons criticised, possibly vigorously, by strong-minded lawyers, acutely sharp academics and informed laypersons within the general community. In this way, the constraints on the judiciary reinforce one another and together provide an effective limit on arbitrary decision-making. The exercise of judicial discretion is constrained, 'not as the result of the doctrine of precedent, but by the felt presence of all the factors which make up the discipline which binds the judiciary.'[15]

Some structural constraints?

As we have seen, formalism or the formalistic approach produces a number of judicial preconceptions, predilections and prejudices that are applied all too blindly, almost as a conditioned reflex on the part of the judge. Many, and certainly the main preconceptions, have been identified; treating certainty as a primary goal of adjudication; adhering to an overly coercive doctrine of precedent; seeking to leave any significant change in the law to Parliament, and demonstrating a commitment to form over substance when the two conflict. Other preconceptions may be added, such as the adoption of a minimalist approach and providing a tight regime of guidelines to circumscribe and curb a judicial discretion. Frequently, a judge's decision will turn on his or her attitude to these issues. Yet, the reason why the judge may prefer one approach to the other is seldom spelt out, at least, not with any pretence at comprehensiveness.

In the new methodology I propose these issues would be explicitly addressed in the context of the particular case. They would not be taken for granted. For example, the question would be asked, is certainty a relevant consideration in this particular case and, if so, why is it relevant? If these issues are addressed specifically, judicial reasoning will again be more transparent and honest, and the law will be likely to be more certain and predictable.[16] These latter qualities would be achieved, not only as a result of the honesty and transparency in the judge's reasoning, but also because a body of principles would develop that would provide litigants and their advisors with a greater appreciation of the courts' likely response to these underlying but nevertheless critical issues.

At the same time, the exercise of addressing these issues in a more explicit and structured manner would act as a constraint on errant or

---

[15] Monograph, at 56. See also Feeley and Rubin, *Judicial Policy Making*, at 246.
[16] See above, Chapter 5, at 121.

aberrant judicial reasoning. With the formalistic blindfold removed the judge would be forced to weigh the relevant factors more deliberately and logically. Furthermore, any automatic or mechanical response to the issues would be exposed for what it is, a reflex expression of the judge's preconception in the matter. If the provision of reasons generally provides a constraint on judicial waywardness, giving reasons on these underlying and frequently basic questions must further the same function.

Each question may be examined in turn. In carrying out this examination it is not my purpose to identify all the relevant considerations relating to each issue. These factors will emerge and develop on a case-by-case basis once the recommended approach is adopted.

A legitimate role for certainty

I have earlier intimated that the fact the law may be inherently indeterminate does not mean that certainty is to be invariably excluded as a legitimate consideration. Rather, it is certainty's status as an unquestioned primary goal of adjudication that is refuted. Certainty becomes a particular consideration in the context of a particular case. The question would be approached pragmatically and the impact of a decision on the community's ability to order its affairs would be taken into consideration and addressed in the context of the circumstances of the particular case. In other words, the relevance of certainty to the case at hand would need to be expressly demonstrated. Thus, the aim of certainty in the law would be directly relevant in any case where the community had for some time acted on a particular basis and that basis was under challenge in the instant case. The preservation of existing proprietary or contractual rights would be another important factor. So, too, it would be relevant to the question whether the notion of certainty was germane in the particular case if it could be demonstrated that a litigant or others had in fact relied upon a past rule or precedent.[17]

In cases where it could not be demonstrated that the notion of certainty is a germane and overriding consideration, the quest for certainty would give way to the interests of justice in the instant case and the capacity for the law in question to meet contemporary requirements and expectations. With certainty ceasing to be intuitively or blindly treated as a goal of adjudication, it would be required to establish its credentials.

---

[17] See above, Chapter 6, at 142–143.

A justifiable role for precedent

From the outset I have been careful not to denigrate a doctrine of precedent. Rather, I have challenged the unthinking and rigid application of that doctrine and the 'attitude of mind' that it engenders. I now propose that the question whether a precedent should be re-evaluated and applied, not followed, or overruled should also be approached on a pragmatic case-by-case basis. As posited before, precedents become 'tools' in the judges' armoury.[18]

Precedents would, of course, continue to be cited in argument. Judges would also continue to be receptive to the wisdom of judges in the past who had traversed much the same ground as they are now required to address. They would also be conscious of the need to establish consistency where the circumstances were such as to require weight to be given to the principle that like should be treated alike. But the precedent should be re-evaluated where it no longer appears to serve the interests of justice or is no longer adequate to meet the contemporary needs and expectations of the community. The coercive element in the doctrine of precedent would no longer prevail over the twin objectives of justice and relevance. Precedents would be like signposts pointing to the possible law or finding in the instant case, rather than rules directing the law or finding. At times, of course, such as where a superior court has indicated a test, or an approach, or a procedure, the value of precedent will continue to be appreciated. But it will be appreciated because the precedent is acceptable and, in the context of the issue in question, it is seen to be sensible for the judge to apply the same test or adhere to a uniform approach or procedure.

Apart from adopting a different and more pragmatic approach to precedent, there are a number of aspects relating to the application of the doctrine which can assist a court, more particularly a lower court, avoid the dominance and severity of the strict doctrine of precedent. Greater flexibility will result.

First, the court needs to be careful not to attribute to an earlier or higher court an intention that its decision is to be binding when that is not necessarily the case. The conclusion that the coercive element is absent could be reached if the higher court was tentative in the view it expressed, or if it is apparent that the point in issue had not been fully argued. In other cases it may be evident that, in the context of the argument before the other or higher court, the significance of the

---

[18] See above, Chapter 9, at 221.

particular issue had not been fully appreciated. The issue may have been dealt with cursorily or without it being realised that the finding would have more far-reaching consequences as a precedent than had been contemplated. Requiring a judge, including a judge at first instance, to blindly follow a precedent that is not for one or other of these reasons truly 'authoritative' cannot be justified.

Secondly, the Continental attitude to precedent has great appeal. Only rules which have been reiterated in a number of cases by a higher court are accepted as precedents. This practice should be accepted; after all, one swallow does not make a summer. In other words, precedents need only obtain so-called 'authoritative' strength after they had been endorsed more than once. Initially, it would be open to a judge, including in appropriate cases a judge at first instance, to hold that the single case did not lay down a rule, however firmly it might have been expressed. While judges at first instance would, of course, need to act with circumspection, the open statement of their reasons for not attributing authoritative force to a single decision they did not consider enduring would be preferable to the present 'backdoor' methods of circumventing an unwanted precedent. This approach is consistent with a pragmatic and principle-oriented approach for it is more likely that the essential principle will emerge from its application in a number of cases.[19]

Thirdly, a decision where appellate judges are not unanimous could well, depending on the nature of the issue, be treated as non-binding. The fact that the court is divided indicates the indefinite or incomplete nature of the law involved. The only compelling reason for following the decision of the majority is *stare decisis* itself. Otherwise, a precedent of a court which is divided provides lower court judges with the opportunity to examine the reasoning of the various judges and elicit or extract the relevant principle for themselves. Occasions when dissenting judgments have eventually prevailed are all too common to ascribe to any majority the blessing of infallibility.

Fourthly, there are cases in which an appellate court will, in the course of its judgment, refer to an earlier decision in such a way as to place a question mark over its authority. The court may indicate that an earlier

---

[19] Recall Sir Anthony Mason's observation when criticising the tendency to apply non-binding decisions without any attempt to analyse their worth, a tendency that he perceived to be an abdication of the judicial function. It is one thing to apply an opinion on a matter of law when the opinion has been accepted after consideration in a later case and in learned writing, but quite another to blindly apply such an opinion when it has not been considered critically. See above, Chapter 6, at 157.

decision will or may be reviewed in an appropriate future case. Sometimes it may be clear that the case's tenure as an authority is limited.[20] In such circumstances, another court need have no compunction about declining to follow the decision as a precedent. The authority of the decision has been questioned or discredited, and it is demeaning to expect a lower court to accept that it is bound to follow an impaired precedent, particularly as the impairment is of the higher court's own making. To perpetuate an unfortunate precedent, and thereby work an injustice in the instant case when the fate, and possibly the fatal fate, of the precedent has been signalled or, at least, where it has been tacitly labelled as a 'precedent pending review', is both unnecessary and undesirable. Such obeisance does nothing for the administration of justice and the reputation of the legal system.

Fifthly, the courts' could and should adopt a less literal approach to the famed 'famous dicta' referred to earlier. These dicta do not amount to the *ratio decidendi*, although they may be an expression of it, and should not be accorded unquestioning fidelity. Where they do not suit or appeal to the judge deciding a case they should simply be disregarded. Rules through precedent are one thing; rules emanating from dicta that do not and cannot have the force of statute are quite another.[21]

In the sixth place, it is suggested that there are times when a court should deliberately make a fresh start. On many issues of law the authorities are in disarray. The chaos may have been widely acknowledged by commentators and, indeed, by the courts themselves. Undue adherence to the doctrine of precedent has created the entangled muddle and it is specious and futile for a subsequent court to endeavour to unravel and extract from its core the appropriate rule or principle. If an attempt is made to make some sort of sense out of the morass of

---

[20] Eg., *McLaren, Maycroft and Co v Fletcher Development Co Limited* [1973] 2 NZLR 100, a decision of the New Zealand Court of Appeal, which held that a claim for negligence in the performance of professional services was a claim in contract only, thus precluding the application of concurrent liability in negligence and contract. The decision was marked for reconsideration by the same Court in *Rowe v Turner Hopkins and Partners* [1982] 1 NZLR 198 and *Day v Mead* [1987] 2 NZLR 443. Nevertheless, *McLaren, Maycroft* was applied in a number of cases at first instance. Sitting at first instance, I declined to follow *McLaren, Maycroft* in *Rowlands & Ors v Colin & Anor* [1992] 1 NZLR 178. *McLaren, Maycroft* was subsequently repudiated by Cooke P, in *Mouat v Clark Boyce* [1992] 2 NZLR 559, at 565. The view precluding concurrent liability in negligence and contract was then effectively put to rest by the House of Lords in *Henderson v Merritts Syndicates Ltd* [1995] 2 AC 145.

[21] See above, Chapter 6, at 154–155.

confused and conflicting cases it is highly unlikely that the outcome will be logical or principled. Rather, it is preferable for the confusion to be treated as if it were unclaimed baggage, and for the court to start afresh.[22] To mix a metaphor, it is better to replough the field.

'Leave it to Parliament'

While all judges acknowledge that judges make law, the question as to when a change in the law should be made by the courts or left to Parliament remains a divisive issue. There are two extremes in judicial thinking on this question; at one extreme are those who shy away from making any significant change in the law, however much they may consider that the change is necessary or desirable, and at the other extreme those who are more expansive and prone to regard the development of the common law as the courts' sole prerogative. The former will recommend that Parliament enact the necessary or desirable change in the law and feel that they have discharged their duty to the litigants and to the community. Any resulting injustice, hardship or irrelevance in the law is no longer perceived to be their responsibility. Parliament becomes the culprit. The latter will overtly make the change content in the knowledge that if Parliament does not like their handiwork it can, if it so wishes, legislate it out of existence.

This sharp division is to be expected. It reflects the different preconceptions and predilections of the judges and their different perception of the judicial role. For that reason, the maxim that a change in the law should be left to Parliament will for the most part be invoked by the more conservative or formalistic judges; it will be slighted by those who are more liberal or creative.

---

[22] A classic example is the decision of the Privy Council in *Royal Brunei Airlines Sdn Bhd* v *Tan* [1995] 2 AC 378. The case law relating to knowing assistance in furtherance of a breach of trust was in a state of chaos. In a brilliant judgment, Lord Nicholls cut through the chaos to the essential principle. The law is now not only more logical and coherent but also much more certain. I had also earlier concluded when sitting at first instance in *Powell* v *Thompson* [1991] 1 NZLR 597 that the law on knowing receipt and knowing assistance was in such a state of disarray that it was necessary to start afresh by reverting to fundamental principles. This approach was expressly approved in *Royal Brunei* with substantially the same outcome. But no one could pretend that starting afresh will resolve a matter for all time. See *Twinsectra* v *Yardley* [2002] UKHL 12; [2002] 2 All ER 377, in which the Law Lords sitting differed as to whether the term 'dishonesty' used by Lord Nicholls meant 'objective dishonesty' or 'subjective dishonesty'.

In my view, there is again no absolute answer. The question that faces judges in practice as to when to leave a proposed change in the law to Parliament is a practical question. In most cases it is a question of when and where to draw the line, and it necessarily falls to the judges to determine when and where to draw that line. A self-imposed restraint is essential. While such judicial restraint provides the framework for the exercise of determining when, or when not, to leave a change in the law to Parliament, it cannot embrace a truckling deference or docility or an unthinking or automatic response on the part of the judiciary. Rather, the decision whether a change in the law should be left to the legislature should follow from a pragmatic appreciation of which institution is the appropriate body to affect the remedy. There are telling considerations that point to Parliament being the appropriate law-making body in certain circumstances, and there are occasions when the judiciary is better placed to develop the law. On the latter occasions the courts can fulfil their constitutional role consistently with the doctrine of legislative supremacy and the rule of law.

To put the point another way; the decision whether to leave a proposed change or development in the law to Parliament is a decision that the court must make in the context of a particular case. It can make that decision mechanically, relying upon a perception of Parliament's legislative omnipotence that virtually confers a law-making monopoly on that institution, or it can make a deliberate decision having regard to the factors that favour leaving the proposed change or development to Parliament and the factors that favour a judicial solution. I regard the latter exercise as the inevitable outcome of the fact that judges make law. A decision whether or not to leave the matter to Parliament is inescapable; what is required is a deliberate and reasoned decision relating to that issue.

In *R (on the application of Prolife Alliance) v British Broadcasting Corporation*,[23] Lord Hoffmann recognised that, in a society based on the rule of law and separation of powers, it is necessary to decide which branch of government has in any particular instance the decision-making power and what are the limits of that power. As a question of law it must be decided by the courts. Lord Hoffmann explicitly states that it is inevitable that the courts themselves often have to decide the limits of their own decision-making power. He seeks to legitimate these decisions by asserting that the principles upon which the decision-making powers are allocated are 'principles of law'. Adverting to the independence of

---

[23] [2003] 2 All ER 977.

the judiciary, he rightly proclaims that this quality makes the courts more suited to deciding some kinds of questions than the legislature and executive. But legislative bodies, being elected, make them more suited to deciding yet other questions. Recognised principles are identified. One is the principle that the independence of the courts is necessary for a proper decision of disputed legal rights or claims of violation of human rights. Another is the principle that majority approval is necessary for a proper decision on policy or the allocation of resources. Adherence to these principles means that, in deciding a decision is within the proper competence of the legislature or executive, a court is not showing deference to the other branches of government. It is 'deciding the law'.[24]

Lord Hoffmann's analysis is an advance in acknowledging that the question of the allocation of decision-making responsibilities between the legislature and the judiciary is ultimately a question that the courts must resolve, and that there are some questions that are more appropriately decided by the courts and some that are more properly resolved by the legislature. But Lord Hoffmann's reasoning is otherwise disingenuous. It is, for example, overly simplistic to claim that the decisions which the courts make regarding the allocation of powers are made in accordance with recognised 'principles of law'. Broad principles exist, of course, but in any given case they leave the question whether the judiciary or the legislature is better suited to resolve the matter largely unanswered. A decision is required in the particular case as to whether the matter in issue is to be perceived as, for example, one relating to 'disputed legal rights', which is for the courts, or one where 'majority approval is necessary', which only the legislature can confer. That decision will require more explicit criteria.

The hard decision as to whether the matter should be left to the legislature or decided by the courts can only be made on a pragmatic basis having regard to all relevant aspects of the case.[25] Nor is it possible to then convert the resulting decision into one of 'deciding the law' as Lord Hoffmann would have it. In reality the court is making the law simply because the decision determining whether the particular issue will be left to the legislature or decided in the courts has never been made before. Ultimately, Lord Hoffmann's disclaimer notwithstanding, the courts must, having regard to the broad constitutional framework, make a pragmatic assessment as to which institution is the appropriate body

---

[24] Ibid., at para. [76].
[25] For an examination of the matters to be taken into account, see below, at 259–263.

to determine the particular issue. The constitutional framework must necessarily include the need for judicial deference, but not truckling deference, to the role and status of the legislature in a representative democracy.

The fact that there are many things which Parliament can do better than the courts does not invariably mean that the courts should abstain. In some circumstances, a tentative lead may be required. In other circumstances it may be clear that Parliament will not be motivated to make the change, at least, in the foreseeable future. This may be because the needed change lacks 'political' appeal. Then, there are many things Parliament and the courts can do together, with Parliament providing the lead. The courts, for example, have the opportunity to implement and develop the principles that have received the imprimatur of Parliament and of public opinion.[26]

I therefore take the view that, notwithstanding the differences in the disposition of judges, the issue should be more regularly considered by the courts as part of the decision-making process, and should be specifically addressed in judgments. Criteria for deciding that the change should be left to Parliament or undertaken by the courts would be quickly identified. Having regard to the differences in the disposition of judges, it may be optimistic to expect that a more uniform or common approach will necessarily emerge. But faith in the common law method, if one is to place any faith in it at all, would suggest that the explicit articulation of criteria by which the issue is to be determined will inform and improve the individual judge's reasoning. It must be possible to draw the outer boundaries of this disagreement closer together where both camps of judicial thought agree that it is appropriate for a change in the law to be made but disagree whether that change should be made by the courts or left to Parliament.

I should at once allow that the pragmatic and principled approach I advance in this book would result in the maxim 'leave it to Parliament' being invoked less often than is presently the case. This reduction in its currency would follow from the fact that much judicial thinking on the issue at present is unrealistic and devoid of any principled reasoning. The identification of the criteria for determining whether or not a change in the law should be left to Parliament, and expressly addressing those criteria, would remove the unthinking

---

[26] See Louis L. Jaffe, *English and American Judges as Lawmakers* (Clarendon Press, Oxford, 1969), at 75–76.

formalism involved in the automatic reaction that any significant change in the law should be left to Parliament.

The taciturn attitude of the judge who is content to define the problem or defect in the law and then step aside in favour of the possibility of a legislative remedy derives from an unrealistic perception of both the legislative process and the legal process. The unreality in respect of the legislative process is the judge's expectation that Parliament will in fact do something about the problem or defect in the law which he or she has thoughtfully highlighted. Law reports are full of judgments where the courts have suggested that it is for Parliament to attend to a problem and rectify the defect, but Parliament has done nothing. The problem or defect remains the law, and any injustices or hardships it has caused or may yet cause remains the reality. It must surely be accepted, on the basis of experience if nothing else, that the possibility Parliament will in fact respond is often remote. In such circumstances, the abdication of the court's law-making function has the appearance of a device to shift responsibility for the decision, and any harsh consequences that result, from the court to the legislature.

The perception of the courts' role in such circumstances is also unrealistic in that it has overtones of the declaratory school of thought in seemingly rejecting the notion that judges make law. Unless, the court can change the law covertly or the circumstances allow for a minor extension to the law, something that is purely fortuitous, the judges balk at making the development themselves. The perception is also unrealistic in denying the inevitable scope for judicial autonomy and in failing to recognise that, in many circumstances, declining to make the change in the law is still to make law in the negative sense described in Chapter 1.[27] The difference is that the law that is made in this negative sense is likely to be highly unsatisfactory. Underlying these deficiencies is a failure to realistically appreciate the extent to which judge-made law permeates the life of the community, in particular the commercial community, and the extent to which the law fails to serve the community.[28]

Indeed, it is not going too far to assert that it is lamentable and inefficient to allow unfortunate and awkward decisions to accumulate to the point that the legislature is compelled to intervene. More often

---

[27] See above, 3–4.
[28] No-one can seriously argue, for example, that the business community is well served by the courts' treatment of agreements to agree. See the discourse below on *Fletcher Challenge Energy Ltd v Electricity Corporation of New Zealand*, Chapter 11, at 289–299.

than not, the resulting legislative reform provides a measure of the inadequacy of the judge-made law – or the absence of judge-made law. Large areas of the law have been overtaken by remedial legislation,[29] or a recognised gap remains waiting for the uninterested or tardy attention of the legislature. When judge-made law lags in this manner judicial modesty is unbecoming.

Of course, it is to be reiterated that this does not mean that the court should behave like 'little legislatures'. I accept that when a court, especially an appellate court, goes beyond what is necessary to decide the instant case and sets out broader principles to guide the application and development of the law in a particular area it can be said that, in a sense, the court is then 'legislating'.[30] But legislating in this sense is to be accepted as part of the courts' law-making role. For the most part, of course, the courts cannot issue edicts or announce policy goals,[31] as distinct from recognising or formulating policies in the application of principles in particular cases. The law-making must continue to be limited to the dispute situations that arise for resolution in the courts, and to that extent it will necessarily be incremental. But undue deference to Parliament in changing the law retards the courts' ability to reform the law long before it has become an embarrassment requiring legislative intervention.

In large areas of the law Parliament is undoubtedly the appropriate law-making body. An indication, and only an indication, of those areas where changes should be left to Parliament will provide some idea of the express inquiry that the courts should carry out.

First, where the law is deeply entrenched in the legal and social fabric of the community, the court should abstain in favour of Parliament, even though the law was judge-made in the first place. I would, for example, place the renunciation of the principle of vicarious liability in this category. With its origins dating back to early medieval law, the doctrine not only is an elemental principle of the common law but also is ingrained in the social consciousness of the community. It has contributed to the shaping of the social and economic pattern of society itself. The notion that 'whoever employs another is answerable for him and

---

[29] See, e.g., in New Zealand: Contributory Negligence Act 1947; Law Reform Act 1936; Minors Contract Act 1969; Illegal Contracts Act 1970; Contractual Mistakes Act 1977; Contractual Remedies Act 1979; Contracts (Privity) Act 1982, and, possibly, the Fair Trading Act 1986.
[30] See Peter Cane, 'Another Failed Sterilisation' (Forthcoming publication).
[31] M. Moore, 'Precedent, Induction, and Ethical Generalization' in L. Goldstein (ed.), *Precedent in Law* (Oxford University Press, Oxford, 1987), at 187.

undertakes for his care to all that make use of him' possesses the force of a social injunction.[32] Intervention by the courts in circumstances where a legal principle has assumed this dominance in the structure and weal of society would be to determine the direction society wishes to take. Such changes are matters for the elected legislature.

Secondly, the courts should opt out where the law in question is controversial or there are divided views as to the appropriate remedy. Lord Bingham makes the point in these terms: judges should avoid the change 'where the question involves an issue of current social policy on which there is no consensus within the community.'[33] At times, of course, this reticence is not possible. The community may be clearly divided on the application of a fundamental human right to a particular situation, but the courts will have no option but to resolve the issue. Whether, for example, the exclusion of same-sex marriages from the law relating to matrimony is discriminatory is a question on which there would be no consensus within the community, but it is a question that the courts have nevertheless been required to confront.[34]

Thirdly, changes in the law that might have an undesirable retrospective effect should be left to Parliament. This reticence must be particularly important where people have ordered their affairs on the basis of what might be regarded as settled law. Indeed, it must constantly be borne in mind that the changes in the law made by the courts will or may have retrospective effect. Parliament, for the most part, legislates prospectively.

Fourthly, there will be other aspects where the change in the law will be something which the legislature can clearly do better than the courts. Parliament will have greater resources and the reform may be one that can only properly follow a thorough investigation and extensive research. The attention of a law commission or law reform body may be highly desirable. In this regard, the courts' capacity is limited and it should again, in all probability, abstain. The same can be said for a law where, although it can be seen to be defective, amending it would call for a detailed legislative code, with qualifications, exceptions and safeguards which cannot feasibly be introduced by judicial decisions.[35]

---

[32] Holt CJ in *Boson v Sandford* (1690) 2 Salk. 440.
[33] Tom Bingham, *The Business of Judging: Selected Essays and Speeches* (Oxford University Press, Oxford, 2000), at 31.
[34] See above, Chapter 4, n. 54 at 102.
[35] Bingham, *The Business of Judging*, at 31.

Fifthly, Lord Bingham has highlighted a further category. He suggests that the court should be slow to intervene where the issue is subject to current legislative activity. If Parliament is actually engaged in deciding what the rule should be in a given legal situation, the courts are generally wise to await the outcome of that deliberation rather than to pre-empt the result by a judicial decision. On such occasions deference to the law-making body is appropriate. It is to be noted, however, that Lord Bingham restricts the limitation to those situations where Parliament is actually engaged in deciding what the law should be, and he posits that it is only then 'generally wise' to await the outcome of that deliberation rather than pre-empt the legislature's decision. Much will depend on the circumstances. In some cases the expression of a prior opinion by the courts may conflict with Parliament's ultimate intention. If the courts opinion then must be, or needs to be, annulled by the legislature, the administration of justice may appear deficient. In yet other cases a premature decision by the court may serve to vest one or other of the participants, or rather their cause or interest, with a weighting in the political arena that is not deserved. Restraint is then required on the part of the judiciary. In yet other circumstances the availability of a decision of a court in advance of the enactment of legislation on the same topic may be an advantage. A court's decision relating to a specific factual situation that has arisen in practice, for example, could well be of assistance to Parliament in legislating for the general circumstances. Even where the matter is under current legislative consideration, it may be prudent for a court to provide the lead in a concrete case knowing, of course, that its decision is subject to review by Parliament in enacting the more general legislation. Consequently, while the question whether a court should intervene in a matter that is under current legislative consideration should ordinarily be weighted in favour of non-intervention, not even that question can escape a pragmatic assessment as to what is the best course in the circumstances.

I would not necessarily extend this principle of non-intervention to situations where the matter in issue in the courtroom is under consideration by a law commission or law reform body if it would otherwise be appropriate for the court to change the law. Yet, many judges shy away from making a decision once it is known that a law commission or law reform body is conducting a general inquiry which would or could bear upon the court's judgment. Again, however, much must depend on the circumstances, particularly, the nature of the law commission or law reform body's inquiry, the law to be amended, and the proximity of, or connection between, the issue before the court and the matter under inquiry. Pragmatically, undue sensitivity to the law reform agency may not be required. Law commission and law reform bodies' delays in completing reports are well known, and the legislature's penchant to defer the implementation of recommendations or not to legislate on them at all is not unusual. Regrettably, law reform reports may be found gathering dust and cobwebs in the basements of legislatures around the world. Moreover, if the law commission or law reform body does not agree with the court's decision it can always recommend that it be reversed.

Finally, and in the sixth place, the court should be slow to intervene and change the law where the subject matter is far removed from ordinary judicial experience. Judges should be alert to recognise their own limitations. But again the point cannot be pressed too far. Courts are frequently confronted with problems well outside the experience of the most expansively rounded judge. Judges master the subject as best they are able. Certainly, however, judicial circumspection is in order.

In other areas of the law the courts can appropriately exert a more effective influence than Parliament.

First, those areas of the law that have historically been the subject of case law can be appropriately developed by the courts just as they were developed by judges in the first place. Contract, tort, trusts and the like, can, and should, be advanced to meet the community's needs and expectations without the necessity of the occasional statutory boost. Such areas of the law lend themselves to an incremental approach in accordance with legal principles. With the principle propounded, the changing law can be then empirically tested as it develops. The common and admirable theme of Canadian cases is that, while major and complex changes to the law with uncertain ramifications should be left to the legislature, the courts can and should make changes to the common law to reflect the changing social, moral and economic fabric of society.[36]

Secondly, in many cases Parliament is clearly uninterested in enacting a measure to reform the law, however desirable the reform may appear to be. The legislature, it should be recalled, is a politically motivated organ of government and many areas of the law requiring reform have little or no 'political' popularity. In such cases, the only effective means by which the law will or may be changed is through the exercise of judicial initiative in the appropriate case. What is required is a realistic assessment of the

---

[36] See *R v Salituro* (1991) 3 SCR 654, at 666–670. See also the cases listed in the judgment at 666.

situation and the exercise of a pragmatic judgement as to whether or not it is appropriate for the court to proceed to make the change.

Thirdly, the courts cannot ignore the consequences of a decision. If a decision would be unjust or harsh to a party, or to any other persons to whom it would apply, the courts should be slow to reject a sound submission requiring a development in the law because it is thought that the change should be left to Parliament. Faced with the injustice or hardship, the court should think again. Unless it is absolutely necessary to rule otherwise, the court should give its decision, possibly making it clear that Parliament may well wish to review it. Judges cannot turn their back on the unfortunate consequences of their decision and, by leaving the law change to Parliament, assume that they have discharged themselves from responsibility for those consequences.

I am indebted to Professor Jaffe for my perception of the optimum working relationship between Parliament and the courts. There is, the learned Professor said, potential for a 'fruitful partnership and interaction' between Parliament and the courts 'in the lawmaking business together ... continually at work on the legal fabric of society.'[37] This formula accommodates the day-to-day legislative supremacy Parliament enjoys in a representative democracy. Although a constitutional mandate may prescribe a special procedure in many countries, legislators can, if they so choose, legislatively correct decisions of the courts they do not like. In Westminster-style democracies, the ease with which this may be done is fettered by political considerations only.[38] For their part, the courts can abide Parliament's legislative prerogative without sacrificing their independent role to develop the law where it is appropriate to do so as part of the fruitful partnership and interaction

---

[37] Jaffe, *English and American Judges*, at 75. Lord Devlin criticises this view in *The Judge* (Oxford University Press, Oxford, 1979), at 16–17, to the effect that, to be effective, it would require the two institutions to converse. His point is self-evidently weak. Jaffe's own acknowledgement of the difficulties in encouraging the judiciary to make law that must be undone by the legislature is more telling (at 20). The author has given judicial recognition to Professor Jaffe's concept of a 'fruitful partnership' between Parliament and the courts: see *R v Hines* [1997] 3 NZLR 529, at 581–582; and *Fulcher v Parole Board* (1997) 15 CRNZ 222, at 242; *R v Poumako* [2000] NZLR 695, at para. [100]; and *R v Pora* [2001] 2 NZLR 37, at para. [167].

[38] Recent cases, for example, where Parliament has reversed the Court of Appeal in New Zealand are *R v Hines* [1997] 3 NZLR 529, by ss. 13B–13J of the Evidence Act 1908, inserted by s. 3 of the Evidence (Witness Anonymity) Amendment Act 1997; and *Daniels v Thomson* [1998] 3 NZLR 22, by s. 396 of the Accident Insurance Act 1998.

between the courts and Parliament in the law-making business together.[39]

There are, of course, those who are or would be antagonistic to the notion of a fruitful working partnership between Parliament and the courts in the law-making business together. On analysis, this antagonism would appear to stem either from a failure to realistically distinguish between Parliament, the institution, and the government or majority in Parliament; or from an unsophisticated version of democracy which does not look beyond the concept of majoritarian rule; or from an unrealistic perception of Parliament as the sole law-making body and the consequential resentment of the courts' acknowledged law-making function. With these misconceptions brushed to one side, there is no reason why a working relationship cannot be developed between Parliament and the courts that in no way impairs the primary role of either institution.[40]

It is to be reiterated, therefore, that it is not deference to the legislature which I revile. Such deference is a healthy attribute in a representative democracy. Rather, it is the truckling deference or docility of so many judges that results in the unthinking automatic approach I have described. Blind adherence to the doctrine of parliamentary supremacy of this kind has had a negative impact on the performance of the judicial function. To refer to Professor Jaffe again; 'A judiciary which too much reminds itself that its power is limited by the dogmas of parliamentary omnicompetence, parliamentary supremacy, and parliamentary responsibility may lose the will to exercise ... [its] great historic function.' He suggests that, while the courts have played a great role in the development of an unwritten constitution, above all in creating safeguards

---

[39] The idea of a fruitful partnership between Parliament and the courts in the law-making business together is a different concept from the dialogue model first originated by Professor Hogg (See P. Hogg and A. Bushell, 'The Charter Dialogue Between Courts and Legislatures', 35 Osgood Hall LJ 75 (1997)) relating to the Canadian Parliament and the Supreme Court of Canada. Applicable where the courts are able to invalidate legislation, the dialogue model retains a tension between Parliament and the courts that the partnership concept seeks to suppress. For the shortcomings of the Canadian system, see Mark Tushnet, 'Judicial Review of Legislation' in Peter Cane and Mark Tushnet (eds.), *The Oxford Handbook of Legal Studies* (Oxford University Press, Oxford and New York, 2004), 164, at 175–176. See also Stephen M. Hunter, 'Democracy Talk: Constitutional Law Debate in New Zealand from the Bill of Rights Act to *Moonen* and *Pora*', unpublished Paper submitted in respect of Master of Laws, Harvard Law School, 30 April 2002, at 61–72.

[40] See the author, 'Parliamentary Supremacy and the Judicial Function' (1996) 112 LQR, at 177.

against the abuse of executive and administrative power,[41] judges who insist on Parliament's monopoly of law and policy-making will be loath to check the executive.[42]

The distinguished Professor is surely correct. Unthinking adherence to parliamentary omnicompetence, supremacy or responsibility can induce a debilitating subservience, which must necessarily impinge on the judiciary's traditional function.

Minimalism

Other predilections are all too often applied automatically. Minimalism is one. Many judges decline to decide more than is absolutely necessary to determine the instant case. They shy away from the articulation of general principles that go beyond the immediate issue even though the articulation of those principles, especially at the appellate level, could provide guidance to the community and improve the certainty and predictability of the law. The boast that one is a 'minimalist judge' can all too easily become a badge of honour to be worn at all times irrespective that there may be good reasons to express the judgment in a case on a broader basis.

Any number of senior practitioners would endorse this view. It will suffice to refer to the comment of a leader of the bar in my own jurisdiction. In a forthright paper, Dr James Farmer QC, commented on the failure of appellate courts to provide guidance where general guidance is required.[43] He contended that over time a minimalist approach to judicial decision-making is likely to stultify the growth of the law and leave practitioners with a body of precedent that is very fact-oriented, giving little guidance as to how future cases will be decided. Farmer pointed out that it is not often the judicial opportunity exists at appellate level to provide definitive rulings of principle that will assist the resolution of future disputes without constant resort to the courts. When those opportunities present themselves, he asserted, the courts should be prepared to take them.[44]

A moment's reflection must be sufficient to confirm that there are occasions when it is appropriate for a court, especially an appellate court, to pronounce general principles that will apply in a particular area

---

[41] Jaffe, *English and American Judges*, at 19.   [42] Ibid., at 26.
[43] Dr James Farmer QC, 'The New Zealand Court of Appeal: Maintaining Quality after the Privy Council' in Rick Bigwood (ed.), *Legal Method* in *New Zealand* (Butterworths, Wellington, 2001), at 237.
[44] Ibid., at 245.

of law in regard to a particular issue. Of course, argument in the case must be adequate for that purpose, but that is usually the case. If that is not the case the court can adjourn the hearing for further argument. The questions which should then be addressed are whether the law on the topic is in need of clarification, whether the articulation of principles would provide guidance in other cases, whether a statement of principles would make the law more and not less certain, and whether it would assist citizens, and their lawyers, to predict the outcome of future disputes. It is not being suggested for one moment that courts should write academic opinions or issue mini-textbooks on particular subjects, but only that in an appropriate case it is neither helpful nor desirable for the court to pursue the narrowest track to a resolution of a case when a wider approach going beyond the minimum boundaries necessary for a decision in the particular case would be useful.

Vanquishing general discretions

A number of other predilections could be mentioned. One such predilection on the part of appellate judges is to automatically seek to provide comprehensive guidelines for the exercise of a general discretion vested in the lower courts. Appellate judges are not 'minimalists' when it comes to laying down guidelines to control the exercise of such a discretion. They sometimes seem driven by an undisclosed demon to curb and restrict a general statutory discretion vested in judges lower in the judicial hierarchy. Indeed, cases where a general statutory discretion is fettered by judicial fiat are not uncommon. The guidelines can eventually become so prolific and contradictory that the exercise of the discretion becomes fraught with difficulty and uncertainty. There are, and will be, circumstances where it is preferable not to spell out restrictive guidelines and to leave the deciding judge with the broad discretion vested in the court by Parliament. It is quite possible and feasible to say that the judge below has wrongly exercised his or her discretion without redefining or limiting the general discretion conferred by Parliament.

The observable drive by appellate judges to confine and control the exercise of the discretionary power conferred on the lower courts by statute is puzzling. It is as though the appellate judges are not prepared to trust the lower court judges to exercise the discretionary power in terms of the statute, or for the purposes of the statute, as they would trust themselves. But the primary reason probably relates back to the traditional legal distrust of general discretions and a feeling that further directions are needed to comply with the rule of law. At times, of course, appellate guidance is required to obtain consistency in the way the discretion is to be exercised by first instance judges and to give concrete effect to the legislature's purpose. To provide guidelines on such occasions is to do no more than contribute to the 'fruitful partnership' between Parliament and the courts in the law-making business together, of which I have already spoken.[45]

There is also, in the interpretation of statutory directions, a natural tendency for the court to use alternative wording in seeking to convey the perceived meaning. The phrases used to explain this meaning can then become the effective direction, and are likely to in turn promote argument as to what is their exact meaning. The irony is that if the legislature had used the alternative phraseology in the first place, the court would in all probability have used the statutory language actually used to explain what it meant!

Two clear situations where an appellate court should exercise deliberate forbearance in circumscribing a lower court's statutory discretion may be identified. One occasion for such forbearance is when the wording or criteria set out in the empowering statute conferring the discretionary power is explicit and simply does not require a judicial gloss. Further elaboration is then redundant and will or may only tend to confuse. It can fairly be said, however, that in contrast to the appellate mania to tie the hands of judges at first instance or lower in the court hierarchy, more judges today are striving to suppress their instincts and to seek to avoid substituting one set of words for the set of words used by the legislature simply for the purpose of explaining what the legislature meant. This trend is healthy. The discretion conferred on the court can properly be exercised in the terms in which it is conveyed.

The second situation where the provision of further guidelines by an appellate court to control the exercise of a discretion should be avoided is where the court has already been overgenerous with its guidance in the past. A welter of guidelines clutters rather than clarifies the discretionary power and leads to much unnecessary argument. In such circumstances, it is preferable not to add to the overwhelming clutter, but to start afresh and resort to the wording of the statute.

Conclusion

Systematically identifying and elaborating the constraints on the judiciary may seem a rather mundane digression in a work directed to the

---

[45] See above, at 263–264.

jurisprudential aspects of judicial reasoning. Yet, I regard the emphasis on the constraints to which the judiciary is subject as being critical to the judicial methodology and conception of the judicial role that are pursued in this book.

The reality is that the judiciary is far from unconstrained, and this is a wholly appropriate state of affairs. A constitutional democracy requires that the third branch of government, and not just the legislature and the executive, should be subject to effective constraints. But the constraints cannot be of the kind to which the legislature and executive are subject. If that were so, or even partially so, the independence of the judiciary would be seriously compromised and democracy would be deprived of a fundamental constitutional imperative. One must look elsewhere than the popular vote or supervision of one kind or another for the constraints that will curb errant or aberrant judicial behaviour.

As traversed in Chapter 9, constraints on the judiciary are essential to preserve the rule of law. Yet, because the law is inherently uncertain, the text of the law or sophistication of legal doctrine cannot provide the decisive constraints. Those constraints are to be found in the methodology that is adopted, and are essentially the constraints that I have traversed in this chapter. Consequently, I have not overstated the importance of these constraints in the context of a contemporary judicial methodology. They are the backbone of a conception of the judicial role which makes the judicial function an elemental component of a constitutional democracy, preserves the rule of law, vests the judiciary with democratic legitimacy, and provides the law with coordination, coherence and direction.

When examined, these constraints turn out to be both real and effective. Looked at in total, they are much more extensive and deep-rooted than is commonly appreciated. They are also interlocking in that they reinforce one another to form a formidable matrix of control and discipline. Thus, a judge whose decisions reflect even a moderately schismatic sense of the judicial role or judicial function is liable to be reversed on appeal, incur the cogent disapproval of his or her colleagues, inspire trenchant criticism from legal practitioners and legal academics alike, and run the risk of being maligned in the forum of public opinion. One or more of the same effects is highly likely to befall the judge who fails to coordinate or integrate his or her decision in the context provided by the totality of the law or legal background. The same can be said of the judge whose conception of the rule of law or parliamentary supremacy, or any other constitutional requirement in a democracy, is found to be wanting. The institution of the law permits no or little scope for judicial heresy, heterodoxy or schismatic dissidents.

This chapter has also been utilised to advance a pragmatic approach to a number of the preconceptions or predilections that presently blemish judicial reasoning. Not only will this approach improve judicial decision-making, but also will inject into that process a further set of structural constraints. These constraints will arise because a judge's underlying preconceptions or predilections will be explicitly addressed rather than remaining submerged below the reasoning that is overtly advanced. Such express attention is required simply because the underlying preconception or predilections more often than not will determine the outcome of a case. What might otherwise be an instinctive, blind or reflexive response to a question becomes a pragmatic and open exercise expressly directed at, and justifying, the judge's decision. No perceptions or predilections will go by default.

In the result, the greater control and discipline that will be introduced into judicial deliberations must necessarily constrain the scope for wayward judicial reasoning. Differences will remain, but those differences will occur within a narrower compass and make the judge's motivation and direction transparent. Judges will be free to adopt a new judicial methodology appropriate to the twenty-first century. That methodology is introduced in the next chapter.

11

Towards a new judicial methodology

A methodology for the twenty-first century

No judge, lawyer or academic is going to agree with all the points made in the preceding chapters. Legal theory and discourse is too diverse and the dispositions of judges, lawyers and academics too divergent to achieve any such unanimity. But it is hoped that some judges will attain sufficient benefit to advance their perception of the judicial role. What should emerge is a refreshingly new judicial methodology that will better serve the interests of society. The various strands pursued in this book can be brought together to form a synthesis of realism, pragmatism and practical reasoning, including in that reasoning a critical role for principles.

Judicial reasoning will be re-invigorated by being less entrammelled by unnecessary and outdated dogmas. It will be at once more realistic and pragmatic, it will be forward looking rather than oriented to the past, it will be more honest and transparent, and it will be more diligent and creative in meeting the particular needs of society. The legal process will be no less, and even more, disciplined than at present, and no less, and again even more, beholden to a realistic and modern conception of the rule of law.

Basic to this fresh approach is the reiterated truism that the law is a social institution that exists to serve society. This subjection to the needs and expectations of society is its ultimate rationale and justification. The notion that the law is an independent and autonomous discipline and a self-sufficient and self-sustaining complex is part of the mystique of the law, and mystique can play no part in a new order. It must succumb to hard reality and determined pragmatism.

While most judges, lawyers and many academics will no doubt accept that the law is a social institution, disagreement, if there is disagreement, will be about the methodology that should be adopted to achieve that end. Those, for example, who are committed to a formalistic approach, may still argue that such an approach best serves the needs, if not the expectations, of society. But such a judgement can only be made by reference to some criterion, and their criterion will undoubtedly be certainty and predicability in the law. Positivists will advance the same or similar benchmarks. Natural law lawyers will press their other-worldly musings. The primary criteria I proffer are, of course, justice and relevance.

A deadlock can be avoided, however, if the various criteria are closely analysed and examined. Those criteria that best withstand close scrutiny must carry the day. It is for this reason that I have sought to stress the inherent uncertainty of the law and the foolhardiness of thinking that the law can be made more certain and predictable by persisting with a formalistic stance or adhering to the rule-bound approach generated by positivism. While these themes appear and reappear throughout the earlier chapters, they reach their zenith in Chapter 5 dealing with certainty and Chapter 6 dealing with precedent. The outcome is a more pragmatic approach in which certainty ceases to be the dominant goal of judicial adjudication and becomes a deliberate consideration in the appropriate case to be balanced against other relevant factors, and the coercive element in the doctrine of precedent is diminished to allow prior cases to be re-evaluated or balanced against the requirements of justice in the individual case and the contemporary needs of the community. Arguably, and it is so argued, greater certainty and predictability is likely to emerge from such a pragmatic approach.

Nor can natural law fare better as a criterion. If natural law is only partly as speculative, profuse, insecure and rootless as I have suggested, it provides nothing more than a panoply of subjective ideals by which to judge the law or legal system. As a criterion it fails, not because it is not a means of judging the law, but because it provides nothing sufficiently concrete to direct the law. For example, a concept of justice may appear in some casts of natural law, but I have yet to find a natural law theorist who has found the need for the law to keep abreast of the times etched in the heavens. Natural law does not provide the intrinsic guidance which valid criteria require.

The realistic perception is to accept that a variety of competing interests and values are involved in the adjudicative process and that a judge will have regard to a number of different and often conflicting considerations in arriving at a decision. If choice is endemic to judicial decision-making, balancing competing interests and values in order to exercise a choice is equally pervasive. Holmes' maxim about where to draw the line[1] in itself requires judges to balance various considerations in order to know where they wish to strike the line. A more generic description would be to acknowledge that the essential function of judicial decision-making is the task of balancing one or more interests or values against one or more other interests or values in order to reach a decision. The much vaunted value judgement is brought to bear in the course of this exercise. Hold judicial decision-making upside down and turn it inside out as you will, but a balancing exercise is an inescapable attribute of that process. It may take place in the context of statutory interpretation or in a common law setting. It may relate to findings of fact or determinations of law or of mixed fact and law. It may be executed impeccably or it may be performed imperfectly. But a balancing exercise will take place.

My critical contention, therefore, is that justice and relevance are the primary considerations to be taken into account in the course of this balancing exercise and the task of reaching a decision. They are not, of course, the only considerations, but they must be the dominant considerations if the law and legal process is to serve its basic function. The community's expectation that justice will be done in the individual case or that the law will keep abreast of the times will not be met if it is otherwise. While again admitting the usefulness and influence of other factors, justice and relevance become the primary normative values by which the law and legal process is to be measured. Those twin virtues must be brought to bear in every case where there is scope for their application.

Justice and relevance

The reality of justice

I do not propose to develop a theory of justice under this heading. In Chapter 15 of this book I advance a personal theory of justice focusing on the ameliorative effect of the law on the excesses of the prevailing creed of liberal individualism and its underlying economic order, capitalism. But I at once allow that there will be other theories of justice, even within the framework of the methodology commended in this work. What I do not allow is a theory that debunks justice as illusory.[2]

---

[1] See above, Chapter 6, at 159.
[2] I am indebted to Christos Mantziaris, then in the Law Program at the Research School of Social Sciences, Australian National University, Canberra, for his patience over a

It is disturbing to find that a small school of academic thought harbours the view that justice is an illusion, an ephemeral perception, a façade for more immediate concerns, a label or a rhetorical flourish designed simply to persuade. Alf Ross's words indicate this scepticism:

> To invoke justice is the same thing as banging on the table: an emotional expression which turns one's demand into an absolute postulate. That is no proper way to mutual understanding. It is impossible to have a rational discussion with a man who mobilises 'justice', because he says nothing that can be argued for or against. His words are persuasion, not argument. The ideology of justice leads to implacability and conflict, since on the one hand it incites to the belief that one's demand is not nearly the expression of a certain interest in conflict with opposing interests, but that it possesses a higher, absolute validity; and on the other hand it precludes all rational argument and discussion of a settlement.[3]

My immediate purpose, therefore, is to establish that the notion of justice is undoubtedly a reality in the legal process and to elaborate its relevance to judicial decision-making.

At first glance, it would seem absurd to deny the reality of justice. Concepts of justice have a long and convoluted history steeped in philosophy and theology and in ancient practices that no doubt preceded recorded history.[4] Extending endlessly back in time every known society has had its conception of right and wrong, the forbidden and the permissible, the commendable and the condemned, the ideal that ought to be and the inexpiable that ought not to be.[5] In the course of history few self-respecting philosophers have neglected to advance a theory of justice. Homer, Plato, Socrates, Aristotle, Hume, Adams-Smith, Hobbes, Locke, Rousseau, Hegel, Kant, Engels, Marx (possibly),[6] John Stewart Mill, Hajek, Dworkin, Rawls, Nozick and many, many others. Admittedly, in this philosophical abundance there are theories which

---

number of exchanges, including memoranda, earnestly endeavouring to convince me that justice is nought but an illusion; a veneer for the many factors that actually influence a judge in reaching a decision; and utilised to make the decision more acceptable to the parties and the community generally.

[3] A. Ross, *On Law and Justice* (Stevens & Sons, London, 1958), at 274–275.
[4] Robert C. Solomon and Mark C. Murphy, *What is Justice? Classic and Contemporary Readings* (Oxford University Press, Oxford and New York, 1990), at 13 *et seq.*
[5] Ibid., at 3–11.
[6] I say 'possibly' because Marx does not address the question; 'What is justice?' But in employing the language of exploitation, Marx is surely condemning capitalism for its injustice.

may be sublime but are indifferent to reality (say, Rousseau) and theories that are little more than elaborate metaphors (say, Socrates). At the risk of hyperbole, one would never complete the list for as fast as one intoned the names from the top a new generation of philosophers would need to be entered at the bottom. These philosophers have not wasted their time. The philosophical preoccupation with justice, which from time to time may have waned only to return to prominence yet again,[7] represents attempts to come to grips with a phenomenon which is entrenched in human activity and discourse. Professors Solomon and Murphy claim that it is safe to say that the subject of justice, perhaps in somewhat altered form or as part of some related concern, perhaps in the guise of a shadow or even in its very absence, has been at the core of social thinking ever since Plato and Aristotle.[8]

To practising judges and lawyers the suggestion that justice is illusory will also seem absurd. It defies all practical experience. To solicitors toiling long hours at the office, the question will be mystifying having regard to the number of occasions when they will have listened to their clients indignantly describing how they have been wronged. To barristers who have spent the better part of their lifetime either backing or seeking to defuse 'the merits', that is, the justice of the case, the question will seem a waste of time. When the merits have been with their client they will have sought to take advantage of that fact by determinedly pressing those merits on the court, or, when the merits have not been with their client, they will have attempted to counter those merits by one of any number of strategies, and when the merits have been even or neutral, they will as often as not have exercised their advocacy to try and persuade the court that in fact the merits lie with their client. To judges who have sat patiently in court day after day and witnessed the sense of grievance, righteousness or indignation with which the parties' versions of events unfolds, or bandied notions of justice about with counsel, or exchanged views as to the merits of a case with their colleagues in conference, or felt dissatisfaction with the law being urged upon the court where it does not accord with common notions of 'decency and fairness',[9] the suggestion will appear fanciful.

But the wonder that practitioners of the law would express would be mild compared with the reaction of laypersons to the suggestion that notions of justice lack substance. They believe that 'fair play' and giving

---

[7] Solomon and Murphy, *What is Justice?*, at 5–6.   [8] Ibid., at 6.
[9] Justice Frankfurter in *Adamson v California* 332 U.S. 46 (1947), at 67.

a person a 'fair go' are real and enduring values which they share with most members of the community. Experience confirms that parties seek justice – admittedly justice as they perceive it – and they expect the judge to provide that justice. They are fully aware that they are not addressing a cipher of the law. They know that it is the judge who is deciding the case, and that the judge has it in his or her hands to decide in their favour or against them. What they look for in the courtroom, therefore, is not any certainty in the law, but an impartial adjudicator possessing a judicial mind and habits trained in the judicial method to assess facts, identify the issues, and resolve the dispute in accordance with common notions of fairness. When they turn to the Bench they would rather see a Solomon than a living embodiment of *Halsbury's Laws of England*.

Justice is real in that it imports a substantive normative value into the operation of the law, which may be decisive in determining how various interests or values will be weighed or which of competing interests and values will prevail in the inevitable balancing exercise. A notion of justice will be invoked by the judge, not simply to persuade others to the 'rightness' of the judge's viewpoint and to justify that viewpoint to the parties and wider community, but because it will enter into the judges' thought processes as they strive to balance one interest or value against one or more other interests or values. Where relevant, therefore, justice or notions of what is just or unjust clearly infect the decision-making process.

Justice is also the yardstick by which the community, or a section of the community, will react, perhaps vociferously, to a decision which is seen to be unjust, however much the court may have clothed it in the respectable mantle of 'the law'. In all, the community expect the law to measure up to its sense of justice. Many examples could be given of decisions in which the community's expectation of justice has been critical. The House of Lords decision in *Pickett v British Rail Engineering Ltd*[10] will suffice. In that decision the House of Lords ruled for the first time that damages from an injury that shortened a person's life should include the earnings that would have accrued to that person during the 'lost years'. As Professor Harris has pointed out, the primary justification for the decision, which overruled earlier authorities, was that the new rule would accord with the ordinary man's expectations about claims against tortfeasors, and was for that reason 'just'.[11]

---

[10] [1980] AC 136.
[11] J. W. Harris, *Legal Philosophies* (2nd edn, Butterworths, London, 1980), at 262.

This is not to say that at times the community may be fractured and fail to speak with one voice or that there will not be differences of opinion as to what is or what is not just in particular circumstances. But notions of justice will exist. They are immanent in the community, and irrespective of the difficulty the judge may have in translating them for the purpose of his or her decision-making, they will inform the judge and be instrumental, if not decisive, in directing the outcome. Some judges, of course, will be more susceptible to the influence of considerations of justice than others. But this fact neither refutes the view that justice is a value immanent in community, nor that it is this sense of justice as a value which will inform and influence judicial thinking. Fuller made the point in these terms:

> [In] a sufficiently homogenous society certain 'values' will develop automatically and without anyone intending or directing their development. In such a society it is assumed that the legal rules developed and enforced by courts will reflect those prevailing 'values'.[12]

For the purpose of the present exposition I do not need to identify the source of the sense of justice immanent in the community. That question is best left to, or addressed in conjunction with, sociologists and psychologists. No doubt it stems in part from generations of rolled-over history and tradition that have by acquiescence or convention applied a sanction to our interpersonal relationships and our interactions with our fellow human beings, and the communitarian obligations we recognise one to the other. It has become part of our culture, and this is no less so simply because other cultures may have reached the same commitment. So ingrained is it in the very fibre of society that it is as much a learned activity as eating, walking or riding a bicycle. Indeed, it may not be entirely learned. The example may be given of the young child with no learning experience sufficient to have inspired a sense of injustice being chastised for something the youngster did not do. His or her innocence, and the injustice of being condemned when innocent, will be relayed to the skies even more lustily than if they were guilty and deserved the chastisement.

Irrespective of the force of history, tradition and cultural acceptance, the endless roll of philosophers and theorists who have advanced theories of justice, the daily experience of the courts, the language of much legal discourse and the patent expectations of the community, scepticism of justice as a value central to judicial decision-making is directed

---

[12] Fuller, 'The Forms and Limits of Adjudication' (1978) 92 Harv. LR 353, at 378.

at the notion that there is, or can be, a conception of substantive justice. I agree, as I have said, and will further develop in Chapter 15, that there is no abstract or universal concept of justice or, at least, one that we are capable of discerning. It cannot be unearthed objectively and does not exist objectively. But to then deny justice a role in the legal process is to confuse the question of its substantiveness as an abstract or universal concept with the substantiveness of its status as an independent value in the balancing exercises undertaken by the judges. Its reality derives, not from any abstract or universal conception of justice, but from the sense of justice or injustice that the community, or a section of the community, brings to concrete situations and that judges then seek to translate into their decision-making. The existence of such notions of justice in concrete situations and their contribution to the decision-making process, not as rhetoric, but as self-standing principles relevant to the outcome is plain to see.

Take the situation where an employer dismisses an employee without notice and without consulting the employee or giving him or her a proper opportunity to be heard. The employee brings proceedings for wrongful dismissal. The employee's immediate concern and interest is in being reinstated or obtaining compensation for the wrongful dismissal. Other motivations and considerations may be present, but let us keep the example simple. The employee's immediate interest does not found an argument in itself. Rather, he or she will claim that the procedure followed by the employer was unfair in that they were dismissed without being heard. The claim is an appeal to a basic concept of procedural justice arising out of the broader concept of natural justice itself. The fact that there is a disparity between the employee's immediate interest and the argument founded on justice does not make the latter a veneer, a label or mere rhetoric. It becomes a major consideration possessing independent value and weight. Without further elaboration there would be widespread agreement among judges that this value outweighed the employer's interest in managing his or her business as they see fit. It is, of course, no answer to say that the court would, in holding for the employee, simply be applying an established legal principle. That principle itself evolved because of the sense of justice – or injustice – involved if an opportunity to be heard is not given in such circumstances. Today, the same values and conception of justice would be relevant to the question whether the principle should apply to the new factual situation in issue.

Assume, however, that it is demonstrated that the employee had in fact committed a breach of his or her conditions of employment so that the employer would have been justified in dismissing the employee had the proper procedure been followed. Now, the respective merits or claims on justice by the employer and employee change. Many, if not most, would regard it as unjust for the employee to benefit from his or her breach notwithstanding that the procedure surrounding the dismissal was unfair. Two conflicting values of justice have come into conflict and both the values and the conflict are anything but an illusion. Again, a sense of what is just or unjust will be an ascertainable value in the case.

Another straightforward example may be given to demonstrate how a sense of what is just or unjust can be elevated to a critical or substantive role in the decision-making process. A landlord gives a tenant notice to quit. Everything is in order under the lease. But the landlord has made a promise to the tenant that he or she will not be given notice if the tenant repairs the leaking roof of the premises, and the tenant has done that at his or her own expense. The tenant's immediate interest is to remain in occupation of the premises under the lease, and this concern will be his or her motivation and purpose in taking or defending proceedings against the landlord. But the substantive argument will ultimately depend on whether it would be an injustice to the tenant to allow the landlord to renege on his or her promise. The landlord's interest in obtaining possession of the premises under the lease is likely to be outweighed by the value of justice – or injustice – inherent in the situation where the landlord has made a promise that the tenant has relied and acted upon to his or her detriment. Again, it is no answer to say that the law of promissory estoppel is now well established. The same sense of justice that demands its application today infused its development in prior cases and will continue to infuse its application in further incremental cases.

But accept that the landlord is the land owner and the occupants are squatters. Requiring the property for his or her own use, the owner wants the squatters out forthwith. The owner's immediate interest in obtaining possession of the premises to which he or she is legally entitled is clear. The squatters do not appear to have any immediate interest outside of keeping a roof over their heads. Both established law and common notions of justice would seem to favour the property owner having the right to the return of his or her own property; the squatters can have no legal or moral claim to occupy someone else's property without consent. They are trespassers. But suppose that the property owner had left the building vacant and neglected for some time and, although aware that homeless persons were likely to occupy poorly secured and dilapidated buildings in that neighbourhood, had failed to secure it or supervise its security or otherwise take any precautions against squatting. Nothing in the immediate concern and interests of the owner and the squatters has altered. But the balance of justice between the two has changed. There is now an argument based on a notion of justice that any order evicting the squatters should be suspended for a short but reasonable period to enable them to obtain other accommodation. Change the facts again so that it is known the squatters have 'trashed' the interior of the building and may well do further damage, and the balance of justice will change yet again. The just citizen, as with the judge sensitive to justice, would now ask why, irrespective of his or her neglect of the building, the property owner should have to face the prospect of the building being further damaged by the squatters staying in occupation one day longer than necessary. It would be thought unfair to subject the property owner to the risk of suffering permanent damage to his or her property for which they would almost certainly be unable to recover compensation. Once again, the basic interest of the parties may not have changed but the justice of the situation has been reversed.

These simple examples illustrate how unreal it is to depict those values that reflect a sense of justice or injustice as illusory, or as ephemeral perceptions, or as a façade, or as a label for more immediate concerns or interests, or as simply a rhetorical table-thumping gesture designed to justify and gather support for a decision that has been made having regard to deeper underlying factors. The notions of justice involved are decisive in determining the outcome. They become the primary considerations in the balancing exercise that the court cannot escape in reaching a decision. To describe them as appendages to some other more basic yardstick is not so much unreal as surreal.

In all these instances, the language used will embrace notions of what is just or unjust. Undeniably, the language of much legal discourse, in the lawyer's office, at interparty conferences, in the courtroom, in the judges' conference room, or in the judges' judgments, is the language of justice. Principles, or even rules, which owe their existence to a concept of justice in a particular factual situation are difficult to refer to without involving the justice value underlying them. Lord Goff in his Maccabean Lecture in Jurisprudence in 1983 said that, if he were asked what was the most potent influence on a court in formulating a statement of legal principle, he would answer that in the generality of instances it is the desired result in the particular case before the court.[13] One reason why

---

[13] Robert Goff 'The Search for Principle', Maccabean Lecture in Jurisprudence, 1983, Proceedings of British Academy, Vol. 69, at 169.

that result may be the 'desired result' is because, on the facts of the case, it would be unjust to reach any other outcome. The parties, counsel and the court will reflect that sense of justice in the expressions that are used. But the reflection is more than a veneer, label or façade, because once it is accepted that the language of justice is a reality, it must surely be accepted that this language will infect the substance of the judge's thinking, the outcome of the case and the law generally.

A variant of the sceptics' argument, still clinging to the notion that concepts of justice are irrelevant to the judge's real reasons for reaching a decision, is to seek to identify yet another set of values allegedly underlying any veneer of justice.[14] Thus, it is argued, that as the judge is the product of his or her background, upbringing and experience, he or she will have a conception of the 'good' or of what is 'right'. This conception, rather than any conception of justice, will direct the judges' thinking. But what is so special or discrete about the 'good' or the 'right' as distinct from the 'just' or the 'unjust'? Why would a judge, as the product of his or her background, upbringing or experience, not also develop a conception of the 'just' or the 'unjust'? What excludes a conception of the 'just' or 'unjust' from being part of a conception of the 'good'? To rest with the conception of the 'good' or what is 'right' is to rest short of an answer which identifies the value that makes that conception 'good' or 'right' in the eyes of the holder. Scepticism of this kind can be reduced to a semantic quibble requiring a pitiable act of faith to fill the void that would be left if concepts of justice were divorced from the many and varied disputes that come before the court for resolution.

Mild curiosity would lead one to speculate why such justice scepticism remains precious to a disaffected handful in legal academia. One possible reason could be that, unlike lawyers and judges, academics are not exposed to the coalface of litigation. They have not seen the plaintiff sob or the defendant wracked with indignation at the charge levelled against him or her, or one or other of the parties faced with ruin or tragedy if, as they would put it, justice is not done. Distance may bring greater objectivity, but it may also bring a greater detachment from the interests of justice as distinct from the perceived requirements of 'the law'. A second reason is more probable. It is the seemingly deep-seated distrust of judicial discretion and a corresponding resistance to accept

---

[14] Again, I am again indebted to Christos Mantziaris for his spirited presentation of this argument. See, above n. 2.

the reality of judicial autonomy. The reaction is to seek to curb the judicial discretion by whatever means possible. Giving justice a more overt role in the judicial decision-making process seemingly enlarges the area of judicial discretion. Better, it is wistfully thought, to confine the judges to administer the law according to the law. This fundamental scepticism is flawed in that it erects a straw man in order to justify the ensuing scepticism. The straw man is the impression that the courts are claiming to appeal to some concept of substantive justice or 'higher order' value when they are not in fact doing so.

I have already made plain in asserting the reality and relevance of concepts of justice to legal reasoning that no concept of substantive justice is involved. Nor is any 'higher order' law or value involved. Indeed, the existence of an abstract or universal concept of justice divorced from concrete situations is disputed. What is real is the everyday common garden sense of justice that is indwelling within the community and bears on or relates to particular situations. It need not be the only consideration which will bear on a dispute or issue and it will not be present in every case. But when some notion of justice is in issue it obtains or should obtain pre-eminence simply because of the community's expectation that justice will be done in the individual case. It provides the court with a normative value with which to exercise the choices required in weighing the competing interests and values in arriving at a determination.

But is justice 'knowable'?

A less fundamental form of scepticism flows from the belief, again not uncommon in legal academic circles, that justice is all too difficult if not impossible to discern. Notions of justice, it is suggested, are too nebulous, multifarious and diverse to claim that any notion of justice can be identified, even in a concrete situation. Further, no sense of justice can be said to be immanent in the community because the community is fractured into many different and often irreconcilable communities. In other words, 'justice' is unknowable. In the result, judges can never know or discern what might be called or thought to be a sense of justice indwelling in the community.[15]

---

[15] I am grateful to Gary Edmond, a Visiting Fellow at the Research School of Social Sciences, the Australian National University, Canberra, for his constructive advocacy of this point.

There is both a small element of truth and a large element of hyperbole in this bleak picture. Of course, notions of justice are nebulous, multifarious and diverse, but the point is that they crystallise, or tend to crystallise, in a concrete situation. There may, perhaps, be disagreement in such a situation as to what is just and unjust. But the principle or notion of justice in issue, or principles or notions if more than one, will either have been identified, or could be identified if the court were so inclined. Moving from the general to the particular carves a path through the nebulous, multifarious and diverse notions of justice to the principle or principles which are relevant to the case in hand. Ultimately, one notion of justice will predominate if the court is to reach a final determination.

Nor is the claim that there is no recognisable community, as such, to nurture notions or a sense of justice lacking in overstatement. Certainly, the community can be broken down into many sections and each sector may have a different perception or interest. But at the same time a community can be sufficiently homogenous to share an impressive bundle of common values reflected in a common language and shared institutions and organisations. As Fuller observed in the quotation given above,[16] in a sufficiently homogenous society certain values develop automatically without any positive intention or direction, and it is assumed that those values will be reflected in the law that is enforced by the courts. It is both realistic and reasonable to accept that, while differences and disagreements certainly exist in our society so, too, there is a large area of homogeneity and large areas of agreement. A commitment to justice, an expectation that courts will administer, or will at least seek to administer, justice and a rough sense of what justice generally requires in particular situations is part of that accord.

The more acute problem, which I have already identified when speaking about community values generally,[17] is essentially one of translation. How is this sense of justice immanent in the community discerned by a judge? If it is discerned, how can the judge's fidelity to that evaluation be assured? In what way can the interference of the judge's own personal notions of justice be curbed? These are valid questions, and I have not suggested that they do not pose real difficulties. Indeed, sceptics who press these questions are likely to conclude that their scepticism is warranted by the only answers that can be given.

---

[16] See above at 276.
[17] See above, Chapter 4, at 84–86; and see Chapter 10, at 242–243 and 245.

The first point to make is that there is no viable alternative. If justice is going to be done in the courts it must be done by the judges. Decision-making is in their hands, and unless the law is to be administered devoid of any concept of justice at all, we cannot escape the reality that conceptions of justice fall within the scope of judicial discretion. It is part of the inevitable judicial autonomy of which I have so often spoken. While critics may, therefore, have a field day with the difficulties involved, they can offer nothing positive in its place. The bleak prospect if one were to succumb to their arguments is a barren adjudicative process bereft of any concept of justice. Yet, such a prospect is a defiant denial of the expectations of the people the law is designed to serve.

Accepting, in the second place, therefore, that the task of translating the values in the community, including the value called justice, into legal principles must fall to the judges, the objective should be to facilitate rather than impede that task. I am not, of course, suggesting that evidence be given as to what a party considers just or unjust or what the community considers just or unjust. Justice is not a subject for Brandeis' briefs. Rather, what can be done is to be more open about the subject of justice itself in legal discourse and exchanges within the adjudicative framework. Judges should reveal and discuss their perception of the justice of the case just as they should seek to identify and explain the value judgement that they believe underlies their decision. More often than not the concept of justice and the value judgement may be one and the same. Indeed, the perception of the justice of the case is likely to be an integral part of the value judgement. In this way the operation of justice in the judicial system would be more transparent and open to comment or criticism and judges would be more responsive in their appreciation and application of the concept accordingly.

Nor, in the third place, is it permissible to deny justice a role in the legal process simply because it is difficult to be assured that the judge's own perception of what is just or fair will not intrude into the process. Indeed, it has been and is acknowledged that the judges' own notions of justice will influence and, in some cases, possibly dominate their perception of what is just or unjust in the circumstances of a particular case. But again, more overt treatment of the subject will assist to provide greater objectivity. Furthermore, concern that the justice administered in the courts will be the judges' personal perception of justice must to some extent be ameliorated by the fact that the judges are members of the community. A shared sense of justice or fairness is likely to be reflected in their personal values. Because it is an immanent property, the community's deep-rooted sense of fairness and that of the judges are more often than not likely to coincide. Experience suggests that this coincidence is real enough. Of course, exceptions can always be found, but case law generally tends to confirm that judges are not removed, or far removed, from the community's sense of justice.

This identification exists notwithstanding that many judges may come from a more advantaged sector of the community and even privileged elite. Justice of the kind that is reflected in legal principles has a habit of transcending such sectional boundaries. The unfairness of not being treated alike, or not being given a fair hearing, or having someone resile from a promise which one has relied and acted upon to one's detriment, or suffering a punishment or penalty or reaction which is disproportionate to the misdemeanour or act, can strike the rich as well as the poor.[18] The judicial process is primarily concerned with corrective justice rather than the wider aspects of social justice and does not therefore have the same extensive scope for irreversible disagreement.[19]

Finally, I would refer to the constraints upon the judiciary that I have traversed in Chapter 10. My avowed purpose in treating that more prosaic topic at such length was to demonstrate that fear of the errant or aberrant judge is misplaced. The constraints serve to keep the judiciary within bounds equally acceptable – or intolerable – to conservative and liberal alike. The constraints also serve to impose upon judges, not just restraint, but a fine regard for their responsibility as judges. That sense of responsibility can embrace the need to confront an issue of justice conscious of the need to subvert one's own predilections and undertake an honest attempt to articulate that sense of justice indwelling in the community.

In my view, the more pressing problem in judicial adjudication is not so much translating the community's sense of justice into concrete situations as ensuring that justice is not in fact ignored; that it is consciously taken into account where considerations bearing on the justice of the case are clearly relevant. The bugbear is the persistence of a formalistic approach. Formalism and justice not only walk on the opposite sides of the river but they also then walk in different directions. A formalistic approach eliminates the judge's choice of a concept of fairness or justice. No justice value is invoked. The balancing exercise is

---

[18] See below, Chapter 15, at 365–366.
[19] See below, Chapter 15, at 361–362, for a brief reference to distributive justice.

then distorted by being channelled into a narrow approach that excludes the very considerations conducive to an outcome likely to do justice in the particular case.

Consequently, the abandonment of formalism would itself bring about a marked improvement. But more than a consequential reaction of this kind is required. As I have sought to stress, justice needs to be deliberately addressed whenever it is relevant to a particular case. The community of considerations of which I will shortly speak must consciously embrace the notions of justice or fairness that are pertinent.[20] More judges must be prepared to give open expression in their judgments to the influence of justice in their reasoning.[21]

This approach does not mean that the Cadi will enter and dominate the courtroom and judicial thinking. The insignia of justice above the judges' bench will not be replaced by a palm tree. As I have said, principles and rules will remain serviceable tools used by judges in the judicial process; where appropriate a rule may be the premise or starting point for judicial reasoning and often it may be the end of the matter; certainty will be a consideration to be taken into account whenever there is a positive reason to do so in the context of a particular case; past cases will be referred to for the guidance they can give and be adhered to where they remain valid; judges will be subjected to the judicial constraints

---

[20] One example, which has just come to hand, of a judge who consciously sought to ask this question, is Justice Stewart H. Hancock, a retired Judge of the New York State Court of Appeals. Not surprisingly, perhaps, that was Cardozo's Court. In his Hugh R. Jones Memorial Lecture delivered to the Albany Law School on 9 March 2004, Justice Hancock related that he asked his law clerks these questions: 'Will the rule you are proposing work? Does it make sense? How will it fit into the existing progression of the law? And, will it operate fairly?' (at 5 and 17). One factor is identified as more influential than all others. It is 'fundamental fairness' (at 7). Applied to a judge it connotes wisdom, even-handedness, perceptiveness and maturity of judgment. But the Judge recognised that these qualities add little to the idea that the judge should be fair. Fairness, he concludes, apart from equality, evenness, reasonableness and a careful balancing of interests, has many dimensions. Justice Hancock then describes two innate attributes of fairness which were of particular importance to him as a judge. One is the moral or ethical component, which he expands at some length (at 8–12). The other is what he describes as the 'human dimension', a dimension that enables judges to perceive a need for a solution and inspires them to find a way to fill that need; to ask, not 'whether' but 'how' (at 12 and 17). For present purposes, the judge's views are not in issue; the immediate point is that the question of justice is deliberately addressed.

[21] See, for example, *Hussey* v *Palmer* [1972] 1 WLR 1286, per Lord Denning at 1790 and *Dextra Bank and Trust Co Ltd* v *Bank of Jamaica* [2002] 1 All ER (Comm) 193, per Lords Bingham and Goff at para. [38]. And see any number of Lord Steyn's judgments. His Lordship's judgment in *Chester* v *Afshar* [2004] UKHL 41, is a recent example.

and, possibly, the further structural constraints I recommend in Chapter 10; a considered judicial methodology and discipline will apply; and the rule of law, based not on a positivist or formalistic notion that there are firm rules to predict and apply, but on the operation of that methodology and discipline will hold good. The Cadi under the palm tree must remain a mirage.

I do not propose to proffer a case study demonstrating how formalism, or the formalistic approach still pursued by many judges, can subvert justice. Examples abound. It is sufficient to point out that each of the cases subjected to close examination for the purpose of illustrating other points in the course of this book also exhibit painful injustices. The first case, utilised to illustrate the shortcomings of formalism itself, was *Sevcon Ltd v Lucas CAB Ltd*.[22] By no stretch of the imagination can it be suggested that it is anything other than a gross injustice that an applicant for a patent who is required by statute to publish details of his or her invention to the world at large cannot then recover damages for infringements committed pending the grant of the patent. The injustice is all the more gross if the delay in granting the patent occurs because the infringer uses – or misuses – court proceedings to bring about that delay. *State Government Insurance Commissioners v Trigwell and Ors*[23] was examined to illustrate the implausibility of Dworkin's assertion that there is a 'right' answer and his consequential attempt to minimise judicial discretion, distinguish principles and rules, separate principles and policy, and justify undue adherence to precedent. In addition, however, the outcome in that decision was as unjust as it was wrong. Following the advent of *Donoghue v Stevenson*[24] it cannot serve justice to exclude from a landowner's liability in tort the consequences of his or her stock negligently permitted to wander on to a public highway. The injustice is singularly acute in that a neighbour would be able to recover claiming the same negligence causing the same damage against the same land owner.

The decision of the Privy Council in *Lewis v Attorney-General of Jamaica*,[25] was selected to confirm the deficiencies in the overly rigid and formalistic application of the doctrine of precedent, but it is not that decision that is unjust. The injustices occurred prior to that decision. In 1999, the Privy Council declined to review a precedent decided twenty-one years earlier, notwithstanding that the principles of administrative

---

[22] See above at, Chapter 3, at 66.   [23] See above, Chapter 8, at 208.
[24] [1932] AC 56.   [25] See above, Chapter 7, at 164.

law had undergone dramatic development in the meantime. As a result, an unknown number of persons were subsequently executed on the basis of reasoning held to be faulty in *Lewis*. That default is an injustice.

Finally, reference may be made to *Fletcher Challenge Energy Ltd* v *Electricity Corporation of New Zealand Ltd*, which will be dealt with later in this chapter. There is no need to rehearse that case at this stage. As will be seen, it has been selected to illustrate many features of the formalistic approach. Suffice to say that among those features resides a rank injustice. Parties who undeniably intended to be bound by a contract that they had entered into, and which the Court otherwise found to be certain in its terms, were held not to have intended to be bound by the contract. In such circumstances it is unjust that the party entitled to the benefit of the contract should be denied that benefit.

No further cases are necessary to demonstrate that justice and formalism are unhappy bedfellows.

The imperative to be relevant

Again, it would seem to be nothing short of a truism that a law and legal process that have the fundamental function of serving society should keep abreast of the times. Certainly, much judicial homage is paid to this objective. But all too often it is lip service. Too many factors in the law and legal system operate to impede the courts ability to develop the law to meet contemporary needs and standards. These factors have all been mentioned; continuing to adopt the judicial style or form appropriate to the belief that there is a law to be discovered and declared; extending positivism into a rule-bound black-and-white approach or, at least, adopting a presumptive approach to rules by virtue of the fact that, courtesy of an earlier court, the rule exists; adhering to a formalistic approach which is backward rather than forward looking; idolising certainty and predictability as the primary goals of judicial adjudication; and accepting an unwanted coercive element in the doctrine of precedent. All these factors combine to create a formidable weighting for the *status quo* irrespective of any pressing need to update the law.

The fell fact remains that a law that is out of step with the needs and expectations of the times is not serving the society it is designed to serve. It is failing in its basic function. All sections of the community suffer as a result of the law being less responsive to their needs than they have a right to expect. No sector suffers more than the commercial community. To be blunt, it is reprehensible that commerce should be subject to a law that is anything other than painstakingly scrupulous in its attempt to match the law with the requirements of commerce. Commerce is central to the social and economic well-being of the community and the law should seek to facilitate rather than impede, or risk impeding, its operation. A deliberate and conscientious judicial effort is required to ensure that the law serves the commercial community.

Apart from the factors that I have already mentioned, I would select three features for specific mention in this context.

The first factor I have already touched upon. It is the formalist's predisposition to try and make commerce operate according to rules which are comfortable to proclaim but difficult to comply with in actual commercial practice. Judges cannot proclaim these rules and then shrug their shoulders and blame commercial people, and their lawyers, for not trying harder when they are shown to be unrealistic. This perception does not mean, of course, that the law is obliged to endorse the morality of the commercial community. The wider community's sense of what is acceptable commercial behaviour would ordinarily override any alleged commercial morality. Rather, I am speaking here of all the common law rules that affect the day-to-day workings of commerce, and particularly because it is so central to commerce, the law of contract. When evaluating the suitability of a rule or prior decision one of the first questions asked must be, what are the requirements of commerce and how well, or badly, does this rule fit those requirements?

The second factor has been dealt with in Chapters 5 and 6; it is the demanding obsession for certainty and predictability. Commercial lawyers, in particular, frequently upbraid the courts, even when the courts are in harmony with their thinking, for not delivering a law that is more certain and predictable. I have already expressed an understanding of their position. Pressed by their clients to advise on what the law is, and what it prohibits or permits, and not what the law may be or what it may permit or may prohibit, their professional lives undoubtedly would be more comfortable if the law was more certain. But we have already accepted that the degree of certainty is sought unattainable. Much bad commercial and contractual law is made in pursuit of that chimerical goal. It is a focus that has deflected the courts from the task of providing a substantive law that is responsive and suitable to the needs of commerce.

Followers of the illusion of certainty, for example, will condemn any move in the courts towards recognising an implication of good faith in contract simply because such an implication has not been plainly spelt out in the case law and, it is alleged, its recognition would lead to uncertainty in the performance of the contract. No finite view as to the desirability of such a concept is required here. What is in point is the narrowness of the thinking involved in resisting the concept. Those who dismiss the notion outright generally omit to note that the largest and most vigorous, competitive private enterprise economy in the world, the United States, has been served by a doctrine of good faith for many years. Similarly, they neglect to note that international commercial instruments governing enormous global transactions invariably incorporate the concept.[26] Even further, they fail to consider that a requirement that a contract be performed by a party with fidelity to the promise made in the contract should promote, not only certainty in the performance of the contract, but also greater stability in the commercial relationship of which the contract is only a part.

The third factor that impedes the ability of the law or legal process to meet the requirements of commerce is more subtle. This factor is the judge's, or many judges', hesitancy to accept that they can know what those requirements are. Not all judges can claim the advantage of a professional lifetime in commercial litigation rubbing shoulders with businessmen and women. Diffidence in purporting to divine the demands of commerce must be accepted and, in any event, such diffidence may be a prudent prescription for those judges who too readily believe they know best the requirements of commerce. Nevertheless, the fact is that, in the context of a litigated dispute, the requirements of commerce are frequently evident to all but the most obtuse of judges. The needs of commerce are frequently inherent in the circumstances and may well have been spelt out in evidence at first instance. Any shortfall in judicial knowledge can, in respect of such a question, be the subject of submissions or more general evidence of the commercial practice relevant to the dispute in issue. It can be no excuse to accept that commerce should not be well served by the law simply because the judge's understanding of its requirements may be initially modest and even inadequate.

A case study: *Fletcher Challenge Energy Ltd* v *ECNZ Ltd*

The city of Wellington in New Zealand is located on an earthquake fault line. It runs through the central city. From time to time, seismic tremors are felt. The Court of Appeal of New Zealand sits in Wellington, its

---

[26] E.g., UNIDROIT Principles of International Commercial Contracts; Article 7(1) United Nations (Vienna) Convention on Contracts for the International Sale of Goods.

unprepossessing courthouse being situated squarely on the fault line. One cannot say with certainty that the Court's decision in *Fletcher Challenge Energy Ltd* v *Electricity Corporation of New Zealand Ltd*[27] delivered in 2001 was a manifestation of this fault line, but it is highly likely that this was the case. There can be no doubt that the decision came as a major shock to the legal and commercial community. It provides an apt case study for what has gone before in this book and, indeed, what is yet to come.

The case concerns the law's approach to preliminary agreements. Because I propose to be harsh in my criticism of the judiciary in cases of this kind it is best that, upon this occasion, the case study come from my own jurisdiction. The decision has been the subject of one of the most scathing criticisms of any court decision by a distinguished academic one would ever – or, rather, never – hope to read.[28] Regrettably, I cannot say that the learned academic's trenchant criticism is unjustified. The decision provides a classic example of the courts' continued adherence to formalism and consequential inability to be realistic; their failure to meet the contemporary needs of commerce when those needs are patent and unchallenged; and their readiness to disregard the justice of the case when it is clearly open to the courts to make the choices that would bring their decisions, and the law, into concordance with that fundamental value.

The question in issue was whether a Heads of Agreement entered into by Fletcher Challenge Energy Ltd (FCE) and Electricity Corporation of New Zealand Ltd (ECNZ) for the long-term supply of gas was a binding contract. The majority of the Court[29] held, in a judgment delivered by Blanchard J, that the heads of agreement was legally complete and sufficiently certain to be a valid contract,[30] but that the parties did not intend it to be legally binding.[31]

FCE was New Zealand's largest oil and gas producer. It held a 68.75 per cent interest in the Maui oil and gas field, which was expected to be depleted by 2009, and a 22.5 per cent interest in the Kupe field, which was expected to be depleted by 2011. ECNZ is the country's major generator of power. In the mid 1990s it faced the prospect of being

---

[27] [2002] 2 NZLR 433.
[28] David McLauchlan, 'The FCE/ECNZ Heads of Agreement: Progress Report or Binding Contract?' (2002) 8 NZBLQ 192.
[29] Richardson P, and Keith, Blanchard and McGrath JJ.
[30] See paras. [85]–[112] and para. [125].   [31] Paragraphs [68]–[84].

short of gas to fuel its gas and coal-fired station situated at Huntly. From 1995 to early 1997, the parties sought to negotiate a contract for the long-term supply of gas but, at that time, FCE could not satisfy ECNZ's wish to secure a long-term supply. Hence, the negotiations were abandoned.

FCE had in the meantime sought to acquire a larger interest in the Kupe field. It purchased a 20 per cent interest held by other joint venture companies. Another shareholder, Western Mining Corporation (WMC), decided to sell its 40 per cent interest in that field by open tender. FCE submitted a bid. Unbeknown to it, ECNZ also submitted a bid. WMC decided to reopen the tenders with a deadline of 28 February 1997. When FCE learned that ECNZ was the only competing bidder, it approached ECNZ 'with a view to a mutually beneficial proposal'. This course was readily accepted by ECNZ.

The Chief Executives of the respective companies negotiated an agreement on 26 and 27 February. They signed a letter the following day recording the terms of the agreement. The validity of this initial agreement was never challenged. Among other matters, the agreement stipulated that the two companies would resubmit their bids to WMC and, if or when either were successful, the resulting interest would be divided between them, 14.25 per cent to FCE and 25.75 per cent to ECNZ. The letter then provided that by the end of the day the parties would enter into a heads of agreement for the long-term supply of gas specifying 'all essential terms for it to be a binding agreement'. The letter concluded by providing that, in the event of ambiguity or uncertainty, the Chief Executives would interpret the current intent and their interpretation would prevail.

Senior executives of the two companies met on 27 February to negotiate the heads of agreement and negotiations continued into the following day. Lawyers were deliberately excluded. By resorting to the matters that had previously been agreed in the aborted negotiations quick progress was made. A Heads of Agreement, fewer than four pages in length, was signed on the afternoon of 28 February. The senior executives reported their success back to the Chief Executives. The Chief Executives shook hands on the deal and had a drink together to celebrate their success in concluding a full supply agreement.

Two matters in the Heads of Agreement were stated to be conditions precedent. The first was to the effect that one or other of the parties had to secure the 40 per cent stake in Kupe; the second was the approval of the ECNZ Board. Two headings were noted with the words, 'not agreed', and one matter was noted, 'to be agreed'. The parties were required 'to use all reasonable endeavours to agree to a full sale and purchase agreement within three months of the date of this agreement.' The words, 'agreed (except where indicated)', appeared above the signatures of the senior executives who signed the Heads of Agreement.

Immediately after the Heads of Agreement had been executed, the companies resubmitted their previous bids for WMC's interest in Kupe. FCE was the successful bidder. Following advice of FCE's success, and for reasons that need not detain us here, the Chief Executives signed a slightly amended version of the preliminary letter on 12 March, that is, *after* the Heads of Agreement had been signed. The revised letter still contained the requirement that the Heads of Agreement was to specify 'all essential terms for it to be a binding agreement', the Chief Executives then knowing exactly what had been agreed and 'not agreed'. Although adopting qualified language, ECNZ's Board purported to approve the Heads of Agreement on the same day, and FCE was advised the next day that the Board had approved the Heads of Agreement.

The parties thereafter completed the purchase of WMC's interest in Kupe and divided that interest between them as had been agreed. Final settlement was completed in terms of the Chief Executive's letter on 27 March. Negotiations for the full supply agreement began and continued until they eventually came to a halt in January of the following year. ECNZ then belatedly claimed that the Heads of Agreement did not constitute a binding agreement and declined to proceed with the purchase of gas. FCE sought a declaration from the Court that the Heads of Agreement was legally binding, and that ECNZ was in breach of its obligation to use all reasonable endeavours to agree to the terms of the full agreement.

As to be expected in a complex commercial cause, and one in which billions of dollars were at stake, many issues were raised and numerous arguments advanced relating to the efficacy of the Heads of Agreement. The only issue which need be addressed here, however, is the critical question whether the Heads of Agreement was intended to be legally binding.

The Judge at first instance had held that, taking into account all the circumstances, including the subsequent conduct of both companies, the parties intended to be bound immediately upon the execution of the Heads of Agreement. Neither party wanted to defer the implementation of their agreement until the full agreement was completed. The Judge also held that the Heads of Agreement was not void for incompleteness and uncertainty. The Court of Appeal agreed with this latter finding but not the first. Notwithstanding that the agreement contained two headings marked 'not agreed' and one heading marked 'to be agreed', the Heads of Agreement was both complete and certain. Blanchard J stated:[32]

> But even where the parties are *ad idem* concerning all terms essential to the formation of a contract ... they still may not have achieved formation of a contract if there are other unagreed matters which the parties themselves regard as a prerequisite to any agreement and in respect of which they have reserved to themselves alone the power of agreement. In such cases, what is missing at the end of the negotiation is the intention to contract, not a legally essential element of a bargain.

Professor McLauchlan considers that informed business people would find this conclusion 'incredible' and 'indeed, bordering on the laughable'.[33] The Professor is driven to suggest that the charitable explanation for this reasoning is that Court 'experienced a mental block'.[34] He points out that, if as would be more common, the parties had simply deleted the provisions marked 'not agreed', the Court would presumably have held that the contract was binding![35] Not without some force, McLauchlan further observes that recording the terms in question as 'not agreed' has an effect which the failure to make any mention of the terms would not have. It prevents (or at least makes very difficult) a later argument that either term was agreed so that the Heads of Agreement should be rectified or that the agreement was a partly written and partly oral contract. It would also preclude an argument that a term in question should be implied.

I agree that it is illogical to deny the Heads of Agreement binding force where the parties set out to reach a 'binding agreement' and thought and acted as if they had done so essentially because they did not agree to certain provisions, the absence of which does not render the agreement incomplete or uncertain. The decision reflects a judicial 'negativism' or aversion to less than comprehensive contracts, which is still evident in the law. In the result, the community, and in particular the commercial community, are poorly served. It is this aspect which

---

[32] Paragraph [52]. [33] McLauchlan, 'The FCE/ECNZ Heads of Agreement', at 204.
[34] Ibid., at 206.
[35] Ibid. This conclusion follows from the fact that the parties set out to reach a 'binding agreement' and undoubtedly thought and acted as though they had, and the finding that, even in the absence of the two 'unagreed' matters, the Heads of Agreement was legally complete and certain.

I particularly wish to stress. To avoid unnecessary contention I will not refer to the large body of extrinsic evidence and evidence of the parties' subsequent conduct that is decisive in establishing that ECNZ, as well as FCE, clearly intended the Heads of Agreement to be binding. For present purposes, questions of fact must give way to the deficiencies in the Court's approach.

The first criticism must be levelled against the Court's formalistic and commercially unrealistic approach to heads of agreement. Heads of agreement are an essential feature of commercial activity. Businessmen and women regularly resort to them. Sometimes the agreements are complete, but more often than not they leave important matters to be decided later. As Lord Lloyd (then Lloyd LJ), who was for a time a distinguished Judge of the Commercial Court in the United Kingdom, has stated, parties may agree to be bound now while deferring important matters to be agreed later. 'It happens', he said, 'every day when parties enter into so-called "heads of agreement".'[36] Whether judges and lawyers like it or not, the reality is that heads of agreement are a vital part of commercial activity.

While commercial agreements are frequently long and complex documents, what is crucial is the essence of the bargain. Completing the initial bargain is the task of senior management. They are the deal-makers. Often the circumstances require the bargain to be 'struck under great pressure of events and time'.[37] Heads of agreement are the means by which the bargain can be converted into a binding transaction. Once completed, the senior managers, the deal-makers, then move to other productive areas of the company's business leaving the core agreement to be expanded into a comprehensive document by subordinate executives and the parties' legal advisers. As is to be expected, the chief executives or deal-makers focus on the essential elements of a proposed agreement. Contingencies will frequently be incompletely dealt with, the contract will fail to specify a party's obligation on the occurrence of a future event, or the future contingency will not be addressed at all.[38] Provisions to cover such contingencies will invariably

---

[36] See *Pagnan SpA* v *Feeds Product Ltd* [1987] 2 Lloyd's Rep 601, at 619.
[37] John Steyn, 'Contract Law: Fulfilling the Reasonable Expectations of Honest Men' (1997) 113 LQR 433, at 439.
[38] See David Goddard, 'Long-term Contracts: a Law and Economics Perspective' [1997] NZLR 423, at 426.

deal with the allocation of risk and, if no explicit provision is agreed, the parties can generally be deemed to have accepted the risk involved.

Moreover, by and large, the essential terms of a contract do not relate to contingencies. There are various reasons why this is so: by definition, the contingency may be a remote possibility and may never occur; the sensible outcome, should the contingency occur, may be able to be determined by agreement or, failing agreement, by resorting to the common law; the appropriate provision may be a 'boiler plate' clause or one that can readily be determined by reference to industry practice; or the parties may simply not be prepared to risk jeopardising a favourable bargain by arguing about a contingency which is remote and may never occur. Thus, it is not uncommon for commercial parties to enter into heads of agreement that have gaps, but that are intended to be binding pending the completion of a more comprehensive agreement. Where heads of agreement are not intended to be binding, but only the forerunner to a formal contract, commercial prudence (if not the sense of self-preservation of executives carrying out the negotiation) would ordinarily dictate that this conditional status be clearly spelled out.[39] The notion that the adversarial ethic prevails in commercial negotiations relating to a prospective deal is misconceived. Indeed, in the context of a prospective deal, it is a myth. More often than not businessmen and women approach such negotiations with a 'win/win' outlook. A bargain can be struck that, certainly overall and notwithstanding the inevitable and unresolved risks involved, will be perceived to be of advantage to both parties.

Apart from a heavy dose of commercial reality, the Court's decision would have also benefited from an economic perspective and law and economics thinking.[40] Of course, the commercial reality just alluded to reflects the underlying economic imperative. Parties who enter into a binding agreement are to be assumed to be making a rational choice. They are seeking a commitment on the part of the other party that will enable them to undertake a course or activity they would be unable or unwilling to undertake without that commitment. The form in which the parties will choose to obtain that binding commitment will

---

[39] See, e.g., Lord Wright's speech in *Hillas & Co Ltd* v *Argus Limited* (1932) 147 LT 503; [1932] All ER 494 (HL), at 503 and 504.

[40] I am impressed by and pay tribute to an unpublished paper, 'Law and Economics Provide a Pragmatic Approach to Preliminary Agreements', by a student, Kate Gundersen. I am indebted to her and confirmed in my view that if a student can master the insights revealed in this paper there can be no excuse for judges not to do so.

necessarily depend on the circumstances. Often those circumstances will require a preliminary agreement. In the present case, for example, the Heads of Agreement was part of a broader agreement recorded in the Chief Executive's preceding letter that the parties would resubmit their bids to acquire WMC's interest in Kupe and that, one of them having succeeded, they would then divide that interest as agreed.

Furthermore, few, if any, contracts can be said to be complete. Parties and their legal advisers have a finite capacity to anticipate and identify future contingencies, or if they do, to necessarily provide an adequate or flawless response to those contingencies. Consequently, imperfect contracts tend to be the norm and not the exception. The fact many contracts are not challenged in the courts does not mean that they are complete; it is more likely to mean that an event or contingency that would result in the completeness of the contract being tested has not occurred.

It would be quite wrong, however, to think that a contract that omits a provision to deal with a particular contingency is due to an oversight or the finite capacity of business people and their legal advisers to predict future events with accuracy. As we have seen, there are sound commercial and economic reasons why the parties may deliberately choose to enter into agreements in which no provision is made for known contingencies. The economic criteria will be the rational objective of efficiency. Parties will accept the omission of a provision to cover an anticipated contingency where the transaction and other costs of meeting the contingency, and devising a response to it, are outweighed by the gains in efficiency achieved in omitting it. It is in their interest to minimise the deadweight loss, that is, the unrealised losses, and other costs involved in the formation of a more comprehensive agreement.

Once it is accepted that most, if not all contracts, are to some extent incomplete, it can be seen that it is the extent of the incompleteness which varies. Thus, the optimal level of completeness required for the parties to intend their agreement to be binding will rest on the judgement of each party as to what is most efficient from their point of view. The decision as to what is most efficient will be made having regard to the factors already adverted to; the time available for further negotiations, the cost of more comprehensive drafting, the risk that the core bargain will be lost, the chances of the contingency actually occurring, and the consequences or alternatives available if the contingency does occur. Further, with long-term or relational contracts, such as the agreement between FCE and ECNZ, the parties may anticipate that some terms of the contract will be renegotiated and developed in the light of experience or necessity. In essence, the decision involves a rough and ready cost-benefit analysis. The point at which the parties decide to be bound is the point at which they decide that the costs of reaching greater completeness outweigh the benefits associated with a less complete contractual document.

It is not difficult to inject such an economic perspective and law and economics thinking into the *FCE* v *ECNZ* case. The parties were under a severe time constraint if they were to resubmit their bids to Kupe on the agreed basis. Efficiency dictated that they prepare a contract having regard to the cost of failing to reach agreement and the time and cost involved in providing for contingencies, the absence of which would not render the agreement unenforceable on the grounds of incompleteness or uncertainty.

The commercial utility of heads of agreement is founded on these economic imperatives. They preclude the courts saying, in effect, that if the parties wish to give effect to their intention to be bound, they can expressly say so, and if they do not say so, they cannot blame the court for not giving effect to their intention. Such a response is as outmoded as it is haughty. It suggests that the law will lay down the rules and commerce can abide by those rules or come asunder; not that the law should serve the realities and needs of commerce. Those of a formalistic persuasion can, from time to time, be heard to applaud such an approach on the basis that it provides 'certainty and predictability' in the law. But how can it be validly claimed that it facilitates certainty and predictability to deny parties who have manifest an actual intention to be bound the binding force which they seek for their contract? On the contrary, if parties manifest an intention to be bound, they deserve the certainty of knowing that the courts will recognise their intention and endeavour to give effect to that intention. Formalism must not be allowed to erode this fundamental principle.

Nothing I have said is to be taken as suggesting that the courts should 'make' or 'remake' the contract for the parties. Of course, the courts cannot and must not do that. Judges must remain scrupulous not to fill in gaps in a contract in a way which may not reflect the intention of the parties. But this caution should not be pressed to the extent that it becomes an argument *in terrorem*. The courts' refusal to 'make' or 'remake' the contract is more critically relevant to the question whether, notwithstanding the parties' actual intention, the contract is so incomplete or uncertain as to be unenforceable at law. Where the court determines that the parties intended to be bound, however, it is not making the contract, or filling in a gap in the contract. The fact that there are matters that have been deferred for future agreement or that a number of significant matters have not been agreed may be an indication that the parties did not have the requisite contractual intention. But sight should not be lost of the fact that the focus of the initial question is the actual intention of the parties and not the content of the contract.

The Court in *FCE v ECNZ* should not have had any difficulty in adopting a realistic approach to the question whether the parties intended their Heads of Agreement to be binding. Alert to the reality of commercial activity, what would then be required would be an objective finding of the facts. Eschewing formalism, the Court would quickly dismiss the notion of seeking to tell parties who had actually intended to be bound that they did not actually intend to be bound. The court's finding would be based on all reliable evidence relevant to the intention of the parties. It would not be crimped by the rules that apply to the interpretation of a contract. With contractual interpretation, the focus is directed at the content of the contract and the wording can be vested with an objective meaning. In respect of the question whether the parties intended the contract to be binding, however, the focus must be directed at the intention of the parties for it is their intention, and not the meaning of the agreement, which is in issue.[41]

A responsive court would also consciously recognise and expunge from its thinking the courts' traditional 'negativism' or aversion to preliminary agreements.[42] Being alert to the realities of commercial activity, it would fully accept the commercial utility of preliminary

---

[41] See *Air Great Lakes Pty Ltd v K S Easter (Holdings) Pty Ltd* [1985] 2 NSWLR 309, per McHugh JA at 337. McHugh JA stresses that the intention to be bound is a jural act separate and distinct from the terms of the bargain.

[42] The Court did state that *May and Butcher Ltd v The King* [1934] 2 KB 17(n) should no longer be regarded as a sound authority (at paras. [60]–[63]) but, in writing the judgment, Blanchard J failed to mention the Court's earlier decisions that were based on the principle that, where a material term has been deferred for future agreement, no binding contract arises. See *Willetts v Ryan* [1968] NZLR 863; *Barrett v IBC International Ltd* [1995] 3 NZLR 170; *Smith v Alex McDonald (Merchants) Ltd* 20/11/ 89, CA 195/84; and *Hinterleitner v Heenan* [1990] 1 NZ Conv. C, 190, 468. Further, the contemporaneous endorsement of the Court's own decision in *Attorney-General v Barker Bros Ltd* [1976] 2 NZLR 495, might suggest that not too much has changed. See McLauchlan, 'The FCE/ECNZ Heads of Agreement', at 201–202, and 'Rethinking Agreements to Agree' (1998) 18 NZULR 77. The fact that *May and Butcher* has withstood challenge for so long is a triumph of servitude to precedent over the recognition of commercial realities and logic and, indeed, plain common sense.

agreements and be cognisant of the economic considerations underlying that utility. A pragmatic approach would be adopted. Reason and common sense would dictate that the parties' actual intention to be bound and some so-called 'objective' intention not to be bound cannot comfortably coexist. The false reasoning involved in the argument that, because two headings had been marked 'not agreed', the parties cannot have intended the Heads of Agreement to be binding would be exposed. The back-to-front notion that it is for commerce to accord with the artificial dictates of the courts would be abandoned in favour of an approach that would seek to bring the law into harmony with the reality and requirements of commerce. Accompanying this approach would be an open acknowledgement that it is unjust to deprive one or other of the parties of the advantages secured in an agreement intended to be binding and otherwise complete and certain.

The fundamental purpose of the law of contract is to give effect to the reasonable expectations of commercial men and women. That purpose is achieved by giving legal effect to their bargains.[43] Within that general purpose the principle that, having found that the parties intended their agreement to be binding, the courts will strive to give effect to their intention is well established.[44] At issue, is the autonomy of the will of the parties. That principle should not be frustrated by the introduction of an artificial barrier or formula which has the effect of negating the parties' actual intention to form a concluded bargain. Hope JA's observation in the *Air Great Lakes* case[45] may sound like an overstatement, but is it?

> If the mutual actual intention of the parties who have signed a document is that it should not have contractual operation, it would be fraudulent on the part of either of them to seek to enforce it as a contract. Consistently, if the *mutual actual intention was that there should be a concluded contract, it would be fraudulent to deny that intent* ... (emphasis added)

Conclusion

In this chapter, I have taken the initial step in spelling out a contemporary judicial methodology. With the dogmas of the past exorcised, the

---

[43] See Lord Tomlin's dicta in *Hillas & Co. Ltd v Arcos Ltd* [1932] All ER 494, at 499.
[44] *Hillas & Co. Ltd v Arcos Ltd*, above n. 39; *R & J Dempster Ltd v The Motherwell Bridge and Engineering Co. Ltd* [1964] SC 308; and *Anaconda Nickel Ltd v Tarmoola Australia Pty Ltd* (2000) 22 WAR 101, at 132–133.
[45] Above n. 41, at 319.

judicial process can be approached afresh. That process requires judges to have regard to a number of different and often conflicting considerations in arriving at a decision. The judicial task is to then balance the competing interests and values in order to exercise the choices which are endemic to the process.

In undertaking that exercise it is essential that judges have at hand a guide as to the weight to be given to the various competing interests and values. Predominant among these criteria must be the twin benchmarks of justice and relevance. Other considerations exist, of course, and may at times prevail, but the twin objectives of meeting the community's expectation that justice will be done in the courts and that the law will meet society's reasonable needs remains the lodestar of the system.

It may seem strange to many readers that in this context I have found it necessary to assert the reality of justice as a value in the legal process. I, myself, find it strange. But the rehabilitation of justice as a primary value is necessary to offset the demands of those who would subjugate it to a more or less formalistic methodology and the norms dictated by an earlier age.

The fact that justice does not exist in the abstract, or that it is beyond our capacity to discern its universal essence, cannot be allowed to obscure its presence in concrete situations. In those situations it imports a normative value into the judicial process that may be decisive in determining how various interests or values are weighed or which of conflicting interests or values will prevail in the inevitable balancing exercise. In this sense justice is itself a value; one that drives the direction in which other values will be ranked in the course of judicial reasoning. No appeal to some concept of substantive justice or 'higher order' law is involved. Justice as a value is the fundamental mechanism in determining the tip of the scales.

Nor is there a credible excuse to justify retarding the law's development to meet the requirements of the community, especially the commercial community. A law or legal process that does not strive to meet the needs or expectations of the society it serves is simply failing in this basic function. It is the community that suffers. A concerted judicial effort, one which is deliberate and conscious, is therefore required to ensure that the law or legal process is directed by a contemporary judicial methodology.

I acknowledge at once that the contemporary judicial methodology which I will proceed to outline in Chapters 12 to 14 and the theory of the judicial role which emerges from it, is not particularly theoretical.

Indeed, a theory that is essentially based on a realistic and pragmatic approach giving effect to a scheme of practical reasoning in which principles predominate may not be worthy of the label 'theory' at all. I accept that it may cast doubt on the need for judges to make themselves familiar with legal theory if, at the end, all that is on offer is an approach of such down-to-earth practicality.

But I have already sought to justify a winding path through jurisprudential theory as a prerequisite for obtaining a sound conception of the judicial role, however mundane it might eventually prove to be. The art is not to get lost along the path suffused with the nirvanaic joy of pure theory. Obviously, it is opportune to turn to the fundamental 'isms' of my theory; realism and pragmatism.

12

Of realism and pragmatism

Hard realism

A new realism

In arguing that judges should adopt a hard realistic approach to judging, I am not advocating a return to the realism of the American Legal Realist movement. But I make that disclaimer without wishing to derogate from the constitutive impact of that movement on jurisprudential theory. A burst of realism was necessary then, just as another injection of more refined realism is necessary now. American legal realism was, in short, very much an insurrection against formalism; the pedantry and artificiality of legal reasoning; the myth of certainty in the law; and the dominance of rules in the legal process. It represented a shift of emphasis from what law is to what law does. In that respect, its success cannot be denied, but the success was partial and erosive. A further revolt in the nature of an insurrection may be more than what is required now, but open and organised judicial protest at formalism's lingering influence is very much in order.

The problem with American legal realism is that it sought to achieve too much. It was believed that it was not enough to expose the excesses and fancies of formalistic thinking. Both realists and their critics looked for a theory to replace that which had been systematically destroyed. Realists responded with a predictive science of law owing much to the experimental methods of the social sciences. Social scientific methods and insights could be employed to understand social change. These methods, however, seemed to be largely based on positive conceptions of social science[1] and failed to take hold. From the mid 1930s onwards, realism suffered a gradual institutional and intellectual demise as its proponents became ever more indifferent and even hostile to 'the

---

[1] Martin Loughlin, 'Rights, Democracy, and Law' in Tom Campbell and K. D. Ewing (eds.), *Special Essays on Human Rights* (Oxford University Press, Oxford, 2001), at 152.

clumsy jargon of the so-called social sciences'.[2] Legal theorists abandoned the movement and it has little support from legal theorists today, certainly in its early twentieth-century form. Nevertheless, its practical contribution cannot be denied. In his outstanding work, *Patterns of American Jurisprudence*, Professor Duxbury acknowledges that his book is more than anything else a testament to the intellectual impact of legal realism. But, he points out, the distinctiveness of the mark that realism has made on modern legal thought is more than matched by the indeterminacy of its conceptual and thematic boundaries.[3]

As will have been apparent, the indeterminacy of twentieth-century realism's conceptual and thematic boundaries does not bother me. In large part, this indeterminacy was due to the numerous and diverse aspects of the legal process that required re-examination. Unsettled and undefined conceptual and thematic boundaries were to be expected. Rather, it is realism's committed fidelity to the reality of the judicial process that matters and that must be accepted as having endured, and to be enduring. Realism was essentially a mood, an attitude of dissatisfaction with 'twentieth century legal thought being dominated by a nineteenth century legal world view'.[4] That mood or attitude is required again, this time being dissatisfaction with twenty-first-century legal thought being dominated by a mid twentieth-century legal world view. Realism must therefore be updated. The realism required is the realism of Holmes, Cardozo and Frank rejuvenated and restored to the twenty-first century. But what does this renovation mean?

In the first place, realism today means the adoption of a judicial mood or attitude that reflects an irritated dissatisfaction with the continued domination and influence of an outdated legal approach, and which is constantly attentive to the demands of the present. This broad mood or attitude must necessarily infiltrate the judges' approach to specific legal issues and concrete situations. It must enable the judge to break through to both the reality of the judicial process and the realities of the instant case. To mix metaphors, realism will then make out on the ground and at the coalface. Some of the respects in which this redirection in legal thinking is required will be traversed shortly.

---

[2] Neil Duxbury, *Patterns of American Jurisprudence* (Clarendon Press, Oxford, 1995), quoting Fred Rodell, 'Legal Realists, Legal Fundamentalists, Lawyer Schools, and Policy Science – Or How Not to Teach Law', (1947) Vanderbilt LR 1, at 6.
[3] Ibid., at 65.   [4] Ibid., at 69.

In the second place, modern realism will not seek, as before, to implant a new legal theory of the kind which realism destroyed in an already overrun garden of such theories. Realism will remain incontrovertibly functional and pragmatic. But this does not mean that there will be no scope for its development by legal theorists. The first contribution may be made by scholars undertaking extensive groundwork and surveys of particular areas of judicial activity and then drawing conclusions from that work and surveys. Feeley and Rubin's book is a prime example of what is required.[5] An exhaustive survey of all federal cases in the United States relating to prison reform and a discussion of what the judges actually did provides the foundation for insightful perspectives on judicial decision-making.

The second contribution that legal theorists can make to the development of a new realism is to undertake much more empirical research. Much of the research may need to involve other disciplines, such as sociology and psychology. The rationale for reference to other disciplines is clear. For the law to serve society and so promote human welfare, it must be grounded in an understanding of society and human behaviour. This understanding requires the help of the social sciences to illuminate the behaviour of the people whom the law regulates, and also the behaviour of the people who do the regulating.[6] Legal theorists, or some legal theorists, have already fully embraced economics. Other disciplines will be even more accessible to the legal mind. For present purposes, however, the point is that the scope for research into the working of the law in society is of gargantuan dimension.

The paper by John Braithwaite already referred to,[7] which demonstrated that, in the area of study undertaken, broad principles were more efficient and predictive than firm rules, illustrates the value of empirical inquiry. The judicial process, including such aspects as the influence of a judge's background and education; the predilections and predispositions of judges; the full extent to which judges make law and formulate policy; the common background and experience of judges that cause them to think alike or, conversely, that lead them to be either 'conservative' or 'liberal' in inclination; whether there is a pattern in the decisions of conservative and liberal judges respectively; the degree and kind of influence exerted on judges by judicial colleagues; the

---

[5] Malcolm M. Feeley and Edward L. Rubin, *Judicial Policy Making and the Modern State: How the Courts Reformed America's Prisons* (Cambridge University Press, Cambridge, 1998).

[6] Daniel A. Farber, 'Toward a New Realism' [2001] Chic. LR, 279, at 280.

[7] John Braithwaite, 'Rules and Principles: A Theory of Legal Certainty' (2002) 27 Aust. Journal of Legal Philosophy 47.

effectiveness of judicial procedures, such as judicial conferences; whether some appellate judges are more likely to overrule lower court judges than others; the values of the community and how they are formed; and judges' perception of the values of the community and whether and, if so, how, the values of the community are translated into judicial reasoning, would all benefit from empirical research.

The work of legal theorists along the above lines will reinforce the experience of judges. Judicial experience, objectively analysed, is itself a form of empirical study. But it can be shaped and supplemented, and even refuted, by studies of the kind I have just endorsed. The judicial mood or attitude of realism of which I have spoken must be greatly strengthened by such studies.

Realism in practice

A number of particular respects in which the new mood of realism would assert itself may be touched upon. Obviously, the list is not exhaustive. I do not intend to refer to all the respects in which it has been suggested realism is presently lacking in the judicial process. The main areas of concern only need be reiterated. More often than not, it is not so much the acceptance of the reality, as recognising and giving effect to the consequences of that reality, which is required at the judicial level.

First and foremost, of course, the inherent uncertainty of the law should be fully accepted. Knowing the extent of uncertainty in the law by virtue of their experience, judges and lawyers must deliberately resist the pressure of critics, commentators and, especially, crusading legal fundamentalists, who elevate certainty to mythical proportions. What is required is a realistic appreciation of the extent to which certainty and predictability in the law can be in fact achieved. With a realistic appreciation of what is possible, the judiciary will be more receptive to taking certainty into account as a consideration in a particular case when that factor is directly relevant.

Part and parcel of accepting that the law is inherently uncertain means more than accepting the American realists' rule-scepticism. It is rules, more than principles or any other component of the law, that are inherently uncertain. Yet, they seem to take on a life of their own. Critical Legal Studies scholars label it 'reification'. Rules appear reified or 'thing-like' and are treated as having a reality distinct from the social, political or other functions that first gave them life and meaning. As Cotterrell points out, legal reasoning becomes a kind of mystification. It becomes possible to theorise about the meaning of such legal concepts as 'corporate personality', 'title' or 'contract' without considering as a central matter the policy, functions or settled practices that these concepts reflect, or, at least, once reflected in their origins.[8] As I have already said when rejecting positivist theory, a rule-oriented analysis is ultimately superficial.[9]

Secondly, and hand in hand with a realistic appraisal of the inherent uncertainty in the law, a full appreciation of the reality of choice in judicial decision-making is essential. The choice is not simply between the option of deciding for one party or for his or her opponent, or of deciding what particular judicial approach to adopt in order to reach or rationalise a decision. The art which realism requires is to recognise the multiple choices involved at every step of the adjudicative process. Finding the facts, for example, involves numerous decisions; what witnesses to hear, what evidence to admit or exclude, what witnesses to believe or disbelieve, how to reconcile conflicting narratives, ascertaining what the probability of the various versions of an incident are from the circumstances of the case, and determining what facts as found are relevant. Determining the issue or issues of law to be resolved can require a number of steps to be taken; are there principles or rules which could assist to identify the issue or issues; what are the rules or principles; are there other considerations bearing on the legal issue or issues; how can the issue or issues be defined; and what are the consequences of adopting different alternative expressions of the issue or issues? Restating the issue as defined then involves a complex process of reasoning; what are the telling facts; what rules or principles bear on the issue or issues; are there any prior cases which are relevant; are any apparently applicable rules, principles or precedents helpful; what are the interests or values involved; what is the value judgement driving the judge to a particular decision; can the existing rules, principles or precedents be applied without doing an injustice; do the rules, principles or precedents require re-evaluation in the light of modern conditions, and so on.

Appreciation of the extensive reality of judicial choice also confirms the need to have regard to the widest possible community of considerations in order to ensure that the choice made is well informed and in accord with current requirements. Open articulation as to how those considerations are dealt with and balanced one against the other and the ultimate decision reached will follow. Acceptance that both the choices and the value judgement underlying those choices must be transparent is or becomes part of the reality of accepting the prevalence of choice in the judicial process. To

---

[8] Roger Cotterrell, *The Politics of Jurisprudence* (Butterworths, London 1989), at 187–188.
[9] See above, Chapter 2, at 29–34.

accept this vast scope for choice is also to accept that judicial autonomy is a reality. The existence of choice presupposes that autonomy. But the realisation that choice is intrinsic to the process also at once generates an appreciation and commitment to a judicial methodology, including judicial constraints, which will avert the errant or aberrant outcome and confine the administration of the law within the rule of law.

Accepting, in the third place, the reality of judicial law-making and the extent to which policy factors enter into that law-making process is essential. As it is now universally accepted that judges make law, realism requires an appreciation of the extent of that law-making and, in particular, the extent to which that process is directed by policy considerations. At the same time it must be accepted as an unavoidable reality that the judicial process is ultimately a 'political' process.[10] Acceptance of these realities is a prerequisite to determining in a pragmatic manner when a change in the law should be left to Parliament or undertaken by the court. Such acceptance also assists judges decide what matters of policy are legitimate matters to which to have regard and which matters should be disregarded in the legal forum. Most importantly, a realistic appreciation of this law-making and policy formulating role of the judiciary, and the 'political' elements that arise in discharging that role, emphasises the need to work within a considered judicial methodology containing comprehensive judicial constraints.

Once again, the importance that attaches to the constraints on the judiciary is readily apparent. Those constraints are themselves part of the reality of the judicial process. Consequently, a conscious appreciation of their extent, content and impact is required on the part of judges. That conscious appreciation will in turn serve to stress how and why the realities of the inherent uncertainty of the law, the vast scope for choice in the judicial process, and the law and policy-making function of the judiciary are kept in check, and why recognition of these realities and acting upon them does not prejudice the administration of the law or any modern concept of the rule of law.

Determined pragmatism

Legal pragmatism

Pragmatism can mean different things to different people. For my purposes, pragmatism is a mix of a number of attributes that again

---

[10] See above, Chapter 4, at 101–104.

add up to an attitude. First and foremost, I regard pragmatism as being essentially functional. The law is viewed as a social institution in its social setting and vested with the social purpose of serving society and furthering the interests and goals of society. Then, pragmatism necessarily embraces realism, its distinct jurisprudential complement.[11] Pragmatism is prepared to rely heavily on experience and values the cumulative product of that experience ahead of abstract theories and obtuse doctrines. For this reason pragmatism is necessarily concerned with the practical consequences of the law and the bearing of the law on the requirements and interests of people. Judgements evaluating any situation, claim or issue are invariably functional and practical.

Being essentially functional and practical, legal pragmatism is irreversibly hostile to unrealistic and abstract theories and ritualistic doctrine alike. Theories which do not accord with reality cannot be reconciled with pragmatism. They will simply get in the way. Similarly, legal doctrines that inhibit the courts adopting a functional and practical bent are incompatible with a pragmatic approach. Indeed, legal pragmatism is the very converse of a doctrinaire approach. It is or tends to be stifled by the dogmatism congenital to doctrinaire legalism. Innate to pragmatism, therefore, is a deep-rooted distrust of the positivistic notion that rationality is a matter of applying criteria.[12]

Legal pragmatism is a by-product of a philosophical movement. Neither legal pragmatism nor its philosophical parent need be accepted in their entirety, but there is much of value to extract from recognised theories of pragmatism to aid in the development of the pragmatic judicial approach for which I contend.

Three philosophers in the United States, John Dewey, William James and Charles Pierce, in particular, were responsible for endeavouring to redirect the course of philosophy away from the prevailing conceptions of truth and knowledge. They were concerned that philosophical theories had become out of touch with contemporary reality.[13] John Dewey, who was particularly influential, claimed that philosophy must abandon abstract metaphysics and apply itself to social engineering. 'Better it is for philosophy,' he said, 'to err in active participation in the living struggles and issues

---

[11] Ian Ward, *An Introduction to Critical Legal Theory* (Cavendish Publishing Limited, London, 1998), at 139.
[12] Richard Rorty 'Solidarity or Objectivity?' in John Rajchman and Cornel West (eds.), *Post-Analytical Philosophy* (Columbia University Press, New York, 1988).
[13] Martin Loughlin, *Public Law and Political Theory* (Clarendon Press, Oxford, 1992), at 126.

of its own age and times than to maintain an immune monastic impeccability, without relevancy and bearing in the generating ideas of its contemporary present.'[14] Thus, Dewey's philosophical position was extremely functional. 'Absolute' truth did not matter as much as whether something was functionally useful or not and facilitated social reform. Dewey accepted that formalism provided only the illusion of certitude. Law did not possess any special timeless legitimacy.[15] He recognised the diversity and novelty of situations which arise in actuality. He defined practical judgment as 'a judgment respecting the future termination of an incomplete and in so far indeterminate situation.'[16]

William James also distrusted abstract rules and regarded them as being of limited assistance in arriving at moral decisions because, as he put it, 'every real dilemma is in literal strictness a unique situation.' No adequate previous rule ever exists as 'the exact combination of ideals realized and ideals disappointed which each decision creates is always a universe without precedent.'[17] The appreciation that problems that arise tend to be unique and that no prior rule will necessarily or adequately cope with that problem has obvious relevance to the practice of the law. Similarly, relevant to the legal process is his description of the pragmatist turning away 'from abstraction and insufficiency, from verbal solutions, from bad *a priori* reasons, from fixed principles, closed systems, and pretended absolutes and origins'.[18]

Charles Pierce also took the view that external community standards rather than internal, private or subjective perceptions constitute the correct basis for philosophical and legal judgments. It is only against the backdrop of generally held beliefs in the community that the perceptions of individuals can be judged. Hence, knowledge is essentially public and communal acquired through shared practical experience. Again, the relevance of Pierce's thinking to a judicial approach that seeks to reflect standards or values external to the law and derived from the community is readily apparent.

The peerless judicial pragmatist was undoubtedly Oliver Wendell Holmes. Although it is not known to what extent he was influenced by

---

[14] J. Dewey, *Philosophy and Civilization* (Littlebrown, New York, 1963), at 55.
[15] Ward, *An Introduction to Critical Legal Theory*, at 140–141.
[16] Dewey, 'The Logic of Judgments of Practice' (1915) 12 Journal of Philosophy 505, at 514.
[17] F. H. Burkhart and others (eds.), *The Will to Believe. The Works of William James* (Harvard University Press, Cambridge, Mass., 1979), at 158, quoted in Loughlin, *Public Law and Political Theory*, at 131.
[18] W. James, *Pragmatism* (Longmans, Green & Co., London, 1907), Lecture 2

them, Holmes was a fellow member with William James and Charles Pierce in the Metaphysical Club in Cambridge, Massachusetts, a gathering of distinguished philosophers, scientists and lawyers. His philosophy was both realistic and pragmatic. Legal formalism, he allowed, might 'flatter the longing for certainty' in the jurisprudential mind, but that certainty was in reality an 'illusion'.[19] Judges can only rarely arrive at a decision based on internal logic. Rather, they are driven by '[t]he felt necessities of the time, the prevalent moral and political theories, intuitions of public policy, avowed or unconscious, even the prejudices which judges share with their fellow-men.'[20] Liability is determined, not by internal or private standards of morality, but by reference to rules that reflect the general shared standards of the community. While it is true that overtones of formalism sometimes entered into Holmes' thinking, he was unquestionably a legal pragmatist of the first order. Were he living today I believe that he would jettison any trace of formalism and favour an even more pragmatic view of pragmatism.

Dworkin's charge that pragmatists are being prescriptive, that is, arguing how judges ought to reason, is only partly correct. He rejects pragmatism, of course, because it does not entrench 'rights' in the law as he would require. The actuality of the judicial process, he claims, is that judges by and large decide cases as if they were upholding existing rights rather than making new law. They look to prior decisions to determine the existence of the legal right in a particular case. They do not, he asserts, look to the future to decide a case on the basis of a social goal. But Dworkin clearly confuses the appearance of judgment writing with the reality of judicial decision-making and, as already shown, ultimately adopts a theory which is itself divorced from reality. In effect, Dworkin's portrayal is a caricature of a pragmatist[21] representing a simplistic view of judicial decision-making.

Nor would anyone seriously contest that, whether Dworkin approves of it or not, pragmatism is already evident in judicial decision-making.[22] Recognition of the critical role of value judgements and the regard to policy considerations and the consequences or impact of a decision confirms that pragmatism. I have not intended to suggest that pragmatism is wholly absent from judicial reasoning at present. Rather, I contend that it

---

[19] O.W. Holmes, *The Common Law* (Little, Brown & Co., Boston, 1981), at 1.
[20] Ibid., at 1.
[21] Hilaire McCoubrey and Nigel White, *Textbook on Jurisprudence* (3rd edn, Blackstone Press, London, 1999), at 161.
[22] See, e.g., Peter Spiller, *New Zealand Court of Appeal 1958–1996: A History* (Thomson Brookers, Wellington 2002).

must find its place in the legal process in a more open, deliberate and determined form.

I would add, however, that a false claim to pragmatism is often made, and that is the claim of law and economics theorists. Certainly, the economic analysis is ostensibly pragmatic. Posner described economic analysis as a form of practical reasoning founded in the wider pragmatic assertion of social science that law is a matter of politics and that legal theory is an expression of a given political ideology.[23] Judges are policy-makers and courts are a policy-making forum.[24] But as Mark Kelman has pointed out,[25] law and economic scholarship suffers the same shortcoming as all other jurisprudential theories that seek to establish some sort of scientific rationale and determinacy for the law. Despite its assertion of pragmatism, law and economics theory is founded on a model of actors and markets that does not exist in the real world. People do not necessarily conform to models dedicated to the rationale maximisation of efficiency or any other economic goal. Nor is the market perfect. Choices are specific responses to a particular context and subject to the constraints operating within the market and upon the person making the choice. In such terms, says Kelman, economic analysis cannot properly distinguish between giving money to a mugger and paying taxes.[26] The rapid development of behavioural economics over the past decade or so is an indication of the lack of pragmatism in pure law and economics thinking.

Nevertheless, I do not deny the value of law and economics theory. My analysis of *Fletcher Challenge Energy* v *Electricity Corporation of New Zealand* in the previous chapter demonstrates its value. Rather, it is the claim that law and economics is itself a pragmatic theory which is to be rejected. That claim is essentially a pretence. Law and economics needs to be handled pragmatically, and true pragmatism insists on working from the reality forwards, not from a thesis or ideology backwards to an allegedly pragmatic basis. The fundamental refusal of law and economic theorists to appreciate the essential unpredictability of human beings serves to limit any intrinsic pragmatic value in an economic analysis of law.[27]

---

[23] Ward, *An Introduction to Critical Legal Theory*, at 133.
[24] R. Posner, *The Problems of Jurisprudence* (Harvard University Press, Cambridge, Mass., 1990).
[25] Mark G. Kelman 'Trashing' (1984) 36 Stanford LR 293, at 606–618.
[26] M. Kelman, *A Guide to Critical Legal Studies* (Harvard University Press, Cambridge, Mass., 1987), at 115–137.
[27] Ward, *An Introduction to Critical Legal Theory*, at 136.

I return, therefore, to the more prosaic definition that I put forward earlier. Legal pragmatism is essentially an attitude or approach possessing certain recognisable attributes; it is essentially functionalist; it emphasises realism; it relies upon and values experience; it eschews abstract theories lacking any functional purpose and shuns a doctrinaire approach; it is concerned with the practical consequences or impact of the law; its evaluation of any issue is both realistic and practical; and its judgments are practical judgments designed to further the objectives of a law obligated to meet the needs and expectations of society. Legal pragmatism of this sort will manifest itself in a variety of ways in judicial practice.

Pragmatism in practice

The respects in which a pragmatic judicial approach will manifest itself in practice have been touched upon in earlier chapters, but can also be briefly reiterated.

Pragmatism will undoubtedly prefer substance over form. This preference will be based on the fact that the substance of the matter represents the reality of that matter. To prefer form over substance is to prefer appearance over truth, ritual over verity, and fiction over fact. All this malarkey is the antithesis of pragmatism. Looking to identify and deal with the substance of a matter would not be confined to tax disputes in which the conflict between form and substance is often acute. It would spread across the whole range of the common law as formalism's more doctrinaire habits and distinctions are put to flight. For example, it is likely that the courts would prefer to interpret a contract in accordance with the actual intention of the parties where that intention can be ascertained rather than impose some objectively discerned 'intention' that may, in fact, be little better than a figment of the court's imagination.

Another feature that would characterise pragmatism is the avoidance of absolute rules or principles. Reflecting philosophical pragmatism's rejection of absolute theories, legal pragmatists would avoid such absolutism. Because of the great diversity of concrete situations, pragmatism would accept that rules and principles must remain incomplete to be of use in the next and different situations. Broad principles better fit a pragmatic approach because they allow scope for a practical judgment designed to fit a particular situation.

Also relating to rules, pragmatism would seek to avoid imposing unrealistic or artificial rules on the community or any sector of the community. The pragmatist would know that, pragmatically speaking, the consequence of doing so is that the law is brought into disrepute. Experience demonstrates that such rules will not work, are constantly challenged and, far from promoting certainty in the law, actually add to indeterminacy and unpredictability as the law and society tango out of step. Pragmatism's focus is on the actual needs of the community and the imperative of meeting those needs if the law is to be properly functional.

It also follows that pragmatism would wish to see an end to legal fictions. Legal fictions are the progeny of formalism and, as that creed is pressed to accept its fate and finally expire, so is the inclination of many judges to eliminate the fictions reinforced. Thus, for example, Lord Bingham recently reaffirmed the wisdom of Lord Wilberforce's early dicta deprecating resort to fictions.[28]

A number of aspects of judicial decision-making have then been identified that require a pragmatic approach. I have suggested that it should be pragmatically determined in the context of each particular case whether certainty in the law is a valid and relevant consideration in that case.[29] The assessment required as to whether the community has relied upon a particular rule or precedent, the extent to which it may have done so, and the likely consequences if the rule is changed or the precedent not followed is also essentially a pragmatic assessment. A similar pragmatic evaluation is required of the authority or weight to be given to a precedent where it is thought that the precedent may not render justice in the instant case or meet contemporary needs. A pragmatic decision is also required where a significant change in the law is contemplated.[30] The question then is whether the legislative process or the judicial process is the most appropriate process to make the change. Certain factors may be identified which would point one way or the other, that is, either to the legislative chamber or to the judges' chambers, but that does not detract from the fact that, in the last resort, the assessment must be one that is obdurately practical. The decision cannot be predetermined by judicial predilection.

Other pragmatic decisions are required in the course of formulating a decision. One example is the decision which must be made whether to frame the court's decision narrowly or to write more expansively clearing away the accumulated and confusing baggage of case law and proclaim the applicable principle or principles for the guidance of the

---

[28] *Fairchild* v *Glenhaven Funeral Services Ltd* [2003] 1 AC 32 per Lord Bingham at para. 35, referring to Lord Wilberforce's dicta in *McGhee* v *National Coal Board* [1973] 1 WLR 1, at 4–5.
[29] See above, Chapter 5, at 135–137.   [30] See above, Chapter 10, at 254–263.

community and the promotion of certainty in the law.[31] The same sort of pragmatic consideration is required in determining whether or not to constrain the exercise of judicial discretion, such as that conferred in statutory powers, by restrictive guidelines.[32]

The methodology advanced is essentially a methodology for the judicial delivery of pragmatism.

Conclusion

The realism I have advanced in this chapter is an updated version of realism that will go beyond a realistic appraisal of the judicial process in action and incorporate a realistic evaluation of the legal theories that inform or infect that process. It is not enough to destroy with scornful realism the shibboleths, myths, fictions and mystique of the law; the theories on which those affectations are based must also be dismantled. Nor should the revised realism seek to implant a new legal theory divorced from reality in the place of those that have been dismantled. It must remain steadfastly functional and pragmatic. Without a doubt there is considerable scope within this framework for extensive groundwork, surveys, empirical research and the close involvement of other disciplines.

The rejuvenated realism I propose will remain essentially a mood, an attitude of dissatisfaction with a law or legal process still heavily influenced by the theories of a bygone age in which justice is rendered imperfectly and that is at times out of step with contemporary needs. It is this attitude which needs to inform and infect the process of judicial reasoning, and that will be the most noticeable feature of the new realism in practice. Much more, of course, will accompany the adoption of this attitude. The inherent uncertainty of the law will be accepted; rule scepticism will develop into a healthy rejection of the 'reification' of rules; the pervasiveness and leviathan latitude for choice in judicial reasoning will be recognised and, with that recognition, judicial autonomy will become accepted orthodoxy; and the scope of law-making and policy formulation in judicial decision-making, subject to the extensive judicial constraints that exist and can yet be developed further, will be acknowledged.

The legal pragmatism that I have advocated incorporates this realistic approach and will manifest itself in a variety of ways in legal practice. It will undoubtedly prefer the reality of substance rather than the pretence at reality provided by adherence to form; it will eschew absolute rules in

---

[31] See above, Chapter 10, at 265–266. [32] See above, Chapter 10, at 266–267.

favour of principles or broad rules; it will avoid imposing unrealistic or artificial rules on the community, including and in particular the commercial community; and it will put an end to the remaining fictions that beset the administration of the law. Questions such as whether to treat certainty as a legitimate consideration in a particular case, whether to re-evaluate the validity and authority of a precedent, whether to leave a change in the law to Parliament, whether to adopt a minimalist approach in a particular case or speak in broader terms, and whether or not to constrain the exercise of a judicial discretion by restricted guidelines, can all be resolved with one foot heavily implanted in the pragmatic camp.

Enough has been said to indicate that, once it has been adopted, a pragmatic approach can usefully permeate many, if not most, facets of judicial decision-making. Of course, it is not foolproof. But pragmatism requiring, as it does, a continuing re-examination of the fitness of the law provides a constant rebuff to judicial predilections, preconceptions and prejudices; a running reminder of the futility of formalism and other outmoded theories and approaches; a continuous check on the functionality and relevance of particular laws as they are made and remade in the courts; and a perpetual prompt to adopt the method of practical reasoning, to which I will now turn.

13

Of ... practical reasoning and principles

Practical reasoning

The theory of practical reasoning

A commendable analysis of judicial reasoning has emerged passing under the name of 'practical reasoning'.[1] In general terms, practical reasoning is normally contrasted with deductive reasoning. It involves the ability to recognise suitable abstractions from particular instances. In a sense, it is a reverse of the traditionally perceived task of applying the general to the particular in that argument proceeds from particular instances of facts to general conclusions. It has been described as that capacity to choose between rules or to decide that no rule works well. Practical reason indicates that the instance connects with all the other instances of the rule, which its fits better than it connects with the instances of any other rule, or indicates that there are no such connections. In the latter case practical reason allows the court to develop a new rule.[2]

The emergence or re-emergence of this line of thinking owes much to Professors McIntyre and Wellman.[3] Professor McIntyre takes the view that the capacity of practical reasoning is not simply the capacity to follow rules but, rather, the capacity to act 'with virtue' when rules do not precisely define the right decision. In his thinking, as in mine, the virtue primarily represented in the decisions is 'justice'.[4] Professor

---

[1] While fully acknowledging the significance of Joseph Raz's analysis of the function of norms in judicial reasoning, I am unable to include his version of practical reasoning in this general commendation. See Joseph Raz, *Practical Reason and Norms* (Oxford University Press, Oxford, 1999). The complexity of his theory of practical reasoning cannot mask its ultimate unreality.

[2] James Penner, 'The Rules of Law: Wittgenstein, Davidson, and Weinrib's Formalism' (1998) Vol. 46, No. 2, T. Fac. LR 488, at 519.

[3] See Alasdair McIntyre, *After Virtue* (2nd edn, University of Notre Dame Press, Notre Dame, Indiana 1984), and Vincent Wellman 'Practical Reasoning and Judicial Justification: Towards an Adequate Theory' (1985) 57 Colo. LR 45.

[4] McIntyre, *After Virtue*, at 152.

Wellman examines the question of the dynamics of such a process: what leads to the development of a new rule? He considers that the answer lies in the perception of an 'unsatisfactory' result. He characterises the result of practical reasoning as 'fiats' that must satisfy a criterion of satisfactoriness rather than a criterion of truth.[5]

Professor Penner has sought to illustrate this view by referring to what has been described as a 'holism of beliefs'.[6] A judge is presented with a situation where the prospect of applying existing rules produces a state of dissatisfaction. A new rule occurs to the judge which produces a state of less dissatisfaction, or perhaps, satisfaction. The new rule is then applied. Holism is then introduced to make sense of the notion of satisfaction. The state of satisfaction arises where a firm, complex, interlocking 'web of beliefs' produces a solid support or meaning for the particular rule in question. Dissatisfaction occurs where a rule's meaning is less well supported by 'connections' and other meanings. Once the new rule is recognised, its validity is justified by the connections it has with this 'web of beliefs'.

While these theories or versions of practical reasoning may explain how judges progress from the existing rule or *corpus* of rules – or connections or 'webs of belief' – to a position of dissatisfaction and from there to a new rule or a new application of a rule, they do not, of course, explain why some judges will feel dissatisfaction and others not. Complacent acceptance of the existing rules or *corpus* of rules may never, or only rarely, produce this dissatisfaction. Dissatisfaction with the existing law as it is perceived to be will be more likely to arise with the judge who shuns a formalistic approach and is driven by a conscious recognition of external sources of reference in the law. Notions of fairness and relevance must necessarily intrude at an earlier point in the reasoning process to produce this state of dissatisfaction.

Unless these notions intrude at an earlier point, there is a danger that practical reason will simply be captured by formalism, as, indeed, it has been captured in Penner's case.[7] Existing rules obtain a weighting not accorded competing and possibly more compelling considerations. The process is essentially historical in the sense that it creates for the judge a

---

[5] Wellman, 'Practical Reasoning', at 504.
[6] Penner, 'The Rules of Law', at 504–505, citing Donald Davidson, 'On the Very Idea of a Conceptual Scheme' in Davidson, *Inquiries into Truth and Interpretation* (Clarendon Press, Oxford, 1984).
[7] Ibid., at 512–521.

presumption in favour of the *status quo*; the existing rules apply, subject to the defeasibility.[8] For that reason, it is also essentially conservative and will not respond as readily to change as the community has a right to expect.[9]

A conception of the legal process that perceives development evolving at the point where a rule or precedent ends will not be as fair or relevant as it should be to meet the needs and expectations of society. Such an approach is too confined. What is required is an approach in which, while the existing rule or *corpus* of rules is seen as the starting point, the judge is prepared at the same time to critically re-evaluate that starting point against the objectives of justice or relevance. As I have said above, the re-evaluation in many cases may be little short of a formality. Further, other considerations, such as the objective of certainty, may bear upon the instant case, but from the outset fundamental conceptions may require to be clearly analysed, basic values explicitly examined, and irrelevant rules excised from consideration. The existing rule or *corpus* of rules will not suggest a reason for dissatisfaction if they are vested with an internal intelligibility thought to be innate to the existing law.

There is, of course, also a risk that practical reasoning will inadvertently exhibit an analytical foible; the assumption that the existing rules or *corpus* of rules can be determined and will be generally acknowledged. More often than not, however, the existing rules or *corpus* of rules will be indeterminate or in conflict and subject to dispute. The wider 'web of beliefs' and 'connections' may be only dimly perceived and, if and when comprehended, differ from one judge to another. Consequently, whether or not a judge develops a sense of dissatisfaction in a particular case is likely to depend on his or her appreciation of the existing *corpus* of rules, web of beliefs or connections. The scope for differences to emerge before the judge turns to consider (if he or she chooses to consider) whether the outcome is satisfactory dispatches a neat and tidy theory.

While, therefore, existing theories of practical reasoning are immensely useful, I do not consider that they are the last word. They seek to be too theoretical for a process that is essentially practical, and they are too oriented to a 'rulish' approach to retain touch with practice. Worse, they provide the vehicle for almost any judicial approach a judge may care to

---

[8] See above, Chapter 3, at 60–62.
[9] This point is elaborated more fully in relation to Frederich Schauer's theory of 'presumptive positivism'. See above, Chapter 3, at 58–62.

adopt without attempting a means by which the outmoded approaches will be revealed as being out of touch or the disparity between acceptable approaches reduced. While the starting point may be the same, practical reasoning does not explain why the web of beliefs and connections of one judge are defined narrowly and yet those of another defy systematic delineation. In each case the reasoning process is intrinsically different. It reflects not so much the choices that are made as the personal approach or attitude of the individual judge, for it is that approach or attitude that will dictate his or her response to the choices. While the non-formalist judge will be at a marked advantage in satisfying the criteria of practical reasoning, the formalist may also purport to mount a claim to meet that criterion.

To improve the judicial process, therefore, practical reasoning must be placed in a conception of the judicial role that embraces the realism and pragmatism advocated above. The reasoning requires direction towards an end: the law must serve society and be just and relevant in that service. What is then required in the practical reasoning process is the deliberate introduction of an evaluative step at an early stage of the process. It is not enough to act with 'virtue' and invoke 'justice' where a rule does not define the 'right' decision. A rule, including a rule which may be directly applicable, should be re-evaluated for its justice or fairness and relevance. More often than not the re-evaluation will probably lead to the rule being confirmed, but the focus on that question will serve to disable the obsolete judicial approaches and make judicial reasoning more pointed and responsive. So, too, the question whether a rule meets the criteria of satisfactoriness, or produces a state of dissatisfaction, must be asked at an initial stage of the reasoning process irrespective of the fact that the rule, principle or standard may be directly applicable and would, if applied, be dispositive of the case. No notion of 'presumptive' application would apply if the rule, principle or standard happened to fit the instant case, as the rule, principle or standard would itself require to be reviewed for its ability to serve the interests of justice and keep the law abreast of the times.[10]

Undertaking this review at an early stage of the reasoning process also serves to replace what would or might be the judge's intuitive feeling as to the proper outcome in the particular case with a deliberate evaluation of the justice and relevance of the rule, principle or standard in point.

---

[10] See above, Chapter 3, at 62.

Not only is the reasoning process given a sound basis or starting point, but it is also made that much more open and transparent.

It would not just be overly optimistic, but absurd, to suggest that this format would eliminate the differences between judges. Some judges will remain more conservative, others will remain more progressive. Nothing will conspicuously change that divergence. But a pattern of practical reasoning that requires judges to reassess the law, as distinct from pretending to simply find it, must serve to bring judges into closer accord. The need to re-evaluate the particular rule or principle in issue will focus the judicial mind and bring to the surface the unseen intuitive 'reasoning' that is not necessarily confronted at present. Differences as to whether the rule, or the application of the rule, would be unjust in the circumstances of the particular case or whether its application would meet the current needs and expectations of the community will still arise, but they will be differences bearing on the interests and values involved and not differences arising out of the different approaches adopted. Having a common purpose and a common question, judicial reasoning can be expected to achieve greater concordance.

Practical, practical reasoning

Once it is accepted that judges face a multiplicity of choices in resolving a dispute, including more particular choices within broader choices, the key function of judicial reasoning is to determine how those choices are to be made. The inevitable balancing exercise must be a reasoned process. Explaining how the choices are made and the competing interests and values weighed provides judicial reasoning with its persuasiveness and respect. Choices begin with the finding of facts. The definition of the legal issue or the identification of the interests and values involved, the determination of the community considerations that must be weighed one against the other, including the underlying value judgement, any analogical reasoning that is appropriate, and the open, reasoned discourse and transparent process of reasoning that follows in arriving at a decision, must all be undertaken in a practical manner. Practical reasoning of this kind lacks any taint of legal formalism.[11]

---

[11] Daniel A. Farber, 'The Inevitability of Practical Reason: Statutes, Formalism, and the Rule of Law' (1992) 45 Vanderbilt LR 533.

The all-important facts

Choices begin in determining the facts. As already noted, a close examination of the facts is essential to adjudication. Fact-finding is a process that receives considerable time and attention in the courts. Counsel who have been impatiently pressed to lead a witness to the point of his or her evidence – and to do so without actually asking a leading question – or to curtail an overlong or discursive cross-examination, may assume a sceptical frown, but the importance of the facts is fully recognised in court procedures that dedicate much time and resources to the finding of those facts.

Professor Atiyah, in stressing the strength of pragmatism in English law, has suggested that the great emphasis placed on precedent requires the facts of the case to be treated as all important. Whether an earlier case is in point or distinguishable necessarily depends on the close examination of the facts.[12] The good professor, I suggest, is only partly correct. The overriding importance of the facts of the case is fully accepted. More often than not, however, a close examination of the facts not only reveals the merits of the case but also points to the appropriate law. But while Professor Atiyah's emphasis on the need for judges to undertake a minute analysis of the facts of a particular case is not misplaced, his claim that this need can be attributed to the dominance of precedent is certainly open to challenge. As we have already seen, if judges want to find a difference in the facts of the instant case and the facts of the precedent it is not difficult for them to do so. No close examination or analysis of the facts is necessary to achieve that simple end. Indeed, there is a danger that a judge who wishes to distinguish an awkward precedent will strain to find a difference in the facts of the two cases and thereby distort the facts of one or the other of them in the process. Conversely, if such a close examination of the facts is necessary to implement the doctrine of precedent, it is difficult to avoid the conclusion that the doctrine is operating in a ponderous or pedantic fashion.

The truth is that a close knowledge of the facts is essential, not because of the precedent system, but as a prerequisite to doing justice in the particular case. The facts are the fount of individual justice. Vast areas of fact are commonly examined by judges which have little or nothing to

---

[12] P. S. Atiyah, *Pragmatism and Theory in English Law* (Hamlyn Lectures – 39th series, Stevens, London, 1987), at 68–69.

do with any question of precedent. But those facts will be intensely examined nonetheless because judicial experience confirms that it is essential to focus on the facts in order to arrive at a just decision.

Close and meticulous attention to the facts also serves to make judges, whether at first instance or at the appellate level, confront the involved, knotty or Byzantine tangles and unexpected twists and turns that characterise the human condition. The real plight of the persons who brought the facts into existence or responded to them cannot be avoided. As has been said; 'forget the facts, and you forget the persons helped and hurt by the [courts'] decisions'.[13] It is simply because the facts are hard to forget that the facts tend to drive the courts' decisions.

No jurist has undertaken a closer examination of the fact-finding process of the courts than Frank. As with many theorists pressing a particular theory, Frank's work contains a touch of overstatement, but it is none the less of great value. His experience as a Federal Court Judge confirmed his belief that trial court fact-finding is the soft spot in the administration of justice.[14] Frank believed that judicial fact-finding constitutes the most difficult part of courthouse government. He lamented the fact that fact-finding has been largely ignored by legal theory, pushed off to the edge in most descriptions of the legal system, and did not receive the study which it deserves. Considerable improvement is required, Frank claimed, if justice is to be made as adequate as humanly possible.[15]

Frank pointed out that a legal rule is a conditional statement referring to facts. In simple terms, if the alleged facts exist, then, this or that legal consequence will or may follow. A judge's decision is therefore the product of both a rule and the facts of the case. Hence, the importance of the facts. He posits a situation arising four years before a dispute relating to that situation comes to court. Even if the applicable rule is relatively clear (and Frank is a stern critic of the claim to certainty in the law), a lawyer cannot at any earlier time prophesy what the decision will eventually be. The facts will not be as the situation actually happened in the past but, at best, only what the trial court thinks happened, and what the judge or jury thinks happened may be hopelessly incorrect.[16] The

---

[13] John T. Noonan Jr., *Narrowing the Nation's Power: The Supreme Court Sides with the States* (University of California Press, Berkley, Calif., 2002), at 144.
[14] Jerome Frank, *Courts on Trial* (Princeton University Press, Princeton, 1973), at 74.
[15] Ibid., at 70.
[16] Ibid., at 14–16. Frank's immediate claim that facts of the case are merely a guess about the actual facts must be taken to be an overstatement for effect.

basic point Frank makes is valid. Certainty and predictability in the law are also subject to the uncertainty and unpredictability of the court's ultimate finding of facts.

Equally helpful is Frank's emphasis on the fact that the judge's findings of fact are subjective, although I would prefer to say, largely subjective. Not being 'given' data or waiting somewhere ready-made for the court to discover or 'find', findings of fact represent the judge's subjective reactions to the witnesses' stories. In this sense, Frank argued, facts are 'made' by the trial judge.[17]

An immediate difficulty in reaching a finding that accords with what actually happened is the fallibility of witnesses. Witnesses must first select from 'the brute, raw events' of the past what they will testify about. Their selection depends on their individual capacity for observation, their emotional condition at the time of selection, the time that transpires before they finally give evidence, the fact their memory may be faulty, and such-like factors. In addition, there is the possibility that the witness will be biased in relating his or her recollection of the events that occurred.[18]

Notwithstanding Frank's attack, and notwithstanding my general agreement with the thrust of his argument, I do not share the same dismal view of trial judges' capacity to find facts in a way that will closely accord with what actually happened. Certainly, there will be occasions when there is a disparity between what actually happened and the finding of facts, or when a finding that is generally correct on some issues may include findings that are astray on others, but overall I consider judges at first instance achieve a remarkably high standard in determining and stabilising the facts of a case. Evidence, often long and tortuous, is listened to with care and patience by most judges and then analysed, assessed and weighed to arrive at an acceptable version of the facts.

Of course, there will be lapses, and those lapses due to the human shortcomings of witnesses or the equally human shortcomings of judges will be difficult to eliminate. But taking evidence from witnesses or inspecting documents and, failing agreement, subjecting that evidence to the assessment of an independent and impartial arbiter, is the only system we have for then arriving at findings of fact. Although they may be improved with judicial education and training, or the like, human shortcomings are here to stay. Shortcomings that are due to defects in

---

[17] Ibid., at 23–24. [18] Ibid., at 318.

the system, however, can be or should be removed or remedied. Those defects which are 'systemic' are persisted in only because of the judges' limited perception of their role and, in particular, the scope of their autonomy. A short digression will illustrate some areas in which there is scope for improvement.

In the first place, far too much weight is placed on the demeanour of witnesses. Findings of credibility, or lack of credibility, play too dominant a part in fact-finding at first instance. Demeanour may be important, and findings based on credibility may tend to make a decision 'appeal-proof', but reliance on the demeanour of a witness may not be particularly helpful in getting at the truth. Very little empirical research has been carried out into the question whether reliance on the demeanour of witnesses is a secure method of assessing the veracity of evidence. Realism suggests that judicial reliance on demeanour should be utilised with great caution.

Caution in regard to assessing the demeanour of witnesses was confirmed by the High Court of Australia in *Fox* v *Percy*.[19] The Court unanimously upheld a decision of the New South Wales Court of Appeal reversing a trial judge's judgment based on the resolution of a factual conflict at trial. In a joint judgment, Gleeson CJ and Gummow and Kirby JJ acknowledged that there is a need for appellate courts to respect the advantages possessed by trial judges, especially when their decisions may be affected by the impression they form as to the credibility of witnesses whom they see, but who are not seen by the appellate court. They pointed out, however, that a number of judges have sounded a caution against the dangers of too readily drawing conclusions as to the truthfulness and reliability of witnesses solely or mainly from their appearance. The observation of Atkin LJ in 1924 is quoted with approval: '... I think that an ounce of intrinsic merit or demerit in the evidence, that is to say, the value of the comparison of evidence with known facts, is worth pounds of demeanour.'[20] The three judges go on to point out that, in recent years, judges have become more aware of scientific research that has cast doubt on the ability of judges, or anyone else, to tell truth from falsehood on the basis of appearances. Judges have been encouraged to limit their reliance on the appearance of witnesses and to reach their conclusions, as far as possible, on the basis of contemporary materials, objectively established facts and the apparent

---

[19] *Fox* v *Percy* (2003) 197 ALR 201.
[20] *Societe d'Advances Commerciales, (Societe Anonyme Egyptienne)* v *Merchants' Marine Insurance Co, The 'Palitana'* [1924] Lloyd's Law Rep 140, at 152.

logic of events. They add that this approach does not eliminate the established principles about witnesses' credibility, but tends to reduce the occasions where those principles are seen as critical.[21]

More often that not, 'truth' as far as the system will permit, can be gleaned from a close reading of the contemporaneous documentation, if any, or an analysis of the probabilities intrinsic to the circumstances and about which there may be little or no dispute, rather than the demeanour of various witnesses. Contemporaneous documentation can often provide a strong, or even conclusive, indication of where the true facts lie. At times, documents may not say what they could be expected to say in the circumstances of the case. Their pointed and selective silence may found a sound inference. Unless self-serving, therefore, documents made at the time are more likely to accurately record or indicate the events of that time than the recollection of witnesses. Either alone or supplemented by oral testimony, the facts can be put together with a high degree of confidence that they at least approximate the truth. Yet, at times, appellate judges are surprised to find that the focus of the judge at first instance has been on the oral evidence to the detriment of what the contemporary documents may have conveyed. A finding of fact in the appellate court at variance with the finding at first instance may then eventuate. Such a disparity as to the facts does nothing for the reputation of the courts or the administration of justice.

What I have just said clearly relates to documents which are admissible. A related point, however, is that the court should be slow to exclude evidence if it would assist arrival at the true facts germane to the issue before the court. Only died-in-the-wool formalists any longer justify the indiscriminate application of the parol evidence rule where that evidence would be of direct and real assistance in ascertaining the truth. Any residual tendency, for example, to exclude evidence that could assist in determining whether the parties intended to be bound by an apparent agreement must be suppressed. It is legally sterile and inexcusable to hold that the parties did not intend to be bound when intrinsic evidence would establish that this was in fact their very intention.[22] Similarly, it seems unduly formalistic to exclude extrinsic evidence that would be of direct assistance in ascertaining

---

[21] See *Johnson v Johnson* (2000) 201 CLR, 488, per Kirby J at para. 5. See also Kirby J's comments in *Whisprun Pty Ltd v Dixon* (2003) 200 ALR 447, at paras. [116]–[120] deprecating the tendency to treat a trial as a tournament and emphasising that a judge's assessment of credibility cannot be permitted to trump rationality.

[22] See *Fletcher Challenge Energy Ltd v Electricity Corporation of New Zealand Ltd* [2002] 2 NZLR 433, at paras. [178] and [191]. See above, Chapter 11, at 289 *et seq.*

the true intention of the parties to a contract where that intention is in dispute. Unreliable or unhelpful evidence can always be sorted out and discarded.

Notwithstanding the assistance of contemporaneous documents, however, or where there is scant or no such documentation, the facts can often be ascertained from an analysis of the probabilities inherent in the circumstances of a case. Having regard to the circumstances and to the agreed, undisputed or unchallengeable evidence, some features or outcomes are likely to be more probable than not. The exercise is to then reconstruct the facts from the viewpoint of the parties; figuratively standing in the shoes of the parties or witnesses at the time of the event or transaction in issue.

If, notwithstanding the judge's best efforts, there is a gap in the evidence, or data, or inferences that can be fairly drawn, judges must do their best to work with and around those gaps. Gaps in the evidence should be acknowledged. Judges must endeavour to resolve disputes in circumstances where the full facts cannot be determined and only resort to the burden or standard of proof as a last resort. Experience, however, tends to show that the occasions when it is necessary to resort to the burden or standard of proof are few and far between. What judges must not do is fill in an unresolvable gap with a judicial 'hunch'. To do so is to succumb in part to what I have perhaps unkindly labelled the 'God Syndrome'. Anecdotal evidence suggests that the God Syndrome settles on some judges shortly after their appointment to the Bench. To some, need it be said, it does not appear to be at all unwelcome. One of its features emerges when, confronted with incomplete evidence, the judge nevertheless intuitively 'knows' the full facts. Those 'facts' will be pronounced with confident assuredness. I entertain little doubt that a number of appeals could be avoided if judges of this ilk were to exchange this instinctive sense of infallibility for a realistic approach.

I also entertain little doubt that, while appellate judges must be alert to error in the trial judge's finding of facts, many appellate judgments would be edified if judges at that level did not show an unhealthy preparedness to adopt a version of the facts which cannot be found in the judge's findings of fact or in the transcript of the evidence itself. Although he focuses on courts of first instance, Frank does not overlook the importance of the facts at the appellate level. Citing Lewellyn, he points out that appellate judges pick over and reorganise the facts so as to make plausible the decision that the court has reached. The God Syndrome does not strike at first instance only.

Part of the problem with getting at the 'truth' in the adversarial system of adjudication is the adversarial system itself. The evidence which is adduced is under the control of the parties, or their counsel, and the 'truth' must be garnered from what they choose to present and how they choose to present it. Counsel are most unlikely to adduce evidence adverse to their clients cause unless it is necessary or strategic for them to do so. Rules of evidence, overly-rigid procedural requirements, and the presentation of the evidence in terms of the lawyers' theory of the case can twist the reflection of the true facts.[23] The outcome may then be the artificial 'truth', which Frank asserts will only coincidentally accord with the actual truth.

This artificiality is unacceptable. As the objective must be to arrive at the actual facts of the case, judges may have to adopt the appropriate case-management devices to ensure full disclosure of all relevant facts by the parties to achieve that objective. They may also need to intervene, circumspectly, of course, in the course of a trial with their own questions directed at ascertaining the truth. Further intervention may be required to ensure that appropriate or essential witnesses are in fact called by one or the other of the parties, or, if by neither, by the court itself.[24] Such a course is warranted and to be encouraged where it is necessary to avoid the situation where incomplete evidence could lead to an erroneous or unjust outcome.

The legal issue

Finding the facts does not exhaust the judges' responsibility in this critical area of adjudication. They must at once decide what facts are relevant. This question will turn on the issue or issues to be resolved. Defining or formulating the issue or issues requiring resolution, however, should not be thought of as a single step in the process of the practical reasoning that we are discussing. Clearly, some idea of the issue or issues is required in advance of the fact-finding exercise so that the judge will not 'find' facts that will have no bearing on the case. Determining the issue or issues is a prerequisite to determining what

---

[23] Frank, *Courts on Trial*, at 76.
[24] See, e.g., *Obacelo Pty Ltd v Taveraft Pty Ltd* (1986) 66 ALR 371. See also *Fallon v Calvert* [1960] 2 QB 201; and *Coulson v Disborough* [1984] 2 QB 316. But see also *Re Enoch and Zaretzky, Bock & Co's Arbitration* [1910] 1 KB 327. See also *Dairy Containers Ltd v NZI Bank Ltd* (1994) 7 PRNZ 465.

evidence is or will be relevant. But I am here speaking of the formulation of the issue in overly precise or finite terms. The danger, if the issue is formulated in such precise or finite terms prematurely, is that valid areas of inquiry in the resolution of the dispute will be closed off. Framing the issue or issues is therefore a task that in many cases can validly extend throughout much of the reasoning process.

Consequently, while, to the extent that diligent and astute counsel have not done so already it may be important to define the issue or issues in general or tentative terms at an early stage, it is also important that the final formulation of the issue or issues remain open. There is a strong tendency, especially at the appellate level, to frame or crystallise the exact issue with great 'legal' precision and set it in concrete too early. All too often this tendency results in the exclusion of the breadth of factors that may be relevant to the proper resolution of the case. Precipitately finalising the issue can then have a confining effect on the court's reasoning. Of course, there will be occasions when the formulation of the issue can be settled with confident finality. All I am saying is that care must be taken not to foreclose the legitimate development of judicial thinking in the decision-making process by seeking to prematurely define the issue in overly precise or finite terms.

The initial formulation should therefore be viewed for the most part as an interim formulation subject to revision as and when the facts develop, or argument is refined, or the judge's thinking matures. This tentative approach to the issue is all the more important simply because the formulation of it can often effectively determine the outcome. Pity the hapless counsel who is led by a judge, like a fly into the spider's web, to accept that the issue is to be formulated in certain terms not realising that, because of the way the issue has just been framed, he or she has just forgone any chance of succeeding!

Framing or crystallising the issue too early so as to effectively put it beyond revision fails to take account of the complexity of legal issues and the extent to which judges' thinking can, and possibly should, change as they become more familiar with all aspects of the case and come closer to the essence of the case. Few experienced counsel today deny that a case or argument undergoes a refining process as it passes through the court hierarchy. This view is basically the reason why most jurisdictions insist upon, at least, a two-tier appellate structure. Frequently, the difference between one court and the next is the difference between the respective courts' perception and formulation of the key issue. The point to note is that the same refining process is possible during the course of a case whether at first instance or on appeal. Thus, the door must be left open for the issue to be redefined as required to match the maturation in the judge's thinking even up to and including the writing of the judgment.

The initial premise

Once the issue has been clarified to the point that the judge may begin the reasoning process, he or she must obviously start with a premise. It may be a rule. It may be a principle. It may be a standard. It may be a policy prescription. It does not much matter. While rejecting formalism, one can still accept Wittgenstein's demonstration that rule following is innate. It is a form of human behaviour or practice.[25] With an all-important qualification it can also be accepted that, if a rule applies, that could be the end of the matter. The all-important qualification, of course, is that the rule or its application would not be accepted if it would lead to injustice in the instance case or would perpetuate a law that is out of step with the contemporary requirements of the community.

Life and the law, however, are seldom so simple. Sheer complexity relegates this basic model to the 'land of never-never'. More often than not, more than a rule is required; the rule may not be adequate or apt to cover the situation; the rule may have been shown not to work in practice; there may be a conflict between two apparently applicable rules; or there may be no rule at all. No particular rule will exist to require re-evaluation. The pre-existing *corpus* of rules would, of course, be relevant, and would be taken into account. But that often amorphous body of pre-existing law, which might otherwise exert an unreasoned magnetic pull, should be regarded as providing the legal backdrop or framework only, and the context into which a judge will seek to place his or her judgment. Which brings me to Professors Hart and Sachs.

A community of considerations

Hart and Sachs perceive the courts' role as one anchored by the pre-existing body of rules, principles, standards and policies from which the courts move by a process of 'reasoned elaboration'.[26] Such a perception

---

[25] Penner, 'The Rules of Law', at 491.
[26] H. Hart and A. Sachs, *The Legal Process: Basic Problems in the Making and Application of Law* (The Foundation Press, Westbury, N.Y., 1994).

is elementary but not entirely complete. While the starting point may be the pre-existing body of rules, principles, standards and policies it is what follows that really counts. A judge of a formalist inclination will seek to work deductively to a conclusion. A judge not of that persuasion, but endowed with practical reason, will accept that those premises are both the starting and finishing point if they meet the tests of relevance and fairness. But if the judge considers that they do not do so, he or she will look further. It is this potential for dissatisfaction which is critical. Guided by the lodestars of justice and relevance, the judge would not reserve that sense of dissatisfaction for those cases which academic theorists might describe as a 'hard case'. The choice to re-evaluate the premise, be it a rule, principle, standard, policy prescription, or whatever, exists from the outset. Unlike a formalist judge, who may deny the choice, or fail to explain his or her choice, or concentrate on precedential-based or narrow conceptual arguments, the judge imbued with practical reasoning would acknowledge the choice and seek to explain his or her decision having regard to the broader implications of the case and the substantive arguments leading to an evaluation of what would be the best legal solution.[27]

In working to this solution, the judge should identify the interests or values involved which must be balanced one against the other. These interests or values will then form part of the 'community of considerations' that the judge is required to take into account. For example, a property interest, a property value, an equitable interest or value, a legal principle, a justice value, a certainty consideration and any number of other considerations may fall within the mix in a particular case. It would be foolhardy to try and specify those other considerations. Obviously, they must be relevant to the issue falling for decision, and equally obviously, therefore, they will not include the colour of the plaintiff's hair! Short of meeting criteria such as relevance and reliability, however, they need not be delineated. They are not delineated at present. In one case, the fact Parliament has indicated its policy in a certain area may be pertinent to the policy which the court is called upon to formulate; in another case the developments in other areas of the law may be critical; in yet another case a need or gap in the law may have been shown to exist that adversely affects commerce; and so on. Regard for the wider consequences of a decision would be

---

[27] John Steyn, 'Does Legal Formalism Hold Sway in England?' (1996) 49 II Current Legal Problems 43, at 54.

automatic.[28] In a sense, the community of considerations may be as wide as Dworkin's definition of principles and just as impossible to exhaustively list. Where I differ from Dworkin, as will be apparent shortly, is that I am not prepared to grace all relevant considerations with the appellation of 'principles'.

Practical reasoning requires the judge to work his or her way through this 'community of considerations' explaining why they prefer one consideration to another or one set of considerations to another set, or why they propound a compromise between competing considerations, if that be the case. Of course, reasoning by analogy, which has been perceived as the basic tool of common law reasoning,[29] would not be discarded, but with the relaxation of the doctrine of precedent its importance and application would tend to diminish. While analogical reasoning could still be of assistance to a judge in carrying out the inevitable balancing exercise and reaching a solution, it would not be permitted to eclipse the judge's true reasoning in preferring one consideration to another or one set of considerations to another. The process would, above all, be one of open and transparent reasoned discourse.

Community values

In the course of this process the judge may need to reflect, or may seek to reflect, a value immanent in the community, or assimilate a public attitude or public opinion, or enter upon a policy consideration of a public character.[30] I have already admitted that this feature of judicial reasoning is one that I find most problematic. If one begins with the objective that judges must not impose their own values or opinions, no formula can be found to secure that end. Almost inevitably the values or opinions advanced by judges will be conditioned by their own make-up, background and experience. If one resorts to a formula requiring judges

---

[28] I do not suggest that regard to the wider consequences of a decision would be intuitive. Realism and pragmatism require that wherever possible reference should be made to empirical evidence as to the probability of projected consequences. See Peter Cane, 'Consequences in Judicial Reasoning' in Jeremy Horder (ed.), *Oxford Essays in Jurisprudence* (4th Series, Oxford University Press, Oxford 2000), at 41.

[29] Lord Steyn 'Perspectives of Corrective and Distributive Justice in Tort Law', John Maurice Kelly Memorial Lecture at University College Dublin (November 2001), (published by the Faculty of Law, 2002).

[30] For an excellent article touching on an important aspect of this topic, see Lizzie Barmes, 'Adjudication and Public Opinion' (2002) LQR 600.

to rely, not on their own values or opinions, but their perception of what are the community's values or opinions, one again faces much the same difficulty. Not only is there little or no empirical evidence available but in many situations the availability of such evidence would erode the judicial constraint which arises out of the judges' awareness that they are not in a position to speak definitively on the point. Thus, a judge's assessment is necessarily subjective.[31] But judges cannot decline to reach a view as to the relevant community values, opinion or policy. To do so would be to leave the balancing process incomplete, if not distorted, and deprive the law of any real prospect of doing justice in the individual case or keeping the law abreast of the times. As Lord Steyn has recently observed; 'judges' "sense" of the moral answer to a question, or the justice of the case, has been one of the great shaping forces of the common law. What may count in a situation of difficulty and uncertainty is not the subjective view of the judge but what he reasonably believes that the ordinary citizen would regard as right.'[32] Of course, what the judge reasonably believes the ordinary citizen would regard as right is still largely subjective.

Nevertheless, a number of basic values that judges attribute to the community are readily identifiable. Notions of personal safety, national security, individual privacy, respect and consideration for the individual, the sanctity of life, the protection of property, equality of treatment before the law, fidelity to the terms of a power or promise, the common good, values underlying recognised human rights, and many other such notions form a respectable bundle of shared values. But in themselves these broad values will seldom be sufficient to explain the foundation of a value judgement. Underlying all these diverse values is the community's basic concept of justice and fairness as discerned by the judges.

The problem of judicial translation of community values is further compounded if it is accepted, as I accept, that at times judges do not reflect the values, and certainly the popular values, of the community, but import values that appeal to the judge as being enduring or enlightened values. These values are attributed to the community, whatever the transient mood of the populace may be. Judges do not set out to reflect a consensus in the community or represent the majority view. Indeed, it would be inconsistent with the concept of judicial autonomy

---

[31] Duncan Kennedy, *A Critique of Adjudication* (Harvard University Press, Cambridge, Mass., 1998), at 144–148.
[32] Lord Steyn, in *McFarlane* v *Tayside Health Board* [2000] 2 AC 59, at 82.

to expect judges to seek out either a consensus or a majority viewpoint. To do so would make judges the interpreters and ciphers of public opinion and the law the slave of the public mood. Something more is required of judges than that they reflect the common denominator.

Once this requirement is acknowledged, it becomes increasingly difficult to divert the charge that the judges have set themselves up as an elite, paternalistic self-appointed guardians of public values and morality.[33] But the charge is greatly overstated. What judges for the most part seek to do in cases that attract this criticism is to extract and apply the underlying value that the community hold firm to in the abstract. Many members of the public may reject the application of the value in a concrete situation, but nevertheless fully accept that value divorced from that concrete situation as a basic democratic or human right. For example, few people would deny that the worth and dignity of minority groups within the community must be recognised and respected. The community may roundly condemn discrimination, and its elected representatives may have endorsed that sentiment in legislation, but many may still succumb to intolerance in a particular case or actual circumstances. The courts will be immune to that intolerance and, to the best of their ability, seek to give effect to the basic value in a particular case or actual circumstances. This task is integral to the judicial process. There is no other way that what may be called populism can be exorcised from the law and the community be assured that the more enduring and enlightened values it upholds in the abstract will inform the administration of justice. In the exercise of their judicial discretion, the felt presence of all the factors that make up the discipline that constrain the judiciary offsets, to a greater or lesser extent, the imposition of personal perceptions and foibles. The constraints forming part and parcel of the judicial methodology that I advance in this book will assist judges to discipline and master those perceptions and foibles.[34]

A practical protection built into this methodology is the insistence that judges articulate in language that is as unabashed as it is unequivocal the values, opinions or policies that they favour; the source of the values, opinions or policies; the limits, if any, they recognise in their assessment; and the reasons for favouring the values, opinions or policies that they select ahead of other considerations. Not being in a state of

---

[33] I have already demonstrated the legitimacy of the judicial function. See above, Chapter 4, at 77–88.
[34] See Chapter 10.

denial, judges suffused with practical reasoning will be conscious of the need to make full disclosure of these basic reasons. They will not seek to 'minimise or camouflage the politically contentious steps in the argument'.[35]

Principles to the forefront

In working through this process the judge would give prominence to principles over rules or precedents. Instead of working deductively with the basic building blocks of legal argument, judges would work with general principles and terms of reference that subjugate form to the objectives of fairness and relevance. Generally speaking, they would endeavour to shun particular rules and cases and seek out the general principle underlying those rules or cases. They would then work from the general principle to the particular case in hand without undue regard to the mass of other particulars that the principle may have also generated. Judges will be conscious that, by focusing on the general principles as distinct from their particular application, those principles will eventually obtain a clarity and force that is likely to make the administration of the law more, and not less, certain and predictable.

The role of principles in practical reasoning can be discussed in more detail later under that particular heading.

Common sense

No reference has yet been made in this discourse on practical reasoning to that universally acclaimed virtue, common sense. Seldom is it decried. No commentators, not even legal fundamentalists, are heard to cry; 'but, what is common sense?' Common sense is a seemingly unchallenged human virtue. Critics who decline to vest judges with a sense of values or sense of justice can seemingly accept that judges are capable of exhibiting common sense. No barrier is erected against its use, save perhaps by those who would have courts interpret statutes with an unshakeable literal commitment, but even then there is an exception if the literal interpretation would render the statute absurd or unworkable. Fortunate indeed the theorist who, at the turn of the next century, discovers that both justice and the law equate with common sense. It

---

[35] Barmes, 'Adjudication and Public Opinion', at 617.

will not be the end of history as Francis Fukuyama would have it,[36] but it could be the end of legal history!

Judges ostensibly share the view that they are more than capable of exhibiting common sense. With apparent modesty many judges can be heard to declaim that they are not equipped with a vast knowledge of the law; or that they struggle with what intellect they may have been blessed; or that they have a simple and straightforward mind; or that sophisticated logic and subtle reasoning are beyond their frail human capabilities; but no judge ever suggests that he or she lacks common sense. Indeed, it may often provide a comfortable refuge for those who feel that they might lack, or might be perceived to be lacking, a generous intelligence. No matter, it is common sense that a judge requires.

Judges of all shapes and sizes are also inclined to conclude that the law embodies common sense. For example, Sir James O'Connor rather grandly claimed that the law of specific performance was 'nothing more than common sense crystallised in the chill atmosphere of a Chancery Court'.[37] To counsel seeking to struggle through the intricacies of the case law relating to specific performance that claim may seem somewhat surprising, and the resulting decision even more so if they have sought to give effect to its uncrystallised core! Optimism that there is a close nexus between the law and common sense nevertheless persists. It is an understandable public expectation that the law should coincide with such common sense. Common sense is often aligned with notions of decency and fair play or fairness. Although I would extend them to peoples other than those who speak English, canons of decency and fairness, Justice Frankfurter said; 'express the notion of justice of English-speaking peoples'.[38] But the law is all too often hopelessly vague, needlessly complex, duly burdened with layers of distinctions, and self-evidently in irretrievable disarray to pretend that the law and common sense invariably coincide. The law, of course, does at times reflect common sense, but that is because it is administered by judges that possess that virtue. But the extent of the coincidence should not be overstated. Formalism, or a formalistic approach, finds it difficult to accommodate common sense, and that approach is all too prevalent for common sense to invariably assert its pragmatic supremacy.

The practical reasoning that I propose would embrace common sense. Common sense is another recognisable value to which a judge would

---

[36] *The End of History and the Last Man* (Penguin, London, 1992).
[37] (1928) 3 Ca LJ, 161, at 164.   [38] *Adamson v California* 332 U.S. 46 (1947).

have regard in the 'community of considerations' that bear upon the resolution of an issue. Rulings which do not measure up to the community's perception of common sense are at risk of earning the epithet, 'the law is an ass'. Moreover, the courts are acutely susceptible to public perceptions of common sense. Judges, or some judges, may raise the mystique of the law or formalism to shield them from criticism that they have been unjust or out of date, but they cannot hide behind that mystique or formalism to protect themselves from the charge of lacking common sense. The gentleman ensconced in his leather chair with a whisky at his side at the club, the working man standing at the bar with a jug of beer at his elbow, the lecturer berating her students in the lecture room, or the woman chatting with her neighbours down at the supermarket all judge, or feel that they can judge, a judge's common sense. Common sense is a great leveller.

This is not to say that common sense has not come under attack. Lord Hoffmann has asserted that the phrase, 'it is a matter of common sense', conceals, or possibly reveals, a complete absence of any form of reasoning. He berates the frequent judicial invocation of common sense in relation to the question of causation.[39] Although I tend to think that causation is essentially a practical question of fact to be approached with common sense, I do not intend to enter upon that controversy. One can readily agree with Lord Hoffmann that judges should be encouraged to give the real reasons for their decisions and that such questions as 'remedial justice and economic policy' should not be submerged under an appeal to common sense.[40] Common sense is not a refuge for sloppy thinking or a façade to screen the predispositions, policy considerations or value judgements at the base of judges' reasoning.

What I would resist, however, is any suggestion that common sense is antipathetic to legal principles. The law is not to be divided into sectors; an area restricted to fact-finding and little beyond where common sense may obtain a consensus, and an area where legal rules and principles reign supreme uncompromised by common sense. On the contrary, common sense reflects a practical approach that should be applied to both the formulation and application of rules and principles. It is a further bulwark against the intrusion of formalism. A reasoned appeal to

---

[39] Lord Hoffmann, 'Common Sense and Causing Loss', Lecture to the Chancery Bar Association, 15 June 1999. See also, Jane Stapleton, 'Law, Causation and Common Sense' (1988) 8 OJLS, 111.
[40] Hoffmann, ibid., at 23–24.

common sense will command universal acceptance simply because a consensus is attracted to the hard reality and practical wisdom demonstrated in the common sense judge's response.

Thus, the application of common sense should not be perceived as a negative feature in judicial reasoning, that is, invoked if and when the law is in danger of publicly being branded an ass, but should be utilised positively to evaluate the law. If the particular rule or principle does not accord with notions of common sense, it would require some particular justification to allow it to stand, or to allow it to stand in an unmodified form. In such circumstances, there would be an unshakeable suspicion that all might not be well with the allegedly settled rule or principle. Common sense, along with justice and relevance, can be the instigator for that sense of dissatisfaction required as part of the exercise of practical reasoning.

The basis for elevating common sense to greater prominence in the reasoning process of the judiciary, of course, is nothing other than its close relationship with realism and pragmatism. It is alien to common sense to proceed in a way which is divorced from reality, and common sense is wholly comfortable about proceeding in a pragmatic fashion having regard to the consequences of the court's ruling. Common sense, in other words, goes hand in glove with realism and pragmatism.

A good example of the way in which common sense has expanded its province in the law is the growth of the principle of proportionality. Proportionality, of course, has always been present in the sentencing of prisoners; the severity of the sentence must be proportionate to the crime that has been committed. But the principle now has a wide-ranging compass in other branches of the law, particularly public and administrative law.[41] Its essential function is to relate means to ends and causes to outcomes. The end must not be disproportionate to the means or the outcome excessive having regard to the cause. The relationship must be within the bounds of reasonableness. No other source for making the requisite value judgement as to the proportionately of the means to the end or the cause to the outcome is available than common sense. Common sense, and probably common sense alone, is all that assists a judge determine whether a given end is reasonably related to the means used to achieve that end or whether an outcome is excessive having regard to the cause of that outcome. No amount of rules or precedents will provide that assistance. In all, it is a mark of the law's

---

[41] See Michael Taggart, 'Administrative Law' [2003] NZLR, 99.

maturity that it is beginning to insist that the common sense objective of keeping things in proportion is integral to the functioning of the legal process.

Finally, this excursion into the nature of common sense may be utilised to introduce an unheralded test, which finds no support, much less any mention, in learned treatises on judicial reasoning. It is what I call the 'stand back' test. The test requires no more than that the judge stand back and take a hard look at what is proposed, whether or not it is his or her own handiwork. What is proposed may be a finely crafted and sophisticated piece of legal reasoning, and yet on a removed and objective examination appear repugnant to common sense. How often has the reader digested a decision and, then, standing back from it at once felt that it could not be right. More often than not, the reaction will be prompted by the reader's common sense. Of course, a more sophisticated analysis may follow.

A summary

Practical reasoning, therefore, is eminently practical. Its judicial adherents will be supremely conscious that the law or legal process is a social institution and that their reasoning must ultimately be directed by the functional objective of serving society's needs and expectations. Chief among these needs and expectations will be the community's requirement that the law be just and contemporaneous. Practical reasoning will not be diverted from these objectives by false and flagging theories or influenced by jaded and fading approaches. At root, practical reasoning will reflect a happy mix of realism, pragmatism and principles. The focus on the facts will be extensive in the knowledge that the best legal solution often emerges from a complete grasp of the facts. Defining the legal issue will be a deliberate exercise in which the initial formulation, however firmly expressed, will yet be subject to review as the case is refined and the judge's thinking matures. No rule, principle or standard put forward, however directly applicable it might be, will be immune from being re-evaluated in terms of its fairness and capacity to do justice and its relevance to modern conditions. Dissatisfaction, if there is to be dissatisfaction, with a rule, principle or standard, or with the apparent pre-existing body of law, will be permitted to manifest itself from the outset. Of extreme importance in the process will be the open identification of the interests and values involved in the case and the judge's assessment of those interests and values. The inevitable balancing process or appraisal as to where to draw the line will be fully and transparently reasoned. While the judge engaged in practical reasoning will identify and have regard to a community of considerations, reference or recourse to basic principles will be a prominent feature. The role of principles therefore falls to be examined next.

Principles

Principles and reason

Legal principle is a phrase that resonates with reassuring connotations of legitimacy. I make no such claim. Principles, properly construed, are the basic tools among the community of considerations to which the judge will have regard in arriving at a decision. By their very nature they warrant pre-eminence in the reasoning process. Generally, they must dominate rules and prevail over precedent, and they provide the means by which 'the law' obtains such cohesion, coherence and continuity as it can command.

The search for principles in the law and legal theory followed closely on the destruction wreaked by the American Realists. A system that implicitly denies the credibility of any theory of objective or interpretative legal values prompted legal scholars to search for a remedial article in which to place their faith.[42] They found that article in reason. A rational dimension that had been absent throughout the realist era was then introduced.[43]

Gray invoked 'principles' largely in the sense of consequences or the means by which hard cases could be resolved. Roscoe Pound noted that, throughout history, the law had been influenced by moral principles concerning what is considered to be fair and just.[44] These principles, he argued, provide the starting point for legal reasoning and become active, as Gray had claimed, in hard cases. John Dickinson defined principles as legal stipulations of basic moral beliefs.[45] Certain core legal principles, he argued, protect a particular interest that, because of the complexity of human life and association, will come into conflict with some other interest. A balance is achieved by resorting to policy considerations that, in law, will be

---

[42] Duxbury, *Patterns of American Jurisprudence*, at 205 *et seq.*
[43] Gray, *The Nature and Sources of Law*, at 286.
[44] Roscoe Pound, 'The Limits of Effective Legal Action' (1917) 3 American Bar Assoc. Journal, 55, at 61.
[45] John Dickinson 'The Law Behind Law' Colum. LR 29 (1929), at 113–46.

arbitrary, as there is no coherent system or policy underlying the rules of the common law. All these theorists regarded principles as providing the basis of the legal process. Rules emerge from principles and it is those rules that judges apply. Where in a hard case there is no applicable precedent, judges are able to develop new rules by resorting to principles.[46]

To some extent, as Duxbury points out, Cardozo anticipated these theories.[47] Being a realist, Cardozo recognised that principles are extracted from the pre-existing law and are constantly being retested and reformulated. 'Principles that have served their day expire and new principles are born.'[48] Judicial reasoning, he claimed, evolves through this process.

Principles, however, serve a more vital function than merely explaining how judicial reasoning evolves. Thus, Cardozo attributed a 'directive force' to principles.[49] Where principles conflict it is the directive force of those principles that the judge will assess in making a choice in favour of one over the other. The great jurist turned to *Riggs* v *Palmer*[50] to illustrate his argument. In *Riggs* v *Palmer* the Court of Appeals of New York was faced with the question whether an heir named in the will of his grandfather could inherit his legacy when he had himself murdered his grandfather. All the statutes governing the making of wills, proof of wills and the devolution of property were satisfied, at least on a literal basis. Two principles clashed. One was the principle that the testator's will should prevail in the devolution of his or her property. The other principle was that no-one should be permitted to profit by their own fraud or take advantage of their own wrong, or found any claim upon their own inequity, or acquire property by their own crime. The court decided that the murderer in this case could not inherit. He could not be permitted to profit from his own wrong. Why was this? The simple answer for Cardozo was that the principle was chosen because it 'led to justice'.[51] 'History or custom or social utility', he said 'or some other compelling sentiment of justice or sometimes perhaps a semi-intuitive apprehension of the pervading spirit of our law, must come to the rescue of the anxious judge, and tell him where to go'.[52]

---

[46] Neil Duxbury, *Patterns of American Jurisprudence* (Clarendon Press, Oxford, 1995), at 222.
[47] Ibid., at 217–220.
[48] Benjamin N. Cardozo, *The Nature of the Judicial Process* (Yale University Press, New Haven, 1921), at 167. See also above, Chapter 8, at 207–208.
[49] Ibid., at 30.   [50] 22 NY, 188 (1889).   [51] Cardozo, *The Judicial Process*, at 41.
[52] Ibid., at 43.

Cardozo's view places less reliance on the power of reason than the more pure theorists who promoted principles. As a realist he perceived the flexibility and developing nature of principles and recognised that, in the last resort, in making a choice between conflicting principles, the judge is forced to resort to a value such as justice. He was, moreover, fully alert to the fact that the perception of justice could be influenced by the judge's own version of that value.

Fuller linked reason and principle. 'Law', he thought, 'was compounded by reason and fiat, of order discovered and order imposed, and that to attempt to eliminate either of these aspects of the law is to denature and falsify it.'[53] Judicial activity is predicated on reason, and when producing a reasoned decision the judge, instead of acting on 'personal predilections', is attempting 'to discover the natural principles underlying group life, so that his decisions might conform to them.'[54] The judge invokes 'external criteria, found in the conditions required for successful group living, that furnish some standard against which the rightness of [the judge's] decisions should be measured.'[55] In Fuller's view, therefore, principles become the foundation of legal reasoning marking the distinction between arbitrary demands and legal rights. 'A right', he proclaimed, 'is a demand founded on a principle.'[56] Thus, Fuller's account leads to a rationalistic and rights-oriented principle-based process of judicial decision-making. Many other theorists, of course, extolled the virtue of reason in the law or legal process; Sachs, Henry Hart, Frankfurter, Bickel, Wellington and Wechsler to name but a few.

It can be accepted that principles should constitute the foundation stones of legal reasoning and demand the 'power of reasoned elaboration'.[57] But reason, or pure reason, should not be raised to the pinnacle of judicial decision-making. The theorists ask too much of it. Reasoning is a means of arriving at and explaining a decision; it is not the substance of the decision itself. Judges must reason within the process, such as identifying and working with the community of considerations involved, and must then give, as far as humanly possible, the true reasons for their decision. But because reason alone will not decide the issue, judges must look beyond its confines and reveal the basis of their decisions as Cardozo did in identifying the touchstone as 'justice'. In

---

[53] Lon L. Fuller, 'Reasons and Fiat in Case Law' (1946) Harv. LR 59, at 382.
[54] Ibid., at 378.   [55] Ibid., at 379.   [56] Ibid., at 404.
[57] Hart and Sachs, *The Legal Process*, at 161; and see Herbert Wechsler 'Towards Neutral Principles of Constitutional Law' (1959) Harv. LR 73, at 15–20.

some cases it may be the dictates of justice, in others the need to update the law to meet modern demands and, yet, in others the requirement of certainty in the law may outweigh both these objectives. But to suggest that the answer can be found in the process by working with reason from principles is not only to simplify the process, but also to truncate it. Principles are vital, but they do not and cannot through reason provide the law with an impersonal existence.

None of this is to mention Dworkin. Yet, to touch upon principles without touching upon Dworkin would be worse than poor scholarship, it would be sacrilege. But, of course, I have already dealt fully with Dworkin's treatment of principles in Chapter 8.[58] No more need be said than to remind the reader of Dworkin's inflationary definition of principles; 'if . . . we tried actually to list all the principles in force we would fail. They are controversial, their weight is all important, they are numberless, and they shift and change so fast that the start of our list would be obsolete before we reached the middle.'[59] Principles, he said, are concerned with the promotion of rights, if necessary, ahead of the general welfare. They are the means by which an individual is treated with the same respect and concern as everyone else. This basic principle is the key to the integrity of the law.[60] The 'adjudicative principle', Dworkin said, 'instructs judges to identify legal rights and duties, so far as possible, on the assumption that they were all created by a single author – the community personified – expressing a coherent conception of justice and fairness.'[61]

Essentially, whatever Dworkin may claim, his theory is a world view rather than a theory of judicial reasoning. His emphasis on principles and the notion that judges can have recourse to a set of principles that are indwelling within the community expressing a coherent conception of justice and fairness are laudable, but far too much, as I have already demonstrated, is unrealistic. His distinction between rules and principles and between principles and policies; his view that principles embrace almost everything in the world that are not rules or policies so that, being bound to consider them, there is always a 'right' answer; and his effort to eliminate or reduce the scope of judicial discretion are all part

---

[58] See above, Chapter 7, at 195–201.
[59] R. Dworkin, 'Is Law a System of Rules?' in Robert S. Summers (ed.) *Essays in Legal Philosophy* (Basil Blackwell, Oxford, 1970), at 58.
[60] Ronald Dworkin, *Taking Rights Seriously* (Duchworth, London, 1977), at 217.
[61] Ibid., at 225.

of a gigantic hoax to sustain a perception of an impersonal law. We must again look elsewhere for a theory that will be both descriptively realistic and pragmatic and yet normative in a principled sense.

Legal principles

How then, do I define a legal principle? I do so with much less precision than the theorists I have discussed. Such flexibility is inevitable in that I fully recognise the unreality of seeking to draw a sharp distinction between rules and principles and policies and principles. Essentially, a legal principle is a norm, interest or value couched in relatively general terms that commands general respect and acceptance in the legal process. It will necessarily reflect and embody values and standards but, because those values and standards will change and vary, a principle cannot be excused repeated re-evaluation against the objectives of the law and legal process. Applied to particular situations a recognised principle can provide a persuasive basis for a decision. But it does not have coercive force. In a real sense, it can be seen to represent the accumulated wisdom and experience of past judges without displacing the wisdom and experience of the present judges who must decide the instant case. Consequently, I regard the true value of general principles to lie, not so much in their content, as in the purpose they serve in the legal process. But before elaborating this purpose let me spell out what I am *not* saying about legal principles.

First, I am not suggesting that principles are not elusive. It would be nonsense not to recognise that, as a matter of reality, the law is inherently uncertain – except for principles which magically acquire a certitude denied all other features of the law! Cardozo was correct in saying that 'cases do not unfold their principles for the asking. They yield up their kernels slowly and painfully.'[62] Because of their generality and reflection of a generally accepted norm, value or standard, however, they are likely to obtain greater permanence than more specific rules directed at particular factual situations, none of which will necessarily be the same. Operating at a higher level, principles are not as subject to the complexities and vagaries of the everyday situations that arise for resolution in the courts as are rules. But principles may still be difficult to discern.[63] Many may,

---

[62] Cardozo, *The Judicial Process*, at 29.
[63] See the dictum of Lord Reid in *Scruttons Ltd* v *Midland Silicones Ltd* [1962] AC 446, at 477.

even when discerned, still be difficult to define with precision, and will still be subject to dispute and argument about both their existence and definition. Nothing will alter the ultimate indeterminacy of any component in the law.

It follows, in the second place, that I am not claiming that principles will not vary or conflict one with the other. Indeed, as principles reflect basic norms or values or standards, they will at times be in conflict. Then, the values underlying a principle must still be weighed and balanced against values underlying a conflicting principle. Just as one value must be chosen over another or compromised to accommodate the other, so too one principle must be preferred ahead of other principles or modified to take account of other competing principles. Cardozo was again undoubtedly correct in accepting that principles are constantly being 'retested' and in asserting that they may be reformulated.[64] Over time, I would add, they will be tested further and possibly reformulated yet again. All this is part of the dynamic of the common law and I am not suggesting that it be stilled. But it is a dynamic better undertaken at the level of general principles than more specific rules.

Nor am I suggesting that, notwithstanding the greater pre-eminence of principles, the point may not be reached where a principle should be allowed to pass away. Principles without exceptions are unlikely, but a principle with many exceptions is barely a principle. When to cry enough and announce the death of a principle will always be a question of judgement. But it is not a question which is entirely open-ended or without direction. If the principle has lost the rationale that brought it into existence and that would guide its extended application and development, it is best consigned to the vast graveyard of law that is no longer law.

In the third place, I am not suggesting that principles fill in the gaps in the law when the law is found wanting. They are not just the starting point for legal reasoning in 'hard' cases as Gray, Pound and many others would have it.[65] Rather, they provide the judge with the coordinating tools by which the objectives of the legal process can be achieved. Nor am I even remotely suggesting that principles will be 'neutral', or capable of neutral application as, for example, claimed by Wechsler.[66] Such a perception is unrealistic because principles are generally laden with values. It would also deny the legal process creativity and be a recipe for inaction.[67] Nor do I suggest that principles give rise to concrete

---

[64] Cardozo, *The Judicial Process*, at 23.   [65] See above, at 339–340.
[66] Wechsler, 'Towards Neutral Principles' (1959) 73 Harv. LR, 1.
[67] See Duxbury, *Patterns of American Jurisprudence*, at 275.

rights. Principles may be called in aid by persons wishing to assert a right to give their claim weight or authority, but they are not definitive of a right.

What, then, gives a principle its 'legal' quality or function? My perception is that principles provide the law or legal process with cohesion and continuity. They cohere one rule and another and one case and another. They provide the link between the present case and the next similar case, even though the principle in the later case may be rejected or reformulated. They provide the mechanism by which the accumulated wisdom and experience of the past is brought forward to be utilised and, if necessary, also updated. They provide the means by which values outside the law are introduced into the law. They, and not precedents, make up the 'glue' that holds the system together and give it its overall identity as a legal order. It is this capacity to provide coherence and continuity in the legal process, and nothing more, that gives principles their primacy in that process.

For the most part, of course, unlike a specific rule, a principle that is not accepted or applied in a particular case will not be rejected outright. Where principles conflict it will be a matter of giving one or the other greater weight. The disappointed principle will not necessarily be discarded but simply held not to be applicable or not to outweigh the competing principle or another interest or value, and be deferred for possible use on another day. In this way a balance is struck between two opposing general principles without either necessarily being dealt a disabling blow. Where the balance is struck will be determined by reference to one or more of the community of considerations as a whole. Thus, while principles obtain a high profile, they do not necessarily 'trump' other considerations. So the judge may refer with favour to policy considerations, to other developments in the law, to extra-judicial but relevant material, to the reasonable expectations of the community or, indeed, to a conception of justice specific to the instant case. Principles may be the primary tools of judicial adjudication, but they do not need to oust other considerations or exercise a coercive influence in the reasoning or decision-making process.

In contrast to principles, other considerations, whether interests or values, may have an identity apart from the particular case, but they need not be regarded as having any relevance outside the particular case. Such considerations can be regarded as specific to the instant case. Principles may not be all that different in their generality to the interests and values these considerations embody, but their value is greater than their mere value to the particular case. They must connect into or relate to other principles so as to provide the cohesion and continuity which the legal process requires. Interests and values, standards or any other consideration, on the one hand, and principles, on the other, are all tools at the judge's disposal, but they are managed differently. The former are immediate and disposable. The latter may be rejected or reformulated, but nevertheless have the independent purpose of connecting with the ongoing body of legal principles. Eventually, and possibly in some areas more so than others, a broad net of principles will be woven from which particular principles may be drawn, as and when required, and others repaired and replaced, as and when required.

From what I have said it can be seen that the way in which principles are managed provides a principled approach. But it is not the 'principled approach' so beloved by judges and lawyers of a formalist persuasion. To them, a 'principled approach' is abiding by a precedent, however out of date and unsuitable it may be for modern conditions. Such an approach is said to be 'principled' because it does not challenge the orthodox methodology. This usage is an ersatz use of the phrase 'principled approach' and comes close to being a synonym for formalism. There is nothing principled about it. The approach simply assumes that the doctrines of precedent and *stare decisis* are paramount and that faithful deference to these doctrines will somehow make the judge's behaviour 'principled'. Chapters 6 and 7 give the lie to this assumption.

As I said when outlining my preferred version of practical reasoning based on realism and pragmatism, principles become a paramount part of that reasoning process. But my emphasis on principles must raise the question whether pragmatism and principles are compatible. I have no difficulty with this question. Certainly, there is a problem if principles are vested with an unnecessary rigidity. Pragmatism is then edged out. It is difficult to both apply a principle because to do so is necessary for the legitimacy or integrity of the legal process and at the same time be pragmatic. But the view of principles that I have put forward does not own this difficulty. Principles are treated pragmatically. They are subservient to the functional objective of the law. They will at times come from sources outside the law. They are subject to being deferred in favour of other interests or values that the judge may wish to take into account in resolving the case. The primacy or ascendancy of principles in the legal order is of a different kind. It is the quality that enables them to bring an overall cohesion and continuity to the legal process, and nothing more, which gives them that higher profile.

Conclusion

The analysis of practical reasoning developed by a number of legal theorists is commendable. Practical reasoning is valuable in recognising that at a certain point in the process of judicial decision-making, a judge may become dissatisfied with the outcome directed by the perceived existing law and wish to modify or extend the law. It is also valuable in that it emphasises the fact that judges look to the body of existing law for support and then seek to fit their decision into that context.

Without jettisoning the need for practical reasoning, however, I have sought to show that the conventional analysis of practical reasoning is deficient in that it is prone to be captured by formalism; it fails to introduce into the reasoning process the criteria that may give rise to the sense of dissatisfaction the judge may experience with an existing rule or body of law; it is too 'rulish' in that it is inclined to accept without re-evaluation an existing rule thus creating a presumption in favour of the application of that rule rather than treating it as a starting point and re-evaluating it from the outset; and it fails to absorb the fact that, as the law is inherently uncertain, doubt is likely to infect the existence, content, and scope of a rule so that dissatisfaction may arise out of nothing more than the uncertainty of the so-called existing law.

It is largely for these reasons that I have rejected the notion of a 'presumptive' application of a rule or principle if it seems to fit the particular case. Certainly, there must be a starting point, and that starting point may be a rule or principle, but to be effective and true to its design, the rule or principle must be open to re-evaluation before being take further in the reasoning process. Judicial reasoning can be expected to be less intuitive and more focused, less legalistic and more open and transparent, and less divergent and more likely to achieve a closer judicial concordance than pertains at present.

Practical reasoning is essentially concerned with the determination of the choices that must be made in the course of judicial decision-making. It provides both the procedure and framework for the exercise of those choices and the means by which those choices can be explained in the most effective and persuasive manner. The choices begin with the determination of the facts of the case, a function that is of overriding importance in the judicial process if justice is to be done in the individual case. For that reason I have exploited the opportunity to provide a practical discourse on the topic. Deciding what facts are relevant, defining the legal issue, selecting the initial premise on which to base the necessary reasoning and identifying the interests or values involved follow. Ultimately, judges are seized of a community of considerations that they must balance one against the other in accordance with their best translation of the community values which underlie those considerations.

Principles assume a pre-eminent position among the community of considerations to which the judge will have regard in reaching a decision. They will dominate rules and prevail over precedent and yet retain the flexibility necessary for a dynamic legal system; one in which there is no sharp distinction between principles and rules and principles and policies. As with other components of the law, I also deny principles any coercive force. They gain such force as they command by virtue of the strength and relevance of the norm, interest or value that they embody. Realism means that they are not absolute, that they do not necessarily 'trump' other considerations, that they can be elusive, that they may often conflict one with the other, and that they are seldom if ever value-neutral. Principles, therefore, no less than any other component of the law, must also be open to constant re-evaluation. Principles, too, are subject to the twin goals of justice and relevance.

I have been concerned to demonstrate, however, that this more elastic definition of principles does not mean that they do not have a critical role in the judicial process. The role I have marked out is one of providing the law or legal process with cohesion and continuity. They provide a framework, albeit a flexible framework, for judicial reasoning enabling the judge to cohere different elements in the law in an ordered and orderly fashion, to take advantage of the wisdom and experience of the past without being cowered by it, and to introduce into the law current values and reconcile those values with what has gone before. It is this unique capacity to provide the judicial process with coherence and continuity that give principles primacy in that process. In a sense, principles serve to do what common lawyers look to the doctrine of precedent to do at present. But they will achieve that goal in a manner that will make the law more sensitive to the achievement of justice in the individual case and to securing a law that is in harmony with the times. The metaphor is optional; principles, and not rules, precedent or any other component of the law, are either the 'glue' that binds, or the 'chain' that links, an otherwise disparate body of law into a coherent whole.

14

Taking law seriously

So, will there be a difference?

The point in seeking to bridge the gap between legal theory and legal practice and evolve a comprehensive perception of the judicial role is that it would make a difference in practice. Changes in the judicial process and judicial methodology should eventuate. But is this wishful thinking? Would acceptance of the conception of the judicial role and approach I have advanced do much more, if anything, than make overt in judicial conduct and reasoning that which is already being done covertly? Will the desired changes in attitude and practice occur in any event? What would the main differences be if more and more judges adopted the judicial methodology I have put forward? These questions can be briefly addressed in this penultimate chapter.

Making overt that which is covert

Certainly, acceptance of the recommended methodology would make overt much that is presently been done by judges covertly. I do not doubt for one moment that those judges who are coerced, condemned or otherwise persuaded to read this book will frequently have said to themselves; 'Well, I already do that', or 'That [criticism] may be so of other judges, but it is not true of me.' Judges do not admit to be lacking in realism, pragmatism, creativity, common sense, a sense of justice or any of the other attributes I have extolled.

To some extent, the disparity between actual practice and the self-perception – or self-deception – is due to the fact that a number of the aspects of the process I propose are being performed unconsciously or furtively. All judges, for example, know that they make law, but many will refuse to acknowledge that to be the case when they do so. They prefer to pretend that they have interpreted 'the law'. Again, judges, or many of them, are concerned to do justice, but they will bury that value in a discussion of principle or policy, or even find that the just outcome can be reached by 'reinterpreting' a precedent without referring to the conception of justice that is driving their decision. Again, most judges know that their decision is based on a value judgement, but more often than not they decline to expose that value to public scrutiny. When judges of intelligence and ability operate within a calling that is centuries old, that clings to an oblique mystique, that is innately backward looking and conservative, and that persists in doubting its own legitimacy, it is to be expected that what is actually done will depart from what is actually said.

Without a doubt, therefore, the adoption of the methodology I have recommended will lead to the judicial process being much more open and transparent. Judges could be more than candid, they could be honest. Their value judgements would be disclosed and discussed. When they change the law they would openly say so and justify the change. Silly pretences, such as placing a slant on the facts or insisting upon a strained distinguishing of a precedent, would be abandoned. The temptation, to which not a few judges succumb, of reaching their decision on the basis of what the law 'ought' to be, but then presenting that decision as being what law actually 'is' would be resisted. Formalised rationalisations of a decision would be replaced by a discussion of the real reasons. All this would be to, at least, make overt much that many covertly desire.

The flow of the river ...

I am tempted to adopt James Lowell's observation made several centuries ago; there is no good in arguing with the inevitable. 'The only argument available with an east wind,' he said, 'is to put on your overcoat.'[1] But I reject the metaphor because a wind can blow in different directions. For the past century and a half there has been an assuredness about the trend of the law that does not suggest that it will change direction, and I believe that the methodology advanced in this book embodies that trend. Better, then, to compare the common law with a mighty river: at times it may flow shallowly, at other times deeply; at times it may flow narrowly, at other times broadly; and at times it may flow swiftly, at other times sluggishly; but at all times it flows in the one direction.

Is it too much to expect, therefore, that in the fullness of time the conception of the judicial role and the methodology outlined in this

---

[1] James Russell Lowell, 1819–1891, *Democracy, and Other Addresses* (Houghton, Mifflin, 1887).

book will develop in any event? Why spell it out? In law, one should never be right too soon. Indeed, the very articulation of that role and methodology may result in a reaction which will retard its progress. Yet, the trend is plainly there. One only has to look at the progress which the law has made over the last two centuries to perceive a trend in both the judicial approach and the content of the law. Judges have moved away from the strict formalism that prevailed at the turn of the twentieth century to embrace a more substantive approach, albeit one exhibiting the residual influence of that creed, and the content of the law has changed correspondingly. Equitable principles and concepts of fairness and justice have ameliorated the rigidity of the black letter law that was the rule. This trend will surely continue. It is a progression that is elemental to the imperative that the law serve society and the demand for law to meet the needs and reasonable expectations of the community. Legal evolution of this kind in this direction is indigenous to the functional requirement for the law to change in a changing society.

At what point, assuming this trend will continue, the judicial process will reach a stage along the lines that I have described in this book is uncertain. The evolution of the proposed methodology, or a methodology closely allied to it, however, does not mean that it should not be foreshadowed. I have already acknowledged the risk that spelling out the methodology may inspire resistance that will retard the evolutionary process. But one must be optimistic and hold to the belief that the articulation of the methodology will hasten the demise of the present formalistically influenced approach and lead to a judicial process in harmony with the requirements of the twenty-first century – sooner rather than later.

The main differences

I am therefore under no illusion that I may be merely anticipating a future legal regime. But I have little interest in prediction. The judicial methodology I have advanced can be justified in its own right. Apart from making overt much that is now covert, it would result in changes that would be of immediate advantage to both the administration of the law and the legal process and be of corresponding benefit to society. With one exception, the main differences may be briefly touched upon.

That exception is the substantive changes that could be expected to occur in the law with the adoption of the new legal order. As this book is about legal theory and practice, and embraces a conception of the judicial role and a particular judicial methodology, it would be an unwarranted digression to seek to project what changes could be expected in the substance or content of the law. Indeed, such a digression could well prove a distraction. Obviously, changes in the content of the law will occur, for it will be relatively easier and simpler to address areas of deficiency in the law and the developments necessary to rectify those deficiencies. But the substantive changes that might eventuate as a result must be left open.

Further, virtually by definition, judges imbued with the new methodology will be more realistic and pragmatic. Those attitudes are a prerequisite to practical reasoning with its primary emphasis on principles. But these changes in large part make up the new methodology. We are here concerned with the main differences that will flow from the adoption of that methodology.

In the first place, more judges will be familiar with legal theory and develop a sound conception of the judicial role. They will cast a critical eye over the historical theories that directed judicial reasoning into the formalist mould. Obsolete approaches will be foresworn. The most dramatic change in judicial outlook will flow from the conscious abandonment of those discredited and outdated theories, including their lingering influence. While not every judge's theory or conception of the judicial role will be the same, judicial discourse will assume a new dimension in which judicial intuition will be more closely monitored. In many respects, judicial reasoning will be more structured as judges confront the basic questions underlying their decisions. The key features of practical reasoning will or should provide greater common ground or a greater common focus for the judges' reasoning. Being better informed and structured, judicial discourse should be more congruent.

Secondly, as already stressed, judges working to the new methodology will necessarily be concerned to make their reasoning more transparent and open. As a result, academic and public debate on the real reasons for a decision would be greatly assisted and judges would at once be more accountable for their decisions. Judges who sheltered behind formalism or formalistic platitudes and did not fully explain their decision-making process would be quickly thought of as belonging to a bygone age. Being more realistic, pragmatic and practical, the open and transparent reasoning of judges adopting the new methodology would be seen to be superior to the reasoning of those judges still unable to face up to the inherent uncertainty of the law and embroiled in the more artificial reasoning deriving from a penchant for formalism and a willing acceptance of the coercive element in the doctrine of precedent. Rationalisation would be exposed for what it is, an attempt to present a plausible but specious explanation for a decision arrived at on another and undisclosed basis. Disclosing the real basis would make judicial discourse accessible to a wider constituency.

The third difference that would result is that judges imbued with the new methodology would tend to be more creative. Justice cannot always be done in the particular case without a measure of creativity. Nor can the law often be developed to meet changing requirements without an open display of such creativity. An innovative capacity to develop the law in both its legal and social context working within the constraints to which the judiciary is subject would be requisite. The 'is' and the 'ought' in the law are more readily conjugated.

On the face of it, a rub emerges. Observation would suggest that not every judge is capable of being creative. The suspicion exists that, at times, a less formalistic approach to judicial decision-making by a judge is resisted because of the judge's fear that his or her limited ability to be innovative will be exposed. As has been indicated, legal training, legal practice and legal theory tends to suppress creativity in the law. But I am not worried about this possible problem for two reasons. First, most judges have the capacity to be creative or to develop that capacity. It is not possible to be intelligent and not be creative unless that intelligence has been captured or cordoned off by a persuasion that is hostile to such creativity. Secondly, the new methodology would tend to make the antithesis between creativity, on the one hand, and non-creativity, on the other, otiose. The notion of creativity in the law is to some extent the product of a rule-oriented and precedent-directed legal process. Creativity is the facility, desirable or undesirable depending on the individual's perspective, to break free from the conservatism of that regime. Once the new methodology is adopted, however, the antithesis or tension between creativity and non-creativity would effectively disappear. The objective of judicial inquiry would be to utilise the relatively settled rules and principles, along with other interests and values forming part of the community of considerations, as tools to achieve a just outcome or to ensure that the law is developed in keeping with the changing requirements of the times. That being the objective of the inquiry, and with no formalistic rule-bound or precedent-directed base to depart from, judicial creativity should not be an issue. It will be subsumed in the methodology itself and contained by the constraints that are explicit in that methodology.

Fourthly, the judge practising the new methodology will be committed to substance ahead of form. This commitment is necessary for the judge cannot know what is just or fair unless the reality or substance of the matter in issue is preferred. As already said, a commitment to substance over form is a key ingredient of the non-formalistic approach.[2] The judge will recognise the open-ended nature of the common law and seek to avoid absolute rules or a near absolute prescription that will tend to crimp the dynamic of the law.[3] He or she will be both cautious and flexible in laying down rules which might fetter scope for the exercise of judicial discretion.[4]

The fifth difference to arise relates to the notions of certainty and predicability in the law. Without doubt, the acclamation of judicial autonomy in the proposed methodology will concern many, and terrify some. They will proclaim that the law will become a formless, amorphous, inchoate, hideous, idiosyncratic pottage of half-baked ideas of no value to anyone seeking to order their personal affairs in accordance with the law or looking to the law to provide stability in an ever-changing world. A keen appreciation of the constraints to which the judiciary is subject, together with those that will develop in accordance with the recommended methodology, will prevent any such proclamation gaining ascendancy. Further, with the elimination or reduction of formalism, or its traces, it is undeniable that the uncertainties that have been shown to attach to that approach will also be eliminated or reduced. Certainty will persist as a valid consideration where certainty and predictability actually matter.

Finally, it is self-evident that justice and relevance would loom larger in judicial reasoning. The courts' output would include more decisions in which a conception of justice is overtly applied in the individual case and rulings given that are deliberately in keeping with the needs and expectations of the times. This concentration on justice and relevance follows automatically from a functional perception of the law and the resulting conception of the judicial role and concomitant judicial methodology.

Taking law seriously

Not a few legal theorists openly, and all too many judges privately, describe the legal process as a game or, by analogy, liken it to a game. Rawls, for one, utilised the analogy of a game to explain his 'practice conception', the establishment of a practice that 'involves the abdication of full liberty to act on utilitarian and prudential grounds.'[5] Hart sought to rebut rule

---

[2] See above, Chapter 12, at 312. [3] See above, Chapter 12, at 312–313.
[4] See above, Chapter 10, at 266–267.
[5] J. Rawls, 'Two Concepts of Rules' (1955) in Rawls' Collected Papers (Harvard University Press, Cambridge, Mass., 1999), at 36–38.

scepticism by comparing legal rules with the rules of a game. Such rules, as with other rules, have a core of settled meaning.[6] Dworkin, too, is fascinated by the analogy. He uses the similarity of legal rules to rules of games to assist in explaining his distinction between rules and principles, and then, later in time when developing his theory of interpretation or 'interpretative attitude.'[7] Although perhaps of a different kind, Allan Hutchinson advances an unnerving account of legal reasoning or adjudication as a way of playing the game of life. There is, he says, no final or privileged way to play law's game that explains and grounds all others that is not a game itself.[8]

Drawing an analogy between the law and rules of a game may be harmless enough in theory. But it is hopelessly astray simply because of the relative certainty of the rules of games and the absence in such rules of underlying or competing moral considerations.[9] Fernando Atria has highlighted the unconvincing nature of this comparison. In games there is little disagreement about what the rules are or about how they should be applied.[10] Rule scepticism would be misplaced. The controversial nature of legal rules sets them apart from the rules of a game. In games hard cases do not arise because the rules are not left open for future settlement, unless they are specifically left open. Participating in the game signifies acceptance of the rules.[11]

For practitioners of the law the analogy has two unfortunate consequences. First, it serves to obscure the reality of the law and legal process. It suggests a regime in which rules obtain a certitude that they are denied in reality. Formalism or a formalistic approach is promoted. Rules in games cannot be described as inherently uncertain as I have defined that phrase. A hulking lock in a game of rugby union would quickly find himself in the sin bin if he chose to challenge the rule against interference in a line out or the referee's interpretation or application of that rule. In short, the analogy prompts a picture of the law which is so simplistic as to be chimerical.

---

[6] H. L. A. Hart, *The Concept of Law* (Clarendon Press, Oxford, 1994), at 144–145.
[7] Dworkin, *Taking Rights Seriously* (Duckworth, London, 1977), at 24, and *Laws Empire*, at 47, respectively.
[8] Allan C. Hutchinson, 'The Reasoning Game: Some Pragmatic Suggestions' (1998) 61 MLR 263, at 264.
[9] Fernando Atria, *On Law and Legal Reasoning* (Hart Publishing, Oxford and Portland Oregon, 2001), at 8.
[10] Ibid., at 6–8. [11] Ibid., at 92.

Secondly, and here I express a personal antagonism, the analogy lends itself to a cynical regard to the law and legal process. Few comments are more irksome than the occasional observation from a bemused or bewildered judge; 'It [the law] is just a game.' One can, of course, understand how the cynicism develops at present. Judges can quite rightly become frustrated with the laws devices; the pretence that there is a recognised rule to apply when the rule in question is in fact contested and controversial; the fiction that there is an impersonal law and that the judge is not making law or policy when the judge knows perfectly well that this is just what he or she is doing; the manipulation involved in purporting to adhere to the doctrine of precedent while straining to distinguish or reinterpret a prior case because it poses an awkward authority standing in the way of the preferred decision; the enforced insincerity of buckling to the goal of certainty knowing, at least deep down, that the court's decision will do nothing to achieve certainty in the law and, indeed, may even add to its uncertainty; the façade involved in rationalising with formal reasoning a decision that is reached on grounds that are not disclosed or that remain obscure, and so on. The pretences, the fictions, the manipulations, the insincerity, the facades and all the other devices that presently beset the legal process must, in the absence of firm resistance, necessarily inculcate the notion that it is all 'just a game'.

But the law and legal process is not a game. Its impact on the lives of people is all too often too dramatic to be likened to a game. Judicial power is properly much less expansive than legislative power, but its exercise can be critical for the individual or groups who resort to the courts. Their lives, their assets, and their future are in the hands of the judge. A decision can make the difference between a person being financially successful or being ruined; it can bring joy or tragedy to a person and his or her household; it can cement or destroy personal, business and family relationships; it can wreak havoc for a person's life when harsh, callous or indifferent in its application; and it can lead to years or a lifetime of regret, anguish, grief, and even paranoia if, generally under the guise of formalism, it effects a real injustice. Having people's lives, assets and futures in their hands; it ill behoves judges to play, or toy, with that responsibility.

I am not, of course, suggesting that the new methodology proposed would eliminate all the deficiencies in the present system. Judges are human and a legal utopia will always elude us. But the legal process can be improved and it is that improvement that should be deliberately pursued by a conscientious and responsible judiciary.

I believe that judges are capable of embracing the proposed methodology with the same intelligence and ability that they have displayed in subjection to the methodologies of the past. In the fullness of time their mastery of the new methodology will be no less comprehensive. This will be so because judges are not bureaucrats applying pre-ordained rules; nor are they fundamentalists applying a rigid gospel unable to question the wisdom, validity and relevance of the law that they are called upon to administer; and nor are they mechanics dealing with the repair of things, but rather humane arbiters dealing with the affairs of people. By shedding the bonds of the past century and adopting a methodology designed for the times they will better perform their judicial role in the service of justice and the law.

15

A theory of ameliorative justice

Our Lady of Justice ... why the sword?

In her traditional posture, our Lady of Justice stands serenely blindfolded holding a pair of scales in the one hand and a sword in the other. The blindfold denotes that justice is blind to prejudice or pressure. Fearing, no doubt, that justice should not be thought to be also blind to the truth, the blindfold is often discarded in more recent portrayals.[1] The scales are invariably held in an outstretched hand enabling them to perform their balancing faculty. The sword is more mobile. It is sometimes brandished aloft and at other times sheathed within the folds of the good Lady's ample skirt.

We all know why justice is blind. Justice is objective and impartial, administered without fear or favour. She bears no ill will to any litigant, and all are equal before the law. Thus, justice is even-handed. The scales, we also know, symbolize the process by which one value or interest must be balanced against another value or interest to ensure that justice is done. A fair weighting is an irredeemable element in achieving justice.

But, why the sword? A weapon? It seems incongruous that our Lady of Justice should bear arms.[2]

Strangely enough, no one seems to know why the Lady of Justice carries a sword. It could be suggested, I suppose, that the sword confirms that justice is fearless; a warrior in the cause of justice. But many a coward has toted a weapon and why, if a show of fearlessness is required, would she on occasions billet it within the folds of her skirt? Justice is, of

---

[1] As Lord Denning said in *Jones* v *National Coal Board* [1957] 2 QB 55, at 64, 'It's all very well to paint justice blind, but she does better without a bandage round her eyes. She should be blind indeed to favour or prejudice, but clear to see which way lies the truth ...'

[2] Juvenal thought so in Roman times. 'There should', he proclaimed, 'be no sword in the hand of justice.' (*'tractanda putabat inermi justicia'*) Juvenal in his Satires (iv, 80), quoted by the Rt. Hon. Lord Denning in *The Closing Chapter* (Butterworths, London, 1983), at 275–276.

course, fearless of intimidation, but that notion is already embraced in the fact our Lady of Justice is blind to pressure, and that must include pressure of any kind. A militaristic symbol is not required to convey that virtue.

Lord Denning in the Epilogue to his book, *The Closing Chapter*,[3] suggests that the sword is the symbol of the authority by which justice is done. No judgment of any court and no order of any judge, he reasons, is of any use unless it can be enforced; and to be enforced it requires the authority of the state behind it. Thus, the sword of justice is the sword of the state. 'It is', Lord Denning states, 'the symbol of authority which must be upheld.'[4]

Lord Denning's conjecture that the sword symbolises the authority of the state can only be accepted in the broad sense that the justice administered in the courts is backed by the authority of the state. But our Lady of Justice holds out the promise that justice will be done in the individual case. It is in that respect that Lord Denning's theory is deficient. The authority of the state may be used to enforce an unjust judgment or order, or fail for a variety of reasons to enforce a just judgment or order. Enforcement or execution is a process that operates after justice has been done – or not done. It is an essential element of law and order, but not an integral facet of the justice administered in the courts. Moreover, the Lady is a lady. If the sword represented the coercive authority of the state one would expect the figure of justice to reflect a virile masculinity. That our less gender-sensitive forbears in ancient times chose to portray justice as a female would, perhaps, lead one to think that they had in mind such fair virtues as sensitivity, compassion and mercy.

I have been led to a less authoritarian explanation than that suggested by Lord Denning. Over the years, and particularly when on the bench, I noted that the common law seemed to possess an underlying design. It repeatedly sought to protect those who were vulnerable from being exploited by those in a position of power or dominance or having an unfair superiority. The law, it seemed, could be founded on an altruistic premise.

I concluded that the basic principles which pervade the law do in fact exhibit this inbuilt sense of justice. Justice, perceived as an extension of the concept of corrective justice, seeks to ameliorate the harsh extremes of liberal individualism and, in particular, the economic order,

---

[3] Ibid., at 275–277.   [4] Ibid., at 276–277.

capitalism, by returning the parties to the position they were in before the impeached transaction. No person may exploit another in the sense of taking or obtaining an unfair advantage at the other's expense. In this way the law serves to protect the weak and powerless from the machinations and unfair domination of the strong and powerful.

So there it is; our Lady of Justice bears a sword to protect those in our society who are vulnerable to exploitation from being unfairly exploited.

The precept of non-exploitation

The thesis of this chapter, therefore, is that a compunction underlies the whole spectrum of the common law that can be fittingly described as the precept of non-exploitation. It is the law's ultimate abhorrence of exploitation. The law insists upon a conception of equality that precludes a person from taking or obtaining an unfair advantage at the expense of another. Exploitation, of course, commonly connotes an oppressive form of one person taking advantage of another for one's own ends. Obviously, I use the phrase more broadly. While it includes this more aggressive form, the focus is on unfairly taking or obtaining an advantage at another's expense. The domination must be excessive. I therefore use, and will continue to use, the word 'exploitation' in a sense which assumes that the advantage taken or obtained is unjust or unfair.

The exploitation of which I speak is to be found in the fact that the freedom of one person, or the free choice which that person could exercise, is subject to the excessive domination of another. There can be no true freedom or free choice with that measure of domination.[5] A survey that reveals the deep and entrenched prevalence of this precept of non-exploitation in all branches of the law administered in the courts forms a substantive part of this chapter.

The theory is an extension of Aristotle's conception of corrective justice. Corrective justice is concerned with the interactions of and between persons (what Aristotle called 'transactions') and is limited to

---

[5] A projection of the idea of domination into the liberal tradition can be found in Philip Pettit's book, *Republicanism: A Theory of Freedom and Government* (Clarendon Press: New York and Oxford, 1997). Pettit advances a theory of freedom which he calls 'freedom as non-domination', and contrasts freedom based on the principle of non-domination with the more straightforward liberal definition of absence of constraints or absence of interference. Consequently, Pettit's theory may be seen as an attempt to import into the concept of freedom the notion that an individual's freedom is limited by and to the extent of the domination of another individual.

the parties to the interaction. Such persons are, for the purpose of the interaction, considered equal, no matter how unequal they may be in terms of their capability, capacity or any other comparative criterion. Thus, corrective justice involves a presumed equality of entitlement to the parties' respective positions prior to the interaction.[6] If any interaction results in an unjust benefit for one or an unjust burden to the other, corrective justice requires that the pre-existing equality be restored. Either the benefit must be disgorged or the loss flowing from the burden must be compensated. Unjust gains or losses are thereby corrected.

The theory does not invoke 'distributive justice', which is to be distinguished from corrective justice. Whereas corrective justice applies to individual transactions and requires that the effects of such interactions on the interacting parties be consistent with each parties' 'equal negative freedom',[7] distributive justice focuses more broadly on a person's status as a member of the political community and requires the community's resources to be distributed to promote the equal positive freedom of each person in the community.[8] Worthwhile efforts have been made to demonstrate that distributive justice enters into various facets of the law, although it has to be said that many attempts are strained and capable of bearing a different analysis.

Peter Cane has confirmed that much of the theoretical literature on distributive justice is huge and complex and pitched at a level of abstraction too high to be of much direct use to lawyers.[9] Cane's theory is to the effect that, when courts make rules about the circumstances in which tort liability to repair harm will arise, they contribute to the establishment of a pattern of distribution of the resources and burdens in society. In other words, his suggestion is that making rules that define the grounds and bounds of tort liability is a distributive task. I imagine

---

[6] See Richard W. Wright, 'Right, Justice and Tort Law' in David G. Owen (ed.), *Philosophical Foundations of Tort Law* (Clarendon Press, Oxford, 1995), at 166–174; and 'Substantive Corrective Justice' (1992) 77 Iowa LR 624, at 691.

[7] The principle of corrective justice expresses important moral values. It contains notions of fairness, equality, responsibility for the outcomes of one's choices and the importance of certain interests to human welfare. Jules Coleman provides an illuminating account of the role of corrective justice with respect to the costs and the misfortunes due to human agency. Jules Coleman, *The Practice of Principle: In Defence of a Pragmatist Approach to Legal Theory* (Oxford University Press, Oxford, 2001), at 5, and notes 4 and 5.

[8] See Owen, Foreword to *Philosophical Foundations of Tort Law*, at 12.

[9] Peter Cane, 'Distributive Justice and Tort Law' (2001) 4 NZLR, 401, at 419

that *Donoghue* v *Stevenson*[10] is itself an example of this pattern. The case involved the interaction between the consumer and manufacturer, but the outcome can be said to have had major distributive consequences. My short criticism of this theory is that the fact a pattern of distribution may emerge says nothing about the justice of the particular cases that make up that pattern. If the individual cases are 'just', the fact they are just cannot be due to the distributive pattern that may eventually emerge. A distributive 'pattern' cannot be automatically equated with distributive 'justice'.

Hence, the concept of distributive justice need not impinge upon the theory advanced in this chapter. That concept may or may not be perceived as a possible basis for another theory of justice existing parallel to or on a different level from the basic precept of non-exploitation. But the precept of non-exploitation rests squarely on the operation of corrective justice.

The presumption of equality of entitlement in the interactions or interpersonal relationships of individuals or groups arising out of corrective justice is fundamental to the precept of non-exploitation. There is a presumption in favour of an equality of deservedness. No-one may exploit or unfairly take advantage of another so as to vitiate that equal entitlement. That equal entitlement would be vitiated, and it would violate our notions of justice or fairness, if one person were able to unilaterally set the terms that govern the interaction or interpersonal relationship, without the other having some means of recourse if that person abused their position of power, dominance or superiority in setting those terms.

The precept of non-exploitation does not necessarily require a deliberate intention or positive act on the part of one party to obtain an advantage at another's expense. It is sufficient that the vulnerable party may suffer an unfair deprivation that, if uncorrected, will benefit the other. A marked example of such 'passive exploitation' is unjust enrichment, where one party would obtain an unexpected windfall if the parties were not restored, as best the law can do, to their respective positions prior to the interaction. In holding that the exploitation is 'wrong' or 'unfair', the courts reflect the expectations of the community as to what is fundamentally required of the law. It becomes an internal acknowledgement of the law's essential function.

---

[10] [1932] AC 56.

Of course, the precept of non-exploitation will not impinge upon every situation. Cases arise requiring resolution that do not involve any element of exploitation but that nevertheless require regulation in an ordered society. But the existence of these situations does not mean that the precept is not the motivating and moral force in achieving justice according to law.

Further, the precept of non-exploitation may be an unarticulated premise of a legal rule or principle. When applying the rule or principle, individual judges will unconsciously or unwittingly, or even mechanically, give effect to the precept. In this sense, the precept can be perceived to be larger than individual judges. They may be insensitive or indifferent to its command, or they may at times spoil or prejudice its delivery, but they cannot destroy its momentum any more than the occasional lapse in our personal behaviour banishes our troublesome conscience from contention.[11]

I am not concerned, however, to identify the theory as being purely descriptive of the law, that is, of the tools at the judge's disposal in resolving a case. Certainly, the precept of non-exploitation is to a greater or lesser extent ingrained in those tools, but it can still provide a judge with the norm by which to consciously develop the law where it is appropriate to do so. The more progressive or creative judges are likely to consciously pursue its mandate. In this way, at one and the same time, the precept is part of the judicial stock in trade and part of the process by which the law is developed in a way that is compatible with justice.

In what way, then, is the theory an 'ameliorative' theory of justice? The theory is ameliorative in that the law is perceived to be the social instrument by which the untrammelled prevalence of exploitation in a society committed to liberal individualism and its underlying economic order, capitalism, is curbed or mitigated. Liberal individualism vaunts individual freedom that, unless checked, can give rise to uncivil and harsh effects that necessarily impinge on the freedom of others. The plight of the latter is alleviated by the intervention of a law in which the precept of non-exploitation is firmly entrenched. Of course, it is not every uncivil or harsh effect that attracts the attention of the law. Liberal individualism and capitalism require a latitude that the courts are pleased to recognise. But the existence of this latitude does not detract from a theory of justice based on the precept of non-exploitation.

---

[11] There are, perhaps, shades of Ronald Dworkin's soundest theory of law in the assertion of a moral premise larger than individual judges. But I would reject the suggestion. See my criticism of Dworkin in Chapter 8.

The ground is cleared – a reconciliation

Any such precept of non-exploitation must, of course, be consistent with the theory of judicial adjudication advanced in the earlier chapters of this book. Three questions or aspects might benefit from immediate clarification.

First, how can it be said that there is no impersonal or transcendent law if a drive or imperative to protect the weak and powerless from unfair exploitation by the strong and powerful is entrenched in the law? Does the precept of non-exploitation not represent a bias that may fairly be described as an immanent property or intelligibility in the law?

As will shortly become clear, I reject this suggestion. The precept of non-exploitation is a theory of justice rather than a theory of the law. In correcting the imbalance between the weak and powerless and the strong and powerful, judges have understandably drawn a line beyond which citizens may not exert the freedom that liberal individualism otherwise confers. To fail to draw that line would be to fail to deliver the justice that the community looks for and expects in the administration of the law. In this manner the interaction of persons within society is regulated in accordance with a basic precept of justice, but that does not mean that the law is impersonal or transcendent. The law and the administration of the law can be infused with a sense of justice without rendering that law an impersonal or transcendent law. Indeed, to the extent that the question as to what is just, or not just, cannot wholly avoid the subjective evaluation of the deciding judge, the opposite is more often the case.

The second aspect requiring preliminary clarification relates to the fact that the common law is judge-made and, because the dynamic of the common law cannot be suppressed, will be made and remade by each generation of judges. Judicial autonomy is, I have argued, both inevitable and desirable. If the law is founded on an altruistic premise, however, does that not mean that this altruism must be ascribed to the judges who administer and develop the law? It has to be said at once that any such ascription would fail miserably to cope with the common perception of judges who administer the law.

By and large, judges are perceived as a conservative, middle to upper class, frequently second or third generational privileged elite.[12] Irrespective of their professed judicial neutrality, judges, it is thought,

---

[12] See Lord Justice Scrutton in an address to the University of Cambridge Law Society on 18 November 1920: 'The Work of the Commercial Courts' (1923) 1 Camb LJ 6, at 8.

mirror the attitudes, beliefs and prejudices of that elite. Professor Griffith concluded that judges are, like the rest of us, 'not all of a piece'.[13] They are liable to be swayed by emotional prejudices. Their 'inarticulate major premises' are not only unarticulated but are also sometimes unknown to themselves. Yet, those unarticulated and at times unknown premises may be strongly, if not passionately, felt.[14]

Cardozo made much the same point, although more benignly. He wrote that, throughout all their lives, forces that judges do not recognise and cannot name have been tugging at them — inherited instincts, traditional beliefs and acquired convictions. The result is an outlook on life and a conception of social needs which, when reasons are nicely balanced, must determine where the judge's choice will fall.[15]

There can be no doubt that judges tend to reflect their relatively privileged background, education, and social and economic grouping. They lean to the traditional, the conventional and the conforming view; they are concerned to preserve and protect the existing order; and they can manifest the prejudices and emotional responses prevalent in the more advantaged and established sections of the community from which they come. To suggest that such judges are imbued with the perception that justice manifests itself in protecting the weak and powerless from the machinations and domination of the strong and powerful would be plainly unrealistic.

What is clear, however, is that, notwithstanding their relatively privileged background, education and social and economic grouping, judges on the whole manage to reflect the values immanent in the community. As we have seen,[16] there are many reasons why this is so: judges are professional people fully conscious of the requirements of independence and impartiality that are vital to the judicial performance of their duties; they work within a judicial methodology and are subject to extensive judicial constraints that are directed to assist them rise above their personal background and experience; and judges, whatever their privilege and standing, live, work and spend their leisure time in the community.

---

[13] J. A. G. Griffith, *The Politics of the Judiciary* (1st edn, Manchester University Press, Manchester, 1977) at 180.
[14] Ibid.
[15] Benjamin N. Cardozo, *The Nature of Judicial Process* (Yale University Press, New Haven, 1921), at 12.
[16] See above, Chapter 13, at 331–334.

Most significantly, values generally, such as a conception of justice in a particular case, tend to be indifferent to different backgrounds, education and social and economic standing. Unfair discriminatory treatment is unfair discrimination whether it applies to train drivers or the chauffeur-driven owners of Mercedes; dishonest and deceitful behaviour is anti-social whether it takes place in the office of an accountant or the office of an influential member of a racing club; natural justice is breached irrespective whether the person denied a hearing is a third-rate pugilist fighting to retain his licence or a distinguished chief executive determined to retain his or her jeopardised status; and a broken promise is a broken promise whether the person who has been duped toils in a clothing factory in the nearby industrial estate or plays cards at the bridge club in the more pleasant environs of the adjoining neighbourhood. In a reasonably homogenous society, values can override sectional or class interests and transcend social and economic barriers.

I do not therefore seek to implant into the present theory a moral shibboleth grandly espoused by judges when carrying out their judicial tasks. On the contrary, it is a search for an imperative or drive infusing the law independently of the temporal responses of mere judges.

The final preliminary point requiring clarification relates to my perception that, apart from it being a deliberative and reflective process, the judicial process is singularly independent and impartial, and that it is those qualities which render the process immune to the relative strength, power and coincident advantages of the respective litigants.[17] This claim must be reconciled with a theory of justice that curbs those who possess the strength or power or other coincident advantage from unfairly using those advantages to exploit those who are vulnerable to their use. Can it be claimed that the administration of the law possesses the independence and impartiality that I have stressed if it favours the vulnerable? Or, to put the point another way, how can it be said that the law is indifferent to the strength, power or coincident advantages of the parties if it works to protect the party who lacks those advantages from exploitation? A quick analysis confirms that any tension or inconsistency in this regard is more apparent than real.

The courts' ever-present touchstone of relevance provides the answer. It is only the strength or power or advantage that is unfairly used to effect the exploitation that is relevant. The element of exploitation must be present and must be directly related to the question in issue.

---

[17] See above, Chapter 4, at 78–79.

Extraneous advantages are ignored. For example, a large corporation may possess disproportionate wealth, economic dominance, political clout, ready access to the media and many other material blessings that can be of value in resolving a dispute in the political process. But these attributes will be of no juridical value in the context of a dispute in the legal arena. Such advantages are irrelevant to the resolution of the question in issue.[18]

Furthermore, the particular strength, power or advantage being exploited may be that of a small company or individual in conflict with a much larger corporation. A relatively impecunious individual, for example, who has taken advantage of inside knowledge or misused confidential information to the detriment of a wealthy corporation, has exploited the advantage he or she has obtained from possessing that inside knowledge or information. In such circumstances, the greater strength, power or wealth of the corporation is irrelevant as is the relative weakness, powerlessness or impecuniosity of the exploiter. As to be expected of a theory based on corrective justice, it is the advantage unfairly taken and in issue in the proceedings and not the overall position or status of the respective parties that is germane to the precept of non-exploitation. More often than not, of course, the strength, power and coincident advantages will be the assets of the larger and wealthier participants in a capitalistic economy. But for the purposes of a theory based on corrective justice, the beneficiary of the law is the party who is vulnerable to unfair exploitation by another.

But before expanding the theory further, I must also venture some general observations about that nebulous concept, justice.

The ground is further cleared – justice?

Justice is an elusive concept. It seems to defy definition. The most intelligent and erudite of philosophers and legal theorists are unable to essay a determinative theory. When a comprehensive theory is attempted, as in the case of John Rawls,[19] the forests of Chile are

---

[18] I do not overlook the advantage an affluent litigant obtains in litigation against a relatively poorer party in being able to prepare and present a stronger case and in being able to use the costs of litigation as a strategic means of obtaining a more favourable outcome or settlement. This is a different kind of advantage outside the scope of corrective justice.

[19] John Rawls, *A Theory of Justice* (Oxford University Press, Oxford, 1972). Rawls assayed a comprehensive theory of justice directed at the fair ordering of resources in society. It

dramatically thinned as paper is produced to cope with the mountainous and never-ending criticism of that theory. It continues to irk us that no more definitive definition of a concept that is so central to society is attainable.

Consider for a moment the vast variety of senses in which we use the word 'justice'. We refer to corrective justice and distributive justice, to substantive or material justice and procedural justice, to social justice and justice in the individual case, to legal or formal justice, to natural justice or due process, and to many more variants of this phenomenon called 'justice'. We take the Justinian precept that 'justice is the set and constant purpose to give every man his due' without agreeing on what is a person's 'due'. We use justice in the sense of righting wrongs, whether by the imposition of punishment, the payment of compensation or by restitution, without being clear on the 'wrongs', or why it is just to right them. We invoke justice to support the idea that a person's expectations should be fulfilled when, clearly, some expectations should not be fulfilled. We utilise justice to promote an ideal, whether a desirable family relationship or a social or political system or institution, and at times we usurp it to bolster an ideology and so provide that ideology with a false legitimacy. We equate impartiality with justice even though an impartial arbiter may arrive at a finding we consider substantively unjust. We recoil in the name of justice at the notion that persons in an equal position should receive less than equal treatment, at least, unless some justification is proffered to explain or mitigate the inequality or different treatment. We insist, in the name of justice, on the ideal of basic human equality or worth, but temper its consequences with notions of merit.[20] We ally justice with notions of basic rights, entitlement, empowerment, and the condemnation of oppression or domination, and all too quickly lapse into the expedient convenience of rhetoric. We assert an absolute or universal concept of justice, but are yet forced to concede that different cultures have different beliefs as to what is just and unjust. But still, as the crescendo of disagreement and variation mounts, we strive for a unifying feature.

I have been brought to the view that there is no such thing as justice in the abstract or, if there is, that it will forever defy our abilities to discern its abstract essence. It is therefore largely a futile exercise for

---

is to be emphasised that the theory which I advance in this chapter is much more limited being relative to the adjudicative process. See below, at 371.

[20] See Tom Campbell, *Justice* (St Martin's Press, LLC, Basingstoke, 1988) for a comprehensive treatment of the subject.

philosophers, legal theorists and other commentators to seek to define justice in the abstract or to seek to identify a unifying feature. Justice exists, of course, but it has no abstract meaning divorced from a particular context. It is so multi-faceted and diverse that no universal or common element emerges for us to seize upon. As already indicated, it is incomplete to say that justice requires that every person be given their due. What, then, is their due? The question is begged, at least until placed in a concrete situation in which an aggrieved person claims not to have received his or her due. Then the argument becomes clear. There is then a reason why it is claimed that the act is that person's due or why that person has received something that is not his or her due. The unfairness is exposed. One only has to take the simple example of a neighbour who has borrowed one's lawnmower and failed or refused to return it to perceive what is one's due.

We do not appear to have the same difficulty distilling the abstract or universal meaning from other concepts such as, to take random examples, 'dignity', or 'humaneness', or 'virtue', or 'utilitarianism', or 'love'. To speak of the 'dignity' of people is to speak of their essential worth as individual human beings; to speak of 'humaneness' is to speak of benevolent or compassionate conduct; to speak of 'virtue' is to speak of moral excellence and goodness; to speak of 'utilitarianism' is to refer to the usefulness of some act for the benefit of the majority; and to speak of 'love' is to speak of an intense feeling of affection or fondness for another person or persons. Even morality, when thought of in abstract terms, connotes the degree of conformity with ideas, practices or principles that are concerned with the goodness or badness of human character or behaviour and with the distinction between right and wrong, and the abstract concept loses nothing in definition because what is good or bad or right or wrong may be open to disagreement. To speak of 'justice', however, is to speak of 'just conduct' or 'fairness' or the assertion or maintenance of 'right'. We may as well say that 'justice' is about justice or what is considered just or unjust. But we are then back to begging the question.

Our discourse reflects this problem. We are much more comfortable with the negative concept of 'injustice' simply because it tends to be associated with a concrete situation in which, it is alleged, injustice resides. We ask why a certain act is unjust in the context in which that act occurs. The fact, for example, that it may be unjust to deprive someone of an expectation in certain specified circumstances does not mean that it is invariably unjust to deprive people of their expectations as those expectations may be unfounded or absurd. Far less do we convert the notion into a positive concept of justice, that is, that it is just to provide people with their expectations without qualifying the expectation with a word such as 'proper' or 'justified', again leaving us lamenting our failure to identify the quality that attracts those qualifications?

Justice, then, in my perception, does not have an identifiable abstract meaning or a discernible essence. No universal or holistic definition is presently possible. Justice, however, certainly exists in specific contexts. It is incorrigibly context-specific. Outside a specific context it loses its identity and attempts to capture its essence founder on its diversity and differentness. Beyond the specific we seem to be left with nothing more than meaningless generalities or mere rhetoric.

But, if justice has no sensible meaning in the abstract, or at least it is beyond our human limitations to perceive it, what are we to do with the question; 'What is justice?' We can, of course, continue to indulge in endless philosophical discourses that somewhere along the way become exercises in linguistics, or semantics, or other word games. We can certainly undertake more empirical research in the hope that a common or unifying element will emerge, although I suspect it will not. It may well be that we will accept that there is no unifying or common element and conclude that justice consists of a number of discrete concepts, each with its own abstract meaning and discernible essence, appearing under the loose banner of 'justice'. In this quest I do not doubt that we can look to the sociologist or psychologist to assist in determining why and when people proclaim that something is unjust. The latter inquiry, I believe, probably represents the most productive avenue for determining whether, and if so why, a vast and diverse group of contexts in which it may be said injustice exists can be legitimately grouped together as a distinctive category or distinctive categories.

Throughout this book I have used the words 'justice' and 'fairness' interchangeably, and will continue to do so. While I am aware of the literature seeking to distinguish between justice and fairness, for all practical purposes I am disinclined to pursue the fine distinction that is drawn. It seems to me that a prerequisite for resolving the question whether there is any difference is to have a relatively firm definition of both concepts. If justice in the abstract defies definition, presumably fairness in the abstract is similarly recondite. How, then, is it possible to draw a sensible distinction between the two? Both terms nurture a sentiment which is deep-rooted in the community, and the community declines to favour the theorist with a convenient distinction between the two terms.

Nor can I proffer the source of justice in the specific context. That is to say, I cannot provide a theoretical answer to the question why it is that the majority of people or many people would describe a certain act in a specific context as unfair or unjust. Their opinion will represent a sentiment immanent in the community and seemingly deeply rooted in the psyche of the individual. Why they adhere to that sentiment, however, admits of no easy answer, and no doubt embraces answers relative to the history, culture, and social and economic order of the society of which they are citizens. At times, indeed, the sense of injustice that can arise in certain circumstances can seem innate.[21] Ultimately, whatever its derivation, what is or is not unjust or unfair in a certain context depends on a consensus within the community. Justice is not so much a political construct, as many hold, as a community construct.

For these reasons I propose to proffer no more than a theory of justice relative to the adjudicative process. The contexts are the disputes or disagreements that arise in social interaction and lead to litigation or the possibility or threat of litigation. What these contexts have in common is that they arise because a person considers that he or she has been wronged. They have a grievance and seek a legal remedy to rectify or atone for that grievance. Many situations will give rise to the claim that the wrong represents an injustice and that the law should provide a cause of action to rectify that injustice. Justice, or their due in the circumstances of their case, will be to have the wrong righted. The theory advanced in this chapter seeks to identify the concept of justice that is involved in the ensuing adjudicative process. What is identified is a precept or underlying value entrenched in the law and the legal process that informs and serves to circumscribe the judges' thinking.

Liberal individualism

The transcendent drive in western industrial society is the desire for freedom of choice and freedom of action. This drive reached its philosophical zenith in the nineteenth century but remained a powerful and resurgent force in the twentieth century.[22] Freedom of choice and action has been proclaimed as the ideal by philosophers and political pundits alike. Thus,

---

[21] See above, at 276.
[22] N. Seddon, 'Compulsion in Commercial Dealings', in P. D. Finn (ed.), *Essays on Restitution* (Law Book Company, North Rhyde, NSW, 1990), at 139–142. See generally P. S. Atiyah, *The Rise and Fall of Freedom of Contract* (Clarendon Press, Oxford and New York, 1979).

the dignity of the individual, on the one hand, and democracy, on the other, are perceived to be diminished to the extent that this freedom is curtailed.[23] Liberal individualism becomes the distinct ideology.

Under such an ideology the individual is afforded primacy over social or collective goals. Not being subordinate to society, each individual is autonomous and independent, enjoying equality of autonomy and an equal right to freedom from interference by other persons in the exercise of that autonomy.[24] Constraints or, perhaps, excessive constraints, on the freedom of the individual are antithetical to this prevalent and enduring creed.[25]

Liberal individualism therefore demands a political system that empowers the individual. Democracy serves this function. But the commitment to democracy cannot avert the imposition of the coercive power of the state. To the sturdy individual, the majority emerging in the political process may present a tyrannical presence and the machinery of government an overwhelming and intimidating bearing. The libertarian ideal also spawns an economic regime, capitalism, in which freedom of choice is endemic. Indeed, liberal individualism is capitalism's captive creed. From the laissez faire economies of the nineteenth century, through the regulated or mixed economies of the mid-twentieth century, to the free market and global economies of today, freedom from interference has been and remains a fundamental premise. Market forces and competition, it is avowed, require freedom of choice and freedom from interference. But, if unrestrained, this freedom means that the strong and powerful will necessarily prevail over the weak and vulnerable. Even its strongest proponents do not deny that capitalism can be a brutal, cruel process.[26] The market place is not an accommodating place for the insecure and frangible.[27]

---

[23] Seddon, ibid., 139–142.
[24] Michael Rosenfeld, 'Contract and Justice: The Relationship between Classical Contract Law and Social Contract Theory' (1985) 70 Iowa LR 769, at 778, cited in R. Bigwood, 'Conscience and the Liberal Conception of Contract: Observing Basic Distinctions' (2000) 6 NZBLQ 1, at 20.
[25] This creed is, as I have stated, the ideal of a western industrial society. It is not the only, or necessarily the best, ideal. Compare for instance traditional New Zealand Maori society, which was based on concepts of unity, community, solidarity and hapu or tribal identity.
[26] Charles Whelan, *Naked Economics* (W W Horton & Company, New York and London, 2002), at 36.
[27] These characteristics have even been hinted at in the courtroom; Mason CJ and Wilson J have said, 'competition by its very nature is deliberate and ruthless' in *Queensland Wine Industries Pty Ltd v Broken Hill Proprietary Co Ltd* (1989) 63 ALJR 181, at 186.

And so the cult of individualism pervades our lives. Of course, the necessity of collective existence imposes many constraints. Freedom of choice and freedom from interference cannot go unrestrained in a civilised society. The plunderings of highwaymen are beyond the pale. But the underlying philosophy remains rooted in liberal individualism and the freedom and independence that it seeks to accord the individual.

Nevertheless, at the same time the bell tolls for us all as we are all 'involved in mankind'.[28] It is a truism that individuals, however free and independent their aspirations, necessarily interact with one another at all levels; in the family, in social and community affairs, in commercial dealings and business relationships, and in political life and governmental activity. Interaction with others is part of the daily grist. It is equally a truism that in these interpersonal relationships there is both the potential for and reality of inequality. Individuals are not equal. A variety of factors, from the chance make-up of one's genes to luckless ill fortune, result in marked and, at times, gross disparities between the capacity and capabilities of people. In rank, capital, wealth and other material resources, disparities are self-evident. So, too, in wisdom, judgement, knowledge, personal skill, will-power, discipline, perception, common sense and a host of other acknowledged personal attributes, some persons will be superior and some will be inferior. These disparities lead to an imbalance of power in the interaction and interpersonal relationships of individuals. Some will be in a position to assert power over others; yet others will be vulnerable to the assertion of that power.

So we arrive at a key point. By virtue of these discrepancies in interpersonal power, one person is or may be in a position to take advantage of another. That other is in a position where he or she may be taken advantage of. The power may take many forms; it may be the coercive power of the state, it may be political power, it may be economic or commercial power, it may be the power of communication and persuasion, or it may simply be the power that any significant advantage invariably confers. But whatever form the power may take, it involves the potential for exploitation. It is here that the law takes a

---

[28] 'No man is an island, entire of itself, every man is a piece of the continent, a part of the Main ... Any man's death diminishes me, because I am involved in Mankind; And therefore never send to know for whom the bell tolls; It tolls for thee' (John Donne (1571–1631), 'For Whom the Bell Tolls').

stand. It will call a halt to the pursuit of individual freedom where that pursuit results in one person exploiting or taking unfair advantage of another as a result of an imbalance of power in their interpersonal relationship. The law will not countenance the excesses of a social, political and economic order committed to liberal individualism. To the law, the weak and vulnerable as well as the strong and powerful are individuals having an equal entitlement to the freedom and autonomy innate to that ideology.

It is, perhaps, as well to clarify that the precept of non-exploitation that emerges does not in itself seek to undermine liberal individualism or destroy capitalism. Nor is it directed at the harsh and cruel features of what might be called the naked economics of capitalism. Competition and free markets means that there will be 'losers'. Thus, for example, the theory will do nothing to inhibit what some economists have termed creative destruction, the process by which existing economic units are destroyed by the creation of new and more efficient orders. As Charles Whelan has noted, we look back and speak admiringly of technological breakthroughs like the steam engine, the spinning wheel, and the telephone. But those advances made it a bad time to be, respectively, a blacksmith, a seamstress or a telegraph operator.[29] These economic adversities will remain unscathed by the theory.

Hence the stand that the law takes is not directed at any perceived excesses of liberal individualism or capitalism as such, but rather at the abuse of the freedom and autonomy that those creeds entail. Based on the notion of corrective justice, the freedom and autonomy of one person cannot be exploited by another person exercising their freedom and autonomy in an unconscionable manner. Harsh and cruel it may be, but capitalism still requires ground rules by which the combatants pursue their economic and entrepreneurial activity. It is the fairness of the manner in which a dealing, transaction or interpersonal relationship is executed and not the dealing, transaction or relationship itself, which is subject to the precept of non-exploitation. Both parties share the presumption in favour of an equality of deservedness.

Obviously, it is now necessary to establish that this stand does in fact permeate the law. Equally obviously, equity is the starting point.

---

[29] Whelan, *Naked Economics*, at 36.

Equity

Equity can readily be equated with conscientious conduct. Conscience is the underlying principle.[30] The old Court of Chancery was a court of conscience, and the standards imported into and developed in the law reflect standards of conscience, fairness and equality in interpersonal relationships. Equitable intervention in dealings between people is principally based on requirements of conscientious conduct, and arises where there is something in the conduct of the one that is exploitative of the other, or in the position of the other that is vulnerable to exploitation. Broad language to give effect to this precept is favoured by equity and has so far resisted the attempts to suppress its flexibility with defined and definite rules.[31]

But the use of words or phrases such as 'conscience', 'unconscionability', 'inequitable', 'unconscientious conduct', 'unfair and oppressive', 'fair dealing', 'good faith', and the like, and the flexibility which they import, should not be permitted to obscure the fact that the common feature that these words or phrases share is equity's concern to protect the weaker and more vulnerable from the exploitative actions of the stronger and more powerful. The historic basis of equity's focus on fraud illustrates this point. At common law, fraud represented an act of wilful deceit by one to gain an advantage over another, but even that broad formula did not protect all those who were harmed as a result of another's breach of an obligation which, as Viscount Haldane said, 'is the sort of obligation which is enforced

---

[30] M. Halliwell, *Equity & Good Conscience in a Contemporary Context* (Old Bailey Press, London, 1977), 1.

[31] Not that the attempt has not been made. See, e.g., R. P. Meagher, W. M. C. Gummow and J. R. F. Lehane, *Meagher, Gummow and Lehane's Equity: Doctrines and Remedies* (4th edn, Butterworths, Sydney, 2002) for a comprehensive endeavour to reduce equity to a set of concrete rules. For a scathing denunciation of this work, see Peter Birks' book review in (2004) 120 LQR, 344. Birks acknowledges that, as an immense repository of accumulated knowledge the book invokes admiration, or even wonder, but then suggests that the awe resembles the awe that in a museum of natural history might be offered to a life-sized but lifeless mammoth. Observing that judgement has to find a path between complex rationality and obfuscating pedantry, Birks asserts that the language and mystique of the book falls on the wrong side of the line and encourages mysticism. Page by page, he says, there lingers the vestige of a suspicion that the argument may be led by 'an angry fundamentalism'. Birks concludes, and it is a conclusion I heartily endorse, that as significant as it is from some important perspectives, the book is not merely not needed but is actually harmful to the law's rational integrity. Readers may care to contrast Meagher, Gummow and Lehane with Sarah Worthington's *Equity* (Oxford University Press, Oxford, 2003), a masterly exposition that focuses on categories of equity in which lawyers today learn and think.

by a Court that from the beginning regarded itself as a court of conscience.'[32] The concept of constructive 'fraud' or 'equitable fraud' emerged to embrace those who failed to take sufficient care to ensure that their actions did not unfairly take advantage of another.

The conscience of equity is expressed in a range of different doctrines. Patrick Parkinson's analysis is helpful. He points out that it is possible to discern five broad categories, at times overlapping, into which these doctrines may be placed. They are: the exploitation of vulnerability or weakness; the abuse of positions of trust or confidence; the insistence upon rights in circumstances that makes such an insistence harsh or oppressive; the inequitable denial of obligations; and the unjust retention of property.[33]

Thus, the exploitation of a person's special vulnerability is regularly treated as unconscionable conduct. The same principle underlies the doctrines of unconscionable dealing and undue influence. Relief against unconscionable bargains is granted where in all the circumstances a transaction is so unconscionable that it cannot be allowed to stand. In respect of such dealings Sir Edward Somers' description of equity is apt: 'It is a jurisdiction protecting those under a disadvantage from those who take advantage of that fact ...'[34]

So, too, with undue influence. Undue influence represents the illicit pressure or persuasion of one person over another. The oppressor benefits at the expense of the victim. Protection of the vulnerable from victimisation is the object of the doctrine.[35]

The fiduciary relationship, of course, has been equity's main means of preventing persons abusing a position of dominance or influence. Fiduciaries are required to act in the best interests of their beneficiaries. They are not permitted to place themselves in a situation where their interests conflict with that duty; nor are they allowed to profit from the opportunities gained in the course of their fiduciary task; and nor are they able to use or disclose confidential information acquired as a

---

[32] *Nocton v Lord Ashburton* [1914] AC 932, at 954.
[33] Patrick Parkinson 'The Conscience of Equity' in Patrick Parkinson (ed.), *The Principles of Equity* (Law Book Company, North Rhyde, NSW, 1996), at 34.
[34] *Nichols v Jessup* [1986] 1 NZLR 226, at 235.
[35] *Allcard v Skinner* (1887) 36 Ch D 145, at 182–183. See also the cases cited in *Wilkinson v ASB Bank* [1998] 1 NZLR 674, especially at 694–695. For a counterview, see generally P. Birks and C. N. Yin, 'On the Nature of Undue Influence', in J. Beatson and D. Friedmann (eds.), *Good Faith and Fault in Contract Law* (Clarendon Press, Oxford, 1995).

fiduciary. The common element underlying these obligations is the imbalance of power between the fiduciary and the beneficiary. A fiduciary is in a position to exploit the relationship, and the beneficiary is vulnerable to the fiduciary's departure from his or her obligation of loyalty. In the fiduciary relationship, the beneficiary is uniquely susceptible to being unfairly disadvantaged.

A further illustration of this principle is equity's treatment of agents, attorneys and company directors. Standing in a position of trust with regard to their principal, such persons are held liable to account for any abuse of their position. They cannot exploit their appointed capacity to the detriment of their principal.[36] Similarly, a power given to one person to affect another person's property must be exercised honestly and for the purposes it was given. Otherwise, it is a fraud on a power and is void. Equity will not countenance the exploitation of the power.[37]

Equity also requires a person to forego the strict application of his or her legal rights where insistence on those rights would be harsh or oppressive to the weaker party. Estoppel, for example, precludes such insistence on legal rights where in the circumstances it would be exploitative for the possessor of those rights to enforce them. By words or conduct, he or she will have led the other party to rely upon their non-enforcement. The possessor of the rights is not then permitted to take advantage of his or her rights at the expense of the person who has acted upon that forbearance.[38]

Promissory estoppel falls into the same broad category. The maker of a voluntary promise cannot exploit the promisee by reneging on the assumption, which he or she has created, that the promise will be fulfilled, thereby disregarding the promise to the promisee's detriment.[39] Such other concepts as equitable set-off and the prevention of reliance upon rights in relation to stipulations of time can be explained

---

[36] R. Pearce and J. Stevens, *The Law of Trusts and Equitable Obligations* (Butterworths, London and Edinburgh 1995) at 118; and G. Fridman, *Law of Agency* (Butterworths, London and Edinburgh, 1996), at 174–188.
[37] *The Laws of New Zealand*, Powers, para. 101.
[38] See *Jorden v Money* (1854) 5 HLC 185; *NB Hunt & Sons Ltd v Máori Trustee* [1986] 2 NZLR 641, at 655–657; and *Thompson v Palmer* (1933) 49 CLR 507, at 547. These cases relate to estoppel by conduct. For an authority on estoppel by deed, see *McCathie v McCathie* [1971] NZLR 58, at 59. See generally Kevin Lingren, 'Estoppel in Contract' (1989) 12 NSWLJ 153, at 155–156.
[39] See *Central London Property Trust Ltd v High Trees House Ltd* [1947] 1 KB 130; *Waltons Stores (Interstate) Ltd v Maher* (1988) 164 CLR 387; and *Gilles v Keogh* [1989] 2 NZLR 327.

in the same way. Equitable set-off is motivated by equity's concern to prevent the harsh exercise of rights. A set-off is permitted where it would be unconscionable to allow the plaintiff to proceed to judgment when a countervailing claim seriously diminishes the merits of the plaintiff's claim without being a substantive defence to that claim. So, too, a plaintiff may not unfairly insist upon his or her rights in relation to a stipulation as to time in a contract where time has not been made of the essence. To allow the plaintiff to succeed would be to allow him or her to obtain an unconscionable advantage.[40]

The repudiation of obligations also attracts relief in equity. Thus, the Statute of Frauds cannot be used as an instrument to shield fraud. The fields in which this general approach has been adopted include the doctrine of part performance; the rule that parol evidence is admissible to show that an absolute conveyance was in truth by way of security only; the rule that oral evidence can establish that a person has taken a transfer of property as trustee or agent for another; and the rule whereby equity will compel beneficiaries who have agreed to accept their interests under communicated trusts to perform those trusts.[41] In all these situations equity will not permit a person in a position of relative power to exploit that power to the disadvantage of the other person involved in the interaction.

Finally, equity will not permit a person to retain property in circumstances in which it was not intended that he or she should have the benefit of it. A constructive trust may be imposed on the property on the basis that the acquisitive holder should be required to share the benefit of it with another having a less formal but nonetheless meritorious claim. Constructive trusts and, possibly, to an even greater extent the courts' proud invention, the remedial trust, are the means by which equity prevents a person exploiting another person's inferior title or interest.

Closely related to the underlying justification of a constructive trust is the concept of unjust enrichment and its consequential product, restitution. Juristic attempts to redefine 'conscience' in terms of an independent principle of unjust enrichment can, at least for present purposes, be

---

[40] See Parkinson, 'The Conscience of Equity', at 40.
[41] *Last v Rosenfeld* [1972] 2 NSWLR 923, at 927–928. See generally *Rocherfoucauld v Boustead* [1897] 1 Ch 196, at 206, and G. E. Dal Pont and D. R. C. Chalmers, *Equity and Trusts in Australia and New Zealand* (Law Book Company, North Rhyde, NSW, 1996), at 329–330.

disregarded. The element that makes the enrichment of one at the expense of another 'unjust' invariably reflects the fact that, to allow the enrichment to stand, would be to permit the defendant to obtain unfairly a benefit at the expense of the plaintiff. This perception is so whether one takes the English approach of presupposing, one, an enrichment of the defendant; two, that the enrichment is at the expense of the plaintiff; and, three, that the enrichment is unjust;[42] or the broader Canadian formulation of, one, an enrichment of the defendant; two, a corresponding deprivation on the part of the plaintiff; and, three, an absence of juristic reason for the enrichment.[43]

All the above doctrines represent different applications of equity's concern to redress unfair exploitation. All have in common a situation in which one person is in a position of relative strength or power and the other is in a position of relative weakness, powerlessness or other vulnerability. Equity prevents the one exploiting or taking unfair advantage of the other.

The common law

Establishing that the precept of non-exploitation is the basic scruple underlying equity's many excursions in the law is not difficult. But it is an essential plank of the theory being pursued that the precept also permeates the common law. Indeed, a number of causes of action have a basis in both common law and equity. Actual fraud, breach of confidence and waiver are in this category.

Actual fraud can be pursued at common law in deceit and also in equity. The same is true of fraudulent misrepresentation, which is both a common law and an equitable wrong.

In like fashion, the uncertain antecedents of breach of confidence straddle both common law and equity. At common law, the cause of action has been analysed by some as being based on either a property right in the confidential information or an implied contractual term.[44] Others have preferred to view breach of confidence as an equitable

---

[42] R. Goff and G. Jones, *The Law of Restitution* (4th edn, Sweet & Maxwell, London, 1993), at 16; and R. B. Grantham and C. E. F. Rickett, *Enrichment and Restitution in New Zealand* (Hart Publishing, Oxford, 2000), at 9–10.
[43] *Pettkus* v *Becker* (1980) 117 DLR (3d) 257, at 254; and *Sorochan* v *Sorochan* [1986] 2 SCR 38.
[44] *Linda Chih Ling Koo* v *Lam Tai Hing* (1992) 23 IPR 607, at 633.

doctrine arising out of breach of trust.[45] But for present purposes, the point is that the underlying objective of the cause of action, whether resting in the common law or equity, is to prevent the person who possesses the ability to appropriate confidential information from doing so at the expense of the person who is exposed to the risk of having his or her confidence abused.

Again, views as to the status of waiver differ. Some commentators argue that waiver is not an independent doctrine but a diffuse concept used in different senses to mean either a variation by contractual novation at common law, or an estoppel in both common law and equity, or an election in equity only.[46] Other writers contend that waiver is a distinct concept that operates in equity.[47] But whether waiver is viewed as a doctrine common to both common law and equity,[48] or as a distinct equitable concept,[49] its foundation is essentially the same: to prevent one person in a position to take advantage of another from doing so by seeking to enforce a right that he or she has earlier released.

In other areas equitable doctrines can be said to have a common law counterpart or genesis. Thus, at common law, a cause of action for interference with a property right is extended by equity to cover interference with an equitable interest, such as an equitable lease.[50] Estoppel by conduct in common law is expanded by proprietary estoppel and promissory estoppel in equity. Then, duress at common law may amount to undue influence in equity. Yet, again, the precept of non-exploitation is the unifying theme.

Common mistake at common law is extended to other types of mistake in equity, including mutual mistake and unilateral mistake where the other party is aware of the mistake.[51] Unilateral mistake may be understood as a doctrine that seeks to correct the unconscionable exploitation of another's position of weakness. In such cases, the

---

[45] *Duchess of Argyll* v *Duke of Argyll* [1967] Ch 302. See generally *Lac Minerals Ltd* v *International Corona Resources Ltd* (1989) 61 DLR (4th) 14; and Dal Pont and Chalmers, *Equity and Trusts*, at 80–81.
[46] See Meagher, Gummow and Lehane, *Meagher, Gummow and Lehane's Equity*, at 433–435.
[47] See Dal Pont and Chalmers, *Equity and Trusts*, at 567–570.
[48] See G. C. Cheshire, C. H. S. Fifoot and M. P. Furmston, *Law of Contract* (12th edn, Butterworths, London, 1991), at 562–565.
[49] See Dal Pont and Chalmers, *Equity and Trusts*, at 567–570.
[50] *Walsh* v *Lonsdale* (1882) 21 Ch D 9.
[51] N. C. Seddon and M. P. Ellinghaus, *Cheshire and Fifoot's Law of Contract* (7th edn, Butterworths, London, 1997) 471.

vulnerability arises from one's own mistake. With common and mutual mistake, both parties are vulnerable as a result of the mistake or mistakes, but one party will in the circumstances obtain an unfair advantage at the expense of the other party if the contract is allowed to stand.

Although supported by equity, agency and powers of attorney are common law concepts.[52] If agents act other than in accordance with the terms of their authority or in breach of the duty of loyalty or care owed to their principals, they will be liable for any loss. In some cases, a third party suffering a loss will also have a right of redress against the agent by way of damages for breach of an implied warranty of authority.[53] In either case, agents cannot trespass beyond the boundaries of the power conferred on them at the expense of another person vulnerable to that power.

A prime example of related causes of action in common law and equity that are clearly founded on the precept of non-exploitation are actions for money had and received at common law and actions for unjust enrichment in equity. Neither will permit the fortuitous recipient to retain the windfall at the expense of the rightful owner.

Finally, reference may be made to legal and equitable set-off. The former, which is statutory in origin, provides a right to set off liquidated mutual debts.[54] The latter is much broader. There is no strict need for mutuality, and unliquidated amounts may be claimed.

In all these cases, while the protection of the common law may not be as potent as that provided by equity, the common law causes of action reflect the same compunction that moved equity to protect those who are vulnerable from the exploitative predations of the strong and powerful.

In pursuing an examination of the common law further, contract, tort and administrative law can usefully be the focus of specific attention. Criminal law and property law have been largely overtaken and codified by statute.[55] But it is not difficult to discern the precept

---

[52] Pearce and Stevens, *The Law of Trusts*, at 118; Beatson and Friedmann (eds.), *Good Faith and Fault in Contract Law*, at 174; and *Laws NZ*, 'Agency', paras. 7 and 34.

[53] Beatson and Friedmann, ibid., at 233–234; and *Laws NZ*, ibid., para. 140.

[54] See the Statutes of Set-Off, comprising the Insolvent Debtors Relief Act 1728 (Imp) and the Set-off Act 1734 (Imp), in force in New Zealand by virtue of s. 3(1) of the Imperial Laws Application of the Act 1988. The principles in these statutes have long since been absorbed into the common law. See, e.g., *Felt and Textiles of New Zealand Ltd v R Hubric Ltd (in receivership)* [1968] NZLR 716, at 713–718.

[55] But, of course, judicial law-making in the criminal law continues. See, A. T. H. Smith, 'Judicial Law Making in the Criminal Law' (1984) 100 LQR 46.

of non-exploitation in the common law that preceded the legislation. The criminal law always subjected a wide variety of activity to penal sanctions where one person exploited or sought to exploit another's person or property. In property, the common law protected the owner's property rights from being diminished by anyone who did not possess or share those rights. Detailed land rights were one of the main legacies of the Norman conquest. The property rights granted under the sophisticated system of tenure were zealously protected so as to prevent one person exploiting the ownership of another, first by customs as applied in local feudal jurisdictions, and later by a common body of principles and a centralised justice system.[56]

Contract

Greater attention can be directed to contract for it is the law of contract that has the greatest impact on interactions where freedom of choice and action and freedom from interference are most coveted.

Adams and Brownsword have stated that contract law in the modern world prescribes good faith and conscionable dealing, confining the parties' freedom to take unfair advantage of one another.[57] That freedom is apparent in the interaction between persons when negotiating a deal. Indeed, the bargaining process is the primary example of interpersonal activity that can give rise to an inequality of power or advantage as between the parties. The law prohibits the unfair exploitation of that inequality.

It must be quickly clarified, of course, that it is not every bargain that might be said to be 'unfair' that the law declines to enforce. Self-interest in contract is a fact of life. The law cannot seek to correct all the inequalities that inevitably affect contracting parties according to their circumstances. It does not seek to assist those who enter into an imprudent or improvident deal. Paternalism forms no part in the law's prescription of contract law. The law is not, to quote Lord Radcliffe,

---

[56] The Statute Quia Emptores, refining the rights of tenants and sub-tenants, was passed in 1290. Actions in seisin and right, and writs of entry and novel disseisin – legal mechanisms supporting the system of tenure – were available from relatively early times in both the lords' and the king's courts. See generally S. F. C. Milsom, *Historical Foundations of the Common Law* (2nd edn, Cambridge University Press, Cambridge, 1981), at 99–150; and R. C. Van Caenegam, *The Birth of the English Common Law* (2nd edn, Butterworths, London 1988), at Chapter 2.

[57] J. N. Adams and R. Brownsword, *Key Issues in Contract* (Butterworths, London and Edinburgh, 1995), at 355.

'a panacea for adjusting any contract between persons when it shows a rough edge to one side or the other.'[58]

This rejection of paternalism is consonant with the autonomy of the individual. As Rick Bigwood has said:

> ... if we are to take autonomy seriously, we must respect the bad bargains that people make as well as the good ones, since to interfere with bad bargains entered into voluntarily is to deny someone the right to self-determination, and hence to deny that person's absolute and equal status as a freely choosing, rationally valuing, specially efficacious moral personality.[59]

For this reason, exploitation that may be branded unfair by many, or even all, people, does not necessarily fall foul of the precept. The exploitation must reach such a degree of unfairness as to warrant the courts' intervention. While the courts through the administration of the law may seek to protect the community from the excesses of liberal individualism and capitalism, a degree of moral latitude is necessarily permitted. In other words, the law allows a margin of unfairness, as it were, before taking a stand against the exploitation involved in the formation and performance of a contract. It is for this reason that the great majority of contracts will never be challenged. As between the parties, the bargaining power or negotiating strength will be equal, or roughly equal, or will even out. The parties will have entered into the contract with their eyes open. Indeed, some eminent jurists have referred to the position between bargaining parties as involving mutual 'coercion'. Robert Hale argues that scarce resources necessitate bargaining, which in turn requires parties to give up some legal rights in exchange for others. He points out that a bargain, once struck, obtains the force of law.[60] Philips observes that 'coerced' agreements are 'an inevitability of our social life'.[61] Consequently, to attract the intervention of the law, the vulnerability of the disadvantaged party must be of a particular kind. It

---

[58] *Bridge v Campbell Discount Co Ltd* [1962] AC 600, at 626.
[59] Bigwood, 'Conscience and the Liberal Conception', at 21. Bigwood has recently expanded his thinking in an excellent book; see R. Bigwood, *Exploitative Contracts* (Oxford University Press, Oxford, 2003). Bigwood makes an outstanding contribution to legal theory in elaborating the law's antithesis to exploitation in contract law. See also the comments of Salmon J in *Brusevitz v Brown* [1923] NZLR 1106, at 1109.
[60] Robert L. Hale, 'Bargaining, Duress and Economic Liberty', 43 Colum. LR 603, at 604.
[61] Michael Philips, 'Are Coerced Agreements Involuntary?' (1984) 3 Law and Phil 133, at 134. See also the comments to like effect in R. Bigwood, 'Coercion in Contract: The Theoretical Constructs of Duress' (1996) 46 U Tor. LJ 201, at 201–203; E. A. Farnsworth,

must bear on the parties' capacity to consent genuinely and voluntarily to the agreement.

A binding contract is grounded in the notion of consent. Doctrines such as *non est factum* and *consensus ad idem* testify to this rudimentary requirement, and it is through this requirement that the precept of non-exploitation principally makes itself felt in contract. Just as liberal individualism requires that people be permitted to enter into binding agreements, it also demands that binding agreements reflect their free and voluntary choices.[62] Thus, the various rules and principles that govern the formation of contracts are essentially designed to deter one party from failing to obtain the other party's genuine and voluntary consent. Such a failure may result in an injustice against the latter party that warrants annulment in the form of corrective justice.[63] So it is that the law sets limits on what constitutes a contract, on when a contract is formed, and on the implication of terms in a contract, all of which leaves without contractual force or redress a significant range of interaction by and between parties purporting to deal consensually with each other.[64]

Voluntariness may be defective in a number of ways. Genuine and voluntary consent is absent where one party induces the other to enter into the contract by fraud, force, or economic duress. In each of these cases the offending party has sought to exploit a position of power or advantage over the other party who, if that party is to succumb, is vulnerable to that fraud, force or duress.

Yet, in other cases, the apparent voluntariness of a party is belied by his or her ignorance, mistake, incapacity, drunkenness or need.[65] In such cases, the stronger party may not intend to take advantage of the defect in the other party's capacity, but the element of exploitation is present and complete should the contract be enforced. The stronger party, for example, obtains an advantage at the expense of the other party whether or not he or she knows of that party's particular incapacity. To permit the contract to be enforced in such circumstances would

'Coercion in Contract Law' (1982) U Ark at Little Rock LJ 329, at 332–333; and Atiyah, *The Rise and Fall of Freedom of Contract*, at 734–735.
[62] R. Bigwood, 'Undue Influence: "Impaired Consent" or "Wicked Exploitation"?' (1996) 16 OJLS 503, at 505.
[63] Ibid., at 507.
[64] P. D. Finn, 'Unconscionable Conduct' (1994) 8 Jnl of Contract Law 37, at 40. Note particularly in this regard the courts' special approach to the interpretation of exemption clauses in standard form contracts: as to this see G. H. Treitel, *The Law of Contract* (Sweet & Maxwell, London, 1999), Chapter 7.
[65] Bigwood, 'Undue Influence', at 507.

be to give effect to the passive exploitation inherent in the weaker party's vulnerability. As Bigwood has put it, that the defendant should be identified as an 'exploiter' relative to the plaintiff is the only publicly convincing way of bringing coherency to the plaintiff–defendant relationship consistent with the major features and true purposes of the liberal conception of contract.[66]

A special category of contract in which the precept of non-exploitation is conspicuously present is the contract of employment. Employment situations are, perhaps, the archetypical example of human interactions where the relatively powerful, be it the employer or the employee's organisation, may exploit or take advantage of the other. Because of the potential for exploitation, the common law has recognised the special nature of the relationship between the employer and the employee. It is a relationship under which the employer and the employee have mutual obligations of confidence, trust and fair dealing.[67] Lord Browne Wilkinson, when Vice Chancellor, called this implied term 'the implied obligation of good faith'.[68] Thus, the unequal power of the employer and the employee is mitigated by the law's insistence that each demonstrate good faith to the other.

Let Professor Kronman have the last say. Speaking of cases where one party claims that his or her promise was not voluntarily given, he stated:

> ... the promisee enjoys an advantage of some sort which he has attempted to exploit for his own benefit. The advantage may consist in his superior information, intellect, or judgment, in the monopoly he enjoys with regard to a particular resource, or in his possession of a powerful instrument of violence or a gift of deception. In each of these cases, the fundamental question is whether the promisee should be permitted to exploit his advantage to the detriment of the other party, or whether permitting him to do so will deprive that other party of the freedom that is necessary, from a libertarian point of view, to make his promise truly voluntary and therefore binding.[69]

---

[66] Bigwood, 'Conscience and the Liberal Conception', at 14.
[67] *Telecom South Ltd v Post Office Union* [1992] 1 ERNZ 711, at 722, and *Lowe Walker Paeroa Ltd v Bennett* [1998] 2 ERNZ 558, at 582.
[68] *Imperial Group Pension Trust Ltd v Imperial Tobacco Ltd* (1991) 2 All ER 596, at 606. For a relatively recent application, see *Mahmud v Bank of Credit and Commerce International SA (in liq)* [1998] AC 20 (HL).
[69] Anthony T. Kronman, 'Contract Law and Distributive Justice' (1980) 89 Yale LJ 473, 480.

Tort

Many jurists would have it that no single normative basis can be attributed to tort law. A plurality of competing norms, such as loss spreading, efficient deterrence, retribution, corrective justice, distributive justice, autonomy and community responsibility may be invoked to explain or justify the law.[70] Having regard to the diversity of torts, there can be no easy answer. Nonetheless, we can again assert that the precept of non-exploitation provides the law of torts with a universal precept.

In many cases, of course, the law's core concern to prevent and deter exploitation is openly apparent. Thus, one person may not use his or her power to harm another by physically assailing that person; a person may not take advantage of the gullibility of another person by perpetuating a deliberate deceit; a person may not trespass on another's land to the detriment of the owner's property rights; a person with special skills may not make a careless representation likely to be relied upon by another person to that person's detriment;[71] and a publisher may not utilise the advantage possessed by the disseminator of information to publish a defamatory comment at the expense of a person's reputation. But the concrete situations in which these torts arise do not always disclose exploitation in the sense that an apparently stronger party has taken advantage of another.

It is necessary to dig deeper into the foundation of tort liability to uncover the precept of non-exploitation: tort law protects the individual against actual or threatened injury to one's person or property by condemning in damages or other relief the person who exerts his or her freedom at the expense of the freedom of the injured party. The parties possess an equality of entitlement regardless of their relative wealth, merit or need. Hence, if one person affects or threatens to affect the person or resources of another by means of an interaction that is inconsistent with that equality, the latter will have a claim for the correction or prevention of that adverse effect.[72] In short, the exploitation lies in the wrongdoer asserting, intentionally or inadvertently, his or her autonomous freedom at the expense of the autonomy and

---

[70] See Wright, 'Right, Justice and Tort Law', at 159–160. See also the author's observations in *Daniels v Thompson* [1998] 3 NZLR 22, at 68.
[71] *Hedley Byrne & Co v Heller & Partners* [1964] AC 465.
[72] Wright, 'Right, Justice and Tort Law', at 167.

freedom of the other party to the interaction, thereby causing him or her loss.[73]

This abstract perception may be given concrete meaning by referring to the pervasive tortious concept of neighbourhood. One person to the interaction will assert his or her autonomy in a way that interferes with the autonomy or another. Where the power of one or the vulnerability of the other in that interaction is such that the one has the capacity to cause harm to the other, the law will impose a 'duty of care' on the possessor of the power to avert or refrain from inflicting that harm.[74] The possessor of the power must respect, and thereby refrain from exploiting, the freedom of other autonomous individuals to be 'free' from such interference.

Public and administrative law

The concept that the law is essentially concerned to prevent abuse of power is clearly evident in administrative law. As is frequently proclaimed, no area of the law has developed so magnificently as administrative law in the twentieth century. Lord Diplock's famous statement that the progress made towards developing a comprehensive system of administrative law was the greatest achievement of the English courts in his lifetime is invariably quoted.[75] Administrative law has been served well by the principle of ultra vires. There are clear signs, however, that a substantive principle of common law is evolving to take the place of the ultra vires principle, which is essentially an adjunct of statutory interpretation.[76] But, however the framework of administrative law is viewed, its essential function is to protect the citizen from the abuse or misuse of governmental or coercive power.[77]

---

[73] Wright uses the language of each party's 'equal negative freedom' to explain the outcome.
[74] Finn, 'Unconscionable Conduct', at 42. See also Jane Stapleton, 'The Golden Thread at the Heart of Tort Law: Protection of the Vulnerable' (2003) 24 Australian Bar Review, 41.
[75] *Inland Revenue Comrs v National Federation of Self-Employed and Small Businesses Ltd* [1981] 2 All ER 93, at 104.
[76] For an early indication of the issue, see the author, 'Administrative Law and the Rule of Law' (1987) NZ Law Conference Papers, at 172. See also Paul Craig, 'Ultra Vires and the Foundations of Judicial Review' (1998) 57 Camb. LJ 63 and the author, 'The Relationship of Parliament and the Courts: A Tentative Thought or Two for the New Millennium' (2000) 31 VUWLR 5 ('Centennial Lecture') at 13–14.
[77] See, e.g., *R v North and East Devon Health Authority, ex parte Coughlan* [2000] 2 WLR 622.

In that relationship, whether described as the interaction between the state and the individual or the government and the citizen, the state or government official is self-evidently in a position of power and able to assert that power. The precept of non-exploitation is therefore at the heart of a system of administrative law designed to prevent or curb the abuse of power over citizens, many or most of whom are relatively powerless within the political or governmental process.[78]

The conclusion is clear. The precept of non-exploitation is entrenched in the law, whether it is equity or the common law, so as to prevent one person unfairly taking advantage of another as a result of an imbalance of power in their interpersonal relationship.

... of Marxism and Critical Legal Studies

Following the publication of a paper[79] setting out in rudimentary form the theory advanced in this chapter, a reader responded asserting that the notion of an altruistic premise in the law was a total refutation of Marx's view of the law as the tool of the ruling class. In curbing the excesses of capitalism, he continued, the premise that I had exposed was the antithesis of the Marxist perception of law and the social order. This refutation, he concluded with a generous bouquet, represented the real value of my theory.

While I would be pleased for my theory to possess real value, I must confess that I do not regard it is a refutation of the Marxist perception at all. I therefore propose to digress for a moment and briefly explain why Marx is unchallenged and, indeed, why to some extent, at least, the theory supports Critical Legal Studies scholarship. I do not, of course, need to defend either perspective but I want to briefly clarify the relationship of the precept of non-exploitation to those theories.

Karl Marx portrayed the law broadly as a set of rules or sanctions by which class relations are mediated in favour of the ruling class and that, ultimately, confirm and consolidate class power. 'Hence, the rule of law is only another mask for the rule of a class.'[80] I do not apprehend Marx's perception that the economic basis of society had a determinative effect over all forms of social activity and the institutions making up the

---

[78] The author, 'Administrative Law and the Rule of Law', at 12–13.
[79] 'The Conscience of the Law' (2000) Waikato LR, Vol. 8, 1.
[80] E. P. Thompson, *Whigs and Hunters: The Origin of the Black Art* (Allen Lane, London, 1975), at 259.

super-structure of society rules out my analysis. Rather, the altruistic premise that I have identified becomes part of the super-structure and serves the purpose of sustaining the basic economic order.

Law, as such, did not receive separate treatment from Marx, and little more from his colleague Engels. Neither conferred prominence on the substance of the law in their analysis of the socio-economic organisation of society. Further, both contemplated that legislation might be enacted which would assist the proletariat and be against the apparent interests of the ruling class. Engels certainly accepted that the law may react on its economic base and, to some extent, warp or temporarily halt the inexorable march towards the collapse of capitalism. For Marx, it was sufficient to point to the law at a general or structural level. It is the state with its agencies of the law and law enforcement that ultimately protect the economic dominance and property of the ruling class. He perceived, however, that the ruling class cannot maintain its control of the economy by coercion but must obtain the active cooperation of the population or most of the population. Religion, philosophy, ethics and law are utilised for this purpose. These instruments or social institutions raise a 'false consciousness' in the community.

One need not accept Marxist terminology, nor endorse his historical and allegedly scientific analysis of society, nor support his prophecies as inevitable, but may yet be disinclined to reject the ultimate economic and social dominance of those who control the empowerment and movement of capital. Ownership of capital may be diverse, and even democratic, but effective control rests with those who have the capacity to direct and manage capital in the economic system, today frequently on a global basis. The power that comes with that control and empowerment possesses a decisive effect on the social norms, organisation, institutions, beliefs and ideologies of society. The law, as one such institution, operates within this framework. It is essentially reflective of capitalism; for example, the concept of private ownership, the fiction of corporate personality, the presumption of equality of bargaining power, and the notion that a person's labour is a commodity or economic unit.

Any law, however, which directly and unduly reflected the interests of this capital-empowered class would cease to obtain the cooperation of the great bulk of the people. It would be harsh and unconscionable, at times deserving of the epithet; 'the law of the jungle'. To serve the ends of the capital-empowered class, the law must therefore temper that harshness and unconscionability. Only then can capitalism survive its moral paganism.

Consequently, the law may be viewed, along with the universal franchise, the growth of a propertied middle class, the advent of the intervention of the state and the development of welfarism, as the means by which the capitalist economic order, together with the liberal individualism necessary for that order, not only prevails but flourishes. To serve this purpose the law must necessarily ameliorate the harsh and unconscionable excesses of that system. It does so to the extent that the amelioration becomes the community's perception of the justice to be delivered by the law or legal process.

It is no answer to say that a true Marxist would reject the ameliorative theory of justice as grossly unjust. Embracing an anaemic, capitalistic notion of non-exploitation, the true Marxist would assert, is merely a technique for tricking the downtrodden into compliance so that capitalists can continue to enrich themselves at the expense of the bulk of the population. So why, he or she would ask, celebrate 'a theory of non-exploitation' as a theory of justice? What is attractive about a theory that permits gross misdistribution of wealth and the exploitation of the working people? To which, one would be tempted to reply, fair comment. But in fact, two points disarm the criticism.

First, the theory of justice advanced in this book does not purport to be a theory of social justice. I have disclaimed that intent and defined a much more modest aspiration. I have hazarded no more than a theory of justice relative to the adjudicative process.[81] The precept of non-exploitation is the underlying notion of justice administered in the courts. The hypothetical Marxist's comment, in contrast, invokes a full-blooded theory of social justice. Moreover, it is one which, whether by virtue of indoctrination, self-interest, enlightenment or any other reason, the bulk of the population do not support. It would be amiss for the courts to reflect that concept of justice as a value in judicial reasoning.

Secondly, the theory is a theory of justice relative to an adjudicative process rooted in and circumscribed by liberal individualism and capitalism. Liberal individualism dictates the judicial system as well as the political system. The precept of non-exploitation applies in that context. As such, it is necessarily a theory that will seem decidedly tawdry to the true Marxist who rejects that context. To those who either endorse liberal individualism and capitalism as the most desirable state of affairs conceivable for humankind or merely accept those 'isms' as realities that

---

[81] See above, at 371.

will not go away, the precept of non-exploitation presents itself as a means by which the harsh excesses of the existing order can be checked.

Nor would I wish the precept of non-exploitation to be perceived as antagonistic to Critical Legal Studies. Far too much of value has come from this scholarship to permit that conclusion. Indeed, Critical Legal Studies scholarship represents a sharp reaction against contemporary formalistic legal thinking; it declines to accept that the text or substance of the law imposes any form of constraint on the judiciary; it too rails against the 'reification' of rules so as to treat them as 'thing-like' having a reality separate from the social context or community values that the rules merely reflect;[82] it rejects the validity of doctrinal logic while at the same time accepting the impact of legal doctrine on the norms, beliefs and ideologies of the community and its role in abetting those norms, beliefs and ideologies;[83] it recognises the ideological positions of liberalism and conservatism;[84] and it recognises the mitigating effect of the law on the harsh, repressive and alienating conditions to be found in contemporary western societies. Typical, and underlying all these aspects, perhaps, is Unger's notion of the domination of people's consciousness by a group or groups of interests or forces with the result that 'society's law may be perceived as the external manifestation of the embeddedness of society's law in its culture.'[85]

The precept of non-exploitation that I have advanced is a lowly and more law-specific variant of Unger's perception of unjustified dominance and the power that dominance produces. That power is ultimately identified as unjustified – or, I would say, unfair – by reference to our established moral intuitions and practices.[86]

But all this, I acknowledge is a digression; a perceived need for a disclaimer lest it be thought that the thesis I have advanced is a refutation, or attempted refutation, of all that which is of value in Marxist theory or of the insights of the Critical Legal Studies Movement. It demonstrates, at least, that a judge who conscientiously and within the bounds of liberal individualism faithfully renders justice in the individual case in administering the precept of non-exploitation may at the

---

[82] Roger Cotterrell, *The Politics of Jurisprudence* (Butterworths, London, 1989), at 188. See also above, Chapter 12, at 305–306.
[83] Cotterrell, ibid., at 211.
[84] Duncan Kennedy, *A Critique of Adjudication* (Harvard University Press, Cambridge, Mass, 1998), esp. Chapter 3.
[85] Roberto Mangabeira Unger, *Knowledge and Politics* (Free Press, New York, 1975), at 242–243.
[86] Ibid.

same time be serving, pawn-like, the ends of the controlling or dominant capital-empowerment sector of society.

Justice and fairness

Has the earlier lightning survey of the ameliorative impact of the law unearthed the answer to the perennial question of what is fair or unfair? The answer is both yes and no.

The question, 'but what is fair?' is repeatedly posed by those who perceive the notion of fairness as notoriously vague and imprecise. Judicial expressions of 'fair-dealing', 'reasonableness', 'good faith', 'unconscionable and unconscientious conduct', 'unfair and oppressive conduct', 'reasonable and legitimate expectations', 'unjust enrichment' and so on, evoke the same response.[87] By and large, these are the same critics who yearn for an impersonal and positive law and a formalistic process. As I have suggested above, they are acutely uncomfortable with and distrustful of the discretion any notion of fairness vests in the judges.[88] The problem that they perceive is essentially one of translation. How is the sense of fairness immanent in the community to be discerned by a judge and, if it is discerned, how can his or her fidelity to that evaluation be assured?

I need not canvas this issue again.[89] It will suffice simply to point to the reality of judicial reasoning and to query what credibility these commentators would obtain if they framed the question in terms of 'but what is just?' By the simple artifice of substituting the word 'fair' for 'just' these critics obtain an audience that would otherwise be quickly dismissive of their claims.

Accepting that the notion of fairness is a reality in judicial decision-making, however, does not mean that efforts to reduce its apparent vagueness should be neglected. The search remains vital to the essential function of the law to serve the community of which it is a part. Identifying the moral sentiment that is universal to all branches of the law must therefore make a worthwhile contribution to that objective. Thus, it is the law's underlying antagonism to the exploitation by one person of another that becomes the key prescription in discerning what is fair or unfair in any particular context. In this way the precept of non-exploitation provides the framework within which the question, or any question, of fairness may be resolved. It reduces the perceived

---

[87] See Bigwood, 'Conscience and the Liberal Conception', at 4.
[88] See above, Chapter 11, at 280–281.   [89] See above, Chapter 11, at 272–287.

abstractness of the question and assists to channel argumentation and reason into a defined frame of reference.

This perception, then, is the affirmative part of the answer to the question, 'what is fair?' But, of course, within that framework, a subjective element remains. It is inherent in the question whether the advantage taken or obtained by the one person over the other in a particular case is unfair or not. An assessment of the circumstances, including the strength and power of the defendant, the weakness, powerlessness and vulnerability of the plaintiff, and the relative position of the two must be made. Eventually, a value judgement is required. The judge must draw the line between what is acceptable and what is unacceptably harsh and unfair requiring amelioration at law.

But, to some extent, this qualification misses the point of our quest. Except where the issue involves an equitable test giving overt and substantive expression to the precept of non-exploitation, the judge does not ask whether in the particular case the exploitation is unacceptable or whether one person has used his or her superior strength, power or dominance unfairly to obtain an advantage at the expense of another. The question before the court may be whether a contract has been partly formed, or whether an agent has acted within the scope of his or her authority, or whether the defendant is estopped from asserting his or her rights or has waived those rights, or it may be any one of the myriad of other questions which come before the courts for resolution. Those questions will be determined by a process of reasoning beginning with the relevant rule or body of law. The law's compunction against harsh and excessive exploitation underlies these particular questions but does not comprise the particular question itself.

In this way justice, or the concept of fairness, can be given effect in accordance with conventional legal methodology. The judge in deciding that a contract is unenforceable or that liability exists in tort, or that a governmental agency has acted ultra vires, may do so having regard to accepted rules, principles and precedent that will in general manifest the law's underlying aversion to exploitation. If it appears that the accepted rules, principles and precedents do not encompass the precept, then, as already indicated, the precept of non-exploitation may provide the more progressive or creative judge with a sure guide as to how the law should be developed.

Are we not, therefore, confirmed in our earlier view? There is a sense in which the precept is larger than the judges. It is akin to being entrenched in the law, or legal tools, and in a self-perpetuating judicial methodology and an imposed and self-imposed judicial discipline, which judges are called upon to administer. Of course, the law that reflects this precept is judge-made, much of it having been made by the judges of old who placed principles before precedent.[90] Equally certain is the inevitability of change and development in the law. But there is no mystery as to how the law was made, or how it is developed, so as to reflect the underlying precept that a person may not use his or her superior strength, power or dominant position to take or obtain an unfair advantage at another's expense. Judges reflect this sense of fairness that is immanent in the community.

It is for this reason that the notion of an altruistic premise underlying the law cannot be debunked. It stems from the community itself. The tension inherent in liberal individualism between the freedom and autonomy of the individual to pursue his or her own ends without interference, on the one hand, and the fact that in the pursuit of his or her own ends the individual must interact with other individuals who seek to assert their freedom and autonomy, on the other, cannot be resolved by reference to morally neutral criteria. A balance must be struck between the two and, unless the arbitrary will of the stronger and more powerful is to prevail, the balance can only be struck by resorting to a premise that will meet the community's sense of what is just and fair. The precept of non-exploitation serves that purpose.

Of course, the administration of the law and legal process will vary at the hands of individual judges. But the precept of non-exploitation remains a constant principle and restricts the scope for judicial diversion or distortion. As already indicated, a progressive or enlightened judge may seek to develop the law in accord with its dictates. But even a conservative or indifferent judge, who rigorously utilises the doctrine of precedent and adheres to the 'logic' of formalism, reinforces and strengthens this long-standing bias in favour of the weak and vulnerable that is entrenched in the law and legal process. It is a voice that cannot be stilled in the service of justice according to the law.

Conclusion

The law and legal process will ensure or, at least, has the capacity to ensure, that the stronger and more powerful do not take unfair

---

[90] E. W. Thomas, *A Return to Principle in Judicial Reasoning and an Acclamation of Judicial Autonomy* 4 (1993) VUWLR Mono. S, at 1.

advantage of the weaker and less powerful, that is, those who are vulnerable to the exercise of that strength and power. Strength and power, which may be decisive in the outside world, are diminished so that such potentially damaging 'assets' will not be permitted to unfairly disadvantage the weak and the powerless. The law insists on placing them on equal terms in the courtroom.

I have been careful to say that the precept of non-exploitation is 'entrenched' in the law or legal process rather than being embedded in it. To say it is 'embedded' would be to suggest that it is innate to the law, and I do not make that suggestion. I have specifically rejected the notion that there is any immanent property or intelligibility in the law. Nor do I wish to vest the theory with overtones of natural law promptings. The precept, therefore, is not embedded in the law. Rather, at least for the most part, I have chosen to say that it is 'entrenched' believing that word carries a more flexible connotation. Consequently, I allow that over time the precept may be ignored, diminished, or even reversed so that it can no longer be said to be entrenched in the law. I would not renounce the proposition that the precept was put there by the judges in the first place and can be taken away by the judges. History has demonstrated that the law may be a force for ill as well as for good.

The point I make is that the common law as it has developed, and as I believe it will continue to develop, does in fact reflect this precept. As demonstrated above, it infuses and informs all fields of judge-made law. It is now so deeply entrenched in the law and legal process that it can fairly be said to vest the administration of the law with an altruistic premise from which it would be difficult to escape. That escape is difficult for no other reason than that the precept is essential to ensure that the cruder excesses of liberal individualism and, in particular, capitalism, are kept to levels that the community deem tolerable.

If we accept, as surely we must, that the law is not an end in itself but exists to serve the needs of society, the conscious or unconscious implementation of the precept becomes part of the judicial function. The law as administered by judges gives effect to the precept. This design forms part of the expectations of the community and becomes the community's mandate to the judges. That mandate and the judicial function therefore merge at the core of the law's stretch to render to all the justice that is their due.

SUBJECT INDEX

academic writing, xxiii, 245
administrative law
   development, 168–169, 175, 387
   discretion, 226
   non-exploitation, precept of, 387–388
   political nature, 103
adversarial system, 327
agency, 377, 381
Air Great Lakes case, 298, 299
ameliorative justice, 363, 390
Amnesty International, 78
analogy, 331
analysis. *See* reasoning
animals, duty of care, 208–213, 286
aphorisms, 167, 168, 172
appeal courts
   constraint on judiciary, 243–244
   and courts of first instance, xx–xxi
   and facts, 326
   guidelines on judicial discretion, 266–267
arbitrariness
   and precise laws, 228
Athena, J, 212–214
Atkin, Lord, 209, 210–211, 324
'attitude of mind', 157–161, 168, 176
Attorney General v *Ortiz*, 98
autonomy. *See* judicial autonomy

Bahamas
   constitution, 169, 170
   death penalty case, 164
Belize, 164
Bingham, Lord, 177, 313
Blanchard, J, 290, 293, 298
blind justice, 358

Boyce and Joseph v *Barbados*, 176, 177
breach of confidence, 379–380
Bridge, Lord, 113
Brind, R. v *Secretary of State for the Home Department, ex parte*, 169, 170
Brown v *Board of Education*, 100
Browne-Wilkinson, Lord, 109, 385
Burger, Justice, 142
Burt v *Governor-General*, 168
business. *See* commerce

Canada
   cases, xxii
   development of law, 262
   human rights jurisprudence, 47
   judicial review of legislation, 264
   Supreme Court jurisprudence, xx, 175
   unjust enrichment, 379
Caparo Industries v *Dickman*, 109
capitalism, 359, 363, 372, 374, 388, 389
Cardozo, Justice, 96–98, 157, 285
Caribbean death penalty cases, 164–173, 176–183
cases, illustrative value, xxii
centipede, 13
certainty
   acknowledged causes of uncertainty, 122–125
   and commercial needs, 288–289
   consequences of uncertainty, 130–131
   Dworkin, 192
   and finality of judgments, 126–128, 229–230

and formalism, xviii–xix, 24, 58, 63, 64, 70, 131, 187–188, 309
as goal of adjudication, xviii, 15–16, 135–137
and imprecise language, 125–126
inherent uncertainty of law, 16, 31–32, 36, 115–121, 271, 305
and judicial discretion, xvi, 131, 354
and justice, 128–130, 136
and multi-jurisdictional approach, 124–125
myth, 118–119
and precedents, 108, 131–135, 140, 145, 149, 165, 213
preservation of property rights, 250
as relevant consideration, 135–137, 250
and rule-scepticism, 305–306
settled law, 119–120, 220
uncertain definition of legal disputes, 123
uncertain exceptions, 124
uncertain facts, 122–123, 132–133
uncertain *ratio decidendi*, 123–124
uncertain world, 115
underlying causes of uncertainty, 125–130
and wealth of precedents, 125
change. *See* development of law
choices in decision-making
acceptance, 306–307
and declaratory theory of law, 25, 27, 184–185
Dworkin's rejection of, 202
facts, 321–327
and formalism, 55–56
and interpretive theories, 7
judicial reasoning, 174, 271, 347–348
legal issues, 306, 327–329
and positivists, 33, 36
practical reasoning, 320
and *ratio decidendi*, 132
and realism, 306–307
scope, 15
transparency, 306
Christianity, 97
commerce

commercial unrealism of judiciary, 294
FCE v *ECNZ*, 289–299
heads of agreement, 289–299
law serving commercial community, 287–289, 297
common law
changes, 135, 140, 156
complacency about, 45
concepts, 139
development. *See* development of law
dynamic, 75, 180, 184–185, 364
importance, xxi–xxii
jurisdictions, 124–125
legacy, 139
non-exploitation precept, 360–367, 379–392, 395
open-ended nature, 354
process, 218
underlying design, 359
common sense, 60, 334–338
community
changed expectations and precedents, 146, 174
concept of justice, 275–277, 282–284
constraints on judiciary, 245, 284
judges' relations with, 87, 283–284, 365
law at service of, 287–289
reliance on rules and precedents, 311, 313
sense of fairness, 141, 371
community values, 140, 204, 282–284, 331–334
comparative law, 125
complacency, 45
confidence, breach of, 379–380
conformity, pressures to conform, 25
Conjwayo case, 171
consistency
inconsistencies of law, 136
meaning, 187
precedents, 139–141, 142, 145–146, 161, 205, 251
constitutions
Bahamas, 169, 170

constitutions (cont.)
  constitutional powers of judiciary, 234
  human rights, 45
  Jamaica, 173
  living instruments, 182–183
  nature, 51–52
  political documents, 103–104
  powers to annul legislation, 233
  reviewability of procedures, 165
  Trinidad and Tobago, 170, 171, 177–180
  United States, xxi, 7, 92, 233
  unwritten constitutions, 49, 83
  written constitutions, xxi, 6, 83
constraints
  appeal structures, 243–244
  community censure, 245, 284
  criticism and comments, 245
  education and training, 245
  effectiveness, 18–19, 86, 87, 268–269
  external constraints, 243–245
  internalised constraints, 245–249
  and judicial autonomy, 57, 266–267
  judicial self-restraint, 246–248
  leaving it to Parliament, 254–265
  legitimate role of certainty, 250
  minimalism, 265–266
  new methodology, 249–250
  other bench members, 244
  parliamentary supremacy, 248
  principles, 249
  purpose, 242
  reasons for decisions, 244–245
  role, 121, 307
  rule of law, adherence to, 248
  significance, 241–243
  social conditioning, 246
  sources, 227, 230
  structural constraints, 249–267
constructive fraud, 376
constructive trusts, 378
contemporaneity *See also* relevance
  essential requirement, 14, 19–20
  and formalism, 65
  and precedents, 139
  realism, 306
  and *Trigwell*, 212–213
Continental approach, 252
contract law
  certainty, 119–120, 250
  coherence, 186
  contingencies, 295, 296
  development by judiciary, 262
  economic imperatives, 294–297
  employment contracts, 385
  heads of agreement, 289–299
  implied good faith, 288–289, 385
  incomplete contracts, 295, 296–298
  intention of parties, 299
  non-exploitation precept, 382–385
  and precedents, 148
  purpose, 299
  time of the essence, 378
Cooke, Lord, 135, 166, 168, 171–172, 174–175
corrective justice, 360–361
Council of Civil Service Unions v *Minister for the Civil Service*, 168, 172
courts, hierarchical structure, 85
creativity
  Dworkin's rejection of, 202
  human rights field, 46
  judicial activism, 84, 88–100
  law as continuum, 218
  law-making judges, 3–4, 26
  and legal fundamentalists, 76, 84
  limits, 254–265
  and nature of law, 18
  new methodology, 353
  and non-exploitation precept, 363
  personal variations, 185
  and positivists, 31
  scope, 7, 18, 21, 32, 229
criminal law, 381
Critical Legal Studies Movement, 118, 305, 388–392
cynicism, 356

de Freitas v *Benny*, 164, 167–169, 174, 175
death penalty

cruel punishment, 180
international law, 177
Privy Council jurisprudence, 167–173, 176–183
declaratory theory of law
  denial of law-making, 26, 258
  discredited, 2, 14, 25–27
  and Dworkin, 189
  formalism, 24
  myth of impersonality, 17, 26, 184–185
  persistence, 52
democracy
  democratic legitimacy of judiciary, 77–88
  democratic positivism, 35
  legislative process, 39–40, 41–42
  and liberal individualism, 372
  and majority government, 79–84
  and minorities, 81–82
  imperfections, 79–84
Denning, Lord, 5, 90, 94–99, 185
development of law
  administrative law, 168–169
  change of values, 180
  flexibility, 145
  future changes, 352
  human rights, 174
  incremental development by judiciary, 144, 262
  legislature v judiciary, 254–265, 313
  and precedents, 135, 150, 155–156
  process, 18, 26, 37–40, 41–42, 140, 217–219, 225
  resistance to change, 146–147
  and rule of law, 228–229
  rules of change, 228–230
  social changes, 184–185, 213
  surreptitious changes, 140
Devlin, Lord, 111
Diplock, Lord, 167, 168, 172, 387
discretion. *See* judicial autonomy
discrimination, 92, 235–236, 333, 366
distributive justice, 361–362
doctrinal disposition, 166, 183
documentary evidence, 325–326
Donoghue v *Stevenson*, 3–4, 113, 209–213, 286, 362

due process, 141, 170, 171, 173
duress, 380
Dutton v *Bognor Regis UDC*, 5
Dworkin, Ronald
  and certainty of law, 126, 127, 192
  concept of law, 189–192
  hard cases, 204–205, 211
  Hercules, J, 192, 202, 203–204, 208
  impersonal law, 188–214
  justification of precedent, 205–208
  and pragmatism, 310
  and principles, 192, 203, 342–343
  principles v policy, 195–201
  principles v rules, 192–195
  rejection of judicial discretion, 202–205
  right answers, 189, 195, 286
  strengths, 215
  and *Trigwell* case, 208, 286

economics, 304, 311
educational constraints, 245
empirical research, 304–305, 324
employment contracts, 385
equal treatment, 145–146, 205, 207, 332
equality, 360, 362, 386
equitable set-off, 377–378, 381
equity, 22, 96, 351, 375–379
Esanda Finance Corporation v *Peat Marwick Hungerfords*, 110
estoppel
  equity principle, 377–378
  promissory estoppel, 96, 278, 377
  proprietary estoppel, 380
European Convention on Human Rights, 235
evidence
  documentary evidence, 325–326
  witnesses, 323–325
executive power, 81, 241
exploitation. *See* non-exploitation
extrinsic evidence, 325

facts
  and adversarial system, 327
  and appeal courts, 326
  documentary evidence, 325–326

facts (cont.)
  extrinsic evidence, 325
  fallibility of witnesses, 323–325
  finding, 306, 321–327
  gaps, 326
  and justice, 321–322
  practical reasoning, 321–327
  subjectivity, 323
  uncertain facts, 122–123, 132–133
Fairchild v *Glenhoven Funeral Services*, 5
fairness. *See* justice
FCE v *ECNZ*, 19, 287, 289–299, 311
fictions, legal fictions, 313
fiduciary relationships, 376–377
finality of judgments, 126–128, 229–230
first instance courts, and precedents, xx–xxi, 143, 251–254
Fisher v *Minister of Public Safety and Immigration (No. 2)*, 164, 165, 167, 169–170, 171, 173, 175
formalism
  absolute rules, 63
  case study, 66–72
  and certainty, xviii–xix, 24, 58, 63, 64, 70, 131, 187–188, 309
  characteristics of formalist judges, 62–66
  and commercial needs, 288, 297
  and common sense, 335
  and contemporaneity, 65
  criteria, 270–271
  dogmatic formalism, 24
  effect, 73–74, 249
  Fletcher case, 294
  and Holmes, 310
  internal logic of law, 186
  judicial reasoning, 74, 352
  and justice, 66, 69, 284–285, 286–287
  legacy, 55–56
  and legal change, 64
  meaning, 56–57
  and minimalism, 65
  and multi-disciplinary approaches, 65
  persistence, xviii–xx, 13, 14, 15, 52, 56–58, 73
  and positivism, 58, 73–74
  and practical reasoning, 317–318
  and precedents, 63, 72, 133, 140, 160, 162
  and presumptive positivism, 58–62
  Privy Council cases, 174, 179
  and public policy-making, 5
  and Realist School, 302
  replacement, 23, 56
  and statutory interpretation, xxii
  and substance, 10, 63, 312, 353–354
  theoretical foundation, 187–188
Fox v *Percy*, 324–325
Frankfurter, Justice, 94, 335
fraud, 375–376, 378, 379
freedom from domination, 360, 372
freedom of speech, 200
fundamental rights
  balancing exercise, 200–201
  community values, 332
  constitutional powers of judiciary, 234
  creativity on, 46
  developing expectations, 174
  Dworkin model of the law, 190
  interpretation requirements, 180–182, 183
  justiciability, 232–233
  and natural law, 45–49
  and parliamentary supremacy, 181–182
  and rule of law, 50–51, 232–233
  supremacy, 45–46
  universality, 47
fundamentalism. *See* legal fundamentalism

games, 21, 168, 183, 354–357
gender discrimination, 235–236
General Tire & Rubber v *Firestone and Rubber*, 69–70
Genghis Khan, 54
Ghaidan v *Godin-Mendoza*, 181, 234–236
Gleeson C J, 324
God Syndrome, 326

SUBJECT INDEX

Goff, Lord, 109, 168
good faith, 120, 288–289, 385
Gummow, J, 324

Haldane, Viscount, 375
Hale, Baroness, 235
hard cases, 202, 204–205, 211
heads of agreement, 289–299
Hedley Byrne v *Heller*, 109
Henderson v *Merrett*, 110
Henry, J, 166
Higgs v *Minister of National Security*, 164, 165, 166, 167, 170–172, 173, 174–175
Hobhouse, Lord, 166
Hoffmann, Lord, 64, 78–79, 165–166, 169, 171, 177–178, 179, 181, 182–183, 255–257
holism, 317
homosexual couples, 181, 234–236
Hope, J A 299
Hope, Lord, 169, 177
human rights. *See* fundamental rights
hunches, 326
Hutton, Lord, 165, 169

impartiality, 77–78, 366–367, 368
impersonal law
  declaratory theory of law, 26, 184–185
  Dworkin, 188–214
  and internal logic of law, 186–188
  myth, 17, 184–186, 214
  and precedents, 160, 161
  right answers, 184, 189–190, 215, 286
independence
  judicial process, 366–367
  judiciary, 77–78
individual, respect for, 332
individualism, liberal individualism, 359, 363, 371–374, 390–391, 393, 394
inhuman or degrading treatment, 165, 169, 171, 177, 180
institutions
  pressures, 25
  stability, 147

Inter-American Commission on Human Rights (IACHR), 164, 169, 170, 173
International Covenant on Civil and Political Rights, 177
international law
  death penalty, 177
  and domestic law, 169–170
  Jamaican obligations, 172, 173
interpretivist theories, 6–7
intuition, 2, 8, 24, 44
issues of law, 306, 327–329

Jamaica
  constitution, 173
  death row appeals, 164–173
  international obligations, 172
jargon, 10
judicial activism
  Cardozo, Justice, 96–98
  conservative activism, 99–100
  Denning, Lord, 94–99
  ersatz concept, 91–94
  generally, 88–100
  or leaving it to Parliament, 254
  and legal fundamentalists, 84
  meaning, 93
  parable, 88–91
judicial autonomy
  and certainty, xvi, 131, 354
  and concepts of justice, 280–281
  constraints, 57, 266–267
  death penalty, 182
  denial, 24, 280–281
  Dworkin's rejection of, 202–205
  fear of, 241–242
  and legal theory, 7, 11
  and positivists, 36
  and precedents, 141, 152–153
  and presumptive positivism, 61
  reality, xviii, 185–186, 307
  and rule of law, 226–231
judicial discretion. *See* judicial autonomy
judicial dishonesty, 27
judicial oath, 217, 238–239, 246–247

judicial process
  balancing exercise, 200–201, 271–272, 284, 320
  deprecation by Waldron, 40–41
  differences, 349–354
  doctrinal dispositions, 183
  greater transparency, 57, 160–161, 163, 214, 249, 349–350, 352–353
  impartiality, 366–367
  inevitability, 350–351
  influences, 304–305
  legitimacy, 195
  majority rulings, 40
  methodology. *See* methodology
  political process, 101–104, 307
  precedential effect of decisions, 158–159
  projected differences, 349–354
  reasoning. *See* reasoning
  self-reinforcing process, 244–245
judicial reasoning. *See* reasoning
judicial restraint, 93, 99–100, 246–248, 254–265
judicial review
  constitutional procedures, 165
  constitutional rights, 49–50
  political process, 103
  prerogative powers, 168, 172
  rule of law in action, 230
  triumph of common law, 50–51
judicial role
  changing concepts, 350–351
  defining, 1, 2–3
  edified conception, 23
  effect of legal theory on, 8–9, 12–13
  individual perceptions of, 246
  legitimacy, 26–27
  making law. *See* law-making
  policy-making. *See* policy-making
judiciary
  boundaries of power, 105
  and commercial world, 289
  constitutional powers, 234
  constraints. *See* constraints
  creativity. *See* creativity
  and credibility of witnesses, 324–325
  democratic function, 83–84
  democratic legitimacy, 77–88
  diversity of functions, 237–238
  experience, 262, 305
  God Syndrome, 326
  hunches, 326
  immaturity, 184
  impartiality, 78–79, 366–367, 368
  independence, 77–78, 241, 255
  and legal fundamentalists, 84
  and legal theory, 352
  limitations, 262
  links with community, 87, 283–284, 365
  littleness of mind, 139
  minimalist judges, 265–266
  personality, 184
  political function, 88, 101–104, 307
  privileged elite, 284, 365–366
  public perceptions, 364–365
  role. *See* judicial role
  self-appointed guardians of public values, 333
  self-perception, 349–350
  stoicism, 245
  training, 86, 245, 353
  values, 84–86, 280
jurisprudence. *See* legal theory
justice
  abstract justice, 368–370
  ameliorative justice, 363, 390
  blind justice, 358
  and Cardozo, 340–341
  cases of injustice, 286–287
  and certainty, 128–130, 136
  and common sense, 335
  community roots, 141, 371
  concepts, 141, 273–274, 367–371, 392–394
  constitutional procedures, 165, 167
  corrective justice, 360–361, 362
  death penalty procedures, 165, 167, 170, 173–174
  Denning, Lord, 95, 97
  distributive justice, 361–362
  Dworkin on, 190
  equity, 375–379
  and facts, 321–322
  and fairness, 274–275, 370

SUBJECT INDEX

Fletcher case, 287, 289–299
and formalism, 66, 69, 284–285, 286–287
goal, 14, 184
illusion, 272–273
individual and collective, 19
judges' values, 280
and judicial activism, 95
knowability, 281–287
Lady of Justice, 358–360
language, 279–280
and law-making by judiciary, 263
and legal fundamentalists, 90
and liberal individualism, 371–374
natural justice, 85, 165, 172, 173–174
new methodology, 351
new methodology benchmark, 271, 354
non-exploitation precept, 360–367, 373–374
personal theory of justice, 21–22
and precedents, 146–147, 155–157, 205, 207
reality, 273–281, 300
scales of justice, 358
status, 128–130
sword of justice, 358–360
wrongful dismissal, 277–278
justiciability
and fundamental rights, 232–233
Justizstaat, 231–238

Kirby, J, 324
knowledge, 309

language
imprecision, 125–126
'justice', 279–280
law
'as is' and 'ought', 224–225
autonomy, 270
change. *See* development of law
commercial function, 287–289, 297, 300
continuum, 43, 218–219, 225
court-defined, 219–222
cynicism, 356
Dworkin's concept, 189–192
end in itself, 186–187, 270
fidelity to, 44
fluidity, 222, 228
formalist approach, 57
game, 21, 168, 183, 354–357
instrument of social policy, 8, 12, 14–15, 19, 43, 102–103
internal logic and coherence, 186–188
law state or judiciary state, 231–238
legitimacy, 30, 32, 33, 42, 43–44
logic, 186–188
meaning, 17–18, 214–215, 217–219
mystique, 336
process, 18, 26, 37–40, 41–42, 140, 217–219, 225
purpose, 12, 186–187, 225, 270–271
rule of law, 50–51, 225–231, 231–238, 248, 286
rule of recognition, 30, 31, 33
settled law, 119–120, 220
social function, 225, 270–271, 287–289
and sources of law, 219–220
tools, 221–222, 229, 346, 353, 363, 393–394
vagueness, 227–229
law commissions, 89, 260, 262
law and economics, 295–297, 311
law-making
and declaratory theory of law, 26, 258
denial by judges, 26–27
and Dworkin, 201
human rights, 48–49
judicial activism, 93
judicial role, 3–4, 25
and justice, 263
leaving to Parliament, 254–265, 313
legislative process, 37–40, 41–42
'fruitful' partnership, 237, 263, 263–265
limits, 254–265
positive and negative forms, 3, 33
and positivists, 31
reality, 27, 213, 307

law-making (cont.)
  and *stare decisis*, 150
law reform
  See also development of law
  future changes, 352
  law commissions, 89, 260, 262
  leaving to Parliament, 254–265
  legislative or judicial process, 64, 313
  pre-empting legislature, 261–262
leases
  inducement payments, 66
  succession, 181, 234–236
legal fictions, 313
legal fundamentalism
  critique, 15
  description, 75–76
  influence, 105
  and judicial activism, 84, 88–100
  legitimacy of judiciary, 84
  and uncertainty, 120
  and 'political' process, 101–104
legal issues, 306, 327–329
legal theory
  bridging practice/theory divide, 12–14, 23
  Denning, Lord, 96
  distrust, 2
  and economics, 304
  jargon, 10
  and judicial autonomy, 11
  and judicial practice, xxii–xxiii, 1–3, 9–12,
  and judiciary, 352
  meaning, 9
  naming rights, 10
  necessity, xxiii, 7, 12–13
  obscurity, 10–11, 23
  and pragmatism, 308
  and Realists, 302–303
  role, 11, 21
  substantive shortcomings, 11
  surfeit of theories, 9
  vacuum, 14
legalism, 172, 174, 175, 178–179
legislation. See law-making
legislatures
  See also parliamentary supremacy
  constraints, 241

judiciary-legislature partnership, 237, 263–265
  leaving law reform to, 254–265, 313
  political bodies, 262–263
  refusal to change law, 262–263
Lewis v *Attorney-General of Jamaica*
  assessment, 173–176
  description, 16–17, 182–183
  injustice, 286–287
  legal history, 164–173
liberal individualism, 359, 363, 371–374, 390–391, 393, 394
life
  right to, 169–170
  sanctity of life, 332
limitation periods, 66–72
Lloyd, Lord, 169, 294
Lochner v *New York*, 99
logic of law?, 186–188

MacNiven v *Westmorland Investments*, 64
MacPherson v *Buick Motor Company*, 210
Marxism, 388–392
Matthew v *Trinidad and Tobago*, 176, 177
Die Meistersinger von Nürnberg, 27–29
mercy, prerogative of mercy, 164–174
Metaphysical Club, 310
methodology
  appeal and first instance courts, xx–xxi
  constraints on judiciary, 249–250
  and creativity, 353
  criteria, 271–272, 300
  Denning, Lord, 96
  differences of new methodology, 349–354
  Dworkin, 191, 195
  FCE v *ECNZ*, 289–299
  judicial autonomy, 185–186
  Lewis case, 174
  new methodology, 249–250, 270–272, 299–301
  pragmatism. See pragmatism
  realism. See realism
  reasoning. See reasoning

and substance, xix
  trends, 350–351
Miller v Jackson, 98
Millet, Lord, 235
minimalism, 65, 249, 265–266
ministerial responsibility, 81
minority groups, 39, 48–49, 81–82, 333
mistake, 380–381
modernity, 75, 95
morality
  abstract morality, 369
  commercial community, 288
  ethical positivism, 34–35, 36–37
  judges as self-appointed guardians of, 333
  and legality, 30, 43, 44
  natural law, 42, 44–45
  and positivists, 30, 33, 34
muddling along, 1, 14, 24–25, 52
multi-disciplinary approaches, 65, 304
Murphy, J, 208
Mustill, Lord, 60, 68

naming rights, 10
national security, 332
natural justice, 85, 165, 172, 173–174
natural law
  authority of law, 42, 43–44
  Denning, Lord, 97
  and Dworkin, 189
  generally, 42–52
  and human rights, 45–49
  other worldliness, 14
  and parliamentary supremacy, 49–52
  speculation, 43, 53
  subjectivity, 271
  superstition, 42–45, 53
  unjust law, 30
natural rights, 43, 45
negativism, 293, 295
negligence
  animals, 208–213, 286
  contractual and tortious, 253
  negligent advice, 108
  principles and policy, 198–199
New Zealand
  cases, xxii
  Court of Appeal jurisprudence, 135
  influence of UK decisions, 125
  Maoris, 372
Nicholls, Lord, 165, 177, 235–236
Nolan, Lord, 109
non-exploitation
  common law, 379–392
  contract law, 382–385
  entrenchment in law, 395
  equity, 375–379
  justice, 392–394
  and capitalism
  and liberal individualism, 359, 363, 371–374, 390–391
  and Marxism, 388–392
  precept, 360–367, 373–374
  public law, 387–388
  tort law, 386–387
notices to quit, 278–279
nuisance, 197, 198

oath, judicial oath, 217, 238–239, 246–247
obiter dicta, 123, 168
O'Connor, James, 335
Oliver, L J, 68
Oliver, Lord, 110
Organization of American States, 164

Parke B, 143
parliamentary supremacy
  See also legislatures
  blind adherence to doctrine 264–265
  constraint on judiciary, 248
  and fundamental rights, 181–182
  and legal fundamentalists, 87–88
  and natural law, 49–52
patents, 286
  causes of action, 66–72
personal responsibility of judges, denying, 27
personality. *See* impersonal law
Pickett v British Rail Engineering, 275
Pinochet case, 78–79n
policy-making
  covert process, 108

policy-making (cont.)
  Dworkin's principles v policy, 195–201
  and formalism, 72
  inevitability, 102
  judicial activism, 93
  judicial role, 4–6
  social policies, 199–200
politics
  legislatures, 262–263
  political function of judiciary, 88
  political process of judicial decision-making, 101–104, 307
positivism
  aspirational positivism, 34–37
  criteria, 271
  critique, 14, 29–34
  crude forms, 2, 24, 29, 34
  democratic positivism, 35
  ethical positivism, 34–35
  and formalism, 58, 58–62, 73–74
  generally, 27–42
  hard cases, 202
  ideology, 29
  law students, 23–24
  and meaning of law, 218
  normative positivism, 34, 36
  and precedents, 32–33
  presumptive positivism, 58–62, 318
  romantic positivism, 36–42
  static concept of law, 225
  superficiality, 30–31, 306
  survival, 33–34, 52–53
  terminology, 10, 34
powers of attorney, 381
practical reasoning. *See* reasoning
practice
  'as is' and 'ought', 224–225
  differences of new methodology, 349–350
  practical reasoning, 320, 338–339
  practical skills and legal theory, 1–3
  pragmatism, 312–314
  realism, 305–307
pragmatism
  and absolute rules, 312
  American philosophers, 308–310
  commercial reality, 299
  consequences of decisions, 312–313
  development of law, 313
  and economic theory, 311
  and legal fictions, 313
  legal pragmatism, 20, 307–312, 314–315
  and legal theory, 308
  necessity, 270
  new methodology, 301
  practice, 312–314
  reasons for decisions, 313
  substance over form, 312
precedents
  assessment by judges, 221–222
  'attitude of mind', 157–161, 168, 176
  broad doctrine, 144
  case study, 164–173
  and certainty, 108, 131–135, 140, 145, 149, 165, 213
  and change, 155–156
  coercive element, 251–252
  consistency, 139–141, 142, 145–146, 161, 205, 251
  Continental approach to, 252
  debunking, 144–153
  decision-making with precedential effect, 158–159
  difference of facts, 132–133, 321
  distinguishing, 150, 151, 152, 321
  doctrine of precedent, 141–144
  Dworkin's justification, 205–208
  efficiency argument, 153
  elasticity, 109, 134
  equality of treatment, 145–146, 205, 207
  famous dicta, 154–155, 157, 253
  first instance courts, xx–xxi, 143
  and flexible development, 145
  flexible use, 160, 162, 182–183
  foolish consistency, 139–141, 161
  force, 121, 205–208
  and formalists, 63, 72, 133, 140, 160, 162
  fresh starts needed, 253–254
  and judicial autonomy, 141, 152–153
  judicial craftsmanship argument, 151–153

SUBJECT INDEX 407

and justice, 146–147, 155–157, 205, 207
and legal fundamentalists, 76
legitimacy argument, 150–151
non-binding precedents, 153–155, 157, 172
non-unanimous judgments, 252
ordinary dicta, 155
overruling, 182
perpetuation of dubious authorities, 174, 175, 253
personal safety, 332
persuasive precedents, 154
and positivism, 32–33
praise and condemnation, 141–142
v principles, xxvi, 158, 233
Privy Council jurisprudence, 167–173, 175–176
and property rights, 148
and public confidence, 150–151
re-evaluation, 251
relevance, 155–157
reliance argument, 148–149, 213, 311, 313
role, xvii–xviii, 160, 161, 251–254
security blanket, 147–148
signposts, 251
stability argument, 145–148
strict adherence to doctrine, 16–17, 24, 63, 116, 147–148, 161, 165
volume of case law, 125, 134
prejudices, xviii–xix, 8, 91, 98–99, 365
preliminary agreements, 289–299
prerogative powers
  case study, 164–173
  justiciability, 167–169, 173–174
presumption of innocence, 141
presumptions, 60–62
principles
  absolute principles, 312
  and common sense, 336–337
  conflict of principles, 340, 345, 348
  constraint on judiciary, 249
  and determinacy of law, 189–190
  Dworkin concept, 190–191, 203
  Dworkin's principle v policy, 195–201

  Dworkin's principles v rules, 192–195
  famous dicta, 155
  judicial reasoning, 182
  legal principles, 343–346, 348
  making principles, 203–204
  obsolescence, 344
  and particulars, 116, 117
  and positivism, 30
  practical reasoning, 334
  v precedent, xvi, 158, 233
  principled approaches, xvii, 346
  and realism, 348
  reason and legal principles, 339–343
  rigidity, 346
  role, 21, 121, 348
privacy, 332
Privy Council
  death penalty jurisprudence, 167–173, 175–176, 236
  injustice, 286
  legalism, 174, 175
  recent Caribbean death penalty cases, 176–183
Profile Alliance v *BBC*, 255–257
promissory estoppel, 96, 278, 377
property rights
  certainty, 250
  common law, 381, 382
  community value, 332
  equity, 380
  and precedents, 148
proportionality principle, 337–338
psychology, 304, 370
public confidence, 150–151
public law, non-exploitation precept, 387–388
Puritanism, 76

Radcliffe, Lord, 382–383
Ramsay (WT) v *Inland Revenue Commissioners*, 64
rape victims, 65
ratio decidendi
  binding precedents, 131–132
  choosing, 132, 214
  uncertainty, 123–124

realism
  commercial reality, 298
  empirical research, 304–305
  functional, 304
  importance of constraints, 307
  judicial mood, 303
  meaning, 20
  multi-discipline approach, 304
  new methodology, 301
  new realism, 302–305, 314
  practice, 305–307
  and principles, 348
  Realist School, 97, 101, 132, 302–303, 305, 339
  reality of choice, 306–307
  reality of judicial autonomy, 307
  reality of judicial law-making, 307
  rule-scepticism, 305–306
  uncertainty of law, 305
reasoning
  analogy, 331
  articulating reasons, 333–334
  choice of facts, 321–327
  choices, 306–307, 320, 347–348
  common sense, 334–338
  and community values, 331–334
  considerations, 329, 336
  deductive reasoning, 316
  determining facts, 306
  determining issues of law, 306, 327–329
  formalists, 74, 352
  initial premises, 329
  justice and relevance, 354
  legal principles, 334, 343–346, 348
  legal principles and reason, 339–343
  limits of practical reasoning, 318–319, 347
  mystification, 305
  new methodology, 347, 354
  practice of practical reasoning, 320, 338–339
  reasons as constraint on judiciary, 244–245
  'stand back' test, 338
  theory of practical reasoning, 20–21, 316–320

transparency, 57, 160–161, 163, 214, 249, 349–350, 352–353
Rechtsstaat, 231–238
Reckley Case, 164, 165, 167–169, 170, 173, 174, 175
recognition, rule of recognition, 30, 31, 33
Rehnquist, Justice W., 99, 100, 142
reification, 305, 391
relevance of law
  certainty, 135–137, 250
  exploitation, 366–367
  imperative, 271, 287–289, 354
  precedents, 155–157
  social policy, 213–214, 236
restitution, 378
retrospectivity, 26, 260
Richardson, Sir Ivor, 135
Riggs v *Palmer*, 340
'right' answers, 184, 189–190, 195, 215, 286
right to life, 169–170
Rodger, Lord, 177, 235
Roe v *Wade*, 100
Roman Law, 142
Roodal v *Trinidad and Tobago*, 182
Roosevelt, F. D., 100
Roskill, Lord, 110
Ross v *McCarthy*, 208
rule of law
  constraint on judiciary, 248
  and fundamental rights, 50–51, 232–233
  and justice, 286
  law state or judiciary state, 231–238
  meaning, 225–231
rules
  absolute rules, 63, 116, 312
  community reliance on, 311, 313
  and formalism, 73–74
  legal fundamentalists, 75
  meaning, 57
  precedents, 142
  presumptive positivism, 58–62
  v principles, 192–195
  reification, 305, 391
  rule-scepticism, 305–306, 354

SUBJECT INDEX

Sachs, Hans, 28–29
same-sex partnerships, 181, 234–236
sanctity of life, 332
Scott, Lord, 177
search powers, 126
Searle v *Wallbank*, 208–213
security, and precedents, 147–148
separation of powers, 75, 77–78, 255
set off, 377–378, 381
settled law, 119–120, 220
Sevcon v *Lucas CAB*, 15, 66–72, 286
Slynn, Lord, 165, 169, 172–173
Smith v *Eric Bush*, 110
social policy
　law as instrument of, 8, 12, 14–15, 19, 43, 102–103
　relevant consideration, 213–214, 236
social sciences, 302
sociology, 304, 370
Somers, Sir Edward, 376
specific performance, 335
squatters, 278–279
stability, 145–148
'stand back' test, 338
stare decisis
　See also precedents
　abandoning, 16, 251–252
　and certainty, 131–135
　doctrine, xv–xvi, 142, 143–144
State Government Insurance Commissioner v *Trigwell*, 17, 208, 286
statute law, xxi–xxii
Statute of Frauds, 228, 378
statutory interpretation
　directions, 267
　requirements, 180–182, 183
　and *stare decisis*, 150, 177
Steyn, Lord, 108, 165, 166, 171, 175, 177, 235
students, substance, xxiii–xxiv
substance, 10, 63, 353–354
succession
　by murderers, 340
　tenancies, 181, 234–236

Tamerlane, 54–55
tenancies, succession, 181, 234–236
terminology
　imprecision of language, 125–126
　jargon, 10
　naming rights, 10
　obscurity, 10–11
　positivism, 34
Thomas v *Baptiste*, 165, 170, 171, 173, 175
time of the essence, 378
Timur, 54–55
tools of law, 221–222, 229, 346, 353, 363, 393–394
tort law, 262, 361–362, 386–387
training, judicial training, 86, 245, 353
transparency
　choices, 306
　effect of legal theory, 9, 21
　judicial reasoning, 57, 160–161, 163, 214, 249, 349–350, 352–353
　law-making by judges, 4
　new methodology, 249, 349–350
　and precedents, 160–161, 163
Trigwell case, 17, 208, 286
Trinidad and Tobago, 164, 167
　constitution, 170, 171, 177–180
trust law
　assisting breach of trust, 254
　constructive trusts, 120, 378
　development by judiciary, 262
　fiduciary obligations, 120, 376–377

uncertainty. See certainty
undue influence, 376, 380
United Kingdom
　cases, xxii
　and death penalty, 166
　House of Lords jurisprudence, xx, 101–102
　influence on New Zealand, 125
United Nations, Human Rights Committee, 164
United States
　cases, xxii
　conservative judicial activism, 99–100
　constitutional powers, 7, 233
　constitutional system, xxi, 92

United States (cont.)
　difficult cases, 126
　good faith in contract, 289
　judicial activism, 92
　judicial policy-making, 6
　Metaphysical Club, 310
　pragmatic philosophers, 308–310
　and precedents, 142
　prison system, 6, 87, 304
　Realist School, 97, 101, 302–303, 305, 339
　Supreme Court, 142
United States v Burns, 175
Universal Declaration of Human Rights, 177
unjust enrichment, 378–379, 381

values
　change, 180
　community values, 140, 204, 282–284, 331–334
　competing values, 102
　judges' personal values, 283–284
　justice, 129–130, 275, 276
　value judgements, 242–243, 306, 350, 394
Vandervell's Trusts (No. 2), Re, 94
vicarious liability, 259–260

Wagner, Richard, 27–29
waiver, 380
Walker, Lord, 177
Warren, Justice Earl, 99, 100, 142
White v Jones, 109
Wilberforce, Lord, 313
Williams v Natural Foods, 108
wills, 340
witnesses, 323–325
wrongful dismissal, 277–278
WT Ramsay v Inland Revenue Commissioners, 64

Zacca, Justice, 177

AUTHORS INDEX

Adams, J. N., 382
Adams, Michael, 84
Allan, James, 43
Allen, C. K., 141
Aristotle, 273, 274, 360
Arthur, W. Brian, 244
Atiyah, Patrick, 120–121, 321, 371, 384
Atkinson, Max, 208, 209–210
Atria, Fernando, 355
Austin, John, 224

Banks, C. P., 133, 148
Baragwanath, W. D., 31
Barker, Kit, 114
Barmes, Lizzie, 331, 334
Beatson, J., 381
Bell, R. S., 204
Benditt, T. M., 31, 145, 152
Bentham, Jeremy, 12, 42–43, 44–45, 118, 224
Bickel, Alexander, xv, xxiv, 341
Bigwood, R., 372, 383, 384, 385, 392
Bingham, Lord, 3–4, 5, 155, 260, 261
Birks, Peter, xxiii, 375, 376
Bix, Brian, 12
Blackstone, 45
Bouckaert, Geert, 81
Braithwaite, John, 101, 304
Browning, Robert, 115
Brownsword, R., 382
Burkhart, F. H., 309
Bushell, A., 264
Butler, Andrew, 234

Campbell, Tom, 34–35, 36–42, 368
Cane, Peter, 9, 259, 331, 361

Cardozo, Benjamin Nathan, 58, 115–116, 134, 153, 155, 207, 219, 248, 303, 340–341, 343, 344, 365
Carter, Lief, 132, 145, 150, 151
Chalmers, D. R. C., 378, 380
Cheshire, G. C., 380
Christie, George, 11, 196
Coleman, Brady, 96, 97
Coleman, Jules, 30, 361
Cooper, C. J., 142
Cotterrell, Roger, 12, 42, 43, 305, 391
Craig, Paul, 387
Cross, R., 119, 142

Dal Pont, G. E., 378, 380
Davidson, Donald, 317
deLeon, Linda, 80, 81
Denning, Lord, 95–96, 97, 133, 358, 359
Devlin, Lord, 116, 117, 124, 152, 263–265
Dewey, John, 308–309
Dias, R. W. M., 26, 122, 142, 218, 219, 220
Dicey, A. V., 50–51
Dickinson, John, 339
Donne, John, 373
Dunn, J., 80
Duxbury, Neil, 224, 303, 339, 340, 344
Dworkin, Ronald, xxi, 12, 17, 43, 126, 127, 188–214, 224, 273, 310, 331, 342–343, 355, 363

Easterbrook, F. H., 141
Eisgruber, Christopher, 39, 40
Ellinghaus, M. P., 380
Emerson, Ralph Waldo, 139–141, 161

411

AUTHORS INDEX

Endicott, Timothy, 7, 119, 126, 127, 227–229
Engels, Friedrich, 273, 389
Evans, J., 148

Fallon, Richard, 59, 61
Farber, Daniel, 304, 320
Farmer, James, 65, 135, 265
Farnham, David, 81
Farnsworth, E. A., 383
Feeley, Malcolm, 4, 6, 7, 77, 82, 83, 87, 186, 225, 230–231, 244–245, 246–249, 304
Fifoot, C. H. S., 380
Finn, P. D., 384, 387
Finnis, John, 44, 224
Fish, Stanley, 12
Fleming, John, 9
Fletcher, George, 12, 226, 232
Frank, Jerome, 123, 146–147, 149, 157, 220, 222–223, 303, 322–323, 326, 327
Frankfurter, Justice, 341
Fredman, Sandra, 80
Friedman, G., 377
Friedmann, D., 381
Fukuyama, Francis, 335
Fuller, Lon, 44, 104, 224, 276, 282, 341
Furmston, M. P., 380

Gava J, 84
Gerhardt, Michael, 142
Goddard, David, 294
Goff, Robert, 279, 379
Grantham, R. B., 379
Gray, John, 219–220, 222–223, 339, 344
Greenawalt, Kent, 198
Griffith, J. A. G., 365
Gummow, W. M. C., 375, 380
Gundersen, Kate, 295

Hajek, Jiri, 273
Hale, Robert, 383
Halliwell, M., 375
Halpin, Andrew, 2, 12, 126, 233
Hancock, Stewart, 285
Hand, Learned, 119, 198–199

Harris, B. V., 160, 161
Harris, J. W., 12, 142, 198, 200, 275
Hart, Henry, 329, 341
Hart, Herbert L. A., 12, 30, 31, 32, 33, 196, 197, 224, 354
Hayne, Kenneth, 143
Hegel, G. W. F., 273
Hepple, Bob, 114
Heuston, R. F. V., 98
Heward, Edmund, 98
Heydon, J. D., 143
Hobbes, Thomas, 273
Hodder, Jack, 75, 160
Hoffmann, Lord, 336
Hogg, P., 264
Holmes, Oliver Wendell, 42, 159, 271, 303, 309–310
Homer, 273
Horton, Sylvia, 81
Hume, David, 224, 273
Hunter, Stephen, 264
Hutchinson, Allan, 193, 204, 355

Jaffe, Louis, 257, 263–265
James, William, 97, 309, 310
Jones, G., 379
Joseph, Philip, 88
Joubert, Joseph, 22
Justice, William Wayne, 91
Justinian, 368
Juvenal, 358

Kairys, David, 100
Kant, Immanuel, 273
Kelman, Mark, 311
Kelsen, Hans, 12, 224, 229
Kennedy, Duncan, 24, 56, 332, 391
Knight, A. H., 141
Kronman, Anthony, 385

Lambert, E. L., 143
Laws, John, 49–50, 51
Lee, T. R., 150, 153
Lehane, J. R. F., 375, 380
Lewis, Norman, 81
Lindlom, Charles, 24
Lindsay, A. D., 39
Lingren, Kevin, 377

AUTHORS INDEX

Llewellyn, Karl, 12, 204, 224, 326
Locke, John, 273
Lockhart, Justice, 143, 148, 151, 155
Longley, Diana, 81
Loughlin, Martin, 80, 302, 308, 309
Lovell, James Russell, 350
Lucke, H., 189
Lyons, David, 148

MacCormick, Neil, 36, 181, 197–198, 231–234, 236
Malik, Maleiha, 81
Malthus, Thomas, 134
Mannon, B., 80
Marx, Karl, 273, 388–392
Mason, Anthony, 16, 131, 133, 144, 148, 150, 151, 156, 157, 162, 252
McCoubrey, Hilaire, 12, 310
McGee, David, 68
McIntyre, Alistair, 316
McLauchlan, David, 290, 293
Meagher, R. P., 375, 380
Mensch, E., 132
Mill, John Stewart, 273
Milsom, S. F. C., 382
Mistry, Rohinston, 115
Monaghan, H. P., 141
Moore, M., 259
Morgan, Jonathan, 5
Mulgan, R., 82
Murphy, Mark, 273, 274

Noonan, John T. Jr, 29, 100, 322
Nozick, Robert, 273

O'Connor, Sandra Day, 13
Oliver, Dawn, 81
Owen, David G., 361

Pannick, David, 190, 192, 206
Parkinson, Patrick, 376, 378
Paterson, Alan, 27, 185
Patterson, Dennis, 188
Pearce, R., 377, 381
Penner, James, 316, 317, 329
Perelman, C., 11
Perry, Stephen, 36
Peters, Christopher, 156

Peters, Guy, 81
Pettit, Philip, 360
Philips, Michael, 383
Pierce, Charles, 309, 310
Plato, 273, 274
Pollitt, Christopher, 81
Posner, Richard, 38, 39, 40, 57, 311
Postema, Gerald, 36
Pound, Roscoe, 76, 139, 145, 339, 344

Radcliffe, Lord, 26–27, 151
Rawls, John, 273, 354, 367
Raz, Joseph, 36, 193, 224, 316
Reid, Lord, 3, 133, 197
Rickett, C. E. F., 379
Robertson, David, 101
Robertson, Geoffrey, 98
Rodell, Fred, 303
Rorty, Richard, 308
Rosenfeld, Michael, 372
Ross, Alf, 273
Rousseau, Jean-Jacques, 273, 274
Rubin, Edward, 4, 6, 7, 56, 77, 82, 83, 87, 186, 225, 230–231, 244–245, 246–249, 304
Ruthven, Malise, 75

Sachs, A., 196, 329, 341
Sager, Lawrence, 38–39, 40, 41
Saul, John Ralston, 115
Savoie, Donald, 81
Scalia, Antonin, 226
Schauer, Frederick, 55, 58–62, 118, 318
Scott, K. J., 52
Scott, Richard, 81
Scrutton, Lord Justice, 364
Sebok, Anthony, 60
Seddon, N. C., 371, 380
Sedley, Stephen, 50–51, 140, 155
Shapiro, Martin, 101
Sheller, C. S. C., 157
Shientag, Bernard, 98
Sim, Stuart, 75
Simmonds, N. E., 200
Smiley, John, 66
Smith, A. T. H., xxii, 381, 382
Smith, Adam, 273
Socrates, 273, 274

Solomon, Robert, 273, 274
Soper, E. P., 30, 194
Spiller, Peter, 310
Stapleton, Jane, 114, 336, 387
Stern, Robert, 100
Stevens, J., 377, 381
Steyn, Johan, 54, 63, 66, 187, 226, 294, 330, 331, 332
Stone, Julius, 123
Summers, Robert, 181, 231–234, 236

Taggart, Michael, 337
Thomas, E. W., xvi–xvii, 10, 22, 139, 144, 246, 249, 264, 387, 388, 394
Thompson, E. P., 388
Todd, Stephen, 113
Treitel, G. H., 384
Turpin, Colin, 81
Tushnet, Mark, 59, 87, 100, 264
Twain, Mark, 143
Twining, William, 204, 217, 223

Uhr, J, 82
Umana, John, 198–200

Unger, Roberto, 12, 118, 189, 391

Van Caenegam, R. C., 382
Van der Vyver, Johan, 232

Wakefield, J. N., 193, 204
Waldron, Jeremy, 34, 35–42, 238
Ward, Ian, 12, 308, 309, 311, 313
Warner, K. A., 116
Wechsler, Herbert, 341, 344
Weeramantry, C. G., 134, 151
Weinrib, Ernest, 56, 187–188
Wellington, Harry, 196, 341
Wellman, Vincent, 316
Whelan, Charles, 372, 374
White, Nigel, 12, 310
Wilberforce, Lord, 135
Wittgenstein, Ludwig, 329
Witting, Christian, 114
Woodhouse, Diana, 81
Worthington, Sarah, 375
Wright, Richard, 361, 386, 387

Yin, C. N., 376

Zines, Leslie, xx